Fodor's

SOUTH
FLORIDA

Welcome to South Florida

From the resorts of Palm Beach to the humblest gingerbread cottages in the Keys, South Florida has something for everyone— romantic retreats for couples, fun activities for families, and hot spots for singles. Whether you're taking a thrilling airboat ride through the Everglades, visiting a world-class art museum, snorkeling off Key Largo, or dancing the night away in a glitzy Miami club, there is plenty to do. Beautiful beaches beckon, so when you're not dining in a great restaurant or playing a round of golf, grab a towel and relax in the tropical warmth.

TOP REASONS TO GO

★ **Miami:** A vibrant, multicultural metropolis that buzzes both day and night.

★ **Palm Beach:** Glamorous and sophisticated, the city offers great dining and shopping.

★ **Beaches:** Sceney in South Beach, buzzing in Fort Lauderdale, quieter in the Keys.

★ **The Everglades:** The River of Grass is home to crocodiles, manatees, and panthers.

★ **Fort Lauderdale:** A glittering and revitalized downtown fronts a gorgeous beach.

★ **Key West:** Quirky, fun, and tacky, it's both family-friendly and decidedly not.

Contents

MAPS

Fodor's Features

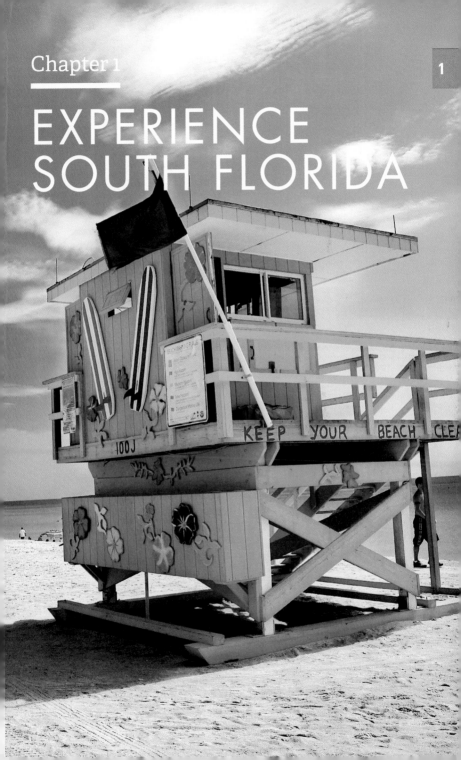

Chapter 1
EXPERIENCE
SOUTH FLORIDA

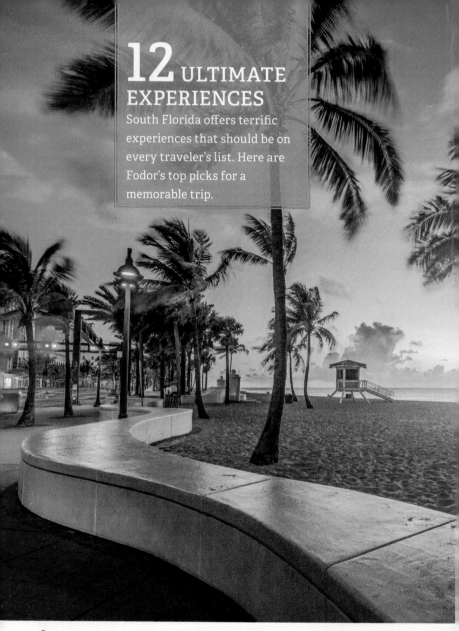

12 ULTIMATE EXPERIENCES

South Florida offers terrific experiences that should be on every traveler's list. Here are Fodor's top picks for a memorable trip.

1 Beaches

Florida's many stretches of sand are just as varied as the state itself. Watch the sun set over Fort Lauderdale Beach, bar hop on South Beach, or snorkel in Key West. If a quiet, more rugged coastline appeals, head to Blowing Rocks Preserve outside of Jupiter. *(Ch. 3, 5, 6, 7)*

2 Art Deco Tour

Learn about Miami's iconic 1920s architecture—the largest collection of art deco buildings in the world, with 800-plus preserved, pastel beauties—at the Art Deco Museum. *(Ch. 3)*

3 Snorkeling and Diving

Swim past a shipwreck and the U.S.'s only living coral reef at John Pennekamp Coral Reef State Park in Key Largo. *(Ch. 5)*

4 The Wynwood Walls

Graffiti artists around the globe create murals for this hip outdoor gallery, with over 80,000 square feet of colorful walls to explore. *(Ch. 3)*

5 Miami Nightlife

Alternate between dancing and people-watching at the late-night lounges that helped earn South Beach its party-heavy rep. *(Ch. 3)*

6 The Everglades

To really experience this national park, zip through the swamp on an airboat and keep your eyes peeled for gators. *(Ch. 4)*

7 High-end Shopping

Miami's Design District, Fort Lauderdale's Las Olas Boulevard, and Palm Beach's Worth Avenue are a shopper's paradise. *(Ch. 3, 6, 7)*

8 Cuban Culture

Little Havana's main drag, Calle Ocho, is where to find Miami's best Cuban restaurants and bars. Don't leave without trying a Cuban sandwich. *(Ch. 3)*

9 Fresh Seafood

It's practically required on your visit to South Florida to eat a fresh catch of the day baked, broiled, or blackened with Cajun spice. *(Ch. 3, 4, 5, 6, 7)*

10 Ernest Hemingway's Home

The legendary American author's Key West home looks nearly the same as it did in the '30s—six-toed cats (descendants of his pet, Snow White) and all. *(Ch. 5)*

11 Sports Games

Cheering for the team is a huge part of Florida culture. Make like a local and catch the Miami Dolphins or Miami Heat in action. *(Ch. 3)*

12 Palm Beach Pampering

In this glam town, you can stay at luxe resorts like The Breakers, shop at chic boutiques, play golf at the PGA National Resort, and gawk at palatial mansions. *(Ch. 7)*

WHAT'S WHERE

1 Miami and Miami Beach. Greater Miami is hot—and we're not just talking about the weather. Art deco buildings and balmy beaches set the scene. Vacations here are as much about lifestyle as locale, so prepare for power shopping, bar-hopping, and decadent dining.

2 The Everglades. Covering more than 1.5 million acres, the fabled "River of Grass" is the state's greatest natural treasure. Biscayne National Park (95% of which is underwater) runs a close second. It's the largest marine park in the United States.

3 The Florida Keys. This slender necklace of landfalls, strung together by a 113-mile highway, marks the southern edge of the continental United States. It's nirvana for anglers, divers, literature lovers, and Jimmy Buffett wannabes.

4 Fort Lauderdale. The town Where the Boys Are has grown up. The beaches that first attracted college kids are now complemented by luxe lodgings and upscale entertainment options.

5 Palm Beach and the Treasure Coast. This area scores points for diversity. Palm Beach and environs are famous for their golden sand and glitzy residents, whereas the Treasure Coast has unspoiled natural delights.

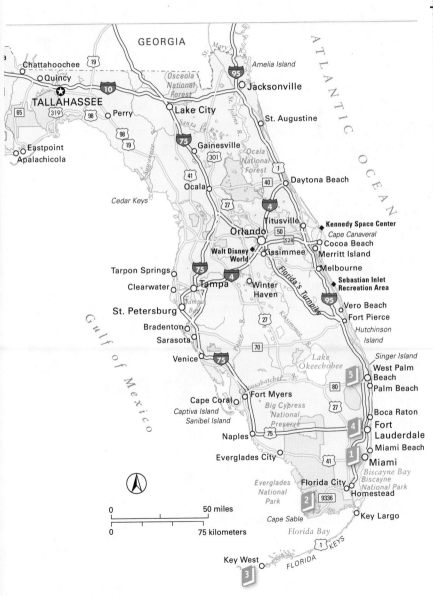

10 Things to Eat and Drink in South Florida

PASTELITOS
Step into any Cuban bakery in Miami and you'll spot these turnover-like pastries proudly displayed (and quickly devoured). The puff pastry treats are as critical to breakfast here as croissants in Paris, with flavors ranging from savory ham to sweet guava and cream cheese. Order one of the flaky confections at family run shops like La Rosa Bakery in Miami.

STONE CRAB
Stone crab season runs from October through May, when you'll find claws served at seafood spots throughout South Florida (one of the best is Joe's Stone Crab in Miami). Claws are presented in similar style to peel-and-eat shrimp, with crackers to help break through to the meaty flesh.

KEY LIME PIE
Florida's official state pie was first baked in the 1860s in Key West, where local Key limes add to the dessert's characteristic tangy taste. The original recipe has three main ingredients—Key lime, egg yolks, and sweetened condensed milk.

MOJITO
Warm weather begs for cold, summertime cocktails, so it's no surprise the classic Cuban mojito is referred to as one of Miami's unofficial drinks. The recipe is easy: a blend of white rum, fresh mint sprigs, sugar, and a splash of club soda. Head to Ball & Chain in Miami's Little Havana for something traditional, or to Ortanique on the Mile in Coral Gables for an award-winning take.

CROQUETAS
Considered Miami's official snack, meat- and cheese-stuffed Cuban croquetas are sold everywhere from fine dining restaurants to drive-through fast food joints and even gas stations. Order the breaded, fried food rolls in classic *jamón* (ham) or a variation like goat cheese and guava jam.

CUBAN SANDWICH
It's said the first *cubano* was invented in 1905 in Tampa's Ybor City, but the classic sandwich is also widespread (and well loved) in South Florida. The historic hoagies are made with two flaky pieces of Cuban bread topped with ham, roast pork, Swiss cheese, yellow mustard, and pickles.

ROCK LOBSTER
Rock Lobster Rock (or spiny) lobster is Florida's answer to the more traditional type you'd find up in Maine. The best way to eat the tender tail meat is grilled and drizzled with rich garlic butter. Head to The Stoned Crab in Key West and order the Baked Half, served in Florida shrimp sauce.

Cafecito

CONCH FRITTERS
Deep-fried conch fritters may have started farther south in the Bahamas, but this popular appetizer dish (typically served alongside tartar sauce) has become a favorite in Florida, especially in the Conch Republic of Key West.

CAFECITO
Cuban coffee, or *cafecito*, is what locals in Miami drink as an afternoon pick-me-up. The strong, espresso-based drink packs a powerful punch thanks to the heavy-handed sugar whipped in. You'll find dedicated cafecito windows, or *ventanillas*, around town, especially in Little Havana.

GATOR TAIL
Just as frog legs are synonymous with France, gator has become a Florida specialty. Bite-sized, deep-fried pieces are served up as nugget-style snacks in the Everglades at Swamp Water Café (a memorable ending to an airboat ride). Tastes like chicken.

10 Best Beaches in South Florida

SOUTH BEACH
The legend of beautiful people is very much a reality on the sands parallel to deco-drenched Ocean Drive and upscale Collins Avenue, lined with luxe boutiques. Pose for pics at the iconic pastel-colored lifeguard stands or take a tour of the city's most historic buildings. *(Ch. 3)*

FORT LAUDERDALE BEACH
The spring break hotspot plays host to a reinvented, more upscale beachfront; however, the buzzy boardwalk and iconic beach bars remain. Stroll and shop along Las Olas or people watch along the beachfront promenade. *(Ch. 6)*

JOHN PENNEKAMP CORAL REEF STATE PARK
Florida's best bet for diving and snorkeling, this state park adjacent to the Florida Keys National Marine Sanctuary encompasses 78 square miles of ecological treasures. The beaches here do attract families, but the real draw is the underwater world. *(Ch. 5)*

DELRAY MUNICIPAL BEACH
This super-popular stretch of sand dotted with trademark royal blue umbrellas intersects trendy Atlantic Avenue in the alluring Village by the Sea; delicious nosh and cute boutiques are a short stroll from the waves. *(Ch. 7)*

HOLLYWOOD BEACH
In between Miami and Fort Lauderdale, this laidback, family-friendly stretch of sand is the star of Broward County, where you can stroll along the 2 ½ mile "Broadwalk," promenade and enjoy beachfront restaurants and bars. *(Ch. 6)*

BAHIA HONDA STATE PARK
Though the Florida Keys aren't renowned for beautiful sand beaches (most are man-made), this is an exception. The 524-acre park has three superb, white sand beaches, including the mile-long, Atlantic-facing Sandspur Beach. *(Ch. 5)*

HAULOVER BEACH PARK
Long known for its clothing-optional stretch of sand (between lifeguard stands 12 and 16), the park, which sits north of Miami Beach, also offers plenty of family-friendly attractions. Food trucks pull up to the Bill Bird Marina on Tuesday nights, and the park often hosts kite-making workshops. *(Ch. 3)*

Bahia Honda State Park

MID-BEACH
This stretch of coastline (which starts at 24th and Collins) sits just a few blocks north of South Beach's nonstop nightlife. Miami Modern buildings sprout across the historic neighborhood, where a few famous faces like Fontainebleau have received billion-dollar revamps in recent years.

Argentinean hotelier Alan Faena is breathing new life into the area, constructing condos and cultural institutions that are as fantastical as his flagship hotel, Faena. *(Ch. 3)*

BLOWING ROCKS PRESERVE
The beauty in Hobe Sound is in the backdrop; the rocky coastline looks like

it's been transplanted from a Greek island, yet this wild strip of mangrove wetlands, turtle nesting beaches, and practically perfect dunes lies less than an hour's drive from Palm Beach. *(Ch. 7)*

BILL BAGGS CAPE FLORIDA STATE PARK
If you're looking to avoid the throngs of tourists sunbathing on South Beach, head to this park in Key Biscayne. Stroll along the shore to the beach's landmark lighthouse—the oldest standing building in the county, originally constructed in 1825—or post up for a picnic at one of the waterfront pavilions. *(Ch. 3)*

10 Best Art Experiences in Miami

ART DECO AND MIMO ARCHITECTURE

In Miami, even the buildings are art. The Art Deco structures on Ocean Drive and Collins Ave, with their pastels and geometric shapes, put South Beach on the map in the '30s and '40s. In North Beach you'll see another iconic style— Miami Modern (MiMo), featuring futuristic, asymmetrical shapes.

ART BASEL

The event around which the Miami Beach art (and social) calendars revolve is this not-to-be-missed art fair, which takes place each December. More than 250 galleries from around the world showcase everything from installations to films, and along with the pricey art comes swanky parties.

THE BASS MUSEUM OF ART

Housed in an art deco gem from the '30s, the museum, renovated and expanded in 2017, spotlights contemporary art and its relationship to culture, design, fashion, and architecture. See whimsical contemporary pieces alongside historical works in the permanent collection.

VIZCAYA MUSEUM AND GARDENS

This European-style villa is an urban oasis where formal gardens meet the edge of Biscayne Bay. Built about 100 years ago, it has survived Miami's hurricanes, economic troubles, and redevelopment. Check out the decorative art spanning the Renaissance to Rococo periods.

The Patricia & Phillip Frost Art Museum

PÉREZ ART MUSEUM MIAMI

Overlooking Biscayne Bay, PAMM's indoor-outdoor venue with hanging gardens, trusses, and steel frames, is a stunning home to international art of the 20th and 21st centuries. The museum is celebrated for sparking much of city's electric arts environment.

THE PATRICIA & PHILLIP FROST ART MUSEUM

Florida International University's free art museum boasts thousands of objects ranging from pre-Columbian era artifacts and American printmaking from the '70s to contemporary works. Note that it's off the beaten path in West Miami.

WYNWOOD ARTS DISTRICT

Once an unremarkable group of warehouses, this now trendy area is an international destination for edgy graffiti and galleries. Check out the Wynwood Walls, an outdoor museum of street art. Your visit will be unique: murals can disappear as quickly as they appear.

LITTLE HAITI AND LITTLE RIVER GALLERIES

Several top-notch galleries—Emerson-Dorsch, Nina Johnson, Mindy Solomon Gallery, Pan American Art Projects—have moved from Wynwood to the neighborhoods of Little Haiti and Little River, so it's no wonder the up-and-coming areas are being referred to as the "new Wynwood."

DESIGN DISTRICT

The Design District is a haven for ultra-high-end fashion houses and boutiques. If you can make it past Louis Vuitton, Hèrmes, and Saint Laurent, you'll find several notable galleries. The Institute of Contemporary Art, Miami (ICA) is the latest add to the city's museums; many pieces in its permanent collection and its major funders were once part of MOCA.

MUSEUM OF CONTEMPORARY ART

MOCA, an intimate museum in North Miami, is home to provocative contemporary art. Its stark gallery spaces are ideal for exhibitions that require time and space to fully understand. Stop by for Jazz at MOCA on the last Friday night of each month.

What to Watch and Read Before Your Trip

FLORIDA BY LAUREN GROFF
This collection of short stories depicts Florida with equal doses fascination and horror, dream world and harsh reality. The state is a recurring character, and the diverse settings, cast of characters, and moods give a full and complex impression of the state.

SWAMPLANDIA! BY KAREN RUSSELL
The story of a young girl growing up in the Florida Everglades among her family's bizarre gator-wrestling entertainment park, Swamplandia! earned Russell the Pulitzer Prize. It has the right amount of fantasy to illustrate the swampy, untamed Everglades.

RAZOR GIRL BY CARL HIAASEN
A con artist works with detectives to find a redneck reality TV star in Hiaasen's most recent novel, but there's plenty more of his Florida-centric work to choose from (Bad Monkey, Tourist Season, and Skin Tight, to name a few).

THEIR EYES WERE WATCHING GOD BY ZORA NEALE HURSTON
Hurston's most-read novel journeys through Reconstruction-era, rural Florida. Through the lens of African American female narrator Janie Crawford, you'll see vivid depictions of small towns, migrant worker communities, and historical events.

TO HAVE AND HAVE NOT BY ERNEST HEMINGWAY
A desperate Key West fishing captain is forced into the illegal smuggling business during the Great Depression in Hemingway's book. It touches on the economic disparity in the Keys during that decade, and the close but complicated relationship with Cuba.

SILENT CITY BY ALEX SEGURA
In the first installment of Segura's murder-mystery series, a man on the edge of personal disaster lands back in his hometown of Miami and into a dark world of peril and past secrets.

MOONLIGHT
A film in three chapters, Moonlight explores violence, identity, and sexuality for two young black males growing up in the Miami area. For a quiet film, it was met with loud praise—the Oscar for best picture. It was the first movie with an all-black cast (and first LGBTQ-themed movie) to win.

THE FLORIDA PROJECT
An indie film that's both heartbreaking and joyous, Florida Project follows a young, struggling mother and her hellion daughter through their days living in a pay-per-week motel in the shadow of Disney World.

BLOODLINE
Taking place on Islamorada in the Florida Keys, this Netflix show begins when a bad-seed brother returns home to stir up trouble. A small family inn serves as the epicenter for so much drama it could be a soap opera—full of family secrets, drug trafficking, and speedboat chases.

SPRING BREAKERS
A dark, highly hyperbolized representation of the wild college trips often associated with Florida, this movie loosely follows a group of teenage girls who go to great lengths to get to St. Petersburg for spring break.

FLIPPER
This feel-good flick stars a young Elijah Wood, who strikes up a friendship with a dolphin while spending the summer at his uncle's marina on Florida's Gold Coast.

MIAMI VICE
A team of undercover detectives take on the shady drug world in South Florida in the 1980s. The show's loud fashion and music, neon lights, palm trees, alligators, and yachts could get anyone into a South Beach mood.

Chapter 2

TRAVEL SMART
SOUTH FLORIDA

Updated by
Galena Mosovich

★ **CAPITAL**
Tallahassee

🚶 **POPULATION**
21,299,325

💬 **LANGUAGE**
English

€ **CURRENCY**
US dollar

☎ **AREA CODE**
239, 305, 561, 786, 754, 954

⚠ **EMERGENCIES**
911

🚗 **DRIVING**
On the right side

⚡ **ELECTRICITY**
120-240 v/60 cycles; plugs
have two or three rectangular
prongs

🕐 **TIME**
Eastern Standard Time (same
as New York); 3 hours ahead
of Los Angeles

🌐 **WEB RESOURCES**
🌐 *www.visitflorida.org*

What You Need to Know Before You Visit Florida

FLORIDA COULD BE SEVERAL STATES.
If you drove from the western stretch of the Panhandle to the state's southern tip in Key West, you'd have traveled more than 800 miles. It's no wonder the state varies so widely in climate, geography, and demography. This massive peninsula's many distinct regions include the Southeast, Southwest, The Keys, Central, Northeast, and the Panhandle—and all have different vibes. Generally, the northern and central regions are more conservative than the coastal communities and the land more akin to Southern Georgia, while the Southeast is by far the most diverse and progressive and the terrain more tropical.

HURRICANE SEASON SPANS HALF THE YEAR.
Florida's annual hurricane season spans from June 1 to November 30. Storms can form within a matter of days, sometimes dissipating or rapidly morphing into monsters. However, big storms are much more likely in August and September. Chances are, you'll be just fine if you travel to Florida in June or July, though it's always a good idea to buy travel insurance in case something does happen. If you're visiting Florida when a storm approaches, fly out as soon as possible or make plans to drive away from the storm's projected path regardless of whether you're in an evacuation zone.

RENTING A CAR IS ESSENTIAL.
Even Florida's urban hubs are sprawling, so a car is the preferred method of transportation. It's also the best way to string a few towns together on a road trip. While a new express train service (formerly Brightline, now called Virgin Trains USA) transports passengers from Miami to Fort Lauderdale to West Palm Beach and has grand plans to expand to Orlando and Tampa in the future, public transit unfortunately isn't an efficient mode in most of the state. Ride sharing services like Uber and Lyft also operate in most areas.

WINTER IS THE BUSIEST AND MOST EXPENSIVE SEASON.
Rates from December to April are high across the board since most try to escape their own winters, avoid the risk of a hurricane, and plan around school breaks. Winter is also the time to visit the Everglades, as temperatures, mosquito activity, and water levels are all lower (making wildlife easier to spot). Northern Florida, conversely, receives the greatest influx of visitors from Memorial Day to Labor Day.

BE PREPARED FOR HUMIDITY AND SUMMER RAIN.
Florida is rightly called the Sunshine State—areas like Tampa Bay report 361 days of sunshine a year! But it could also be dubbed the Humid State. From June through September, 90% humidity levels aren't uncommon, nor are accompanying thunderstorms. In fact, more than half of the state's rain falls during these months.

TAKE THE SUN SERIOUSLY.
Sunburn and heat exhaustion are concerns, even in winter. So hit the beach or play outdoor sports before 10 am or after 3 pm. Even on overcast days, ultraviolet rays shine through the haze, so use a sunscreen with an SPF of at least 15, and have children wear a waterproof SPF of at least 30 or higher. Some sunscreens are banned. Before you buy sunscreen make sure your choice doesn't have oxybenzone or octinoxate. These two chemicals, known to cause coral bleaching, will be banned in Key West starting in 2021.

PROTECT YOURSELF FROM MOSQUITOES.
Mosquitoes are most active in the wet summer months but are present year-round due to the state's climate. Even if the bugs aren't infected by diseases like West Nile or Zika (there was an outbreak in Miami in 2016), humans and pets are still susceptible to their itchy bites. Pack a repellent or lemon eucalyptus oil to ward off the pests, and wear long sleeves, pants, and socks when spending time

in nature. Also, avoid the outdoors at dawn and dusk.

RESPECT THE WILDLIFE.
Much of Florida's wildlife is protected or endangered due to overpopulation and development. While there are plenty of opportunities to commune with nature during your adventures (Everglades National Park to the west of Miami, for example, comprises 1.5 million acres of tropical and subtropical wetlands with one of the world's most diverse ecosystems), they should always come in the form of watching and appreciating from afar.

TOURING BY BOAT HAS ITS PERKS.
A boat ride can help you fully understand the majestic characteristics that make the state so popular. Fort Lauderdale, for example, has long been dubbed the "Venice of America" because of its many waterways, and seeing the city through this lens makes you feel like a local. In Central and Northern Florida, touring natural springs by glass-bottomed boat will help you spot manatees, who enjoy cruising slowly through the aquamarine waters.

PLAN AHEAD FOR THE THEME PARKS.
Make sure your trip is long enough to fit in all desired attractions and parks (Magic Kingdom alone features six lands and 40 attractions!). Select a hotel as close as possible to the park you're visiting, and purchase park tickets in advance so you can look

for discounts and consider upgrading to fast passes that reduce wait times. Packing the most comfortable shoes you own will go a long way. Food inside the parks can be expensive, so read up on the food policy before you go. Some allow you to bring snacks, and refillable water bottles are usually allowed. Once you're inside the park, use free mobile apps such as the My Disney Experience, which provide navigation tools, purchasing capabilities, and tips for making your visit stress-free.

WHEN CHOOSING A BEACH, CONSIDER THE ATLANTIC OCEAN VERSUS THE GULF OF MEXICO.
Not sure which beach to pick? East Coast (Atlantic) beaches can be narrow and crowded or wide and empty depending on the location, while West Coast (Gulf) beaches are sprawling, peaceful respites. East Coast beaches can be havens for parties; Gulf beaches are usually sleepier and more casual. East Coast beaches tend to have oceanfront hotels and high rises that are just steps from the water; on the Gulf side, developments and other buildings are set back from the shoreline. East Coast beaches can be inundated with seaweed for lengthy periods; Gulf beaches can at times be overwhelmed by toxic red tide.

CHECK BEACH CONDITIONS FOR RED TIDE.
A harmful algae bloom that discolors the water and causes eye and respiratory irritations in humans, red

tide isn't new to Florida, but scientists believe nutrient runoff from agricultural activities and the release of Lake Okeechobee's dirty water into the Gulf has increased the intensity of the blooms. Check for blooms from August to December, when the beaches and waterways of Southwest Florida struggle with the harmful algae.

SAVE MONEY BY FLYING INTO SECONDARY AIRPORTS.
Flying into a major city may be convenient, but it can cost more. If you're headed to Miami, for example, search fares for Fort Lauderdale and you can find significant savings. Just be sure to factor in on-the-ground transportation costs.

ACCOUNT FOR RESORT TAXES.
Florida has no state personal income tax, instead heavily relying on tourism revenues. The state sales tax in Florida is 6% (with the exception of most groceries and medicine); when combined with local taxes, the total sales tax rate is as high as 8%. Hotel taxes, often called "resort taxes," vary.

Palm Beach County's resort tax is 6%, for a combined total of 13% with state sales tax (7%). In Greater Fort Lauderdale the resort tax is 5%, for a combined total of 11%. In Miami Beach visitors pay 7% sales tax, 3% Miami resort tax, plus 3% Miami Beach resort tax, for a total of 13%.

Getting Here and Around

✈ Air Travel

Average flying time to South Florida's international airports is 3 hours from New York, 4 hours from Chicago, 2¾ hours from Dallas, 4½–5½ hours from Los Angeles, and 8–8½ hours from London.

AIRPORTS

South Florida has three major airports listed from south to north: Miami International Airport (MIA), Fort Lauderdale–Hollywood International Airport (FLL), and Palm Beach International Airport (PBI). Subtropical, and often chaotic, Miami International Airport is known as the gateway to Latin America and the Caribbean, a hub for American Airlines, and the third-busiest airport for international travelers. The Miami International Airport (MIA Hotel) is within Concourse E and has 260 soundproof rooms.

Fort Lauderdale–Hollywood International Airport offers more than 700 flights a day, including nonstop flights to over 100 U.S. and international cities. South of downtown Fort Lauderdale and north of Hollywood, it's adjacent to Port Everglades, the major cruise complex that hosts approximately four million passengers a year.

Palm Beach International Airport offers flights to and from about 30 destinations from many major airlines with more than 200 flights daily. PBI has parking at assorted pricing levels, including an economy lot. In addition, Key West International Airport (EYW) is a single-runway facility serving carriers large and small. There are more than a dozen car-rental options on arrival.

■TIP➡ **Flying in and out of MIA requires more time and patience due to the sheer volume of travelers. Expect long lines at security, customs, and baggage claim.**

GROUND TRANSPORTATION

SuperShuttle service operates from several Florida airports: Fort Lauderdale, Miami, and West Palm Beach. That said, most airports offer some type of shuttle like GO Airport Shuttle or public bus service. There are also rental-car agencies, ride-sharing services, and taxis.

Cab fares from Florida's larger airports into town can be high. Note that in some cities airport cab fares are a single flat rate (MIA to South Beach is $32); in others, flat-rate fares vary by zone; and in others still, the fare is determined by the meter. Private car service fares are usually higher than taxi fares.

🚗 Car Travel

Three major interstates lead to Florida. Interstate 95 begins in Maine, runs south through the Mid-Atlantic states, and enters Florida just north of Jacksonville. It continues south, ending just south of Miami.

Interstate 75 begins in Michigan at the Canadian border and runs south to Tampa. It follows the west coast south to Naples, then crosses the state through the northern section of the Everglades, and ends in Miami. The Interstate 75 stretch between Naples and just west of Fort Lauderdale levies a toll each way per car.

California and most Southern and Southwestern states are connected to Florida by Interstate 10, which moves east from Los Angeles. It enters Florida at Pensacola and runs straight across the northern part of the state, ending in Jacksonville.

SUNPASS

To save time and money while on the road, you may want to purchase a SunPass for your personal vehicle; many rentals come equipped with their own SunPass transponder or a process for paying through the rental car agency. SunPass provides a discount on most tolls, and it's pretty much mandatory across the state. You also can use it to pay for parking at Palm Beach, Miami, and Fort Lauderdale airports. (SunPass now interfaces with North Carolina's Quick Pass and Georgia's Peach Pass.) Transponders can be purchased online or at 3,100 retailers for $19.99 (SunPass portable is the way to go if you want to switch cars). For more info, check out ⊕ *www.sunpass.com.*

RENTAL CARS

Unless you're going to plant yourself at a beach or theme-park resort, you really need a vehicle to get around in Florida. Rental rates, which are loaded with taxes, fees, and other costs, sometimes can start around $55 to $110/day. In Florida you must be 21 to rent a car, must have a credit card, and need to know rates are higher if you're under 25.

Ride-Sharing Services like Uber and Lyft have revolutionized the way people get around while traveling. Download their respective apps before you go out of town, and add your payment method. This will help make using these tools a lot smoother when you're in an unfamiliar place. Rates vary depending on the type of car you select, whether it's a private ride or a carpool, and how far you're going.

ROAD CONDITIONS

All major cities in Florida can get extremely congested during rush hours, usually 7–9 am and 3:30–6:30 pm or later on weekdays. ■ TIP→ **Due to construction and overdevelopment, expect delays to occur at any time of day. Plan accordingly. For real-time traffic conditions statewide, download the Florida 511 Travel Information app to your smart phone.**

RULES OF THE ROAD

Speed limits are generally 60–65 mph on state highways, 30–35 mph within city limits and residential areas, and 70 mph on interstates, some Orlando-area toll roads, and Florida's Turnpike. Supervising adults must ensure that children under age seven are positioned in federally approved child car seats.

Florida's Alcohol/Controlled Substance DUI Law is one of the toughest in the United States. A blood-alcohol level of 0.08 or higher can have serious repercussions even for a first-time offender.

Cruise Travel

Florida is home to two of the busiest cruise ports in the U.S., the Port of Miami and Fort Lauderdale's Port Everglades, both of which are major ports of embarkation for Caribbean itineraries. Outside of Orlando, cruisers embark from Port Canaveral; Tampa and Jacksonville also have ports.

⊕ Train Travel

Consider riding Virgin Trains USA (formerly called Brightline) if you prefer to avoid road traffic; the routes run from Miami to Fort Lauderdale to West Palm Beach— with future expansion to Orlando. Each leg takes approximately 30 minutes on this passenger rail system, which is the only private train travel company in the country. Virgin Trains USA offers Wi-Fi, full ADA accessibility, a pet-friendly policy, and premium food and beverages. Stations and parking garages are located in the three downtown city centers. ⊕ *www.virgin.com* Amtrak's Atlantic Coast service serves Florida from Jacksonville to Miami.

Before You Go

Passport

American travelers never need a passport to travel domestically. Non-American travelers always need a valid passport to visit Florida. Passengers on cruises that depart from and return to the same U.S. port aren't currently required to carry a passport, but it's always a good idea to bring one if your ship travels through Caribbean waters in the unlikely event that you must fly out of a Caribbean airport during your trip.

Visa

For international travelers, a tourism visa is required for traveling to Florida and the rest of the United States. If you're cruising from Florida to Cuba, you must have a passport and visa.

✎ Immunizations

No specific immunizations or vaccinations are required for visits to Florida.

▦ When to Go

HIGH SEASON $$$$

High season in South Florida spans December to April. Snowbirds migrate down then to escape frosty weather back home, and festivalgoers flock in because major events are held this time of year to avoid summer's heat and high humidity. High season in North Florida is from May to September.

LOW SEASON $

You'll find the lowest rates in the summer months from June to September, but you'll trade savings for scorching summer temperatures and the unpredicability of hurricane season.

VALUE SEASON $$

In addition to good rates, shoulder season in April and May as well as October and November create some of the fairest beach conditions across the state. Most kids are still in school, so you'll miss the family crowds that head here for spring break and summer vacation.

➕ Safety

Don't leave valuables unattended—and that can include food and drink—while you walk the beach or go for a dip. And never leave handbags, cameras, etc., in your vehicle. Don't blatantly stow valuables in your car trunk just before walking away, either, since thieves can be adept at popping lids.

If you're visiting Florida during the June through November hurricane season and a storm is imminent, be sure to follow safety orders and evacuation instructions from local authorities.

What to Pack for Florida

CASUAL CLOTHING

Dress is relaxed throughout the state—sundresses, sandals, or shorts are appropriate. Even beach gear is accepted at a lot of places, but just make sure you've got a proper outfit on (shirt, shorts, and shoes). Clothes should be breathable or better yet, made of fabric that will drip-dry, since you will be facing a hot and humid climate.

A NICER "RESORT CHIC" OUTFIT FOR NIGHTS OUT

A very small number of restaurants request that men wear jackets and ties but most don't. Where there are dress codes, they tend to be fully adhered to. Take note that the strictest places are golf and tennis clubs. Women should be fine with a dress or a nice top and dark jeans.

A SWEATER OR LIGHT JACKET

Even in summer, ocean breezes can be cool, so it's good to have a lightweight sweater or jacket. You should be prepared for air-conditioning in overdrive anywhere you go. Northern Florida is much cooler in winter than Southern Florida (when the mercury can drop to, say, 50), so pack a heavy sweater or more.

PRACTICAL SHOES

You'll need your flip-flops for the beach, but also pack a pair of comfortable walking shoes. Florida's non-beach destinations (think: the Everglades and Orlando's theme parks) are no place to go with open toes.

SUN PROTECTION

Sunglasses, a hat, and sunscreen are essential for protecting yourself against Florida's strong sun and UV rays, even in overcast conditions. Consider waterproof sunscreens with an SPF of 15 or higher for the most protection. And to protect marine life and coral reefs, choose one without harmful chemicals such as oxybenzone and octinoxate.

A CHANGE OF CLOTHES FOR YOUR BEACH BAG

There's nothing worse than a car ride in a wet bathing suit. Avoid it by packing underwear and a casual outfit (shorts or a sundress) that's easy to change into in your beach bag. Don't forget a plastic bag for your wet bathing suit. Note that you can generally swim year-round in peninsular Florida from about New Smyrna Beach south on the Atlantic Coast and from Tarpon Springs south on the Gulf Coast.

RAIN GEAR

Be prepared for sudden storms all over in summer, and note that plastic raincoats are uncomfortable in the high humidity. Often, storms are quick, in the afternoons, and the sun comes back in no time.

INSECT REPELLENT

Mosquitoes are always present in Florida, but especially so in the wet summer months. Pack a DEET-based bug spray for the most effective protection.

PORTABLE SPEAKER

The perfect addition to your beach time? Music. Pack waterproof speakers that sync to your phone via Bluetooth.

WATERPROOF PHONE CASE

Whether you want to snap photos while snorkeling or simply protect your device from kids splashing by the pool, pack a waterproof phone case, or (in a pinch) a Zip-loc bag, to protect electronics.

Essentials

Lodging

In general, peak seasons are during Christmas/New Year's holidays and January through April. Holiday weekends at any point during the year are packed, so if you're considering home or condo rentals, minimum-stay requirements might be longer during these periods, too. Fall is the slowest season, with only a few exceptions (Key West is jam-packed for the 10-day Fantasy Fest at Halloween). Rates are low and availability is high, but this is also prime time for hurricanes.

Children are generally welcome throughout Florida, except for some Key West B&Bs and inns; however, the buck stops at spring breakers. Although many hotels allow them—and some even cater to them—most rental agencies won't lease units to anyone under 25 without a guardian present.

Pets, although welcome at many hotels (Kimpton, The Ritz-Carlton, The W, and others), often carry an extra flat-rate fee. Inquire ahead if Fido is coming with you.

APARTMENT AND HOUSE RENTALS

The state's allure for visiting snowbirds (Northerners "flocking" to Florida in winter) has always made private home and condo rentals popular, particularly for families who want to have some extra space and cooking facilities. In some destinations, home and condo rentals are more readily available than hotels. Fort Myers, for example, doesn't have many luxury hotel properties downtown. Everything aside from beach towels is provided during a stay, but some things to consider are that sizable down payments must be made at booking (15%–50%) and the full balance is often due before arrival. Check for any cleaning fees (usually not more than $150). If being on the beach is of utmost

importance, carefully screen properties that tout "water views," because they might actually be of bays, canals, or lakes rather than of the Gulf of Mexico or the Atlantic Ocean.

Finding a great rental agency can help you weed out the junk. Target offices that specialize in the area you want to visit, and have a personal conversation with a representative as soon as possible. Be honest about your budget and expectations. For example, let the rental agent know if having the living room couch pull double-duty as a bed is not okay. Do research on sites like Airbnb, HomeAway, and VRBO to see if it makes more sense to book through them instead. Florida rental agency companies include Endless Vacation Rentals, Florida Keys Rental Store, Freewheeler Vacations, Interhome, and Villas International.

BED-AND-BREAKFASTS

Small inns and guesthouses in Florida range from modest, cozy places with homestyle breakfasts and owners who treat you like family to elegantly furnished Victorian houses with four-course breakfasts and rates to match. Since most B&Bs are small, they rely on various agencies and organizations to get the word out and coordinate reservations.

HOTELS AND RESORTS

Wherever you look in Florida, you'll find lots of plain, inexpensive motels and luxurious resorts, independents alongside national chains, and an ever-growing number of modern properties. All hotels listed have a private bath unless otherwise noted.

🍴 Dining

Smoking is banned statewide in most enclosed indoor workplaces, including restaurants. Exemptions are permitted for stand-alone bars where food takes a backseat to libations.

One caution: raw oysters in particular pose a potential danger for people with chronic illness of the liver, stomach, or blood, or who have immune disorders. All Florida restaurants that serve raw oysters must post a notice in plain view warning of the risks associated with their consumption.

MEALS AND MEALTIMES
Unless otherwise noted, you can assume that the restaurants we recommend are open daily for lunch and dinner.

RESERVATIONS AND DRESS
We discuss reservations only when they're essential (there's no other way you'll ever get a table) or when they're not accepted. It's always smart to make reservations when you can, particularly if your party is large or if it's high season. It's critical to do so at popular restaurants (book as far ahead as possible, often 30 days, and reconfirm before arrival).

We mention dress only when men are required to wear a jacket or a jacket and tie. Expect places with dress codes to truly adhere to them.

⊕ Tipping
Tip airport valets or hotel bellhops $1–$3 per bag (there typically is also a charge to check bags outside the terminal, but this isn't a tip). Housekeeping gets $1–$2 per night per guest, more at high-end resorts or if you require special services, ideally left each morning since the person servicing your room or suite could change during your stay. In-room dining servers hope to receive a 15% tip despite hefty room-service charges and service fees, which often don't go to the waiters. Check the bill to see if gratuity is automatic before signing. A door attendant or parking valet hopes to get $1–$3. Waiters generally count on 18%–20% or more, depending on your demands for special service. Bartenders get $1 or $2 per round of drinks but not if you're imbibing at a fancy cocktail bar. Those bartenders get 18%–20%. Golf caddies get 15% of the greens fee.

⊕ Health
Sunburn and heat exhaustion are concerns, even in winter. So hit the beach or play tennis, golf, or another outdoor sport before 10 am or after 3 pm.

Even on overcast days, ultraviolet rays shine through the haze, so use a sunscreen with an SPF of at least 15 and UVA and UVB protection.

While you're frolicking on the beach, steer clear of what look like blue bubbles on the sand. These are Portuguese men-of-war, and their tentacles can cause an allergic reaction. Also be careful of other large jellyfish, some of which can sting.

As climate change accelerates and intensifies, portions of Florida's coastal areas may be dealing with harmful algal blooms (red tide). It can kill a massive amount of marine life and pose a huge threat to the respiratory health of humans and pets. For the latest updates, check the Florida Fish and Wildlife Conservation Commission's red tide status website. ⊕ *www. myfwc.com* Mosquito-borne illnesses are also cause for concern. Standing water is prime breeding ground for these insects, and they can carry diseases like Zika, chikungunya, dengue, and encephalitis. You can stay informed by visiting the Florida Department of Health website. ⊕ *www. floridahealth.gov*

Great Itineraries

3 Days: Miami

DAY 1 (FRIDAY)

Fly into Miami International Airport as early as possible on Friday morning to maximize the day at the beach or your hotel's pristine pool. Staying directly on the beach is the right move, because you'll want to avoid traffic and other delays that might eat up your R&R time. Grab lunch from the outdoor counters at La Sandwicherie or My Ceviche in South Beach and have lunch on the sand a couple blocks away. While you're in the neighborhood, go in search of art deco, Miami Modern (MiMo), and Mediterranean Revival gems on a walking tour with the Miami Design Preservation League (MDPL) through the historic architectural district. The MDPL also maintains a museum dedicated to the subject on Ocean Drive and 10th Street. Pop by The Wolfsonian-FIU's iconic 1930s building for a dive into a unique collection of objects defining the modern area of world history. Later, dinner at Macchialina, a hip independent Italian eatery, will fuel you for the rest of the weekend. If you're not wiped out, join in the nightlife that makes Miami so famous: pick from Sugar, a swanky rooftop bar amidst the high rises of Brickell, Blackbird Ordinary for dancing with a younger set Downtown in Brickell, or LIV at the Fontainebleau for the quintessential nightclub experience on Mid Beach.

DAY 2 (SATURDAY)

Grab a late breakfast at Joe's Stone Crab (a Miami institution that's open only October–July). You can take it away for a picnic to South Pointe Park, where cruise ships and other boats go in and out of Government Cut at the confluence of the Atlantic Ocean and Biscayne Bay. Head over to the Miami Beach Marina and hitch a boat ride with Ocean Force Adventures. You'll cruise into Biscayne Bay and Biscayne National Park for an awe-inspiring glimpse of a protected saltwater world that's home to four distinct ecosystems and 500 species of wildlife (fish, birds, turtles, plants, etc.), while marveling at a cluster of wood houses from the 1930s in Stiltsville. Then head to Coconut Grove by car to take a walk back to 1891 under the old trees of a tropical hammock overlooking the bay. The Barnacle Historic State Park is a five-acre slice of the past, and you shouldn't miss the preserved bungalow known as the oldest house in Miami-Dade County still standing in its original location. Here, you'll find a peaceful place to catch your breath. Drive to Little Havana for a late-late lunch at El Exquisito, where authentic Cuban fare awaits in the Calle Ocho community. Exploring the area will result in a deeper understanding of the Cuban exile experience and its influence on Miami culture from the 1960s till now. While there are some kitschy tourist traps, you'll find legitimate tributes to the heritage at Cubaocho Museum & Performing Arts Center, Tower Theater, and Domino Park. Happy hour and live music at Ball & Chain continues the history lesson: Ball & Chain originally opened in 1935 and evolved along with the neighborhood. Expertly crafted mojitos and salsa dancing will bring you full circle at this vivacious bar and restaurant. To cap off the night, visit Azucar Ice Cream Company next door for artisanal ice cream and sorbet flavors inspired by Cuban-American culture.

DAY 3 (SUNDAY)

Your last day in Miami starts with an extraordinary brunch at Zuma in the Epic Hotel on the Miami River. The modern Japanese izakaya's brunch from 11:30 a.m. to 2:30 p.m. features all of the signature dishes from the kitchen, sushi bar, and robata grill in an all-you-can-eat situation known as baikingu in Japanese. But this isn't your typical buffet—it's super-premium and sophisticated ($95–$395 per person). From here, head to the Pérez Art Museum Miami (PAMM) for modern and contemporary works of art inside an impressive building on Biscayne Bay. Its neighbor in Museum Park, the Phillip and Patricia Frost Museum of Science, stands as another great option if a three-story aquarium with a gigantic oculus is more your speed. Before you venture back to the airport, take a drive through the Wynwood Arts District to see Wynwood Walls, the world's largest outdoor graffiti museum, and a swath of ephemeral murals by international street artists on literally every street. Grab a snack before the airport at Zak the Baker, Wynwood's favorite kosher bakery and café with sweets (chocolate babka!) that will make the airport security line less sour.

2 to 3 Days: Gold Coast and Treasure Coast

The opulent mansions of Palm Beach's Ocean Boulevard give you a glimpse of how the top of the 1% lives. For exclusive boutique shopping, art gallery browsing, and glittery sightseeing, sybarites should wander down "The Avenue" (that's Worth Avenue to non–Palm Beachers). The sporty set will find dozens of places to tee up (hardly surprising given that the PGA is based here), along with tennis courts, polo clubs, and even a croquet center. Those who'd like to see more of the Gold Coast can continue traveling south through Boca Raton to Fort Lauderdale (known as the Yachting Capital of the World). But to balance the highbrow with the low-key, turn northward for a tour of the Treasure Coast. You can also look for the sea turtles that

Tips

Now that one-way airfares are commonplace, vacationers visiting multiple destinations can fly into and out of different airports. Rent a car in between, picking it up at your point of arrival and leaving it at your point of departure. If you do these itineraries as an entire vacation, your best bet is to fly into and out of Miami and rent a car from there.

lay their own little treasures in the sands from May through October.

2 to 3 Days: Florida Keys

Some dream of "sailing away to Key Largo," others of "wasting away again in Margaritaville." In any case, almost everybody equates the Florida Keys with relaxation. And they live up to their reputation, thanks to offbeat attractions and that fabled come-as-you-are, do-as-you-please vibe. Key West, alternately known as the Conch Republic, is a good place to get initiated. The Old Town has a funky, laid-back feel. So take a leisurely walk; pay your regards to "Papa" (Hemingway, that is); then rent a moped to tour the rest of the island. Clear waters and abundant marine life make underwater activities another must. After scoping out the parrot fish, you can always head back into town and join local "Parrotheads" in a Jimmy Buffett sing-along. When retracing your route to the mainland, plan a last pit stop at Bahia Honda State Park (it has ranger-led activities plus the Keys' best beach) or John Pennekamp Coral Reef State Park, which offers unparalleled snorkeling and scuba-diving opportunities.

Contacts

📍 Visitor Information

Visit Florida. ✉ *Visit Florida—Corporate Office, 2540 W. Executive Center Cir., Tallahassee* ☎ *850/488-5607* ⊕ *www. visitflorida.com.*

✈ Air Travel

AIRPORT INFORMATION Fort Lauderdale–Hollywood International Airport (*FLL*). ✉ *100 Terminal Dr., Fort Lauderdale* ☎ *866/435–9355* ✉ *ContactFLL@ broward.org* ⊕ *www. broward.org/airport.*
Key West International Airport (*EYW*). ✉ *3491 S. Roosevelt Blvd., Key West* ☎ *305/809–5200* ⊕ *eyw.com.* **Miami International Airport** (*MIA*). ✉ *2100 NW 42nd Ave., Miami* ☎ *305/876–7000, 800/825-5642 International* ⊕ *www.iflymia.com.*
Palm Beach International Airport (*PBI*). ✉ *1000 Palm Beach International Airport, West Palm Beach* ☎ *561/471–7400* ⊕ *www. pbia.org.*

SHUTTLE SERVICE Super-Shuttle. ☎ *800/258–3826* ⊕ *www.supershuttle.com.*

FLIGHTS American Airlines. ☎ *800/433–7300* ⊕ *www.aa.com.* **Delta.** ☎ *800/221–1212 for U.S. reservations, 800/241–4141 for international reservations* ⊕ *www. delta.com.* **Frontier.** ☎ *800/432–1359* ⊕ *www. frontierairlines.com.* **JetBlue.** ☎ *800/538–2583* ⊕ *www.jetblue.com.* **Spirit Airlines.** ☎ *801/401–2200* ⊕ *www.spirit.com.* **United.** ☎ *800/864–8331 for U.S. reservations, 800/538-2929 for international reservations* ⊕ *www. united.com.*

🚌 Bus Travel

Red Coach USA. ⊕ *www. redcoachusa.com.*

🚗 Car Travel

Avis. ☎ *973/496–3500* ⊕ *www.avis.com .* **Budget.** ✉ *6 Sylvan Way, Parsippany* ☎ *800/218–7992* ⊕ *www.budget.com.* **Hertz.** ☎ *800/654–3131* ⊕ *www.hertz.com .* **Sunshine Rent A Car.** ✉ *321 W. State Rd. 84, Fort Lauderdale* ☎ *888/786–7446, 954/467–8100* ⊕ *www. sunshinerentacar.com.*

🚢 Cruise Travel

Carnival Cruise Line. ☎ *888/227–6482* ⊕ *www. carnival.com.* **Disney Cruise Line.** ☎ *800/370–0097* ⊕ *www.disneycruise. com.* **Norwegian Cruise Line.** ☎ *866/234–7350* ⊕ *www.ncl.com.* **Oceania.** ☎ *345/505–1920 in U.K.,* ⊕ *www.oceaniacruises. com.* **Regent Seven Seas Cruises.** ☎ *954/776–6123, 800/477–7500* ⊕ *www. rssc.com.* **Royal Caribbean International.** ☎ *800/398–9819 in U.S., 0844/493-4005 in U.K.* ⊕ *www. royalcaribbean.co.uk.*

🚆 Train Travel

Virgin Trains USA (*Formerly Brightline*). ⊕ *www.virgin. com.* **Amtrak.** ☎ *800/872–7245* ⊕ *www.amtrak.com.*

🛏 Lodging

Airbnb. ⊕ *www.airbnb. com.* **Endless Vacation Rentals.** ☎ *877/782–9387* ⊕ *www.evrentals.com.* **Interhome.** ☎ *954/791–8282, 800/882–6864* ⊕ *www.interhomeusa. com.* **Vacation Rentals By Owner.** ⊕ *www.vrbo.com.*

Chapter 3

MIAMI AND MIAMI BEACH

Updated by
Paul Rubio

⊙ Sights	🍴 Restaurants	🛏 Hotels	⊖ Shopping	🍸 Nightlife
★★★★★	★★★★★	★★★★★	★★★★★	★★★★★

WELCOME TO
MIAMI AND MIAMI BEACH

TOP REASONS TO GO

★ **The beach:** Miami Beach has been rated as one of the 10 best beaches in the world. White sand, warm water, and bronzed bodies everywhere provide just the right mix of relaxation and people-watching.

★ **Dining delights:** Miami's eclectic residents have transformed the city into a museum of epicurean wonders, ranging from Cuban and Asian fare to fusion haute cuisine.

★ **Wee-hour parties:** A 24-hour liquor license means clubs stay open until 5 am, and after-parties go until noon the following day.

★ **Picture-perfect people:** Miami is a watering hole for the vain and beautiful of South America, Europe, and the Northeast. Watch them—or join them—as they strut their stuff and flaunt their tans on the white beds of renowned art deco hotels.

★ **Art Deco District:** Iconic pastels and neon lights accessorize the architecture that first put South Beach on the map in the 1930s.

1 Downtown. Glass and steel labyrinth of high rises and cool lounges.

2 Coconut Grove. Known for bohemian shops and live music.

3 Coral Gables. Dine and shop on family-friendly Miracle Mile.

4 Key Biscayne. Explore parks and beaches by boat or kayak.

5 Wynwood. Trendy, creative area with colorful murals.

6 Midtown. Experience yuppie life and fab restaurants.

7 Design District/ Buena Vista. Browse design rooms and haute boutiques.

8 Little Haiti/Upper East Side. Practice Creole or sample Haitian food.

9 Little Havana. The heart and soul of Cuba's exile community.

10 South Beach. People-watch, admire art deco, and party 'til dawn.

11 Mid-Beach. Booming hotel scene just beyond SoBe.

12 Fisher and Belle Isle. Exclusive private island.

13 North Beach. Quieter northern end of Miami Beach with luxe hotels.

14 Aventura. Known for high end shopping and golf.

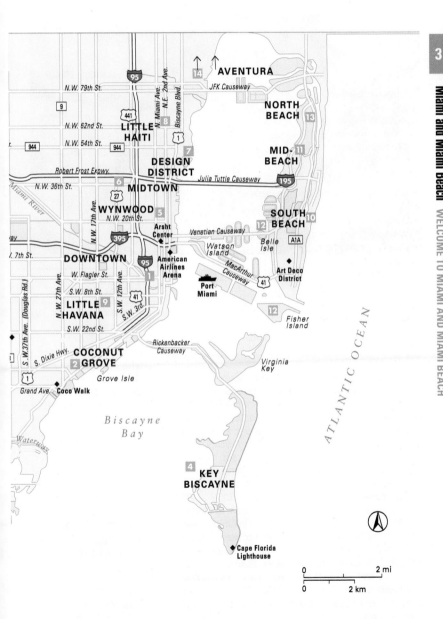

N.W. 79th St.

9

441

N.W. 62nd St.

944

LITTLE
HAITI

N.W. 54th St.   944

N. Miami Ave.   N.E. 2nd Ave.

Biscayne Blvd.

8

1

AVENTURA

14

JFK Causeway

**NORTH
BEACH**   13

**MID-
BEACH**   11

7

**DESIGN
DISTRICT**

Robert Frost Expwy.

6

Miami River

N.W. 36th St.

27   **MIDTOWN**

WYNWOOD   5

N.W. 17th Ave.   N.W. 20th St.

Julia Tuttle Causeway   195

Arsht
Center

Venetian Causeway

Watson
Island

**SOUTH
BEACH**   10

12   Belle
Isle   A1A

way

/. 7th St.

395

DOWNTOWN

95

W. Flagler St.

S.W. 8th St.

**LITTLE
HAVANA**   9

S.W. 22nd St.

N.W. 27th Ave.

N.W. 12th Ave. (Douglas Rd.)

S.W. 12th Ave.   41

S.W. 3rd.

American
Airlines
Arena

1

Port
Miami

MacArthur
Causeway

41

**Art Deco
District**

12   Fisher
Island

ATLANTIC OCEAN

S. 37th Ave.

S. Dixie Hwy.

**COCONUT
GROVE**   2

Rickenbacker
Causeway

1

Grand Ave.   Coco Walk

Grove Isle

*Virginia
Key*

*B i s c a y n e
B a y*

Waterway

4   **KEY
BISCAYNE**

Cape Florida
Lighthouse

0   2 mi

0   2 km

CUBAN FOOD

If the tropical vibe has you hankering for Cuban food, you've come to the right place. Miami is the top spot in the country to enjoy authentic Cuban cooking.

The flavors and preparations of Cuban cuisine are influenced by the island nation's natural bounty (yuca, sugarcane, guava), as well as its rich immigrant history, from near (Caribbean countries) and far (Spanish and African traditions). Chefs in Miami tend to stick with the classic versions of beloved dishes, though you'll find some variation from restaurant to restaurant, as recipes have often been passed down through generations of home cooks. For a true Cuban experience, try either the popular **Versailles** (✉ 3555 S.W. 8th St. ☎ 305/444–0240 ⊕ www.versaillesrestaurant.com) or classic **La Carreta** (✉ 3632 S.W. 8th St. ☎ 305/444–7501) in Little Havana, appealing to families seeking a home-cooked, Cuban-style meal. For a modern interpretation of Cuban eats, head to Coral Gable's **Havana Harry's** (✉ 4612 S. Le Jeune Rd. ☎ 305/661–2622). South Beach eatery **Puerto Sagua Restaurant** (✉ 700 Collins Ave. ☎ 305/673–1115) is the beach's favorite Cuban hole-in-the-wall, open daily from 7 am to 2 am.

THE CUBAN SANDWICH

A great *cubano* (Cuban sandwich) requires pillowy Cuban bread layered with ham, garlic-citrus-marinated slow-roasted pork, Swiss cheese, and pickles, with butter and/or mustard. The sandwich is grilled in a press until the cheese melts and the elements are fused together. Try one at **Enriqueta's Sandwich Shop** (✉ 186 N.E. 29 St. ☎ 305/573–4681) in Wynwood, or **Exquisito Restaurant** (✉ 1510 S.W. 8th St. ☎ 305/643–0227) in Little Havana.

KEY CUBAN DISHES

ARROZ CON POLLO

This chicken-and-rice dish is Cuban comfort food. Found throughout Latin America, the Cuban version is typically seasoned with garlic, paprika, and onions, then colored golden or reddish with saffron or achiote (a seed paste), and enlivened with a splash of beer near the end of cooking. Green peas and sliced, roasted red peppers are standard toppings.

BISTEC DE PALOMILLA

This thinly sliced sirloin steak is marinated in lime juice and garlic and fried with onions. The steak is often served with *chimichurri* sauce, an olive oil, garlic, and cilantro sauce that sometimes comes with bread. Also try *ropa vieja,* a slow-cooked, shredded flank steak in a garlic-tomato sauce.

DESSERTS

Treat yourself to a slice of *tres leches* cake. The "three milks" come from the sweetened condensed milk, evaporated milk, and heavy cream that are poured over the cake until it's an irresistible gooey mess. Also, don't miss the *pastelitos,* Cuban fruit-filled turnovers. Traditional flavors include plain guava, guava with cream cheese, and cream cheese with coconut.

DRINKS

Sip *guarapo*, a fresh sugarcane juice that isn't really as sweet as you might think, or enjoy a *batido*, a Cuban-style milk shake made with tropical fruits like mango, *piña* (pineapple), or *mamey*. For a real twist, try the *batido de trigo*—a wheat shake that will remind you of sugar-glazed cereal.

FRITAS

If you're in the mood for an inexpensive, casual Cuban meal, have a *frita*—a hamburger with Cuban flair. It's made with ground beef that's mixed with chopped chorizo, spiced with pepper, paprika, and salt, topped with sautéed onions and shoestring potato fries, and then served on a bun slathered with a tomato-based ketchup-like sauce.

LECHÓN ASADO

Fresh ham or an entire suckling pig marinated in *mojo criollo* (parsley, garlic, sour orange, and olive oil) is roasted until tender and served with white rice, black beans, and *tostones* (fried plantains) or yuca, a starchy tuber with a mild nut taste that's often sliced into fat sticks and deep-fried like fries.

Three-quarters of a century after the art deco movement, Miami remains one of the world's trendiest and flashiest hot spots. Luckily for visitors, South Beach is no longer the only place to stand and pose in Miami. North of Downtown, the growing Wynwood and Design districts are home to Miami's hipster and fashionista movements, and the South Beach "scene" continues to extend both north and west, with the addition of new venues north of 20th Street, south of 5th Street, and along the bay on West Avenue.

Visit Miami today and it's hard to believe that 100 years ago it was a mosquito-infested swampland, with an Indian trading post on the Miami River. Then hotel builder Henry Flagler brought his railroad to the outpost known as Fort Dallas. Other visionaries—Carl Fisher, Julia Tuttle, William Brickell, and John Sewell, among others—set out to tame the unruly wilderness. Hotels were erected, bridges were built, the port was dredged, and electricity arrived. The narrow strip of mangrove coast was transformed into Miami Beach—and the tourists started to come. They haven't stopped since!

Greater Miami is many destinations in one. At its best it offers an unparalleled multicultural experience: melodic Latin and Caribbean tongues, international cuisines and cultural events, and an unmistakable joie de vivre—all against a beautiful beach backdrop. In Little Havana the air is tantalizing with the perfume of strong Cuban coffee. In Coconut Grove, Caribbean steel drums ring out during the Miami/Bahamas Goombay Festival. Anytime in colorful Miami Beach, restless crowds wait for entry to the hottest new clubs.

Many visitors don't know that Miami and Miami Beach are really separate cities. Miami, on the mainland, is South Florida's commercial hub. Miami Beach, on 17 islands in Biscayne Bay, is sometimes considered America's Riviera, luring refugees from winter with its warm sunshine; sandy beaches; graceful, shady palms; and tireless nightlife. The natives know well that there's more to Greater Miami than the bustle of South

Beach and its Art Deco Historic District. In addition to well-known places such as Ocean Drive and Lincoln Road, the less-reported spots—like the burgeoning Design District in Miami, the historic buildings of Coral Gables, and the secluded beaches of Key Biscayne—are great insider destinations.

Planning

When to Go

Miami and Miami Beach are year-round destinations. Most people come from November through April, when the weather is close to perfect; hotels, restaurants, and attractions are busiest; and each weekend holds a festival or event. High season kicks off in December with Art Basel Miami Beach, and hotel rates don't come down until after the college kids have left after spring break in late March.

It's hot and steamy May through September, but nighttime temperatures are usually pleasant. Also, summer is a good time for the budget traveler. Many hotels lower their rates considerably, and many restaurants offer discounts—especially during Miami Spice in August and September, when a slew of top restaurants offer special tasting menus at a steep discount.

FESTIVALS AND ANNUAL EVENTS
Art Basel Miami Beach
ARTS FESTIVALS | The most prestigious art show in the United States is held every December, with plenty of fabulous parties to go along with the pricey art. This is a who's who of the art world where collectors, emerging artists, renowned artists, curators, gallerists, and art aficionados convene alongside novices, trendsetters, and glitterati. Although the main exhibition is held at the Miami Beach Convention Center, dozens of smaller exhibitions are set up on the beach, Downtown, and in the Wynwood District at galleries, event spaces, and in hotel lobbies. The exquisite art and sensational people-watching more than soften the blow of exorbitant hotel prices, heavy traffic, and long waits. ■TIP→ **Plan ahead to make the most of Art Basel, which includes purchasing tickets or securing your name on guest lists in advance.** ⊕ *www.artbasel.com.*

Art Deco Weekend
ARTS FESTIVALS | This annual weekend of all things art deco was started by the Miami Preservation League in the 1970s to draw attention to and celebrate Miami Beach's Art Deco Historic District. Tours, lectures, film screenings, and dozens of other 1930s-themed events are on tap over this January weekend. Festivities—many of them free—begin on Friday, followed by a car show and street fair (with over 140 vendors) on Saturday and Sunday. More than a quarter of a million people join in the action, which centers on Ocean Drive between 5th and 15th streets. ⊕ *www.artdecoweekend.com.*

Carnaval Miami
CULTURAL FESTIVALS | The Caribbean and Latin America know how to celebrate Carnival in style, so it's only natural their tropical stepsister does, too! Each year, Miami's pre-Lenten celebrations in February and/or March climax during Carnaval Miami. One of the main celebrations is held every year on Calle 8. The wild and fun street festival in the heart of Little Havana is the last blowout before Lent begins. This Sunday street party attracts over a million people, who dance in the streets and enjoy more than two dozen stages of DJs and live music. ⊕ *www.carnavalmiami.com.*

South Beach Wine and Food Festival
FESTIVALS | The Food Network and Cooking Channel's star-studded four-day weekend each February showcases the flavors and ingenuity of the country's top chefs and wine and spirits producers.

Personalities like Anne Burrell, Guy Fieri, and Bobby Flay headline brunches, lunches, dinners, and seminars across Miami Beach. The festival attracts more than 60,000 attendees annually. To avoid disappointment, book your choice events far in advance. ☎ *877/762–3933 for ticketed events* ⊕ *www.sobefest.com.*

The White Party
FESTIVALS | The White Party began in 1985 as a pioneering fund-raiser for AIDS research and awareness. Nowadays, Thanksgiving weekend is one of the most anticipated weekends of the year in the LGBTQ community thanks to the White Party (and another reason not to have that extra scoop of stuffing). On Saturday evening, thousands of gay men, women, and their friends get decked out in white and party the night away under the stars to the sounds of world-famous DJs and recording artists. The event remains a charitable event to support Care-Resource, a nonprofit, community-based AIDS service organization. ⊕ *www.whiteparty.org.*

Winter Music Conference
MUSIC FESTIVALS | Since 1985, the largest DJ showcase in the world has rocked Miami every March, when South Beach truly turns into one big ol' party with more than 100,000 attendees. The latest and greatest in electronic music (to the tune of 2,000 performers and 400 events) diffuses through the lobbies and pools of Miami's most iconic hotels, public spaces, and local event arenas. ⊕ *www.wintermusicconference.com.*

Getting Here and Around

You'll need a car to visit many attractions and points of interest. If possible, avoid driving during the rush hours of 7–9 am and 5–7 pm—the hour just after and right before the peak times also can be slow going. During rainy weather, be especially cautious of flooding in South Beach and Key Biscayne.

AIR TRAVEL
Miami is serviced by Miami International Airport (MIA), 8 miles northwest of Downtown, and Fort Lauderdale–Hollywood International Airport (FLL), 26 miles northeast. Many discount carriers, like Spirit Airlines, Southwest Airlines, and JetBlue, fly into FLL, making it a smart bargain if you're renting a car. Otherwise, look for flights to MIA, which has undergone an extensive face-lift, improving facilities, common spaces, and the overall aesthetic of the airport.

CAR TRAVEL
Interstate 95 is the major expressway connecting South Florida with points north; State Road 836 is the major east–west expressway and connects to Florida's Turnpike, State Road 826, and Interstate 95. Seven causeways link Miami and Miami Beach, with Interstate 195 and Interstate 395 offering the most convenient routes; the Rickenbacker Causeway extends to Key Biscayne from Interstate 95 and U.S. 1. The high-speed lanes on the left-hand side of Interstate 95—often separated by confusing orange poles—require a prepaid toll pass called a Sunpass, available in most drug and grocery stores, or it can be ordered by mail before your trip. It is available with all rental cars (but you are billed for the tolls and associated fees later).

PUBLIC TRANSPORTATION
Some sights are accessible via the public transportation system, run by the **Metro-Dade Transit Agency,** which maintains 800 Metrobuses on 95 routes; the 25-mile Metrorail elevated rapid-transit system; and the Metromover, an elevated light-rail system. Those planning to use public transportation should get an EASY Ticket available at any Metrorail station and most supermarkets, or download the EASY PAY MIAMI app to buy daily passes. Fares are discounted, and transfer fees are nominal. The bus stops for the **Metrobus** are marked with blue-and-green signs with a bus logo and

route information. The fare is $2.25 (exact change only if paying cash). Cash-paying customers must pay for another ride if transferring. Elevated **Metrorail** trains run from Downtown Miami north to Hialeah and south along U.S. 1 to Dadeland. The system operates daily 5 am–midnight. The fare is $2.25 and accessible only by EASY Ticket or the EASY PAY MIAMI app (no cash). The free **Metromover** resembles an airport shuttle and runs on three loops around Downtown Miami, linking major hotels, office buildings, and shopping areas. The system spans about 4½ miles, including the 1-mile Omni Loop, the 1-mile Brickell Loop, and the smaller Inner-Loop. **Tri-Rail,** South Florida's commuter-train system, stops at 18 stations north of MIA along a 71-mile route. There's a Metrorail transfer station two stops north of MIA. Prices range from $2.50 to $6.90 for a one-way ticket.

CONTACTS Metro-Dade Transit Agency. ☎ 305/891–3131 ⊕ www.miamidade. gov/transit/. **Tri-Rail.** ☎ 800/874–7245 ⊕ www.tri-rail.com.

TAXI TRAVEL

These days, most use Uber or Lyft to get around Miami, but old-school taxis still exist. Except in South Beach, it's difficult to hail a cab on the street; in most cases you'll need to call a cab company or have a hotel doorman hail one for you. Taxi drivers in Miami are notorious for bad customer service and not having credit card machines in their vehicles. If using a regular taxi, note that fares run $4.50 for the first 1/6 of a mile and $0.40 for every additional 1/6 of a mile. Waiting time is $0.40 per minute. Flat-rate fares are also available from the airport to a variety of zones (including Miami Beach) for $35. Expect a $2 surcharge on rides leaving from MIA or the Port of Miami. For those heading from MIA to Downtown, the 15-minute, 7-mile trip costs around $21. Some but not all cabs accept credit cards, so ask when you get in.

TAXI COMPANIES Central Cab. ☎ 305/532–5555 ⊕ www.centralcab. com. **Uber.** ⊕ www.uber.com. **Yellow Cab.** ☎ 305/444–4444.

TRAIN TRAVEL

New high-speed train service via Virgin Trains USA (formerly called Brightline) began in summer 2018, connecting Downtown Miami, Fort Lauderdale, and West Palm Beach. The trip from Downtown Miami to Fort Lauderdale takes about 30 minutes; it's another 40 minutes to West Palm Beach.

Amtrak provides service from 500 destinations to the Greater Miami area. The trains make several stops along the way; north–south service stops in the major Florida cities of Jacksonville, Orlando, Tampa, West Palm Beach, and Fort Lauderdale, but stations are not always conveniently located. The Auto Train (where you bring your car along) travels from Lorton, Virginia, just outside Washington, D.C., to Sanford, Florida, just outside Orlando. From there it's less than a four-hour drive to Miami. Fares vary, but expect to pay between around $275 and $350 for a basic sleeper seat and car passage each way. ■TIP→ **You must be traveling with an automobile to purchase a ticket on the Auto Train.**

CONTACTS Virgin Trains USA (*Formerly Brightline*). ⊕ www.virgin.com.

Sights

If you'd arrived here 50 years ago with a guidebook in hand, chances are you'd be thumbing through listings looking for alligator wrestlers and you-pick strawberry fields or citrus groves. Things have changed. While Disney sidetracked families in Orlando, Miami was developing a unique culture and attitude that's equal parts beach town/big business, Latino/Caribbean meets European/American— all of which fuels a great art and food scene, as well as exuberant nightlife and myriad festivals.

To find your way around Greater Miami, learn how the numbering system works (or better yet, use your phone's GPS). Miami is laid out on a grid with four quadrants—northeast, northwest, southeast, and southwest—that meet at Miami Avenue and Flagler Street. Miami Avenue separates east from west, and Flagler Street separates north from south. Avenues and courts run north–south; streets, terraces, and ways run east–west. Roads run diagonally, northwest–southeast. But other districts—Miami Beach, Coral Gables, and Hialeah—may or may not follow this system, and along the curve of Biscayne Bay the symmetrical grid shifts diagonally. If you do get lost, make sure you're in a safe neighborhood or public place when you seek guidance; cabdrivers and cops are good resources.

Restaurants

Miami's restaurant scene has exploded in the past few years, with new restaurants springing up left and right every month. The melting pot of residents and visitors has brought an array of sophisticated, tasty cuisine. Little Havana is still king for Cuban fare, and Miami Beach is swept up in a trend of fusion cuisine, which combines Asian, French, American, and Latin cooking with sumptuous—and pricey—results. Locals spend the most time in Downtown Miami, Wynwood, and the Design District, where the city's ongoing foodie and cocktail revolution is most pronounced. Since Miami dining is a part of the trendy nightlife scene, most dinners don't start until 8 or 9 pm, and may go well into the night. To avoid a long wait among the late-night partiers at hot spots, come before 7 pm or make reservations. Attire is usually casual-chic, but patrons like to dress to impress. Don't be surprised to see large tables of women in skimpy dresses—this

is common in Miami. Prices tend to be extra inflated in tourist hot spots like Lincoln Road, but if you venture off the beaten path you can find better food for more reasonable prices. When you get your bill, check whether a gratuity is already included; most restaurants add between 18% and 22% (ostensibly for the convenience of, and protection from, the many Latin American and European tourists who are used to this practice in their homelands), but supplement it depending on your opinion of the service.

Restaurant reviews have been shortened. For full information, visit Fodors. com. Use the coordinate (✛ C2) at the end of each review to locate a property on the Where to Eat and Stay in the Miami Area map.

What It Costs			
$	$$	$$$	$$$$
RESTAURANTS			
under $15	$15–$20	$21–$30	over $30

Hotels

Room rates in Miami tend to swing wildly. In high season, which is January through May, expect to pay at least $250 per night, even at value-oriented hotels. In fact, it's common nowadays for rates to begin around $500 at Miami's top hotels. In summer, however, prices can be as much as 50% lower than the dizzying winter rates. You can also find great deals between Easter and Memorial Day, which is actually a delightful time in Miami. Business travelers tend to stay in Downtown Miami, and most vacationers stay on Miami Beach, as close as possible to the water. South Beach is no longer the "in" place to stay. Mid-Beach and Downtown have taken the hotel scene by storm in the past few years and become home to some of the region's most avant-garde and luxurious properties to date. If money is no object, stay in one of the glamorous hotels lining Collins Avenue between 15th and 23rd streets or between 29th and 44th streets. Otherwise, stay on the quiet beaches farther north, or in one of the small boutique hotels on Ocean Drive, Collins, or Washington avenues between 10th and 15th streets. Two important considerations that affect price are balcony and view. If you're willing to have a room without an ocean view, you can sometimes get a much lower price than the standard rate, even at an oceanfront hotel.

Hotel reviews have been shortened. For full information, visit Fodors.com.

What It Costs			
$	$$	$$$	$$$$
HOTELS			
under $200	$200–$300	$301–$400	over $400

Nightlife

One of Greater Miami's most popular pursuits is barhopping. Bars range from intimate enclaves to showy see-and-be-seen lounges to loud, raucous frat parties. There's a New York–style flair to some of the newer lounges, which are increasingly catering to the Manhattan party crowd who escape to Miami and Miami Beach for long weekends. No doubt, Miami's pulse pounds with nonstop nightlife that reflects the area's potent cultural mix. On sultry, humid nights with the huge full moon rising out of the ocean and fragrant night-blooming jasmine intoxicating the senses, who can resist Cuban salsa with some disco and hip-hop thrown in for good measure? When this place throws a party, hips shake, fingers snap, bodies touch. It's no wonder many clubs are still rocking at 5 am. If you're looking for a relatively

nonfrenetic evening, your best bet is one of the chic hotel bars on Collins Avenue, or a lounge away from Miami Beach in Wynwood, the Design District, or Downtown.

The *Miami Herald* (⊕ www.miamiherald. com) is a good source for information on what to do in town. The Weekend section of the newspaper, included in the Friday edition, has an annotated guide to everything from plays and galleries to concerts and nightclubs. The "Ticket" column details the week's entertainment highlights. Or you can pick up the *Miami New Times* (⊕ www.miaminewtimes. com), the city's largest free alternative newspaper, published each Thursday. It lists nightclubs, concerts, and special events; reviews plays and movies; and provides in-depth coverage of the local music scene. *MIAMI* (⊕ www. modernluxury.com/miami) and *Ocean Drive* (⊕ www.oceandrive.com), Miami's model-strewn, upscale fashion and lifestyle magazines, squeeze club, bar, restaurant, and events listings in with fashion spreads, reviews, and personality profiles. Paparazzi photos of local party people and celebrities give you a taste of Greater Miami nightlife before you even dress up to paint the town.

The Spanish-language *El Nuevo Herald* (⊕ www.elnuevoherald.com), published by the *Miami Herald,* has extensive information on Spanish-language arts and entertainment, including dining reviews, concert previews, and nightclub highlights.

Shopping

Beyond its fun-in-the-sun offerings, Miami has evolved into a world-class shopping destination. People fly to Miami from all over the world just to shop. The city teems with sophisticated malls—from multistory, indoor climate-controlled temples of consumerism to sun-kissed, open-air retail enclaves—and bustling avenues and streets, lined at once with affordable chain stores, haute couture boutiques, and one-off, "only in Miami"–type shops.

Following the incredible success of the Bal Harbour Shops in the highest of the high-end market (Chanel, Alexander McQueen, ETRO), the Design District and Downtown have followed suit. Beyond fabulous designer furniture showrooms, the Design District's tenants now include Hermès, Dior Homme, Rolex, and Prada. Downtown's mega Brickelly City Centre is the latest arena for high-end retail, with a number of European brands making their U.S. debuts in the chic open-air mall.

Beyond clothiers and big-name retailers, Greater Miami has all manner of merchandise to tempt even the casual browser. For consumers on a mission to find certain items—art deco antiques or cigars, for instance—the city streets burst with a rewarding collection of specialty shops.

Stroll through Spanish-speaking neighborhoods where shops sell clothing, cigars, and other goods from all over Latin America, or even head to Little Haiti for rare vinyl records.

Activities

Sun, sand, and crystal-clear water mixed with an almost nonexistent winter and a cosmopolitan clientele make Miami and Miami Beach ideal for year-round sunbathing and outdoor activities. Whether the priority is showing off a toned body, jumping on a Jet Ski, or relaxing in a tranquil natural environment, there's a beach tailor-made to please. But tanning and water sports are only part of this sun-drenched picture. Greater Miami has championship golf courses and tennis courts, miles of bike trails along placid canals and through subtropical forests, and skater-friendly concrete paths amidst

the urban jungle. For those who like their sports of the spectator variety, the city offers up a bonanza of pro teams for every season.

Visitor Information

For additional information about Miami and Miami Beach, contact the city's visitor bureaus.

CONTACTS City of Coral Gables. ✉ *Coral Gables City Hall, 405 Biltmore Way, Coral Gables* ☎ *305/446–6800* ⊕ *www.coralgables.com.* **Coconut Grove Business Improvement District.** ✉ *3390 Mary St., Suite 130, Coconut Grove* ☎ *305/461–5506* ⊕ *www.coconutgrove.com.* **Greater Miami Convention & Visitors Bureau.** ✉ *701 Brickell Ave., Suite 2700* ☎ *305/539–3000, 800/933–8448 in U.S.* ⊕ *www.miamiandbeaches.com.* **Key Biscayne Chamber of Commerce and Visitors Center.** ✉ *88 W McIntyre St., Suite 100, Key Biscayne* ☎ *305/361–5207* ⊕ *www.keybiscaynechamber.org.* **Visit Miami Beach.** ✉ *Visitor Center, 530 17th St., Miami Beach* ☎ *305/672–1270* ⊕ *www.miamibeachguest.com.*

Downtown

Downtown Miami dazzles from a distance. America's third-largest skyline is fluid, thanks to the sheer number of sparkling glass high-rises between Biscayne Boulevard and the Miami River. Business is the key to Downtown Miami's daytime bustle. Nevertheless, the influx of massive, modern, and once-affordable condos has lured a young and trendy demographic to the areas in and around Downtown, giving Miami much more of a "city" feel come nightfall. In fact, Downtown has become a nighttime hot spot in recent years, inciting a cultural revolution that has fostered burgeoning areas north in Wynwood, Midtown, and the Design District, and south along Brickell Avenue. The pedestrian streets here tend to be very restaurant-centric, complemented by lounges and nightclubs.

The free, 4½-mile, elevated commuter system known as the Metromover runs inner and outer loops through Downtown and to nearby neighborhoods south and north. Many attractions are conveniently located within a few blocks of a station.

 ## Sights

Adrienne Arsht Center

ARTS VENUE | Culture vultures and other artsy types are drawn to this stunning performing arts center, which includes the 2,400-seat Ziff Ballet Opera House, the 2,200-seat John S. and James L. Knight Concert Hall, the black-box Carnival Studio Theater, and the outdoor Parker and Vann Thomson Plaza for the Arts. Throughout the year, you'll find top-notch performances by local and national touring groups, including Broadway hits like *Wicked* and *Jersey Boys,* intimate music concerts, and showstopping ballet. Think of it as a sliver of savoir faire to temper Miami's often-over-the-top vibe. The massive development was designed by architect César Pelli. Complimentary one-hour tours of the Arsht Center, highlighting the architecture and its public art, are offered every Saturday and Monday at noon. Arrive early for your performance to dine at BRAVA By Brad Kilgore, a top Miami restaurant located within the Arsht center. ⊠ *1300 Biscayne Blvd., at N.E. 13th St., Downtown* ☎ *305/949–6722 box office* ⊕ *www.arshtcenter.org.*

Bayside Marketplace

MARKET | **FAMILY** | The Bayside Marketplace, a waterfront complex of entertainment, dining, and retail stores, was en vogue circa 1992 and remains popular due to its location near Port Miami. You'll find the area awash in cruise-ship passenger chaos on most days (it's definitely *not* a draw for locals but a place to kill time in between airport arrival and cruise embarkation), so expect plenty of souvenir shops, a Hard Rock Cafe, and stores like Gap and Sunglass Hut. Many boat tours leave from the marinas lining the festival marketplace. ⊠ *401 Biscayne Blvd., Downtown* ☎ *305/577–3344* ⊕ *www.baysidemarketplace.com.*

Fredric Snitzer Gallery

MUSEUM | The gallery of this longtime figure in the Miami arts scene highlights emerging and mid-career artists, providing them that tipping point needed for national and international exposure and recognition. The newly relocated space maintains its warehouse roots, letting the art speak for itself amid the raw walls and ample natural light. Though a commercial gallery, the selection is highly curated. Rotating monthly exhibitions are usually thematic, with works by one of its represented artists including Hernan Bas, Alice Aycock, Enrique Martinez Celaya, Rafael Domenech, and Jon Pylypchuk. For the art novice, the team, including Snitzer himself, are readily available and willing to share their knowledge. ⊠ *1540 N.E. Miami Ct., Downtown* ☎ *305/448–8976* ⊕ *www.snitzer.com.*

Freedom Tower

BUILDING | In the 1960s this ornate Spanish-baroque structure was the Cuban Refugee Center, processing more than 500,000 Cubans who entered the United States after fleeing Fidel Castro's regime. Built in 1925 for the *Miami Daily News,* it was inspired by the Giralda, an 800-year-old bell tower in Seville, Spain. Preservationists were pleased to see the tower's exterior restored in 1988. Today it is owned by Miami Dade College (MDC), functioning as a cultural and educational center; it's also home to the MDC Museum of Art + Design, which showcases a broad collection of contemporary Latin art as well as works in the genres of minimalism and pop art. ⊠ *600 Biscayne Blvd., at N.E. 6th St., Downtown* ☎ *305/237–7700* ⊕ *www.mdcmoad.org* 🎟 *$12* ⊗ *Closed Mon.–Tues.*

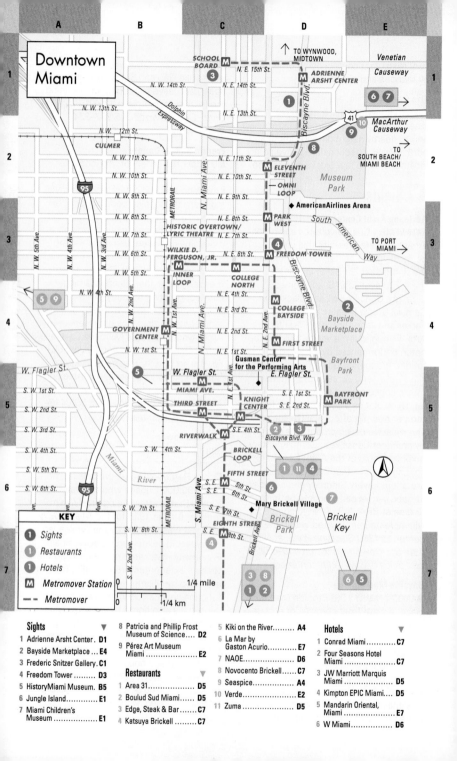

Downtown Miami

TO WYNWOOD, MIDTOWN

Venetian Causeway

TO SOUTH BEACH/ MIAMI BEACH

TO PORT MIAMI

Museum Park

AmericanAirlines Arena

South American Way

Bayside Marketplace

Bayfront Park

Gusman Center for the Performing Arts

BAYFRONT PARK

Mary Brickell Village

Brickell Park

Brickell Key

KEY

- **1** Sights
- **1** Restaurants
- **1** Hotels
- **M** Metromover Station
- - - Metromover

1/4 mile

1/4 km

Sights ▼

1 Adrienne Arsht Center . **D1**
2 Bayside Marketplace ... **E4**
3 Frederic Snitzer Gallery. **C1**
4 Freedom Tower **D3**
5 HistoryMiami Museum. **B5**
6 Jungle Island **E1**
7 Miami Children's
   Museum **E1**

8 Patricia and Phillip Frost
   Museum of Science.... **D2**
9 Pérez Art Museum
   Miami **E2**

Restaurants ▼

1 Area 31.................... **D5**
2 Boulud Sud Miami...... **D5**
3 Edge, Steak & Bar...... **C7**
4 Katsuya Brickell **C7**

5 Kiki on the River......... **A4**
6 La Mar by
   Gaston Acurio............ **E7**
7 NAOE...................... **D6**
8 Novocento Brickell...... **C7**
9 Seaspice.................. **A4**
10 Verde..................... **E2**
11 Zuma **D5**

Hotels ▼

1 Conrad Miami **C7**
2 Four Seasons Hotel
   Miami **C7**
3 JW Marriott Marquis
   Miami **D5**
4 Kimpton EPIC Miami.... **D5**
5 Mandarin Oriental,
   Miami **E7**
6 W Miami.................. **D6**

★ **HistoryMiami Museum**

MUSEUM | FAMILY | Discover a treasure trove of colorful stories about the region's history. Exhibits celebrate the city's multicultural heritage, including an old Miami streetcar and unique items chronicling the migration of Cubans to Miami. Truth be told, the museum is not wildly popular with tourists; however, the museum's tours certainly are. You can take a wide range of walking, boat, coach, bike, gallery, and eco-history tours with varying prices, including culture walks through Little Haiti, informative and exciting Little Havana Arts and Culture Walks, and an evening of storytelling during the Moon Over Miami tour led by HistoryMiami historian Dr. Paul George, where you'll float through Downtown on the Miami River, learning all about Miami's early history circa the Tequesta Indians' days. ⊠ *101 W. Flagler St., Downtown* ✛ *Between N.W. 1st and 2nd Aves.* ☎ *305/375–1492* ⊕ *www.historymiami.org* ⊠ *$10; tour costs vary* ☾ *Closed Mon.*

Jungle Island

ZOO | FAMILY | This interactive zoological park is home to just about every unusual and endangered species you would want to see, including a rare albino alligator, a liger (lion and tiger mix), and myriad exotic birds. With an emphasis on the experiential versus mere observation, the park now offers several new attractions and activities, including private beaches, treetop zip-lining, aquatic activities, adventure trails, cultural activities, and enhanced VIP packages where you mingle with an array of furry and feathered friends. Jungle Island offers complimentary shuttle service to most Downtown Miami and South Beach hotels. ⊠ *Watson Island, 1111 Parrot Jungle Trail, Downtown* ✛ *Off MacArthur Causeway (I–395)* ☎ *305/400–7000* ⊕ *www.jungleisland.com* ⊠ *$39.95, plus $10 parking.*

Miami Children's Museum

MUSEUM | FAMILY | This Arquitectonica-designed museum, both imaginative and geometric in appearance, is directly across the MacArthur Causeway from Jungle Island. Twelve galleries house hundreds of interactive, bilingual exhibits. Children can scan plastic groceries in the supermarket, scramble through a giant sand castle, climb a rock wall, learn about the Everglades, and combine rhythms in the world-music studio. ⊠ *Watson Island, 980 MacArthur Causeway, Downtown* ✛ *Off I–395* ☎ *305/373–5437* ⊕ *www.miamichildrensmuseum.org* ⊠ *$20, parking $1/hr.*

★ **Patricia and Phillip Frost Museum of Science**

MUSEUM | FAMILY | Equal parts style and science, this hypermodern, $300 million-plus museum along Biscayne Bay is totally worth foregoing time at the beach. The high design museum transitions the indoors and outdoors over multiple levels and an impressive 250,000 square feet, crowned by a see-through, shark-filled, 500,000-gallon aquarium. Beyond exhibitions dedicated to oceans, engineering, and the Everglades, look forward to one of the most sophisticated planetariums in the country, which uses 16-million-color 8K projection. ⊠ *1101 Biscayne Blvd., Downtown* ☎ *305/434–9600* ⊕ *www.frostscience.org* ⊠ *$30.*

★ **Pérez Art Museum Miami** (*PAMM*)

MUSEUM | FAMILY | This über-high-design architectural masterpiece on Biscayne Bay is a sight to behold. Double-story, cylindrical hanging gardens sway from high atop the museum, anchored to stylish wood trusses that help create this gotta-see-it-to-believe-it indoor-outdoor museum. Large sculptures, Asian-inspired gardens, sexy white benches, and steel frames envelop the property. Inside, the 120,000-square-foot space houses multicultural art from the 20th and 21st centuries. Most of the interior space is devoted to temporary exhibitions, which have included the likes of *Ai Weiwei: According to What?* and *Grids: A Selection of Paintings by Lynne Golob*

Gelfman. Even if you aren't a "museum type," come check out this magnum opus over lunch at Verde at PAMM, the museum's sensational waterfront restaurant and bar. ■ TIP→ **Admission is free every first Thursday of the month and every second Saturday of the month.** ✉ *1103 Biscayne Blvd., Downtown* ☎ *305/375–3000* 🌐 *www.pamm.org* 🎟 *$16* 🕒 *Closed Wed.*

🍴 Restaurants

Area 31

$$$$ | SEAFOOD | High atop the 16th floor of Downtown Miami's Kimpton Epic Hotel, memorable and sustainable ocean-to-table cuisine is prepared in the bustling, beautiful open kitchen. Look forward to a seafood-centric menu with innovative flavors and a hefty portion of ethos—all fruits of the sea here are certified by the Monterey Bay Aquarium's Seafood Watch. **Known for:** great raw bar; excellent bay-side views; artisanal cocktails. [$] *Average main: $35* ✉ *Kimpton Epic Hotel, 270 Biscayne Blvd. Way, 16th fl., Downtown* ☎ *305/424–5234* 🌐 *www.area31restaurant.com.*

Boulud Sud Miami

$$$ | MEDITERRANEAN | One of America's most celebrated French chefs, Daniel Boulud brings his renowned cooking to the Miami scene with a menu that pays homage to a melange of Mediterranean cuisines, from France's Côte d'Azur to Turkey. Begin, for example, with mezze and octopus *a la plancha*; then feast on seared Mediterranean branzino with a side of patatas bravas. **Known for:** prix-fixe power-lunch menu; beautiful interiors; Hawaij spiced swordfish. [$] *Average main: $29* ✉ *JW Marriott Marquis Miami, 255 Biscayne Blvd. Way, Downtown* ☎ *305/421–8800* 🌐 *www.bouludsud.com/miami.*

Edge, Steak & Bar

$$$$ | STEAKHOUSE | It's farm-to-table surf and turf at this elegantly understated restaurant in the Four Seasons Hotel Miami, where hefty portions of the finest cuts and freshest seafood headline the menu, prepared by renowned chef Aaron Brooks. For a more casual experience, enjoy your meal and the restaurant's artisanal cocktails under the skies on the alfresco terrace. **Known for:** charcuterie boards; Sunday brunch; five-course tasting menu. [$] *Average main: $32* ✉ *Four Seasons Miami, 1435 Brickell Ave., Downtown* ☎ *305/381–3190* 🌐 *www.edgesteakandbar.com.*

★ **Katsuya Brickell**

$$$$ | JAPANESE FUSION | From the high design, photogenic Japanese-inspired interiors to the artistically presented dishes, trays, and cocktails, this restaurant by master sushi chef Katsuya Uechiis is the ultimate Instagram darling. Feast on sushi, sashimi, robata-grilled meats and veggies, and Katsuya legendary signatures like the Wagyu tenderloin, miso-marinated black cod, and baked crab hand rolls; wash it all down with top-tier sake or craft cocktails like the spicy-and-sweet Burning Mandarin. **Known for:** crispy rice with spicy tuna; cool lanterns and massive sake barrels; option of seating around sushi kitchen. [$] *Average main: $41* ✉ *8 S.E. 8th St., Downtown* ☎ *305/859–0200* 🌐 *www.katsuyarestaurant.com/brickell.*

Kiki on the River

$$$$ | GREEK FUSION | In a contemporary waterfront garden setting along the Miami River, Kiki is a daily celebration of fabulous Greek food (hello: olive oil-braised octopus), steamy and sceney Miami nights, and an overall Greece-meets-the-tropics *joie de vivre*. Expect to people-watch, eat a lot, drink even more, and dance (especially if coming for the weekly Sunday Funday party). **Known for:** lobster pasta; tomato salad; great happy hour. [$] *Average main: $38* ✉ *450 N.W. North River Dr., Downtown* ☎ *786/502–3243* 🌐 *www.kikiontheriver.com.*

La Mar by Gaston Acurio

$$$$ | **PERUVIAN** | **FAMILY** | Peruvian celebrity-chef Gaston Acurio dazzles with a sublime menu and an atmospheric, bay-side setting to match. Tour the far corners of Peru through La Mar's signature *cebiches* (ceviche) and *tiraditos* (similar to crudo), freshly grilled skewers of street-style *anticuchos*, *causa* dishes (mashed potato topped with meat and vegetable toppings), and national libations, like the pisco sour. **Known for:** edgy interior design; alfresco dining; desserts served in dollhouses. $ *Average main: $35* ✉ *Mandarin Oriental, Miami, 500 Brickell Key Dr., Downtown* ⊕ *www.mandarinoriental.com/miami.*

NAOE

$$$$ | **JAPANESE** | By virtue of its petite size (eight patrons max) and strict seating times (at 6 and 9:30 nightly), the Japanese gem will forever remain intimate and original. Chef Kevin Cory prepares an *omakase* extravaganza a few feet from his patrons, using only the best Japanese ingredients and showcasing family treasures, like the renowned products of his centuries-old family *shoyu* (soy sauce) and sake brewery. **Known for:** freshest of fresh fish from Japan; authenticity in taste and delivery; $220-per-person price tag plus 20% gratuity. $ *Average main: $240* ✉ *661 Brickell Key Dr., Downtown* ☎ *305/947-6263* ⊕ *www.naoemiami.com* ⊗ *Closed Sun. No lunch.*

Novecento Brickell

$$$ | **ARGENTINE** | **FAMILY** | This popular Argentinian restaurant is the place to go for *empanadas* (tender chicken or spinach-and-cheese), simply grilled meats from the *parrilla* (including luscious grilled skirt steak with chimichurri sauce), and the innovative Ensalada Novecento (grilled skirt steak, french fries, baby mixed greens, and dijon vinaigrette). It's a power-lunch and happy-hour spot for Brickell's business crowd and frequented by families in the evening. **Known for:** daily bottomless sangria or bubbles for

$20; range of Italian dishes; neighborhood hangout of Miami's Latin bourgeoisie. $ *Average main: $26* ✉ *1414 Brickell Ave., Downtown* ☎ *305/403-0900* ⊕ *www.novecento.com.*

Seaspice

$$$$ | **CONTEMPORARY** | Half the fun in dining at this sophisticated brasserie on the Miami River is watching stylish patrons arrive by yacht. Reserve a table outdoors on the patio for the best views of Downtown, and rest assured that a knowledgeable server will guide you through an eclectic menu highlighting fresh seafood, wood-fired casseroles, and refreshing cocktails. **Known for:** waterfront dining; impeccable service; octopus a la plancha. $ *Average main: $35* ✉ *422 N.W. North River Dr., Downtown* ☎ *305/440-4200* ⊕ *www.seaspicemiami.com.*

Verde

$$ | **ECLECTIC** | The slick, contemporary waterfront restaurant at Pérez Art Museum Miami (PAMM) offers seating both indoors and out, with chic decor and accessories true to its "green" name that blend seamlessly with the living walls and hanging gardens strewn across the museum's exterior. The exceptionally affordable, one-page menu features eclectic epicurean lunch plates that include shrimp tacos *al pastor*, tuna tartare, a house chopped salad (with green goddess dressing), and a gourmet cheeseburger with applewood-smoked bacon. **Known for:** fabulous bay views; light lunching; artisanal pizzas. $ *Average main: $18* ✉ *Pérez Art Museum Miami, 1103 Biscayne Blvd., Downtown* ☎ *305/375-3000* ⊕ *www.pamm.org/dining* ⊗ *Closed Wed. No dinner Fri.–Tues.*

Zuma

$$$$ | **JAPANESE FUSION** | This izakaya-style restaurant is known the world over for its sleek design, lounge atmosphere, and contemporary Japanese cuisine. On the ground floor of the Kimpton EPIC hotel, the Miami location promises excellent bay-side views, Zuma's signature menu items, such as roasted lobster with shizo-ponzu butter, and dishes exclusive to Miami (previous exclusives included the 24-ounce bone-in rib-eye.) **Known for:** incredible Sunday brunch; own line of sake; excellent sashimi. Ⓢ *Average main: $47* ✉ *Kimpton EPIC Hotel, 270 Biscayne Boulevard Way, Downtown* ☎ *305/577–0277* ⊕ *www.zumarestaurant.com.*

 Hotels

Miami's skyline continues to grow by leaps and bounds. With Downtown experiencing a renaissance of sorts, the hotel scene here isn't just for business anymore. In fact, hotels that once relied solely on their Monday–Thursday traffic are now bustling on weekends, with a larger focus on cocktails around the rooftop pool and less on the business center. These hotels offer proximate access to Downtown's burgeoning food and cocktail scene, and historic sights, and are a short Uber ride away from Miami's beaches.

Conrad Miami

$$$$ | **HOTEL** | Occupying floors 16 to 26 of a 36-story skyscraper in Miami's burgeoning, business-centric city center, this hotel offers easy access to the best of Downtown and ubiquitous, jaw-dropping views of Biscayne Bay. Like many of its sister Downtown hotels, the lobby is located high in the sky—on the 25th floor to be exact. **Pros:** walking distance to most Downtown sights; great views from some bathrooms; rooftop tennis courts. **Cons:** poor views from some rooms; expensive parking; rooms lack personality. Ⓢ *Rooms from: $489* ✉ *Espirito Santo Plaza, 1395 Brickell Ave., Downtown* ☎ *305/503–6500* ⊕ *www.conradmiami.com* ⮣ *201 rooms* ⧉ *No meals.*

Four Seasons Hotel Miami

$$$$ | **HOTEL** | A favorite of business travelers visiting Downtown's bustling Brickell Avenue, this plush sanctuary offers a respite from the nine-to-five mayhem—a soothing water wall greets you, the understated rooms impress you, and the seventh-floor, 2-acre-pool terrace relaxes you. **Pros:** sensational service; window-side daybeds; amazing gym and pool deck. **Cons:** no balconies; not near the beach; mostly a business crowd. Ⓢ *Rooms from: $599* ✉ *1435 Brickell Ave., Downtown* ☎ *305/358–3535* ⊕ *www.fourseasons.com/miami* ⮣ *221 rooms* ⧉ *No meals.*

JW Marriott Marquis Miami

$$$$ | **HOTEL** | The Miami marriage of Marriott's JW and Marquis brands creates a truly high-tech, contemporary, and stylish business-minded hotel—from the three-story crystal chandelier in the entry to the smart and symmetric guest rooms, rife with electronic gadgets. **Pros:** entertainment and fitness amenities; amazing technology; pristine rooms. **Cons:** swimming pool receives limited sunshine; lots of conventioneers on weekdays; congestion at street entrance. Ⓢ *Rooms from: $499* ✉ *255 Biscayne Blvd. Way, Downtown* ☎ *305/421–8600* ⊕ *www.jwmarriottmarquismiami.com* ⮣ *313 rooms* ⧉ *No meals.*

★ Kimpton EPIC Miami

$$$ | **HOTEL** | In the heart of Downtown, Kimpton's pet-friendly, artful EPIC Hotel has 411 guest rooms with spacious balconies (many of them overlook Biscayne Bay) and fabulous modern amenities to match the sophistication of the common areas, which include a supersexy rooftop pool. **Pros:** sprawling rooftop pool deck; balcony in every room; complimentary wine hour, coffee, and Wi-Fi. **Cons:** some rooms have inferior views; congested valet area; sometimes windy around pool area. Ⓢ *Rooms from: $375* ✉ *270 Biscayne Blvd. Way, Downtown* ☎ *305/424–5226* ⊕ *www.epichotel.com* ⮣ *411 rooms* ⧉ *No meals.*

★ Mandarin Oriental, Miami

$$$$ | **HOTEL** | At the tip of prestigious Brickell Key in Biscayne Bay, the

Mandarin Oriental feels as exclusive as it does glamorous, with luxurious rooms, exalted restaurants, and the city's top spa, all of which marry the brand's signature Asian style with Miami's bold tropical elegance. **Pros:** impressive lobby; intimate vibe; top-notch spa. **Cons:** man-made beach; small infinity pool; traffic getting on/off Brickell Key. $ *Rooms from: $579* ✉ *500 Brickell Key Dr., Downtown* ☎ *305/913–8288, 866/888–6780* ⊕ *www.mandarinoriental.com/miami* ⌁ *357 rooms* ⦿ *No meals.*

W Miami

$$$$ | **HOTEL** | Formerly the Viceroy, Miami's second W hotel cultivates a brash, supersophisticated Miami attitude, likely stemming from its whimsically decorated guest rooms, floor-to-ceiling marble bathrooms, and the Philippe Starck–designed 28,000-square-foot Iconbrickell Spa. Rooms are available in a host of categories, ranging from 440-square-foot "Wonderful" rooms to a 1,550-square-foot "Wow" suite that has a living room, dining room, and sweeping views of Biscayne Bay. Each room, though, is furnished with a private balcony, a W Signature bed with down comforter and pillows, safe, Wi-Fi, and TV. **Pros:** smart design elements; exceptional spa; great gym. **Cons:** serious traffic getting in and out of hotel entrance; the amazing 15th floor pool is for residents not hotel guests; many rooms allow only two persons maximum. $ *Rooms from: $659* ✉ *485 Brickell Ave., Downtown* ☎ *305/503–4400* ⊕ *www.wmiamihotel.com* ⌁ *168 rooms* ⦿ *No meals.*

⍟ Nightlife

★ Blackbird Ordinary

BARS/PUBS | With a vibe that's a bit speakeasy, a bit dive bar, a bit hipster hangout, and a bit Miami sophisticate, this local watering hole is hands down one of the coolest places in the city and appeals to a wide demographic. Mixology is a huge part of the Blackbird experience—be

prepared for some awesome artisanal cocktails. There's something going on every night of the week, and the stylish outdoor space is great for cocktails under the stars, movie screenings, and live music. ✉ *729 S.W. 1st Ave., Downtown* ☎ *305/671–3307* ⊕ *www.blackbirdordinary.com.*

E11EVEN Miami

DANCE CLUBS | After a $40-million cash infusion, the former Gold Rush building has been transformed into an ultraclub with LED video walls, intelligent lighting, and a powerful sound system that pulses sports by day and beats by night, providing partygoers the 24/7 action they crave. Hospitality and VIP experiences are ample throughout the private lounges and second-level champagne room; however, the real action is in The Pit, featuring burlesque performances and intermittent Cirque du Soleil–style shows from a hydraulic-elevating stage. The fusion of theatrics and technology attracts an A-list clientele. Head up to the roof to find an intimate restaurant that serves tapas as well as a live music lounge. ✉ *29 N.E. 11th St., Downtown* ☎ *305/829–2911* ⊕ *www.11miami.com.*

★ Komodo

CAFES—NIGHTLIFE | This swank, triple-story indoor/outdoor resto-lounge is the apex of the Downtown Miami scene, whether standing and posing at one of the three bars, dining in the floating birds nests of the 300-seat restaurant, or partying alongside celebs to DJ-led tunes inside the top-floor Komodo Lounge. The brains behind this hedonistic treehouse complex is David Grutman, the impresario behind Miami Beach's legendary LIV nightclub. ✉ *801 Brickell Ave., Downtown* ☎ *305/534–2211* ⊕ *www.komodomiami.com.*

★ Sugar

BARS/PUBS | This skyscraping rooftop bar, hands down the best in the city, is the essence of the new Downtown Miami: futuristic, worldly, and beyond sleek. It crowns the 40th floor of East, Miami, the luxury hotel tucked inside one of Miami's most ambitious multiuse endeavors: the billion-dollar-plus Brickell City Centre complex. The sunsets here are spectacular, as are the Southeast Asian bites and the exotic cocktails. ⊠ *788 Brickell Plaza, Downtown* ☎ *305/805–4655* ⊕ *www. sugar-miami.com.*

 ## Shopping

★ Acqua di Parma

PERFUME/COSMETICS | Downtown Miami's Brickell City Centre houses the one and only stand-alone store of this Italian fragrance and skin-care brand in the United States. But there's so much more than scents and fragrances for sample and sale in the 1,000-square-foot, marble-clad boutique; consumers can also purchase the brand's line of leather bags, travel accessories, and candles. Additionally, an in-store barbershop offers razor shaves with Acqua di Parma's coveted men's grooming products, the Collezione Barbiere. ⊠ *Brickell City Centre, Level 1, 701 S. Miami Ave., Downtown* ☎ *786/220–8840* ⊕ *www.acquadiparma.com.*

★ Brickell City Centre

SHOPPING CENTERS/MALLS | A billion dollars in the making, this sleek, three-city-block, mixed-use complex in the heart of Downtown is rife with multiple levels of designer stores, restaurants, food halls, hotel rooms, and residences. The high-end retail rivals that in Bal Harbour and the Design District, solidifying Miami's status as a true shopping destination. The center is a grand fusion of indoor and outdoor space and futuristic architectural design, underscored by the striking, glass-and-steel Climate Ribbon, which controls the enclave's microclimate. ⊠ *701 S. Miami Ave., Downtown* ☎ *786/704–0223* ⊕ *www.brickellcitycentre.com.*

Fabiana Filippi

CLOTHING | Although most cities have to settle for a simple rack or section of famed Umbria-based women's wear Fabiana Filippi at high-end department stores, Brickell City Centre houses the one and only stand-alone Filippi boutique in the United States. Browse through a vast range of the current collections that may include resort wear, skinny jeans, pullovers, silhouettes, knitwear, overcoats, and jersey joggers, depending on the season. ⊠ *Brickell City Centre, Level 1, 701 S. Miami Ave., Downtown* ☎ *786/574–9621* ⊕ *www.fabianafilippi. com/us_en.*

 ## Activities

HistoryMiami Public City Tours

TOUR—SPORTS | Cultural institution HistoryMiami Museum runs some fabulous walking tours of Little Havana (spiked with plenty of Cuban coffees and cigars, of course), Little Haiti, the Design District, and Wynwood. Most tours run 90-minutes to one hour and are led by HistoryMiami historian Dr. Paul George, the authority on all things Miami. ⊠ *101 W. Flagler St., Downtown* ☎ *305/375–1492* ⊕ *www.historymiami.org* ☜ *$30.*

Island Queen Cruises

SAILING | **FAMILY** | Experiences on the very touristy Island Queen Cruises run the gamut—sunset cruises, dance cruises, fishing cruises, speedboat rides, and their signature tours of Millionaires' Row, Miami's waterfront homes of the rich and famous. The *Island Queen, Island Lady,* and *Miami Lady* are three double-decker, 140-passenger tour boats docked at Bayside Marketplace that set sail daily for 90-minute narrated tours of the Port of Miami and Millionaires' Row. ⊠ *401 Biscayne Blvd., Downtown* ☎ *844/295–8034* ⊕ *www.islandqueencruises.com* ☜ *From $19.*

Miami Heat

BASKETBALL | **FAMILY** | The 2006, 2012, and 2013 NBA champs play at the 19,600-seat, waterfront AmericanAirlines Arena. The downtown venue features restaurants, a wide patio overlooking Biscayne Bay, and a silver sun-shaped special-effects scoreboard with rays holding wide-screen TVs. Home games are held November through April. ✉ *AmericanAirlines Arena, 601 Biscayne Blvd., Downtown* ☎ *800/745–3000 ticket hotline, 786/777–1000 arena* 🌐 *www.nba.com/heat/tickets* 🎫 *$11–$385.*

Coconut Grove

A former haven for writers and artists, Coconut Grove has never quite outgrown its image as a small village. You can still feel the bohemian roots of this artsy neighborhood, but it has grown increasingly mainstream and residential over the past 20 years. Posh estates mingle with rustic cottages, modest frame homes, and stark modern dwellings, often on the same block. If you're into horticulture, you'll be impressed by the Garden of Eden–like foliage that seems to grow everywhere without care. In truth, residents are determined to keep up the Grove's village-in-a-jungle look, so they lavish attention on exotic plantings even as they battle to protect any remaining native vegetation.

The center of the Grove still attracts its fair share of locals and tourists who enjoy perusing the small boutiques, sidewalk cafés, and cute galleries that remind us of the old Grove. Activities here are family-friendly with easy access to bay-side parks, museums, and gardens.

👁 Sights

★ **Vizcaya Museum and Gardens**

HISTORIC SITE | **FAMILY** | Of the 10,000 people living in Miami between 1912 and 1916, about 1,000 of them were gainfully employed by Chicago industrialist James Deering to build this European-inspired residence. Once comprising 180 acres, this National Historic Landmark now occupies a 30-acre tract that includes a rockland hammock (native forest) and more than 10 acres of formal gardens with fountains overlooking Biscayne Bay. The house, open to the public, contains 70 rooms, 34 of which are filled with paintings, sculpture, antique furniture, and other fine and decorative arts. The collection spans 2,000 years and represents the Renaissance, baroque, rococo, and neoclassical periods. The 90-minute self-guided Discover Vizcaya Audio Tour is available in multiple languages for an additional $5. Moonlight tours, offered on evenings that are nearest the full moon, provide a magical look at the gardens; call for reservations. ✉ *3251 S. Miami Ave., Coconut Grove* ☎ *305/250–9133* 🌐 *www.vizcaya.org* 🎫 *$22* ⏲ *Closed Tues.*

🍴 Restaurants

Glass & Vine

$$$$ | **MODERN AMERICAN** | **FAMILY** | With a design that fuses the indoors and outdoors in the middle of Coconut Grove's residential Peacock Park, this charming, family-friendly restaurant by celebrity-chef Giorgio Rapicavoli (a champion on Food Network's *Chopped*) is as picturesque as it is unexpected. Parents can sit back and enjoy some incredible gourmet-style sharing plates (featuring local catch and produce) and the sensational wine selection, while the little ones are thoroughly entertained outside (there's even a playground). **Known for:** local fish tiradito; charred cauliflower appetizer; beautifully plated dishes. [$] *Average main: $34* ✉ *2820 McFarlane Rd., Coconut Grove* ☎ *305/200–5268* 🌐 *www.glassandvine.com.*

GreenStreet Cafe

$$ | **MEDITERRANEAN** | A tried-and-true locals' hangout since it was founded in

Sights ▼

1	Bill Baggs Cape Florida State Park **G9**
2	The Biltmore............. **B6**
3	Crandon Park Beach ... **G8**
4	Cuban Memorial Boulevard................. **E5**
5	Domino Park............. **E5**
6	El Titan de Bronze **F5**
7	Fairchild Tropical Botanic Garden **C8**
8	Margulies Collection at the Warehouse **F3**
9	Miami Seaquarium **G6**
10	Rubell Family Collection................. **F3**
11	Venetian Pool **C5**
12	Vizcaya Museum and Gardens.................. **E6**
13	Wynwood Walls **F3**
14	Zoo Miami **A8**

Restaurants ▼

1	Alter **F3**
2	Azucar Ice Cream Company................. **E5**
3	Cantina Beach **H8**
4	Chez Le Bebe............. **F2**
5	eating house **C5**
6	El Exquisito Restaurant................. **E5**
7	El Palacio de los Jugos..................... **D3**
8	Glass and Vine **D6**
9	GreenStreet Cafe **D6**
10	Harry's Pizzeria........... **F2**
11	Havana Harry's........... **C6**
12	Joey's **F3**
13	KYU...................... **F3**
14	Los Piñarenos Fruteria.................... **E5**
15	Mandolin Aegean Bistro..................... **F2**
16	Michael's Genuine Food & Drink **F2**
17	Monty's Raw Bar **D6**
18	Ortanique on the Mile ... **C5**
19	Panther Coffee........... **F3**
20	Peacock Garden Café............. **D6**
21	Plant Miami.............. **F3**
22	Rusty Pelican............ **G6**
23	Sugarcane Raw Bar Grill **F3**
24	Wynwood Kitchen & Bar..................... **F3**
25	Versailles **D5**

Hotels ▼

1	The Biltmore............. **B6**
2	Hyatt Regency Coral Gables.............. **C5**
3	The Mayfair at Coconut Grove **D6**
4	The Ritz-Carlton Coconut Grove, Miami **D6**
5	The Ritz-Carlton Key Biscayne, Miami **G8**

JFK Causeway
Biscayne Blvd.
MIAMI BEACH
DESIGN DISTRICT
Julia Tuttle Causeway
195
MIDTOWN
W. 29th St.
WOOD DISTRICT
Venetian Causeway
Belle Isle
SOUTH BEACH
A1A
Jungle Island
Watson Island
Miami Children's Museum
MacArthur Causeway
Art Deco District
Alton Rd.
Collins Ave.
Ocean Dr.
Port Miami
41
OCEAN
Fisher Island
nbacker
22
Causeway
9
Virginia Key
Crandon Park
Crandon Park
KEY BISCAYNE
3
ATLANTIC
5 3
1
KEY
1 Sights
1 Restaurants
1 Hotels
Bill Baggs Cape Florida State Park
Cape Florida Lighthouse

the early 1990s—with regulars including athletes, politicians, entrepreneurs, artists, and other prominent area names—this cozy café serves simple French-Mediterranean delights. Despite the restaurant's see-and-be-seen reputation, diners are encouraged to sit back and simply enjoy the experience with relaxed decor, good food, and friendly service. **Known for:** fruity cocktails; great breakfast; late-night lounging and noshing. $ *Average main: $19* ⊠ *3468 Main Hwy., Coconut Grove* ☎ *305/444–0244* ⊕ *www.greenstreetcafe.net.*

Monty's Raw Bar

$$$ | **SEAFOOD** | **FAMILY** | Monty's has a Caribbean flair, thanks especially to live calypso and island music on the outdoor terrace. Consider it a fun, tropical-style, kid-friendly place where Mom and Dad can kick back in the early evening and enjoy a beer and the raw bar while the kids eat conch fritters and dance to the beats. **Known for:** palapa-topped outdoor seating; tropical cocktails; waterfront views. $ *Average main: $23* ⊠ *Prime Marina Miami, 2550 S. Bayshore Dr., at Aviation Ave., Coconut Grove* ☎ *305/856–3992* ⊕ *www.montysrawbar.com.*

Peacock Garden Café

$$ | **AMERICAN** | **FAMILY** | Reinstating the artsy and exciting vibe of Coconut Grove circa once-upon-a-time, this lovely spot offers an indoor-outdoor, teatime setting for light bites like salads, soups, and sandwiches. By day it's one of Miami's most serene lunch spots, as the lushly landscaped courtyard is lined with alfresco seating, drawing some of Miami's most fabulous ladies who lunch. **Known for:** old-school charm; idyllic setting for lunch; daily homemade soups. $ *Average main: $17* ⊠ *2889 McFarlane Rd., Coconut Grove* ☎ *305/774–3332* ⊕ *www. peacockspot.jaguarhg.com.*

Hotels

Although this area certainly can't replace the draw of Miami Beach or the business convenience of Downtown, about 20 minutes away, it's an exciting bohemian-chic neighborhood with a gorgeous waterfront.

The Mayfair at Coconut Grove

$$$ | **HOTEL** | Some 30 years strong, this five-story hotel still reflects Coconut Grove's bohemian roots, best exemplified by its eclectic exteriors: handcrafted wooden doors, one-of-a-kind decorative moldings, mosaic tiles inspired by Spain's Alhambra, and Gaudí-like ornaments adorning the rooftop pool deck. **Pros:** in the heart of walkable Coconut Grove; details in exterior design; rooftop pool. **Cons:** limited lighting within rooms; interior design looks dated; construction nearby. $ *Rooms from: $359* ⊠ *3000 Florida Ave., Coconut Grove* ☎ *800/433–4555* ⊕ *www.mayfairhotelandspa.com* ⊅ *179 rooms* ⊙| *No meals.*

★ The Ritz-Carlton Coconut Grove, Miami

$$$$ | **HOTEL** | In the heart of Coconut Grove, this business-oriented hotel was completely reimagined in 2018 to create an elegant and modern design masterpiece that rivals top leisure properties in Miami Beach and Downtown. **Pros:** elevated pool deck; fresh from renovation; in an easily walkable area. **Cons:** near residential area; not on beach; lots of conventioneers. $ *Rooms from: $577* ⊠ *3300 S.W. 27th Ave., Coconut Grove* ☎ *305/644–4680* ⊕ *www.ritzcarlton.com/ coconutgrove* ⊅ *115 rooms* ⊙| *No meals.*

Shopping

The Griffin

SHOES/LUGGAGE/LEATHER GOODS | This small boutique packs a big punch with today's most coveted womens' shoe styles, with the latest from Aquazarra to Chloe to Valentino and Loeffler Randall. Walk around once, then do it again, and you're sure to find another style urging you to try it on. Need help pulling the trigger? The boutique's stocked bar eases the pain of pricey purchases. ✉ *3112 Commodore Plaza, Coconut Grove* ☎ *786/631–3522.*

Unika

CLOTHING | A longtime fashion resident of Coconut Grove (circa 1989), Unika takes shoppers from day to night, and all affairs in between, with a wide range of inventory for men and women. The contemporary boutique has an it-girl vibe, but the cool, relaxed one you'd actually want to be friends with. High–low pricing appeases all budgets; expect to uncover up-and-coming designer gems tucked within the racks of well-known brands. Bonus: the staff is great with styling for a head-to-toe look. ✉ *3432 Main Hwy., Coconut Grove* ☎ *305/445–4752.*

Coral Gables

You can easily spot Coral Gables from the window of a Miami-bound jetliner—just look for the massive orange tower of The Biltmore hotel rising from a lush green carpet of trees concealing the city's gracious homes. The canopy is as much a part of this planned city as its distinctive architecture, all attributed to the vision of George E. Merrick more than a century ago.

The story of this city began in 1911, when Merrick inherited 1,600 acres of citrus and avocado groves from his father. Through judicious investment he nearly doubled the tract to 3,000 acres by 1921. Merrick dreamed of building an American Venice here, complete with canals and homes. Working from this vision, he began designing a city based on centuries-old prototypes from Mediterranean countries. Unfortunately for Merrick, the devastating no-name hurricane of 1926, followed by the Great Depression, prevented him from fulfilling

many of his plans. He died at 54, an employee of the post office. Today Coral Gables has a population of about 51,000. In its bustling downtown more than 150 multinational companies maintain headquarters or regional offices, and the University of Miami campus in the southern part of the Gables brings a youthful vibrancy to the area. A southern branch of the city extends down the shore of Biscayne Bay through neighborhoods threaded with canals.

◉ Sights

The Biltmore

BUILDING | Bouncing back stunningly from its dark days as an army hospital, this hotel has become the jewel of Coral Gables—a dazzling architectural gem with a colorful past. First opened in 1926, it was a hot spot for the rich and glamorous of the Jazz Age until it was converted to an army–air force regional hospital in 1942. Until 1968 the Veterans Administration continued to operate the hospital after World War II. The Biltmore then lay vacant for nearly 20 years before it underwent extensive renovations and reopened as a luxury hotel in 1987. Its 16-story tower, like the Freedom Tower in Downtown Miami, is a replica of Seville's Giralda Tower. The magnificent pool is reportedly the largest hotel pool in the continental United States. ∎TIP→ **Because it functions as a full-service hotel, your ticket in—if you aren't staying here—is to patronize one of the hotel's several restaurants or bars. Try to get a courtyard table for the Sunday champagne brunch, a local legend.** ✉ *1200 Anastasia Ave., Coral Gables* ✛ *Near De Soto Blvd.* ☎ *855/311–6903* ⊕ *www.biltmorehotel.com.*

Fairchild Tropical Botanic Garden

GARDEN | **FAMILY** | With 83 acres of lakes, sunken gardens, a 560-foot vine pergola, orchids, bellflowers, coral trees, bougainvillea, rare palms, and flowering trees, Fairchild is the largest tropical botanical garden in the continental United States.

The tram tour highlights the best of South Florida and exotic flora; then you can set off exploring on your own. The 2-acre Simons Rainforest showcases tropical plants from around the world complete with a waterfall and stream. The conservatory is home to rare tropical plants, including the Burmese endemic *Amherstia nobilis,* flowering annually with orchidlike pink flowers. The Keys Coastal Habitat, created in a marsh and mangrove area in 1995 with assistance from the Tropical Audubon Society, provides food and shelter to resident and migratory birds. The excellent bookstore-gift shop carries books on gardening and horticulture, and the Garden Café serves sandwiches and, seasonally, smoothies made from the garden's own crop of tropical fruits. ✉ *10901 Old Cutler Rd., Coral Gables* ☎ *305/667–1651* ⊕ *www. fairchildgarden.org* ✐ *$25.*

Venetian Pool

POOL | FAMILY | Sculpted from a rock quarry in 1923 and fed by artesian wells, this 820,000-gallon municipal pool had a major face-lift in 2018. It remains quite popular because of its themed architecture—a fantasy version of a waterfront Italian village—created by Denman Fink. The pool has earned a place on the National Register of Historic Places and showcases a nice collection of vintage photos depicting 1920s beauty pageants and swank soirées held long ago. Paul Whiteman played here, Johnny Weissmuller and Esther Williams swam here, and you should, too (note: children must be at least three years old and 38 inches tall). A snack bar, lockers, and showers make these historic splash grounds user-friendly as well, and there's free parking across De Soto Boulevard. ✉ *2701 De Soto Blvd., at Toledo St., Coral Gables* ☎ *305/460–5306* ⊕ *www.coralgables.com/venetian-pool* ✐ *$20.*

Zoo Miami. Don't miss a visit to this top-notch zoo, 14 miles southwest of Coral Gables in the Miami suburbs. The only subtropical zoo in the continental United States, it has 320-plus acres that are home to more than 2,000 animals, including 40 endangered species, which roam on islands surrounded by moats. Amazon & Beyond encompasses 27 acres of simulated tropical rain forests showcasing 600 animals indigenous to the region, such as giant river otters, harpy eagles, anacondas, and jaguars. The Wings of Asia aviary has about 300 exotic birds representing 70 species flying free within the junglelike enclosure. Kids love visiting the meerkats and participating in the thrice-daily camel feedings at the Critter Connection exhibit. ✉ *12400 S.W. 152nd St. (1 Zoo Blvd.), Richmond Heights* ☎ *305/251–0400* ⊕ *www. zoomiami.org* ✐ *$22.95; 45-min tram tour $6.50.*

 Beaches

Matheson Hammock Park and Beach

BEACH—SIGHT | FAMILY | Kids love the gentle waves and warm (albeit often murky) waters of this beach in Coral Gables's suburbia, near Fairchild Tropical Botanic Garden. But the beach is only part of the draw—the park includes a boardwalk trail, a playground, and a golf course. Plus, the park is a prime spot for kiteboarding. The man-made lagoon, or "atoll pool," is perfect for inexperienced swimmers, and it's one of the best places in mainland Miami for a picnic. Most tourists don't make the trek here; this park caters more to locals who don't want to travel all the way to Miami Beach. The park also offers a full-service marina. ■TIP→ **With an emphasis on family fun, it's not the best place for singles. Amenities:** parking (fee); toilets. **Best for:** swimming. ✉ *9610 Old Cutler Rd., Coral Gables* ☎ *305/665–5475* ⊕ *www.miamidade.gov/parks/matheson-hammock.asp* ✐ *$5 per vehicle weekdays, $7 weekends.*

🍴 Restaurants

eating house

$$$ | ECLECTIC | Check your calorie counter at the door when you enter this hip, small-plates restaurant, featuring an ever-changing menu that teems with extreme culinary innovation and unexpected flavor combinations. Save room for the famous "dirt cup" dessert, a "soil-filled" flowerpot, which is really crushed Oreos anchored by roots of pretzels, hazelnuts, and *tierra nueva* chocolate ice cream. **Known for:** chicken and waffles; intimate setting; foodie crowd. Ⓢ *Average main: $28 ⊠ 804 Ponce de León Blvd., Coral Gables ☎ 305/448–6524 ⊕ www.eatinghousemiami.com ☾ No lunch weekends.*

El Palacio de los Jugos

$ | CUBAN | FAMILY | To the northwest of Coral Gables proper, this small but boisterous indoor-outdoor market is one of the easiest and truest ways to see Miami's local Latin life in action. Besides the rows of fresh, tropical exotic fruits and vegetables—and the shakes you can make with any of them—Miami's original food hall has numerous counters where you can get a wide variety of Latin American food from *pan con lechón* (roast pork on Cuban bread) to fried pork rinds. **Known for:** fresh, cold coconut water in the shell; no-frills feel; picnic-style tables. Ⓢ *Average main: $8 ⊠ 5721 W. Flagler St., Flagami, Coral Gables ☎ 305/264–1503 ⊕ www.elpalaciodelosjugos.com/en ▤ No credit cards.*

Havana Harry's

$$ | CUBAN | FAMILY | When Cuban families want an affordable home-cooked meal with a twist but don't want to cook it themselves, they come to this big, unassuming restaurant. The fare is traditional Cuban: long, thin, panfried steaks known as *bistec palomilla*, roast chicken with citrus marinade, and fried pork chunks; most dishes come with white rice, black beans, and a choice of ripe or green plantains. **Known for:** mariquitas (plantain chips) with mojo; acclaimed flan; "tres leches overdose" dessert. Ⓢ *Average main: $17 ⊠ 4612 Le Jeune Rd., Coral Gables ☎ 305/661–2622 ⊕ www.havanaharrys.com.*

Ortanique on the Mile

$$$$ | CARIBBEAN | Cascading *ortaniques*, a Jamaican hybrid orange, are hand-painted on columns in this warm, welcoming, yellow dining room, setting an ideal stage for chef-partner Cindy Hutson's "cuisine of the sun." Food is vibrant in taste and color, imbued with island flavors, with dishes like the West Indian–style bouillabaisse and the daily fresh-catch ceviche. **Known for:** creative, tropical cocktails; passionate staff; excellent seafood. Ⓢ *Average main: $41 ⊠ 278 Miracle Mile, Coral Gables ☎ 305/446–7710 ⊕ www.ortaniquerestaurants.com ☾ No lunch weekends.*

Hotels

Beautiful Coral Gables is set around its beacon, the national landmark Biltmore hotel. The University of Miami is nearby.

The Biltmore

$$$$ | HOTEL | Built in 1926, this landmark hotel has had several incarnations over the years—including a stint as a hospital during World War II—but through it all, this grande dame has remained an opulent reminder of yesteryear, with its palatial lobby and grounds, enormous pool (largest in the Lower 48), and distinctive 315-foot tower, which rises above the canopy of trees shading Coral Gables. **Pros:** breathtaking history-steeped lobby; gorgeous pool; great golf. **Cons:** in the suburbs; a car is necessary to get around; nonrenovated rooms look tired. Ⓢ *Rooms from: $549 ⊠ 1200 Anastasia Ave., Coral Gables ☎ 855/311–6903 ⊕ www.biltmorehotel.com ⟲ 312 rooms ꕤ No meals.*

Hyatt Regency Coral Gables

$$ | **HOTEL** | Within walking distance to the shops and businesses of Miami's most prestigious suburb and just 4 miles from Miami International Airport, this Moorish-inspired property mingles European charm with functionality. **Pros:** pet-friendly (for a fee); meets rigorous green standards; walking distance to several local restaurants. **Cons:** small bathrooms; bland design; no spa. [$] *Rooms from: $259* ✉ *50 Alhambra Plaza, Coral Gables* ☎ *305/441–1234* 🌐 *www.coralgables.regency.hyatt.com* 🛏 *253 rooms* 🍴 *No meals.*

Nightlife

The Bar

BARS/PUBS | One of the oldest bars in South Florida (est. 1946), the old Hofbrau has been reincarnated a few times and now goes by the name "The Bar." A massive American flag hangs on the wall of this locals' hangout, arguably the only cool nightlife in suburban Coral Gables. The Bar delivers DJ-led tunes Wednesday through Saturday night and karaoke on Tuesday night. Oh, and they have pretty awesome, farm-fresh bar food, too. ✉ *172 Giralda Ave., at Ponce de León Blvd., Coral Gables* ☎ *305/442–2730* 🌐 *www.gablesthebar.com.*

El Carajo

TAPAS BARS | The back of a Mobil gas station is perhaps the most unexpected location for a wine bar, yet for 30 years a passion for good food and drink has kept this family-run business among Miami's best-kept secrets. Tables are in the old-world-style wine cellar, stocked with bottles representing all parts of the globe (and at excellent prices). A waiter takes your order from the menu of exquisite cheeses and charcuterie, hot and cold tapas, paellas, and, of course, wine. ✉ *2465 S.W. 17th Ave., Coral Gables* ☎ *305/856–2424* 🌐 *www.el-carajo.com.*

Shopping

★ **Books & Books, Inc.**

BOOKS/STATIONERY | **FAMILY** | Greater Miami's only independent English-language bookshop specializes in contemporary and classical literature as well as in books on the arts, architecture, Florida, and Cuba. The Coral Gables store is the largest of seven South Florida stores. Here, you can sip 'n' read in the courtyard lounge or dine at the old-fashioned in-store café while browsing the photography gallery. Multiple rooms are filled with myriad genres, making for a fabulous afternoon of book shopping; plus there's an entire area dedicated to kids. There are book signings, literary events, poetry, and other readings, too. ✉ *265 Aragon Ave., Coral Gables* ☎ *305/442–4408* 🌐 *www.booksandbooks.com.*

Miracle Mile

SHOPPING NEIGHBORHOODS | The centerpiece of the downtown Coral Gables shopping district, lined with trees and busy with strolling shoppers, is home to a host of exclusive couturiers and bridal shops as well as some men's and women's boutiques, jewelry, and home-furnishings stores. The half-mile "mile" runs from Douglas Road to LeJeune Road and Aragon Avenue to Andalusia Avenue, but many of the Gables' best nonbridal shops are found on side streets, off the actual mile. In addition, the street itself teems with restaurants—more than two dozen—facilitating a fabulous afternoon of shopping and eating. **TIP→ If debating Miracle Mile versus Bal Harbour or the Design District, check out the others first.** ✉ *Miracle Mile (Coral Way), Coral Gables* ✥ *Douglas Rd. to LeJeune Rd., and Aragon Ave. to Andalusia Ave.* 🌐 *www.shopcoralgables.com.*

Nic Del Mar

CLOTHING | **FAMILY** | Attending one of Miami's famed pool parties practically requires a trip to this upscale swimwear boutique. From the teeny weeny to innovative one-pieces to sporty cuts, the varied suit selection includes Mara Hoffman, Acacia, and Zimmerman, many of which include matching children's styles for mini beach babes. Flowy cover-ups by the same labels and more can easily double as dinner dresses, while hats, totes, lotions, and even metallic temporary tattoos add a sun-kissed touch. Men's styles are also available. ⊠ *475 Biltmore Way, Suite 105, Coral Gables* ☎ *305/442–8080* ⊕ *www.nicdelmar.com* ☾ *Closed Sun.*

Ramon Puig Guayaberas

CLOTHING | This clothing shop sells custom-made Ramon Puig guayaberas, the natty four-pocket dress shirts favored by older Cuban men and hipsters alike. Ramon Puig is known as "the King of Guayaberas," and his shirts are top of the line as far as guayaberas go. Hundreds are available off the rack. There are styles for women, too. ⊠ *5840 S.W. 8th St., Coral Gables* ☎ *855/ 482–9223* ⊕ *www. ramonpuig.com.*

Silvia Tcherassi

CLOTHING | The famed, Miami-based Colombian designer's signature boutique in the Shops at Merrick Park features ready-to-wear, feminine, and frilly dresses and separates accented with chiffon, toile, and sequins. You'll see plenty of Tcherassi's designs on Miami's Latin power players at events and A-list parties. A neighboring atelier at 270 San Lorenzo Avenue showcases the designer's bridal collection. ⊠ *Shops at Merrick Park, 350 San Lorenzo Ave., No. 2140, Coral Gables* ☎ *305/461–0009* ⊕ *www. silviatcherassi.com.*

Shops at Merrick Park

SHOPPING CENTERS/MALLS | At this open-air Mediterranean-style, tri-level, shopping-and-dining venue, Neiman Marcus and Nordstrom anchor over 100 specialty shops. Outposts by Jimmy Choo, Tiffany &Co., CH Carolina Herrera, and Gucci fulfill most high-fashion needs, and haute-decor shopping options include Brazilian contemporary-furniture designer Artefacto. ⊠ *358 San Lorenzo Ave., Coral Gables* ☎ *305/529–0200* ⊕ *www.shop-satmerrickpark.com.*

🏃 Activities

★ Biltmore Golf Course

GOLF | On the grounds of the historic Biltmore hotel, the championship Biltmore Golf Course was designed in 1925 by Scotsman Donald Ross, the "it" golf designer of the Roaring Twenties. Today, after an extensive renovation and expansion in 2018, the lush course looks better than ever and is easily accessible thanks to its advanced online booking system. There's a pro shop on-site, and golf instruction is available through the Biltmore Golf Academy or the more extensive on-site Golf Channel Academy. ⊠ *The Biltmore, 1210 Anastasia Ave., Coral Gables* ☎ *305/460–5364* ⊕ *www. biltmorehotel.com/golf* 🖾 *$122 for 9 holes, $200 for 18 holes* 🏌 *18 holes, 7800 yards, par 71.*

Key Biscayne

Once upon a time, the two barrier islands that make up the village of Key Biscayne (Key Biscayne itself and Virginia Key) were outposts for fishermen and sailors, pirates and salvagers, soldiers and settlers. The 95-foot Cape Florida Lighthouse stood tall during Seminole Indian battles and hurricanes. Coconut plantations covered two-thirds of Key Biscayne, and there were plans as far back as the 1800s to develop the picturesque island as a resort for the wealthy. Fortunately, the state and county governments set much of the land aside for parks, and both keys are now home to top-ranked beaches and golf, tennis, softball, and picnicking facilities. The long and winding bike paths that run through the islands are favorites for in-line skaters and cyclists. Incorporated in 1991, the village of Key Biscayne is a hospitable community of about 13,200, even though Virginia Key remains undeveloped at the moment. These two playground islands are especially family-friendly.

Sights

Miami Seaquarium

ZOO | FAMILY | This classic family attraction promotes environmental education and raises conservation awareness yet stages shows with sea lions, dolphins, and other marine animals (including killer whales). Discovery Bay, an endangered-mangrove habitat, is home to sea turtles, alligators, herons, egrets, and ibis. You can also visit a shark pool, a tropical reef aquarium, and West Indian and Florida manatees. A popular interactive attraction is the Stingray Touch Tank, where you can touch and feed cow-nose rays and southern stingrays. Another big draw is the Dolphin Interaction program, including the quite intensive Dolphin Odyssey ($210) experience and the lighter shallow-water Dolphin Encounter ($150). ⊠ *4400 Rickenbacker Causeway, Virginia Key* ☎ *305/361–5705* ⊕ *www.miamiseaquarium.com* ⊠ *$46.99, parking $10 (cash only).*

Beaches

★ Bill Baggs Cape Florida State Park

BEACH—SIGHT | FAMILY | Thanks to inviting beaches, sunsets, and a tranquil lighthouse, this park at Key Biscayne's southern tip is worth the drive. In fact, the 1-mile stretch of pure beachfront has been named several times in Dr. Beach's revered America's Top 10 Beaches list. It has 18 picnic pavilions available as daily rentals, two cafés that serve light lunches that include several Cuban specialties, and plenty of space to enjoy the umbrella and chair rentals. A stroll or ride along walking and bicycle paths provides wonderful views of Miami's dramatic skyline. From the southern end of the

Sail Away

If you can sail in Miami, do. Blue skies, calm seas, and a view of the city skyline make for a pleasurable outing—especially at twilight, when the fabled "moon over Miami" casts a soft glow on the water. Key Biscayne's calm waves and strong breezes are perfect for sailing and windsurfing, and although Dinner Key and the Coconut Grove waterfront remain the center of sailing in Greater Miami, sailboat moorings and rentals sit along other parts of the bay and up the Miami River, too.

park you can see a handful of houses rising over the bay on wooden stilts, the remnants of Stiltsville, built in the 1940s and now protected by the Stiltsville Trust. The nonprofit group was established in 2003 to preserve the structures, because they showcase the park's rich history. Bill Baggs has bicycle rentals, a playground, fishing piers, and guided tours of the **Cape Florida Lighthouse,** South Florida's oldest structure. The lighthouse was erected in 1845 to replace an earlier one damaged in an 1836 Seminole attack, in which the keeper's helper was killed. Free tours are offered at the restored cottage and lighthouse at 10 am and 1 pm Thursday to Monday. Be there a half hour beforehand. **Amenities:** food and drink; lifeguards; parking (free); showers; toilets. **Best for:** solitude; sunset; walking. ⊠ *1200 S. Crandon Blvd., Key Biscayne* ☎ *305/361–5811* ⊕ *www.floridastateparks.org/park/Cape-Florida* ⊠ *$8 per vehicle; $2 per pedestrian.*

Crandon Park Beach

BEACH—SIGHT | FAMILY | This relaxing oasis in northern Key Biscayne offers renowned tennis facilities, a great golf course, a family amusement center, and 2 miles of beach dotted with palm trees. The park is divided by Key Biscayne's main road, with tennis and golf on the bay side, the beaches on the ocean side. Families really enjoy the beaches here—the sand is soft, there are no riptides, there's a great view of the Atlantic, and parking is both inexpensive and plentiful. Nevertheless, on weekends be prepared for a long hike from your car to the beach. There are bathrooms, outdoor showers, plenty of picnic tables, and concession stands. The family-friendly park offers abundant options for those who find it challenging simply to sit and build sand castles. Kite-board rentals and lessons are offered from the northern-end water-sports concessions, as are kayak rentals. Eco-tours and nature trails showcase the myriad ecosystems of Key Biscayne including mangroves, coastal hammock, and sea-grass beds. Bird-watching is great at the southern end of the park. **Amenities:** food and drink; lifeguards; parking (fee); showers; toilets; water sports. **Best for:** swimming; walking. ⊠ *6747 Crandon Blvd., Key Biscayne* ☎ *305/361–5421* ⊕ *www. miamidade.gov/Parks/crandon.asp* ⊡ *$5 per vehicle weekdays, $7 weekends.*

🍴 Restaurants

Cantina Beach

$$$ | **MEXICAN** | Discover a small, sumptuous piece of coastal Mexico at this feet-in-the-sand Mexican restaurant at The Ritz-Carlton Key Biscayne, Miami. (Note: non–hotel guests are welcome.) Order the guacamole, prepared tableside, a few tequila-infused cocktails (like the sour black cherry Black Diamond margarita), and then move onto heartier plates of fajitas and enchiladas. **Known for:** top-shelf margaritas; ceviche; family-friendly setting. Ⓢ *Average main: $25* ⊠ *The Ritz-Carlton Key Biscayne, Miami, 455 Grand Bay Dr., Key Biscayne* ☎ *305/365–4500* ⊕ *www.ritzcarlton.com/ keybiscayne.*

Rusty Pelican

$$$$ | **MODERN AMERICAN** | Vistas of the bay and Miami skyline are sensational—whether you admire them through the floor-to-ceiling windows or from the expansive outdoor seating area, lined with alluring fire pits. The menu is split between tropically inspired small plates, ideal for sharing, and heartier entrées from land and sea. **Known for:** sunset views; crispy fried, whole local red snapper; protein-rich Rusty Pelican Board for Two. Ⓢ *Average main: $35* ⊠ *3201 Rickenbacker Causeway, Key Biscayne* ☎ *305/361–3818* ⊕ *www.therustypelican. com.*

Hotels

There's probably no other place in Miami where slowness is lifted to a fine art. On Key Biscayne there are no pressures, there's no nightlife outside of the Ritz-Carlton's great live Latin music weekends, and the dining choices are essentially limited to the hotel (which has five dining options, including the languorous, Havana-style RUMBAR).

⭐ **The Ritz-Carlton Key Biscayne, Miami**

$$$$ | **RESORT** | **FAMILY** | In an ultra-laid-back setting on serene Key Biscayne, it's only natural to appreciate the Ritz hallmarks of pampering with luxurious rooms (renovated in 2017), attentive service, five on-property dining options, and ample recreational activities for the whole family. **Pros:** a world away from city life; feet-in-the-sand restaurants; an adults-only pool. **Cons:** outside noise may permeate thin, sliding glass doors; beach sometimes seaweed-strewn; limited nearby dining options off-property. Ⓢ *Rooms from: $599* ⊠ *455 Grand Bay Dr., Key Biscayne* ☎ *305/365–4500* ⊕ *www.ritzcarlton.com/keybiscayne* 🛏 *402 rooms* ⦿❘ *No meals.*

⚡ Activities

Perfect weather and flat terrain make Miami–Dade County a popular place for cyclists; however, biking here can also be quite dangerous. Be very vigilant when biking on Miami Beach, or better yet, steer clear and bike the beautiful paths of Key Biscayne instead.

Crandon Golf at Key Biscayne

GOLF | On the serene island of Key Biscayne, overlooking Biscayne Bay, this top-rated, championship municipal golf course is considered one of the state's most challenging par-72 courses. Enveloped by tropical foliage, mangroves, saltwater lakes, and bay-side waters, the course also happens to be the only one in North America with a subtropical lagoon. The Devlin/Von Hagge–designed course has a USGA rating of 75.4 and a slope rating of 129 and has received national awards from both *Golfweek* and *Golf Digest*. The course is located on the south side of Crandon Park. ✉ *Crandon Park, 6700 Crandon Blvd., Key Biscayne* ☎ *855/465–3305 for tee times* ⊕ *www. golfcrandon.com* 🍴 *$140* 🏌 *18 holes, 7400 yards, par 72.*

Divers Paradise of Key Biscayne

SCUBA DIVING | This complete dive shop and diving-charter service, next to the Crandon Park Marina, includes equipment rental and scuba instruction with PADI and NAUI affiliation. Half-day (four-hour) dive trips and snorkel trips are offered Tuesdays through Sundays. ✉ *Crandon Park Marina, 4000 Crandon Blvd., Key Biscayne* ☎ *305/361–3483* ⊕ *www.keydivers.com* 🍴 *$65.*

Key Cycling

BICYCLING | On an island where biking is a way of life, this Key Biscayne bike shop carries a wide range of amazing bikes in its showroom, as well as any kind of bike accessory imaginable. Out-of-towners can rent mountain or hybrid bikes for $20 for two hours, $25 for the day, and $100 for the week. ✉ *Galleria Shopping Center, 328 Crandon Blvd., Suite 121, Key Biscayne* ☎ *305/361–0061* ⊕ *www. keycycling.com.*

Wynwood

North of Downtown, the formerly downtrodden Wynwood neighborhood has arrived, with an impressive mix of one-of-a-kind shops and art galleries, public art displays, see-and-be-seen bars, slick restaurants, and plenty of eye-popping graffiti. Wynwood's trendiness has proven infectious, also taking root in proximate neighborhoods. One thing is still missing from the emerging landscape: a decent hotel. On a positive note, it's kept the Wynwood vibe more local and less touristy. The downside: you'll need a vehicle to get here, and though in close proximity to one another, you'll also need a vehicle to get to nearby Midtown and the Design District.

Between Interstate 95 and Northeast 1st Avenue from 29th to 22nd streets lies the centerpiece of the edgy Wynwood neighborhood—the funky and edgy **Wynwood Art District** (⊕ *www.wynwood-miami.com*), which is peppered with galleries, art studios, and private collections accessible to the public. Though the neighborhood hasn't completely shed its dodgy past, artist-painted graffiti walls and reinvented urban warehouses have transformed the area from plain old grimy to supertrendy. The Wynwood Walls on Northwest 2nd Avenue between Northeast 25th and 26th streets are a cutting-edge enclave of modern urban murals. Nevertheless, these avant-garde graffiti displays by renowned artists are just the beginning; almost every street is colored with funky spray-paint art, making the neighborhood a photographer's dream. Wynwood's retail space is a hodgepodge of cheap garment stores, upscale boutiques, and contemporary galleries (some by appointment only). First-timers may want to visit during

Continued on page 71

DECO LANE

by Susan MacCallum Whitcomb

"It was an age of miracles, it was an age of art,
it was an age of excess, and it was an age of satire."

—F. Scott Fitzgerald, *Echoes of the Jazz Age*

The 1920s and '30s brought us flappers and gangsters, plunging stock prices and soaring skyscrapers, and plenty of headline-worthy news from the arts scene, from talking pictures and the jazz craze to fashions where pearls piled on and sequins dazzled. These decades between the two world wars also gave us an art style reflective of the changing times: art deco.

Distinguished by geometrical shapes and the use of industrial motifs that fused the decorative arts with modern technology, art deco became the architectural style of choice for train stations and big buildings across the country (think New york's Radio City Music Hall and Empire State Building).

Using a steel-and-concrete box as the foundation, architects dipped into art deco's grab bag of accessories, initially decorating facades with spheres, cylinders, and cubes. They later borrowed increasingly from industrial design, stripping elements used in ocean liners and automobiles to their streamlined essentials.

The style was also used in jewelry, furniture, textiles, and advertising. The fact that it employed inexpensive materials, such as stucco or terrazzo, helped art deco thrive during the Great Depression.

MIAMI BEACH'S ART DECO DISTRICT

With its warm beaches and tropical surroundings, Miami Beach in the early 20th century was establishing itself as America's winter playground. During the roaring '20s luxurious hostelries resembling Venetian palaces, Spanish villages, and French châteaux sprouted up. In the 1930s, middle-class tourists started coming, and more hotels had to be built. Designers like Henry Hohauser chose art deco for its affordable yet distinctive design.

An antidote to the gloom of the Great Depression, the look was cheerful and tidy. And with the whimsical additions of portholes, colorful racing bands, and images of rolling ocean waves painted or etched on the walls, these South Beach properties created an oceanfront fantasy world for travelers.

Many of the candy-colored hotels have survived and been meticulously restored. They are among the more than 800 buildings of historical significance in South Beach's art deco district. Composing much of South Beach, the 1-square-mile district is bounded by Dade Boulevard on the north, the Atlantic Ocean on the east, 6th Street on the south, and Alton Road on the west.

Because the district as a whole was developed so rapidly and designed by like-minded architects—**Henry Hohauser, L. Murray Dixon, Albert Anis,** and their colleagues—it has amazing stylistic unity. Nevertheless, on this single street you can trace the evolution of period form from angular, vertically emphatic early deco to

aerodynamically rounded Streamline Moderne. The relatively severe Cavalier and more curvaceous Cardozo are fine examples of the former and latter, respectively.

To explore the district, begin by loading up on literature in the **Art Deco Welcome Center** (✉ *1001 Ocean Dr.* ☎ *305/763–8026* ⊕ *www.mdpl.org*). If you want to view these historic properties on your own, just start walking. A four-block stroll north on Ocean Drive gets you up close to camera-ready classics: the **Clevelander** (1020), the **Tides** (1220), the **Leslie** (1244), the **Carlyle** (1250), the **Cardozo** (1300), the **Cavalier** (1320), and the **Winter Haven** (1400).

ARCHITECTURAL HIGHLIGHTS

FRIEZE DETAIL, CAVALIER HOTEL
The decorative stucco friezes outside the Cavalier Hotel at 1320 Ocean Drive are significant for more than aesthetic reasons. Roy France used them to add symmetry (adhering to the "Rule of Three") and accentuate the hotel's verticality by drawing the eye upward. The pattern he chose also reflected a fascination with ancient civilizations engendered by the recent rediscovery of King Tut's tomb and the Chichén Itzá temples.

Cavalier Hotel

LOBBY FLOOR, THE RALEIGH HOTEL
Terrazzo—a compound of cement and stone chips that could be poured, then polished—is a hallmark of deco design. Terrazzo floors typically had a geometric pattern, like this one in the The Raleigh Hotel, a 1940 building by L Murray Dixon at 1775 Collins avenue.

The Raleigh Hotel

CORNER FACADE, ESSEX HOUSE HOTEL
Essex House Hotel, a 1938 gem that appears permanently anchored at 1001 Collins Avenue, is a stunning example of Maritime deco (also known as Nautical Moderne). Designed by Henry Hohauser to evoke an ocean liner, the hotel is rife with marine elements, from the rows of porthole-style windows and natty racing stripes to the towering smokestack-like sign. With a prow angled proudly into the street corner, it seems ready to steam out to sea.

Essex House Hotel

NEON SPIRE, THE HOTEL
The name spelled vertically in eye-popping neon on the venue's iconic aluminum spire—Tiffany—bears evidence of the hotel's earlier incarnation. When the L. Murray Dixon–designed Tiffany Hotel was erected at 801 Collins Avenue in 1939, neon was still a novelty. Its use, coupled with the spire's rocket-like shape, combined to create a futuristic look influenced by the sci-fi themes then pervasive in popular culture.

The Hotel

ENTRANCE, SEÑOR FROG'S
Inspired by everything from car fenders to airplane noses, proponents of art deco's Streamline Moderne look began to soften buildings' hitherto boxy edges. But when Henry Hohauser designed Hoffman's Cafeteria in 1940 he took moderne to the max. The landmark at 1450 Collins Avenue (now Señor Frog's) has a sleek, splendidly curved facade. The restored interior echoes it through semicircular booths and rounded chair backs.

Señor Frog's

ARCHITECTURAL TERMS

The Rule of Three: Early deco designers often used architectural elements in multiples of three, creating tripartite facades with triple sets of windows, eyebrows, or banding.

Eyebrows: Small shelf-like ledges that protruded over exterior windows were used to simultaneously provide much-needed shade and serve as a counterpoint to a building's strong vertical lines.

Tropical Motifs: In keeping with the setting, premises were plastered, painted, or etched with seaside images. Palm trees, sunbursts, waves, flamingoes, and the like were particularly common.

Banding: Enhancing the illusion that these immobile structures were rapidly speeding objects, colorful horizontal bands (also called "racing stripes") were painted on exteriors or applied with tile.

Stripped Classic: The most austere version of art deco (sometimes dubbed Depression Moderne) was used for buildings commissioned by the Public Works Administration.

(top) Hotel Marlin; (left) Sherbrooke Hotel; (right) U.S. Post Office in Miami Beach.

Wynwood is famous for its walls covered by murals from famous contemporary artists, including these by Shepard Fairey.

Wynwood's monthly gallery walk on the second Saturday evening of each month, when studios and galleries are all open at the same time.

👁 Sights

Margulies Collection at the Warehouse

MUSEUM | Make sure a visit to Wynwood includes a stop at the Margulies Collection at the Warehouse. Martin Margulies's collection of vintage and contemporary photography, videos, and installation art in a 45,000-square-foot space makes for eye-popping viewing. Admission proceeds go to the Lotus Village, a local facility for homeless women and children. ✉ *591 N.W. 27th St., Wynwood* ✛ *Between N.W. 5th and 6th Aves.* ☎ *305/576–1051* ⊕ *www.margulieswarehouse.com* ▧ *$10* ⊘ *Closed May–Dec.*

★ Rubell Family Collection

MUSEUM | Fans of edgy art will appreciate the Rubell Family Collection. Mera and Don Rubell have accumulated work by artists from the 1970s to the present,

including Jeff Koons, Cindy Sherman, Damien Hirst, and Keith Haring. New, thematic and topical exhibitions debut annually during Art Basel in December. (For example, a previous exhibition *Still Human* delved into the impact of the digital revolution on the human condition.) Admission always includes a complimentary audio tour; however, true art lovers should opt for a complimentary guided tour of the collection, offered Wednesday through Saturday at 3 pm. The collection plans to move to a new, larger home on the outskirts of Wynwood by 2020. ✉ *95 N.W. 29th St., Wynwood* ✛ *Between N. Miami and N.W. 1st Aves.* ☎ *305/573–6090* ⊕ *www.rfc.museum* ▧ *$10* ⊘ *Closed Sept.–Nov.*

★ Wynwood Walls

LOCAL INTEREST | Between Northeast 25th and 26th streets on Northwest 2nd Avenue, the Wynwood Walls are a cutting-edge enclave of modern urban murals, reflecting diversity in graffiti and street art. More than 50 well-known and lesser-known artists have transformed

80,000 square feet of warehouse walls into an outdoor museum of sorts (bring your camera). The popularity of the walls spawned the neighboring Wynwood Doors and Garden, an industrial space rife with metal roll-down gates also used as blank canvases, complemented by a garden with singular pieces of art and an eye-popping indoor gallery. ✉ *2520 N.W. 2nd Ave., Wynwood* 🌐 *www.thewynwoodwalls.com.*

🍴 Restaurants

★ Alter

$$$$ | ECLECTIC | James-Beard finalist and local superstar chef Bradley Kilgore is always changing the menu based on ingredient availability and then taking on the awesome task of transforming food into edible art. The best way to experience Kilgore's one-of-a-kind taste sensations is through the five- or seven-course tasting menu or, better yet, the wine-paired full chef's experience. **Known for:** interactive chef's counter; locavore patrons; tzatziki ice cream. [$] *Average main: $34* ✉ *223 N.W. 23rd St., Wynwood* ☎ 🌐 *www.altermiami.com.*

Joey's

$$ | ITALIAN | This small, modern Italian café offers a full line of flatbread pizzas, including the legendary *dolce e piccante* with figs, Gorgonzola, honey, and hot pepper—it's sweet-and-spicy goodness through and through. Joey's also serves the full gamut of Italian favorites in an intimate indoor space or on the buzzing patio. **Known for:** fresh burrata; true local feel; affordable wine selection. [$] *Average main: $19* ✉ *2506 N.W. 2nd Ave., Wynwood* ☎ *305/438–0488* 🌐 *www.joeyswynwood.com* 🕒 *No dinner Mon.*

★ KYU

$$$$ | ECLECTIC | Foodies and locavores love this eco-minded restaurant in the heart of Wynwood, which plants five trees for every tree burned in its Japanese wood-fired grill. The Asian-inspired, small-plates menu wows through creative dishes such as the epic roasted cauliflower with goat cheese and shishito-herb vinaigrette and sizzling Thai fried-rice stone pot with king crab. **Known for:** living walls; apex of Wynwood atmosphere; flavor-rich small plates. [$] *Average main: $32* ✉ *251 N.W. 25th St., Wynwood* ☎ *786/577–0150* 🌐 *www.kyurestaurants.com.*

★ Panther Coffee

$ | CAFÉ | The original location of the Miami-based specialty coffee roaster is smack in the center of the Wynwood Arts District (it has now expanded into Miami Beach and other South Florida neighborhoods), attracting a who's who of hipsters, artists, and even suburbanites to indulge in small-batch cups of joe and supermoist muffins and fresh-baked pastries. Baristas gingerly prepare every order, so expect to wait a little for your macchiato. **Known for:** cool clientele; strong coffee; fabulous people-watching. [$] *Average main: $5* ✉ *2390 N.W. 2nd Ave., Wynwood* ☎ *305/677–3952* 🌐 *www.panthercoffee.com.*

★ Plant Miami

$$$$ | VEGETARIAN | Among Miami's new wave of plant-based, vegan restaurants, Plant Miami ranks tops in terms of both cuisine and design. While taking in the zen surrounds of The Sacred Space Miami, an indoor-meets-outdoor expansive wellness zone near the hubub of Wynwood, feast on hypercreative, hyperfresh dishes with global influences including those with an oh-so-Miami Latin flair (Think: Mexican-inspired jackfruit tacos *al pastor*, Cuban-inspired *sous vide* mushroom *ropa vieja*, and Argentinian-inspired cauliflower steak with chimichurri.). **Known for:** gorgeous open kitchen; biodynamic and organic spirits; serene outdoor space with reflection pool. [$] *Average main: $34* ✉ *The Sacred Space Miami, 105 N.E. 24th St., Wynwood* ☎ *305/814–5365* 🌐 *www.thesacredspacemiami.com/plant-miami.*

★ **Wynwood Kitchen & Bar**

$$$ | ECLECTIC | At the center of Miami's urban arts scene within the Wynwood Walls, Wynwood Kitchen & Bar offers an experience that includes both cultural and gastronomic excitement. Enjoy sharing-style, Latin-inspired small plates and artisanal cocktails while marveling at the powerful, hand-painted interiors and exterior murals by Shepard Fairey (of Obama *Hope* poster fame). **Known for:** ropa vieja empanadas; bacon-wrapped dates; graffiti art displays. [$] *Average main: $22* ✉ *2550 N.W. 2nd Ave., Wynwood* ☎ *305/722–8959* 🌐 *www.wynwoodkitchenandbar.com.*

Nightlife

Cafeina Wynwood Lounge

BARS/PUBS | For those in the know, on any given Miami weekend, the evening either begins or ends at this seductive, design-driven lounge with a gorgeous patio and plenty of art on display. It's simply a great place to hang out and get a true feel for Miami's cultural revolution. It's open only Thursday–Saturday (5 pm to 3 am Thursday and Friday, 8 pm to 3 am Saturday). ✉ *297 N.W. 23rd St., Wynwood* ☎ *305/438–0792* 🌐 *www.cafeinamiami.com.*

Wood Tavern

BREWPUBS/BEER GARDENS | This is a neighborhood hangout where anything—and anyone—goes: suits mix with hoodies, fashionistas mingle with hipsters, musicians chill with groupies, but everyone in the crowd gives off a warm, welcoming vibe. The outdoor terrace is a block party scene with Latin bites served from grafitti-covered car countertops and bleacher-style stairs from which to people-watch or bob to the beats as the DJ jumps from Cypress Hill to Led Zepplin. The scene is a bit of a welcomed, artsy departure from the sultry nightlife typically associated with the Magic City (wine and cocktails are served in red plastic cups). ✉ *2531 N.W. 2nd Ave., Wynwood* ☎ *305/748–2828* 🌐 *www.woodtavern.com.*

Wynwood Brewing Company

BREWPUBS/BEER GARDENS | This family-owned craft brewery is hidden among the towering walls of graffiti arts of Wynwood. Communal tables and ever-changing pop-up galleries by neighborhood artists make the taproom cozy; however, a peek through the window behind the bar reveals there is much more to the establishment: 15 pristine silver vats are constantly brewing variations of blond ale, IPA, barrel-aged strong ales, seasonal offerings, and national Gold Medalist the Robust Porter. All staff members are designated "Beer Servers" under the Cicerone Certification Program, ensuring knowledgeable descriptions and recommendations to your liking. ✉ *565 N.W. 24 St., Wynwood* ☎ *305/982–8732* 🌐 *www.wynwoodbrewing.com.*

Shopping

Base

CLOTHING | This is the quintessential fun-and-funky Miami boutique experience. Stop here for men's eclectic clothing, shoes, jewelry, and accessories that mix Japanese design with Caribbean-inspired materials. Constantly evolving, this shop features an intriguing magazine section, a record section, groovy home accessories, and the latest in men's swimwear and sunglasses. The often-present house-label designer may help select your wardrobe's newest addition. ✉ *2215 N.W. 2nd Ave., Wynwood* ☎ *305/531–4982* 🌐 *www.baseworld.com.*

Midtown

Northeast of Wynwood, Midtown (🌐 *www.midtownmiami.com*) lies between Northeast 29th and 36th streets, from North Miami Avenue to Northeast 2nd Avenue. This subcity is anchored by a multitower residential complex with prolific retail space, often housing great dining and trusted shopping brands.

 Restaurants

Sugarcane Raw Bar Grill

$$$$ | JAPANESE FUSION | The vibrant, supersexy, high-design restaurant perfectly captures Miami's Latin vibe while serving eclectic Latin American tapas and modern Japanese delights from three separate kitchens (*robata* grill, raw bar, and hot kitchen). Begin the Sugarcane experience in the alfresco lounge, engaging in a fabulous mix of standing, posing, flirting, and sipping on delicious cocktails, and then move on to a few of the some 60 small bites in the equally chic dining room. **Known for:** night crab sushi roll; crispy pig ear; great weekday happy hour. $ *Average main: $36* ✉ *3252 N.E. 1st Ave., Midtown* ☎ *786/369–0353* ⊕ *sugarcanerawbargrill.com.*

Nightlife

Lagniappe

GATHERING PLACES | Live musicians croon from the corner, with different bands each evening. Shelves house a selection of boutique-label wines with no corkage fee. Artisanal cheeses and meats are also available for the plucking and can be arranged into tapas-board displays. Once your selection is complete, take it back into the "living room" of worn sofas, antique lamps, and old-fashioned wall photos. Additional socializing can be found out in the "backyard" of mismatched seating and strung lighting. ✉ *3425 N.E. 2nd Ave., Midtown* ☎ *305/576–0108* ⊕ *www.lagniappehouse. com.*

Design District

North of Midtown, from about Northeast 38th to Northeast 42nd streets and across the other side of Interstate 195, the Design District (⊕ *www. miamidesigndistrict.net*) is yet another 18 blocks of clothiers, antiques shops, design stores, and bars and eateries. The real draws here are the interior design and furniture galleries as well as über-high-end shopping that's oh-so Rodeo Drive (and rivals Bal Harbour in North Beach).

Restaurants

★ Harry's Pizzeria

$$ | PIZZA | FAMILY | Harry's is a neighborhood spot with some seriously good pizza, as one would expect from Miami culinary darling Michael Schwartz and his team. The casual, friendly-yet-funky setting is inviting for all diner matchups, and seasonally inspired pizzas highlight locally sourced ingredients as unexpected, yet delicious, combinations as toppings for wood-fired, thin crusts. **Known for:** polenta fries; braised short rib pizza; warm chocolate chunk cookies. $ *Average main: $16* ✉ *3918 N. Miami Ave., Design District* ☎ *786/275–4963* ⊕ *www.harryspizzeria.com.*

★ Mandolin Aegean Bistro

$$$ | MODERN GREEK | A step inside this 1940s house-turned-bistro transports you to *ya-ya*'s home along the Aegean Sea. The Greek and Turkish cuisine is fresh and the service warm, matching its charming dining garden enlivened by an awning of trees, a rustic wooden canopy, and traditional village furnishings. **Known for:** signature Greek salad; bucolic courtyard; spectacular meze. $ *Average main: $29* ✉ *4312 N.E. 2nd Ave., Design District* ☎ *305/576–6066* ⊕ *www.mandolinmiami.com.*

★ Michael's Genuine Food & Drink

$$$ | ECLECTIC | Michael's is often cited as Miami's top tried-and-true restaurant, and it's not hard to see why: this indoor-outdoor bistro in Miami's Design District is an evergreen oasis for Miami dining sophisticates. Owner and chef Michael Schwartz aims for sophisticated eclectic cuisine with an emphasis on local and organic ingredients, and he gets it right (Think: crispy, sweet-and-spicy pork belly with kimchi and steamed mussels in coconut milk.). **Known for:** house-smoked bacon cheddar burger; sceney alfresco dining area; Sunday brunch. $ *Average main: $27 ⊠ 130 N.E. 40th St., Design District ☎ 305/573-5550 ⊕ www. michaelsgenuine.com.*

Shopping

Miami is synonymous with good design, and this ever-expanding visitor-friendly shopping district—officially from Northeast 38th to Northeast 42nd streets, between North Miami Avenue and Northeast 2nd Avenue (though unofficially beyond)—is an unprecedented melding of public space and the exclusive world of design. High-design buildings don the creativity of architects like Aranda & Lasch, Sou Fujimoto, and the Leong Leong firm. Throughout the district, there are more than 100 home design showrooms and galleries, including Bulthaup, Kartell, Ann Sacks, Poliform, and Luminaire Lab. Upscale retail outposts also grace the district. Cartier, Dolce & Gabbana, Fendi, Valentino, Giorgio Armani, Louis Vuitton, Prada, and Rolex sit next to design showrooms. Meanwhile, restaurants like Michael's Genuine Food & Drink and Mandolin Aegean Bistro also make this trendy neighborhood a hip place to dine. Unlike most showrooms, which are typically the beat of decorators alone, the Miami Design District's showrooms are open to the public and occupy windowed, street-level spaces. The area also has its own website: ⊕ *www. miamidesigndistrict.net.*

The Bazaar Project

ANTIQUES/COLLECTIBLES | Those looking for the rare and special need look no further than this boutique, curated by owner and Turkey-native Yeliz Titiz via her travels around the globe. Fashions, beauty, decor, and the wonderfully unusual exude the culture and craft akin to their respective regions. Highlights include whimsical housewares from Selab by Seletti, soaps by Haremlique, French wallpapers by Koziel, and intriguing jewelry by Titiz's own line, Sura. ⊠ *4308 N.E. 2nd Ave., Design District ☎ 786/703-6153 ⊕ www.thebazaarprojectshop.com.*

COS

CLOTHING | This Scandinavian fashion label, famous throughout all of Europe, presents its one and only retail outpost in Miami's Design District in a chic, bi-level, 3,700-square-foot space. The brand is the most exclusive arm of H&M brands, which translates to wardrobe essentials with youthful sophistication at affordable prices (a rarity in the Design District). Shop options for men, women, and children. ⊠ *Miami Design District, 3915 N.E. 1st Ave., Design District ☎ 786/857-5923 ⊕ www.cosstores.com.*

En Avance x Maison Francis Kurkdjian

CLOTHING | This Forall Studio–designed space commingles the Design District's first multibrand boutique and a French-fragrance luxury house. En Avance offers a feminine compilation of on-the-cusp designers like Protagonist and Anjuna. The owner's close connection with decorative artist Fornasetti brings to the store an extensive and exclusive selection of fashion-inspired furniture and accessories for the home. Style and beauty enthusiasts will also enjoy the table displays of lotions and potions by the iconic Maison Francis Kurkdjian. ⊠ *151 N.E. 41st St., Suite 129, Design District ☎ 305/576-0056 ⊕ www. enavance.com.*

Galerah Mizrahi

SPECIALTY STORES | Shop for the most stylish handbags by designer Galerah Mizrahi at her only brick-and-mortar boutique in the world. (Other than here, her bags are sold exclusively at Barneys New York.) Browse through Mizrahi's namesake collection of quirky python clutches, shoulder bags, and wallets, sometimes even running into the designer herself. ✉ *Miami Design District, 151 N.E. 41st St., Suite 119, Design District* ☎ *301/787–5209* 🌐 *www.gelarehmizrahi.com* 🕒 *Closed Sun.*

Genius Jones

GIFTS/SOUVENIRS | **FAMILY** | This is a modern design store for kids and parents. It's the best—and one of the few—places to buy unique children's gifts in Miami. Pick up high-design high chairs, strollers, and luggage by Bugaboo, vintage-rock onesies, and cool toys, ranging from rattles to dolls to hard-to-find Japanese imports. ✉ *170 N.E. 40th St., Design District* ☎ *305/571–2000* 🌐 *www.geniusjones.com.*

Little Haiti

Once a small farming community, Little Haiti is the heart and soul of Haitian society in the United States. In fact, Miami's Little Haiti is the largest Haitian community outside of Haiti itself. Although people of different ethnic backgrounds have begun to move into the neighborhood, people here are still surprised to see tourists. Nevertheless, owners of shops and restaurants tend to be welcoming. Creole is commonly spoken, although some people—especially younger folks—also speak English. Its northern and southern boundaries are 85th Street and 42nd Street, respectively, with Interstate 95 to the west and Biscayne Boulevard to the east in its southern reaches, then Northeast 4th Court to the east (two blocks west of Biscayne Boulevard). The best section to visit is along North Miami Avenue from 54th to 59th streets.

Right outside Little Haiti's boundaries, running from 50th to 77th streets along Biscayne Boulevard, is the MiMo Biscayne Boulevard Historic District, known in short as the MiMo District. This strip is noted for its Miami modernist architecture and houses a number of boutiques and design galleries. Within this district and in the neighborhoods to the east—collectively known as Miami's Upper East Side—several new restaurants are beginning to open.

🍴 Restaurants

Chez Le Bebe

$$ | **CARIBBEAN** | Chez Le Bebe offers a short menu of Haitian home cooking—it's been going strong for over 30 years and has been featured on shows like the Travel Channel's *Bizarre Foods with Andrew Zimmern* and *The Layover with Anthony Bourdain*. Try the stewed goat (the speciality) or the tender and flavorful chicken, fish, oxtail, or fried pork; each plate comes with rice, beans, plantains, and salad, for around $15. **Known for:** authentic Haitian eats; no-frills atmosphere; hefty portions. [$] *Average main: $15* ✉ *114 N.E. 54th St., Little Haiti* ☎ *305/751–7639* 💳 *No credit cards.*

🛍 Shopping

There's no shopping "scene" in Little Haiti—unless *botanicas* and voodoo supply shops are your thing. Nevertheless, farther east in Miami's Upper East Side lie several eclectic boutiques.

Fly Boutique

ANTIQUES/COLLECTIBLES | After 13 years on South Beach, this hip vintage clothing store moved to the up-and-coming MiMo District in Miami's Upper East Side. This resale boutique is where Miami hipsters flock for the latest arrival of used clothing. Glam designer pieces from the

1980s fly out at a premium price, but vintage camisoles and Levi's corduroys are still a resale deal. You'll find supercool art, furniture, luggage, and collectibles throughout the boutique. And be sure to look up—the eclectic lanterns are also for sale. ⊠ *7235 Biscayne Blvd., Upper East Side* ☎ *305/604–8508* ⊕ *www.flyboutiquevintage.com.*

Rebel

CLOTHING | Half new, half vintage consignment, the goods offered here make you feel as if you are raiding your stylish friend's closet. Racks are packed with all different types of styles and designers—from Lauren Moshi to Indah—requiring a little patience when sifting through. The store has a particularly strong collection of jeans, funky tees, and maxi dresses. ⊠ *7648 Biscayne Blvd., Upper East Side* ☎ *786/803–8828.*

Sweat Records

MUSIC STORES | For a timeless version of an old-fashioned favorite, visit Sweat Records, one of Miami's last remaining record stores. Sweat sells a wide range of music—rock, pop, punk, electronic, hip-hop, and Latino—as well as turntables and vinyl accessories; there's also Miami's only vegan, organic coffee shop on the premises. ⊠ *5505 N.E. 2nd Ave., Little Haiti* ☎ *786/693–9309* ⊕ *www.sweatrecordsmiami.com.*

Little Havana

First settled en masse by Cubans in the early 1960s, after Cuba's Communist revolution, Little Havana is a predominantly working-class area and the core of Miami's Hispanic community. Spanish is the principal language, but don't be surprised if the cadence is less Cuban and more Salvadoran or Nicaraguan: the neighborhood is now home to people from all Latin American countries.

If you come to Little Havana expecting the Latino version of New Orleans's French Quarter, you're apt to be disappointed—it's not about the architecture here. Rather, it's a place to soak in the atmosphere. Little Havana is more about great, inexpensive food (not just Cuban; there's Vietnamese, Mexican, and Argentinean here as well), distinctive affordable Cuban-American art, cigars, and great coffee. It's not a prefab tourist destination—this is real life in Spanish-speaking Miami.

Little Havana's semiofficial boundaries are 27th Avenue to 4th Avenue on the west, Miami River to the north, and Southwest 13th Street to the south. Much of the neighborhood is residential; however, you'll quickly discover the area's flavor, both literally and figuratively, along Calle Ocho (Southwest 8th Street), between Southwest 11th and 17th avenues, which is lined with cigar factories, cafés selling guava pastries and rose-petal flan, *botanicas* brimming with candles, and Cuban clothes and crafts stores. Your "Welcome to Little Havana" photo op shines on 27th Avenue and 8th Street. Giant hand-painted roosters are found scattered throughout the entire neighborhood, an artistic nod to their real-life counterparts that roam the streets here. You'll need to drive into Little Havana, since public transportation here is limited; but once on Calle Ocho, it's best to experience the neighborhood on foot.

 Sights

Cuban Memorial Boulevard

MEMORIAL | Four blocks in the heart of Little Havana are filled with monuments to Cuba's freedom fighters. South of Calle Ocho (8th Street), Southwest 13th Avenue becomes a ceiba tree–lined parkway known as Cuban Memorial Boulevard, divided at the center by a narrow grassy mall with a walking path through the various memorials. Among them is the *Eternal Torch of the Brigade 2506*, blazing with an endless flame and commemorating those who were killed in the failed Bay of Pigs invasion of 1961. Another is a bas-relief map of Cuba depicting each of its *municipios*. There's also a bronze statue in honor of Nestory (Tony) Izquierdo, who participated in the Bay of Pigs invasion and served in Nicaragua's Somozan forces. ✉ *S.W. 13th Ave., Little Havana* ✣ *Between S.W. 8th and S.W. 12th Sts.*

★ Domino Park

CITY PARK | If you're not yet ready to take advantage of the relaxed restrictions on travel to Cuba, watch a slice of Old Havana come to life in Miami's Little Havana. At Domino Park, officially known as Maximo Gomez Park, guayabera-clad seniors bask in the sun and play dominoes, while onlookers share neighborhood gossip and political opinions. ■ **TIP→ There is a little office at the park with a window where you can get information on Little Havana; the office also stores the dominoes for the older gents who play regularly, but it's BYOD (bring your own dominoes) for everyone else.** ✉ *801 S.W. 15th Ave., Little Havana* ☎ *305/859–2717 park office.*

El Titan de Bronze

LOCAL INTEREST | A peek at the intently focused cigar rollers through the windows doesn't prepare you for the rich, pungent scent that jolts your senses as you step inside the store. Millions of stogies are deftly hand-rolled at this family-owned cigar factory and retail store each year. Visitors are welcome to watch the rolling action (and, of course, buy some cigars). ✉ *1071 S.W. 8th St., Little Havana* ☎ *305/860–1412* 🌐 *www.eltitancigars.com.*

🍴 Restaurants

★ Azucar Ice Cream Company

$ | CAFÉ | FAMILY | More crafty than churning, flavors at this Cuban ice-cream shop are inspired and derived from ingredients at nearby fruit stands, international grocery shops, and farmers' markets. The menu features creations that nod to the culturally rich, Little Havana location (*café con leche*, flan, and the signature Abuela Maria—made with Maria cookies, cream cheese, and guava) as well as seasonal specialites (like sweet creamed corn and egg nog). **Known for:** Abuela Maria ice cream; flan ice cream; one-of-a-kind frozen indulgences. [$] *Average main: $6* ✉ *1503 S.W. 8th St., Little Havana* ☎ *305/381–0369* 🌐 *www.azucarice-cream.com.*

El Exquisito Restaurant

$ | LATIN AMERICAN | For a true locals' spot and some substantial Cuban eats in the heart of Little Havana, pop into this local institution that's been popular since the 1970s. The unassuming Cuban café serves up delectable, authentic Cuban favorites, including a great *cubano* (a grilled Cuban sandwich layered with ham, garlic-and-citrus-marinated slow-roasted pork, Swiss cheese, and pickles) and succulent yuca with garlic sauce. **Known for:** chatty regulars; 75 cent Cuban coffee; quick serve to-go window. [$] *Average main: $14* ✉ *1510 S.W. 8th St., Little Havana* ☎ *305/643–0227* 🌐 *www.elexquisitomiami.com* 💳 *No credit cards.*

Las Pinareños Fruteria

$ | CUBAN | If you're looking for something refreshing or a high-octane jolt while touring Little Havana, try this *fruteria* (fruit stand) that serves *coco frio* (fresh, cold coconut juice served in a whole coconut), mango juice, and other *jugos* (juices), as well as Cuban coffees and Cuban finger foods. You can order from the walk-up window and enjoy your drink at one of the tables inside the market. **Known for:** exotic juices; coco frio; friendly staff. [$] *Average main: $7* ✉ *1334 S.W. 8th St., Little Havana* ☎ *305/285–1135.*

★ Versailles

$$ | CUBAN | FAMILY | Miami visitors looking for that "Cuban food on Calle Ocho" experience, look no further: the storied eatery, where old émigrés opine daily about all things Cuban, is a stop on every political candidate's campaign trail, and it should be a stop for you as well. Order a heaping platter of *lechon asado* (roasted pork loin), *ropa vieja* (shredded beef), or *picadillo* (spicy ground beef), all served with rice, beans, and fried plantains. **Known for:** gossipy locals at takeout window; old-school Little Havana setting; guava-filled pastelitos. $ *Average main: $16* ✉ *3555 S.W. 8th St., Little Havana* ☎ *305/444–0240* ⊕ *www.versaillesrestaurant.com.*

Nightlife

★ Ball & Chain

MUSIC CLUBS | Established in 1935 and steeped in legends of gambling, Prohibition protests, the rise of budding entertainers Billie Holiday and Chet Baker, and the development of Cuban-centric Calle Ocho, this storied nightlife spot has been reestablished under its original name. The high-vaulted ceilings, floral wallpaper, black-and-white photos, and palm-fringed outdoor lounge nod to its torrid history and the glamour of Old Havana. Live music flows freely, as do the Latin-inspired libations and tapas of traditional Cuban favorites. ✉ *1513 S.W. 8th St., Little Havana* ☎ *305/643–7820* ⊕ *www. ballandchainmiami.com.*

Activities

Miami Marlins

BASEBALL/SOFTBALL | **FAMILY** | Miami's baseball team, formerly known as the Florida Marlins, then the Miami Marlins, then simply the Marlins, and now again as the Miami Marlins plays at the state-of-the-art Marlins Park—a 37,442-seat retractable-roof, air-conditioned baseball stadium on the grounds of Miami's famous Orange Bowl. Go see the team that came out of nowhere to beat the New York Yankees and win the 2003 World Series. Home games are

April through early October. ✉ *Marlins Park, 501 Marlins Way, Little Havana* ☎ *305/480–1300* ⊕ *www.marlins.com* ✉ *$10–$395; parking from $20 and should be prepurchased online.*

South Beach

The hub of Miami Beach is South Beach (better known as SoBe), with its energetic Ocean Drive, Collins Avenue, and Washington Avenue. Here life unfolds 24 hours a day. Beautiful people pose in hotel lounges and sidewalk cafés, bronzed cyclists zoom past palm trees, and visitors flock to see the action. On Lincoln Road, café crowds spill onto the sidewalks, weekend markets draw all kinds of visitors and their dogs, and thanks to a few late-night lounges, the scene is just as alive at night. Farther north (in Mid-Beach and North Beach), the vibe is decidedly quieter and more sophisticated.

◉ Sights

Art Deco Welcome Center and Museum
BUILDING | Run by the Miami Design Preservation League, the center provides information about the buildings in the district. An official Art Deco Museum opened within the center in October 2014, and a gift shop sells 1930s–'50s art deco memorabilia, posters, and books on Miami's history. Several tours also start here, including a self-guided audio tour and regular morning walking tours at 10:30 every day. On Thursdays a second tour takes place at 6:30 pm. ✉ *1001 Ocean Dr., South Beach* ☎ *305/672–2014, 305/531–3484 for tours* ⊕ *www.mdpl.org* ✉ *Tours $25.*

★ The Bass

MUSEUM | Special exhibitions join a diverse collection of international contemporary art at this museum whose original 1930s art deco building was designed by Russell Pancoast and

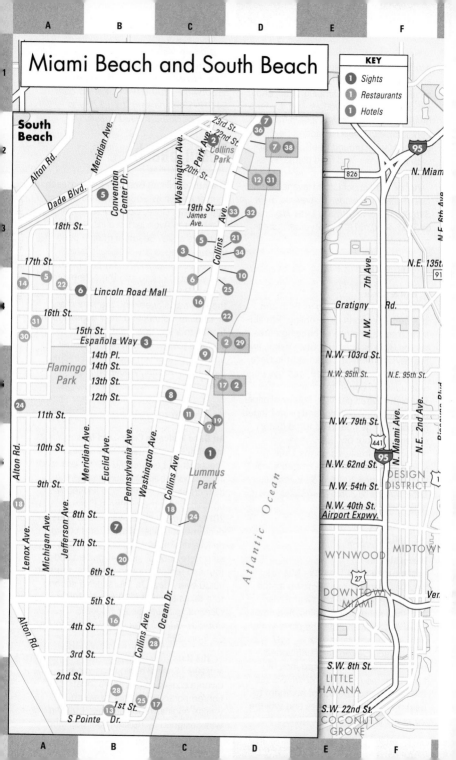

Sights ▼

1 Art Deco Welcome Center and Museum **C6**
2 The Bass.................**C2**
3 Española Way............**C5**
4 Haulover Beach Park **I3**
5 Holocaust Memorial.... **B3**
6 Lincoln Road Mall **A4**
7 South Beach **B7**
8 World Erotic Art Museum (WEAM)..................**C5**

Restaurants ▼

1 AQ Chop House by Il Mulino **I2**
2 Byblos.....................**C4**
3 Carpaccio Restaurant....**I4**
4 Cecconi's Miami Beach...**I7**
5 Chotto Matte Miami **A4**
6 Dolce Italian..............**C3**
7 The Dutch Miami **D2**
8 The Forge.................**I7**
9 Gianni's **C5**
10 Hakkasan Miami.........**I7**
11 Il Mulino New York-Sunny Isles **I2**
12 Jaya **D2**
13 Joe's Stone Crab........ **B9**
14 Juvia **A4**
15 Le Zoo.....................**I4**
16 Lobster Bar Sea Grille.. **B8**
17 LT Steak & Seafood **C5**
18 Macchialina.............. **A7**
19 Makoto...................**I4**
20 Malibu Farm..............**I6**
21 Matador Room **I7**
22 Meat Market **A4**
23 NaiYaRa..................**H8**
24 News Cafe................**C7**
25 Prime 112 .... **B9**
26 Pubbelly Noodle Bar ... **H7**
27 Pubbelly Sushi-South Beach **H7**
28 Red, the Steakhouse ... **B9**
29 Smith & Wollensky Miami Beach............. **H9**
30 Via Emilia 9 .... **A4**
31 Yardbird Southern Table & Bar.............. **A4**

Hotels ▼

1 Acqualina Resort & Spa on the Beach............ **I2**
2 The Betsy–South Beach **C5**
3 Cadet Hotel..............**C3**
4 Carillon Miami Wellness Resort **I5**
5 Catalina Hotel & Beach Club **C3**
6 Circa 39 Hotel **I7**
7 COMO Metropolitan Miami Beach............. **D2**
8 The Confidante............**I7**
9 Crowne Plaza South Beach -Z Ocean Hotel............**C5**
10 Delano South Beach **C4**
11 Dream South Beach.....**C5**
12 Eden Roc Miami Beach..**I6**
13 Faena Hotel Miami Beach..............**I7**
14 The Fisher Island Hotel and Resort........ **H9**
15 Fontainebleau Miami Beach..............**I7**
16 Gale South Beach **C4**
17 Hilton Bentley Miami/South Beach **C9**
18 The Hotel of South Beach.........**C7**
19 Hotel Victor..............**C5**
20 Kimpton Angler's Hotel **B7**
21 Kimpton Surfcomber Miami **D3**
22 Loews Miami Beach Hotel..................... **D4**
23 The Miami Beach EDITION...................**I7**
24 Mondrian South Beach **A5**
25 National Hotel............**C4**
26 The Palms Hotel & Spa ..**I7**
27 The Ritz-Carlton, Bal Harbour **I4**
28 Room Mate Lord Balfour............. **B8**
29 Royal Palm South Beach Miami **C4**
30 The St. Regis Bal Harbour Resort.......**I4**
31 The Setai Miami Beach............ **D2**
32 Shelborne South Beach **D3**
33 Shore Club................ **D3**
34 SLS South Beach **D3**
35 Soho Beach House.......**I7**
36 South Beach Hotel **D2**
37 The Standard Spa, Miami Beach............. **H8**
38 W South Beach **D2**

Did You Know?

From sidewalk cafés, diners enjoy the bohemian atmosphere of Miami Beach's Española Way.

constructed entirely of Florida keystone (material with a coral base). A years-long, $12-million expansion by noted architects Arata Isozaki and David Gauld was completed in 2017, increasing internal space nearly 50% and adding four new galleries. The majority of exhibitions are temporary, but works on permanent display include *Chess Tables,* a sculpture by Jim Drain, and *Miami Mountain,* a sculpture by Ugo Rondinone. For free, docent-led tours of the temporary exhibitions, visit on Saturday and Sunday at 2 pm or 4 pm. ⊠ *2100 Collins Ave., South Beach* ☎ *305/673–7530* ⊕ *www.thebass. org* ⊠ *$10* ☽ *Closed Mon.–Tues.*

Española Way

NEIGHBORHOOD | There's a bohemian feel to this street lined with Mediterranean-revival buildings constructed in 1925 and inspired by New York's Greenwich Village. Al Capone's gambling syndicate ran its operations upstairs at what is now the Clay Hotel, a value-conscious boutique hotel. At a nightclub here in the 1930s, future bandleader Desi Arnaz strapped on a conga drum and started beating out a rumba rhythm. Visit this quaint pedestrian-only way nowadays and find a number of personality-driven restaurants and bars, and enjoy weekly programming, which includes the likes of salsa dancing, flamenco dancing, and opera performances. ⊠ *Española Way, South Beach* ✛ *Between 14th and 15th Sts. from Washington to Pennslyvania Aves.* ⊕ *www.visitespanolaway.com.*

Holocaust Memorial

INFO CENTER | A bronze sculpture depicts refugees clinging to a giant bronze arm that reaches out of the ground and 42 feet into the air. Enter the surrounding courtyard to see a memorial wall and hear the music that seems to give voice to the 6 million Jews who died at the hands of the Nazis. It's easy to understand why Kenneth Treister's dramatic memorial is in Miami Beach: the city's community of Holocaust survivors was once the second largest in the country. ⊠ *1933–1945 Meridian Ave., at Dade Blvd., South Beach* ☎ *305/538–1663* ⊕ *www.holocaustmemorialmiamibeach. org* ⊠ *Free.*

★ Lincoln Road Mall

BUILDING | FAMILY | This open-air pedestrian mall flaunts some of Miami's best people-watching. The eclectic interiors of myriad fabulous restaurants, colorful boutiques, art galleries, lounges, and cafés are often upstaged by the bustling outdoor scene. It's here among the prolific alfresco dining enclaves that you can pass the hours easily beholding the beautiful people. Indeed, Lincoln Road is fun, lively, and friendly for everyone—old, young, gay, and straight—and their dogs. A few of the shops on Lincoln Road are owner-operated boutiques carrying a smart variety of clothing, furnishings, jewelry, and decorative elements, but more often you'll find typical upscale chain stores.

Two landmarks worth checking out at the eastern end of Lincoln Road are the massive 1940s keystone building at 420 Lincoln Road, which has a 1945 Leo Birchanky mural in the lobby, and the 1921 mission-style Miami Beach Community Church, at Drexel Avenue. The Lincoln Theatre (541–545 Lincoln Rd.), at Pennsylvania Avenue, is a classical four-story art deco gem with friezes, which now houses H&M. ⊠ *Lincoln Rd., South Beach* ✛ *Between Washington Ave. and Alton Rd.* ⊕ *www.lincolnroadmall.com.*

World Erotic Art Museum (WEAM)

MUSEUM | Late millionaire Naomi Wilzig's collection of some 4,000 erotic items is on display at this unique museum. Expect sexy art of varying quality—fertility statues from around the globe and historic Chinese *shunga* books (erotic art offered as gifts to new brides on the wedding night) share the space with some kitschy knickknacks. If this is your thing, an original phallic prop from Stanley Kubrick's *A Clockwork Orange* and an over-the-top Kama Sutra bed is worth the price of admission. Kids 17 and under are not admitted. ✉ *1205 Washington Ave., at 12th St., South Beach* ☎ *305/532–9336* 🌐 *www.weam.com* 🎟 *$15.*

Beaches

★ South Beach

BEACH—SIGHT | A 10-block stretch of white sandy beach hugging the turquoise waters along Ocean Drive—from 5th to 15th streets—is one of the most popular in America, known for drawing unabashedly model-like sunbathers and posers. With the influx of new luxe hotels and hot spots from 1st to 5th and 16th to 25th streets, the South Beach stand-and-pose scene is now bigger than ever and stretches yet another dozen-plus blocks. The beaches crowd quickly on the weekends with a blend of European tourists, young hipsters, and sun-drenched locals. Separating the sand from the traffic of Ocean Drive is palm-fringed **Lummus Park,** with its volleyball nets and chickee huts (huts made of palmetto thatch over a cypress frame) for shade. The beach at **12th Street** is popular with gays, in a section often marked with rainbow flags. Locals hang out on 3rd Street beach, in an area called **SoFi** (South of Fifth). **Amenities:** food and drink; lifeguards; parking (fee); showers; toilets. **Best for:** partiers; sunrise; swimming; walking. ✉ *Ocean Dr., South Beach* ✥ *From 5th to 15th Sts., then Collins Ave. to 25th St.*

Restaurants

★ Byblos

$$$ | **MIDDLE EASTERN** | Dynamic and delicious flavors of the Eastern Mediterranean merge over traditional and new-fashioned dishes at this photogenic local hot spot. Feast on *pides* (Turkish flat breads baked in a stone oven), Middle Eastern fried chicken (with tahini, za'atar, and house hot sauce) and *fattouche* (crunch salad) in between Instagram stories and Snapchats of the breezy, art deco surrounds and colorful interiors. **Known for:** creamed-spinach pide; yogurt-baked fluke; trendsetting crowd. [$] *Average main: $28* ✉ *1545 Collins Ave., South Beach* ☎ *305/508–5041* 🌐 *www.byblos-miami.com.*

Chotto Matte

$$$ | **JAPANESE FUSION** | With bright graffiti walls, a buzzing bar, and an open-air roof, this trendy Japanese-Peruvian fusion restaurant has brought sophistication and edge to Lincoln Road. Order a pisco or Japanese whisky and settle in for flavor-packed Nikkei-style cuisine and some of the best sushi in town. **Known for:** excellent sharing menu; glow-in-the-dark bathrooms; flaming Holy Water cocktail. [$] *Average main: $25* ✉ *1664 Lenox Ave., South Beach* ☎ *305/690-0743* 🌐 *www.chotto-matte.com/miami.*

Dolce Italian

$$$ | **MODERN ITALIAN** | Best known as a top contender on the Bravo TV show *Best New Restaurant,* Dolce Italian buzzes in the center of the South Beach action, doling out an irresistible ménage à trois: great food, great setting, and an easy-on-the-eyes crowd. Italian-born chef Paolo Dorigato's menu is packed with modern incarnations of Italian classics that would make *Nonna* proud. **Known for:** homemade mozzarella and pastas; Neopolitan-style pizzas; smart design. [$] *Average main: $28* ✉ *Gale South Beach, 1690 Collins Ave., South Beach* ☎ *786/975–2550* 🌐 *www.dolceitalianrestaurant.com/miami.*

The Dutch Miami

$$$$ | **MODERN AMERICAN** | Loft meets cozy kitchen at the Miami outpost of chef Andrew Carmellini's NYC foodie hot spot in the swank W South Beach. There's a bit of everything on the "roots-inspired American menu," from local line-caught fish to homemade pastas and 28-day dry-aged steaks. **Known for:** great oyster selection; chef's tasting menu for the table; lobster Benedict for breakfast.

$ *Average main: $32* ⊠ *W. South Beach, 2201 Collins Ave., South Beach* ☎ *305/938–3111* ⊕ *www.thedutchmiami. com.*

Gianni's

$$$$ | ITALIAN | Set within the glitz and ostentation of Gianni Versace's former mansion, the Villa Casa Casuarina, this restaurant doles out pricey Italian-Mediterranean eats across the mansion's most prized nooks. It's more about the atmosphere here than the food, which includes caviar selections, filet mignon, and black-truffle risotto. **Known for:** haute dining; wow-factor surrounds; only-in-Miami experience. $ *Average main: $52* ⊠ *The Villa Casa Casuarina, 1116 Ocean Dr., South Beach* ☎ *786/485–2200* ⊕ *www.vmmiamibeach.com/gianni* ⊘ *Closed Mon.*

Jaya

$$$$ | ASIAN FUSION | At the flagship restaurant of The Setai Miami Beach hotel, expect a pan-Asian extravaganza, representing the countries of Thailand, Vietnam, Singapore, Korea, India, China, and Japan, through dishes that range from sea bass tikka to Peking duck to lobster curry. Before or after dinner, be sure to enjoy a cocktail around the harmonious courtyard reflecting pool. **Known for:** beautiful interiors; kimchi fried rice; dim sum. $ *Average main: $41* ⊠ *The Setai, 2001 Collins Ave., South Beach* ☎ *855/923–7899* ⊕ *www.thesetaihotel. com/jaya.php.*

★ Joe's Stone Crab

$$$$ | SEAFOOD | In South Beach's decidedly new-money scene, the stately Joe's Stone Crab is an old-school testament to good food and good service. Stone crabs, served with legendary mustard sauce, crispy hash brown potatoes, and creamed spinach, remain the staple at South Beach's most-storied restaurant (which dates to 1913). **Known for:** the-best-of-the-best stone crab claws; Key lime pie; no reservations (arrive very early). $ *Average main: $46*

⊠ *11 Washington Ave., South Beach* ☎ *305/673–0365, 305/673–4611 for takeout* ⊕ *www.joesstonecrab.com* ⊘ *Closed mid-May–mid-Oct. No lunch Sun. and Mon.*

★ Juvia

$$$$ | JAPANESE FUSION | High atop South Beach's design-driven 1111 Lincoln Road parking garage, rooftop Juvia commingles urban sophistication with South Beach seduction. Three renowned chefs unite to deliver an amazing eating experience that screams Japanese, Peruvian, and French all in the same breath, focusing largely on raw fish and seafood dishes. **Known for:** city and beach views; sunset cocktails on the terrace; bigeye tuna poke. $ *Average main: $35* ⊠ *1111 Lincoln Rd., South Beach* ☎ *305/763–8272* ⊕ *www.juviamiami.com* ⊘ *No lunch weekdays.*

Lobster Bar Sea Grille—Miami Beach

$$$$ | SEAFOOD | As the name implies, lobster is the center of attention at this seafood-centric restaurant, where the Nova Scotian good stuff is perfectly prepared in a variety of ways: steamed and cracked, stuffed (with lobster stuffing), angry (in spicy, chili lobster sauce), flash-fried, or over lemon risotto. There's also a range of other fresh fruits of the sea and custom-aged prime steaks to be enjoyed in a seductive setting that at the same time recalls New York's Grand Central Station and a superyacht. **Known for:** jumbo lobster for two; shellfish towers; caviar selections. $ *Average main: $48* ⊠ *404 Washington Ave., South Beach* ☎ *305/377–2675* ⊕ *www. buckheadrestaurants.com/restaurant/ lobster-bar-sea-grille-miami-beach.*

★ LT Steak and Seafood

$$$$ | STEAKHOUSE | Miami is filled with great steak houses, but this is arguably the best. Located in the glamorous art deco open lobby of Ocean Drive's Betsy Hotel, noted chef Laurent Tourondel (of BLT Steak fame) presents a seasonally inspired menu that includes fresh

seafood, sushi, the highest-quality cuts of USDA prime and certified Black Angus beef, and decadent sides (don't miss the hand-cut Parmesan truffle fries with truffle aioli). **Known for:** massive popovers; The Besty crabcake; cocktails inspired by literary greats. $ *Average main: $38* ⊠ *The Betsy Hotel—South Beach, 1440 Ocean Drive, South Beach* ☎ *305/673–0044* ⊕ *www.thebetsyhotel. com/lt-restaurant.*

Macchialina

$$$ | ITALIAN | Framed by exposed-brick walls, decorated with daily specials on chalkboards, and packed with gregarious patrons, this local foodie hangout feels like a cozy, neighborhoody tavern. Owner and chef Michael Pirolo nails the concept of modern Italian cuisine through a small but special selection of antipasti (try the local burrata and creamy polenta with sausage) and daily homemade pastas (like tagliolini *al funghi* and spaghetti *con vongole).* **Known for:** Italian-imported salumi; house panna cotta; devoted local following. $ *Average main: $27* ⊠ *820 Alton Rd., South Beach* ☎ *305/534–2124* ⊕ *www.macchialina.com.*

Meat Market

$$$$ | STEAKHOUSE | Indeed, this is a meat market in every sense of the phrase, with great cuts of meat and plenty of sexy people passing by in skimpy clothes and enjoying fruity libations at the bar. Hard-core carnivores go wild over the 16-ounce center-cut prime New York steak and pescatarians love the wood-grilled Scottish salmon, topped with red wine cherry butter. **Known for:** outdoor seating on Lincoln Road; great happy hour daily; strong cocktails. $ *Average main: $42* ⊠ *915 Lincoln Rd., South Beach* ☎ *305/532–0088* ⊕ *www.meat-market.net.*

NaiYaRa

$$$ | THAI | Combine the pulse of Bangkok with the glitz of South Beach and under-tones of Tokyo, and you get this hyper-cool, Thai-meets-Japanese restaurant with a sleek, retro-contemporary design in the heart of Miami's burgeoning Sun-set Harbour area. The lovable and highly talented owner, Piyarat Potha Arreeratn (aka Chef Bee), guarantees a memorable night of fun, fruity and wild cocktails, and a diverse menu that spans classic Thai dishes perfected to more daring maki creations. **Known for:** Ab Zaab fried chick-en dumplings; dynamic atmosphere; salmon-belly filled Naiyara roll. $ *Average main: $28* ⊠ *1854 Bay Rd., South Beach* ☎ *786/275–6005* ⊕ *www.naiyara.com.*

News Café

$$ | AMERICAN | Twenty years strong, this 24-hour café attracts a late-night and early-morning crowd with diner-es-que meals, drinks, periodicals, and the people parade on the sidewalk out front. Although service can be indifferent to the point of laissez-faire and the food is mediocre at best, News Café is just one of those places visitors love. **Known for:** post-drinking eats; people-watching; newspaper selection. $ *Average main: $15* ⊠ *800 Ocean Dr., South Beach* ☎ *305/538–6397* ⊕ *www.newscafe.com.*

★ Prime 112

$$$$ | STEAKHOUSE | This wildly busy steak house is particularly prized for its highly marbleized prime beef, creamed corn with black truffles, lobster macaroni and cheese, and buzzing scene. While you stand at the bar awaiting your table—everyone has to wait, at least a little bit—you'll clamor for a drink with all facets of Miami's high society, from the city's top real estate developers and philanthropists to striking models and celebrities. **Known for:** reservations made by phone only; decadent side dishes; stellar service. $ *Average main: $53* ⊠ *112 Ocean Dr., South Beach* ☎ *305/532–8112* ⊕ *www. mylesrestaurantgroup.com.*

★ Pubbelly Noodle Bar

$$$ | ASIAN FUSION | This petite eatery, on a residential street in SoBe's western reaches, attracts the who's who of beach socialites, hipsters, and the occasional tourist coming to chow down on inventive Asian-Latin small plates, ramen noodle bowls, dumplings, and bao buns by executive chef–owner José Mendin. From uni pasta to short-rib tartare, the menu constantly pushes the envelope on inventive cuisine, and locals simply can't get enough. **Known for:** long waits; omakase tasting menu; lechon asado bao bun. $ *Average main: $28* ✉ *1418 20th St., South Beach* ☎ *305/532–7555* 🌐 *pubbellyglobal.com/restaurants/pubbelly-noodle-bar.*

Pubbelly Sushi—South Beach

$$$$ | **JAPANESE** | At this contemporary, Japanese-inspired canteen by Miami's famed Pubbelly team, expect grade-A sashimi, meats from the *robata* (Japanese charcoal) grill, and flavor-rich Pubbelly Rolls like the bigeye tuna (spicy tuna over squares of crispy rice) and Navarro salmon (salmon, crab, melted mozzarella, and fried onions). Wash it all down with refreshing house sake cocktails like the Teasy Bear (green tea, honey, ginger, and sake). **Known for:** Sun.–Thurs. late-night happy hour (10 pm to closing); chocolate miso bread pudding; tuna pizza. $ *Average main: $31* ✉ *1424 20th St., South Beach* ☎ *305/531–9282* 🌐 *www.pubbellysushi.us.*

Red, the Steakhouse

$$$$ | **STEAKHOUSE** | The carnivore glamour den seduces with its red-and-black dominatrix color scheme and overloads the senses with the divine smells and tastes of the extensive menu. Red boasts an equal number of seafood and more traditional meat offerings, each delicately prepared, meticulously presented, and gleefully consumed. **Known for:** tuna tartare; decadent, caloric side dishes; mussels diavolo. $ *Average main: $55* ✉ *119 Washington Ave., South Beach* ☎ *305/534–3688* 🌐 *www.redthesteakhouse.com.*

Smith and Wollensky Miami Beach

$$$$ | **STEAKHOUSE** | Enjoy one of America's premier tried-and-true steak houses in one of Miami's best locations. Situated at the tip of South Pointe Park with fabulous views of Biscayne Bay, this waterfront outpost doles out the full range of signature cuts of 28-day, dry-aged beef and hefty sides, though the beach-conscious crowd skews toward the chilled shellfish platters and savory vegetable dishes. **Known for:** award-winning wine list; shellfish towers; 44-ounce rib eye, charred tableside. $ *Average main: $52* ✉ *1 Washington Ave., South Beach* ☎ *305/673–2800* 🌐 *www.smithandwollensky.com/our-restaurants/miami-beach.*

★ **Via Emilia 9**

$$ | **ITALIAN** | If you're longing for a *true* taste of Italy's Emilia Romagna region and a respite from the overpriced SoBe dining scene, head to this adorable hole-in-the-wall restaurant off Alton Road, owned and operated by Italian chef Wendy Cacciatori and his lovely wife. The pastas and sauces are made fresh daily, using only the best ingredients imported from the chef's homeland supplemented with local produce. **Known for:** ravioli of the day; homemade flatbreads; variety of stuffed pastas. $ *Average main: $18*

Cheap Eats on South Beach 🍴

Miami Beach is notoriously overpriced, but locals know that you don't always have to spend $30 for lunch or $45 for a dinner entrée here to have a good meal. **Pizza Rustica** (✉ *8th St. and Washington Ave. and 667 Lincoln Rd.*) serves up humongous slices overflowing with mozzarella, steak, olives, and barbecue chicken until 4 am. **La Sandwicherie** (✉ *14th St. between Collins and Washington Aves.*) is a South Beach classic that's been here since 1988, serving gourmet French sandwiches and salads.

✉ *1120 15th St., South Beach* ☎ *786/216–7150* 🌐 *www.viaemilia9.com.*

Yardbird Southern Table & Bar

$$$ | **SOUTHERN** | There's a helluva lot of Southern lovin' from the lowcountry at this lively and funky South Beach spot, where Miami's A-list puts calorie-counting aside for decadent nights filled with comfort foods and innovative drinks. The family-style menu is divided between "small plates," "the bird," "plates," and "sides and snacks," but have no doubt "the bird" takes center stage (or plate) here: you'll rave about Llewellyn's fine fried chicken, which requires a 27-hour marination and slow-cooking process, for weeks to come. **Known for:** smoked brisket biscuits; peppered gnocchi pot pie; chicken 'n' watermelon 'n' waffles. [$] *Average main: $27* ✉ *1600 Lenox Ave., South Beach* ☎ *305/538–5220* 🌐 *www.runchickenrun.com.*

Hotels

If you are looking to experience the postcard image of Miami, look no further than South Beach. Most of the hotels along Ocean Drive, Collins Avenue, and Washington Avenue are housed in history-steeped art deco buildings, each one cooler than the next. From boutique hotels to high-rise structures, all South Beach hotels are in close proximity to the beach and never far from the action. Most hotels here cost a pretty penny and for good reason. They are more of an experience than a place to crash (think designer lobbies, some of the world's best pool scenes, and unparalleled people-watching).

★ **1 Hotel South Beach**

$$$$ | **RESORT** | This snazzy eco-minded hotel delivers a picturesque, nature-inspired aesthetic throughout the common spaces and room interiors (Think: heavy use of repurposed wood, living walls, preserved moss, and glassware from recycled wine bottles.) and offers a choice of four swimming pools (including the best rooftop one in Florida) and an excellent swath of beach. **Pros:** even basic level rooms are great; vibrant crowd; sustainability mantra. **Cons:** many rooms face street; constantly busy; balcony furniture a bit worn. [$] *Rooms from: $499* ✉ *2341 Collins Ave., South Beach* ☎ *305/604–1000* 🌐 *www.1hotels.com/south-beach* 🛏 *426 rooms* 🍴 *No meals.*

★ **The Betsy—South Beach**

$$$$ | **HOTEL** | After a massive expansion, the original Betsy Ross Hotel (christened the "Colonial" wing) has been joined with what was the neighboring, historic Carlton Hotel to create a retro-chic, art deco treasure that delivers the full-throttle South Beach experience with style, pizzazz, and a big-time cultural bonus: year-round programs include poetry readings, live jazz, and art shows. **Pros:** unbeatable location; superfashionable; great beach club. **Cons:** confusing hotel layout; great pet-friendly program but fee attached; pool sometimes crowded. [$] *Rooms from: $477* ✉ *1440 Ocean Dr., South Beach* ☎ *844/539–2840* 🌐 *www.thebetsyhotel.com* 🛏 *130 rooms* 🍴 *No meals.*

Cadet Hotel

$ | **HOTEL** | A former home to World War II air force cadets, this gem has been reimagined as an oasis in South Beach, offering the antithesis of the sometimes maddening jet-set scene, with 34 distinctive rooms exuding understated luxury. **Pros:** excellent service; lovely garden; historical value. **Cons:** tiny swimming pool; limited appeal for the party crowd; small bathrooms. [$] *Rooms from: $169* ✉ *1701 James Ave., South Beach* ☎ *305/672–6688* 🌐 *www.cadethotel.com* 🛏 *34 rooms* 🍴 *No meals.*

Catalina Hotel & Beach Club

$ | **HOTEL** | The Catalina is a fun, budget party spot in the heart of South Beach, attracting plenty of early twenty-somethings who value freebies like a nightly drink hour, airport shuttles, fitness classes, two fun pools, and beach chairs over posh digs. **Pros:** cool crowd; free airport shuttle; good people-watching. **Cons:** service not a high priority; late-night debauchery; worn rooms. [$] *Rooms from: $153* ✉ *1720–1756 Collins Ave., South Beach* ☎ *877/762-3477* 🌐 *www.catalinahotel.com* 🛏 *190 rooms* 🍴 *No meals.*

COMO Metropolitan Miami Beach

$$$ | **RESORT** | The luxury COMO brand brings its Zen-glam swagger to South Beach, reinventing the art deco Traymore hotel into a 74-room, Paola Navone–designed boutique hotel that commingles brand signatures (excellent, health-driven cuisine, and myriad spa elements) with Miami panache. **Pros:** easy access to both South Beach and Mid-Beach; Como Shambhala toiletries; stylish "P" and "C" door magnets signal "Clean" or "Privacy". **Cons:** two people per room max; limited number of rooms with good views; small bathrooms. [$] *Rooms from: $383* ✉ *2445 Collins Ave., South Beach* ☎ *305/695-3600* 🌐 *www.comohotels.com/metropolitanmiamibeach* 🛏 *74 rooms* 🍴 *No meals.*

Crowne Plaza South Beach—Z Ocean Hotel

$$$ | **HOTEL** | This is definitely not your grandmother's Crowne Plaza: the lauded firm of Arquitectonica designed this glossy and bold all-suites hideaway, including 27 rooftop suites endowed with terraces, each complete with Jacuzzi, plush chaise lounges, and a view of the South Beach skyline. **Pros:** across street from beach; huge rooms; green, earth-friendly hotelwide initiatives. **Cons:** tiny gym; lack of privacy on rooftop suite decks; rooms could use refresh. [$] *Rooms from: $304* ✉ *1437 Collins Ave., South Beach* ☎ *305/672-4554* 🌐 *www.ihg.com* 🛏 *79 suites* 🍴 *No meals.*

Delano South Beach

$$$ | **HOTEL** | The hotel that single-handedly made South Beach cool again in the 1990s is still making waves across the beach as this Philippe Starck powerhouse immortalizes a glorious moment in South Beach's glamour revival. **Pros:** iconic design; lounging among the beautiful; trippy ornaments like the ladder-to-nowhere. **Cons:** pricey drinks; in need of a refresh; some smaller rooms. [$] *Rooms from: $365* ✉ *1685 Collins Ave., South Beach* ☎ *305/672-2000* 🌐 *www.morganshotelgroup.com/delano/delano-south-beach* 🛏 *208 rooms* 🍴 *No meals.*

Dream South Beach

$$ | **HOTEL** | This trendy boutique hotel, which is right in the center of the South Beach action, merges two refurbished, archetypal, 1939 art deco buildings into a single project of eclectic modernism, with whimsically decorated interiors that are at once trippy and cool. **Pros:** chef Ralph Pagaon's Naked Taco restaurant downstairs; heated rooftop pool; complimentary sparkling wine on arrival. **Cons:** limited natural light in some rooms; lack of bathroom privacy; not on the beach. [$] *Rooms from: $209* ✉ *1111 Collins Ave., South Beach* ☎ *305/673-4747* 🌐 *www.dreamhotels.com/southbeach* 🛏 *108 rooms* 🍴 *No meals.*

Gale South Beach

$$ | **HOTEL** | Though it's not directly on the beach—it's across the street—this boutique hotel offers fabulous, style- and value-conscious accommodations in the heart of South Beach with plenty of art deco history to boot. **Pros:** Regent Cocktail Club downstairs; Pizza Room Service button on guestroom phones; crisp, clean-lined rooms. **Cons:** smaller rooms; busy pool area; crowded hallways. [$] *Rooms from: $299* ✉ *1690 Collins Ave., South Beach* ☎ *305/673-0199* 🌐 *www.galehotel.com* 🛏 *87 rooms* 🍴 *No meals.*

Hilton Bentley Miami/South Beach

$$$ | **HOTEL** | **FAMILY** | Not to be confused with the budget Bentley Hotel down the street, the Hilton Bentley Miami is a contemporary, design-driven, and artsy boutique hotel in the emerging and

trendy SoFi (South of Fifth) district, offering families just the right mix of South Beach flavor and wholesome fun while still providing couples a romantic base without any party madness. **Pros:** quiet location; rooms redeemable with points; family-friendly. **Cons:** small pool; small lobby; daily resort charge. $ *Rooms from: $389* ⊠ *101 Ocean Dr., South Beach* ☎ *305/938–4600* ⊕ *www.hilton. com* ⊷ *109 rooms* ⦿ *No meals.*

The Hotel of South Beach

$$ | HOTEL | This value-conscious art deco property inhabits the historic Tiffany building on Collins Avenue as well as a second building along Ocean Drive with interiors by fashion designer Todd Oldham. **Pros:** original terrazzo floors; room service from nearby News Café; rooftop pool deck. **Cons:** in need of a refresh; poor views from many rooms; no full dining restaurant. $ *Rooms from: $249* ⊠ *801 Collins Ave., South Beach* ☎ *305/531–2222,* ⊕ *www.thehotelofsouthbeach.com* ⊷ *73 rooms* ⦿ *No meals.*

Hotel Victor

$$$ | HOTEL | At the sleek Hotel Victor, guest rooms are equipped with Yabu Pushelberg–designed interiors invoking a post-century beach cabana vibe, and a sexy infinity-edge pool overlooks Ocean Drive and the beach. **Pros:** late-night pool deck; complimentary bikes; complimentary fruit and water by pool. **Cons:** small rooms; noisy crowds at restaurants downstairs; no dedicated area on beach. $ *Rooms from: $329* ⊠ *1144 Ocean Dr., South Beach* ☎ *305/908–1462* ⊕ *www. hotelvictorsouthbeach.com* ⊷ *91 rooms* ⦿ *No meals.*

★ Kimpton Angler's Hotel

$$$ | HOTEL | This boutique hotel is an enclave of old and new South Beach: a contemporary, 85-room tower with a rooftop swimming pool (opened in summer 2018) neighbors a number of personality-driven villas (built in 1930 by architect Henry Maloney and renovated in 2018) and several modern low-rise

units, together capturing the feel of a sophisticated private villa community. **Pros:** gardened private retreat; pet-friendly (no fee); daily complimentary wine hour. **Cons:** no gym; not directly on beach; most units have only showers. $ *Rooms from: $327* ⊠ *660 Washington Ave., South Beach* ☎ *305/534–9600* ⊕ *www. anglershotelmiami.com* ⊷ *132 rooms* ⦿ *No meals.*

Kimpton Surfcomber Miami, South Beach

$$ | HOTEL | As part of the hip Kimpton Hotel group, South Beach's legendary Surfcomber hotel reflects a vintage luxe aesthetic and an ocean-side freshness as well as a reasonable price point that packs the place with a young, sophisticated, yet unpretentious crowd. **Pros:** frozen spiked cappuccino at High Tide Bar; no pet fee; daily complimentary activities offered. **Cons:** small bathrooms; front desk often busy; last renovated in 2012. $ *Rooms from: $206* ⊠ *1717 Collins Ave., South Beach* ☎ *305/532–7715* ⊕ *www.surfcomber.com* ⊷ *186 rooms* ⦿ *No meals.*

Loews Miami Beach Hotel

$$$$ | HOTEL | FAMILY | This two-tower megahotel has 790 rooms (all redesigned in 2018 with a soothing, sea-inspired motif), top-tier amenities, a massive spa, a great pool, and direct beachfront access, making it a great choice for families, businesspeople, groups, and pet lovers. **Pros:** excellent on-site seafood restaurant; resort atmosphere; pets welcome. **Cons:** insanely large size; constantly crowded; pets desperate to go will need to wait several minutes to make it to the grass. $ *Rooms from: $459* ⊠ *1601 Collins Ave., South Beach* ☎ *305/604–1601, 855/757–2061 for reservations* ⊕ *www. loewshotels.com/miami-beach* ⊷ *790 rooms* ⦿ *No meals.*

Mondrian South Beach

$$ | HOTEL | Located along the beach's lesser-known western perimeter and overlooking the bay, this hotel is a living and functioning work of art, an ingenious vision of provocateur Marcel Wanders. **Pros:** great pool scene; perfect sunsets; party vibe. **Cons:** could use a refresh; a short walk from most of the action; no direct beach access. [$] *Rooms from: $299* ✉ *1100 West Ave., South Beach* ☎ *305/514–1500* 🌐 *www.meninhospitality.com/collection/hotels/mondrian-south-beach* 🛏 *335 rooms* 🍴 *No meals.*

National Hotel

$$ | **HOTEL** | The National Hotel is a glorious time capsule that honors its distinct art deco heritage (the building itself and wood pieces in the lobby date back to 1939 and new chocolate- and gold-hued furnishings look period-appropriate) while trying to keep up with SoBe's glossy newcomers (rotating art installations complement the throwback glamour). **Pros:** cabana suites; beautiful night lights around pool area; art deco Blues Bar. **Cons:** street noise on the weekends; gym located downstairs in back of house; no spa. [$] *Rooms from: $255* ✉ *1677 Collins Ave., South Beach* ☎ *305/532–2311* 🌐 *www.nationalhotel.com* 🛏 *152 rooms* 🍴 *No meals.*

Room Mate Lord Balfour

$ | **HOTEL** | In South Beach's SoFi (South of Fifth) neighborhood, the boutique Lord Balfour hotel—part of Spain's Room Mate brand—is a great fit for young travelers who actually desire to go out and experience South Beach (as opposed to sitting at the resort all day) and still want to return to stylish digs. **Pros:** great European crowd; whimsical interior design; affordable pricing. **Cons:** small rooms and smaller bathrooms; occasional street noise from some rooms; no pool. [$] *Rooms from: $175* ✉ *350 Ocean Dr., South Beach* ☎ *855/471–2739* 🌐 *www.room-matehotels.com/en/lordbalfour* 🛏 *64 rooms* 🍴 *No meals.*

★ Royal Palm South Beach Miami

$$$ | **RESORT** | The Royal Palm South Beach Miami, now part of Marriott's individualistic Tribute Portfolio, is a daily celebration of art deco, modernity, and design detail. **Pros:** design blending contemporary style with South Beach identity; photogenic pool areas; social lobby. **Cons:** small driveway for entering; older elevators; maintenance issues. [$] *Rooms from: $321* ✉ *1545 Collins Ave., South Beach* ☎ *305/604–5700, 866/716–8147 reservations* 🌐 *www.royalpalmsouthbeach.com* 🛏 *393 rooms* 🍴 *No meals.*

★ The Setai Miami Beach

$$$$ | **RESORT** | This opulent, all-suites hotel feels like an Asian museum: serene and beautiful, with heavy granite furniture lifted by orange accents, warm candlelight, and the soft bubble of seemingly endless ponds complemented by three oceanfront infinity pools (heated to different temperatures) that further spill onto the beach's velvety sands. **Pros:** quiet and classy; beautiful grounds; both couple- and family-friendly. **Cons:** TVs are far from the beds; busy pool area; many rooms lack ocean views. [$] *Rooms from: $878* ✉ *2001 Collins Ave., South Beach* ☎ *305/520–6111, 888/625–7500 reservations* 🌐 *www.thesetaihotel.com* 🛏 *130 suites* 🍴 *No meals.*

Shore Club

$ | **HOTEL** | In terms of poolside lounging and people-watching, the Shore Club still ranks high in South Beach; the mod yet minimalist rooms aren't bad either (especially given the reasonable entry-level price point). **Pros:** complimentary beach chairs; multiple bars; direct beach access. **Cons:** old elevators; general wear and tear; thin walls. [$] *Rooms from: $185* ✉ *1901 Collins Ave., South Beach* ☎ *305/695–3100* 🌐 *www.morganshotelgroup.com* 🛏 *309 rooms* 🍴 *No meals.*

Shelborne South Beach

$$ | **RESORT** | The iconic Morris Lapidus–designed Shelborne hotel is a retro-chic art deco treasure with stylish yet functional rooms and plenty of oh-so-South Beach amenites, including the beach's most oversized poolside cabanas (which also happen to be air-conditioned); a

Cars whiz by the Avalon hotel and other art deco architecture on Ocean Drive, Miami South Beach.

slick pool deck; a private beach club; and a location that offers direct access to downy sands, art deco, and superlative shopping. **Pros:** Saturday morning meditation classes on the beach; in-house restaurant by Top Chef alums Jeff McInnis and Janine Booth; Oasis Beer Garden features local brews in a beautiful outdoor space. **Cons:** entry-level rooms small; lack of balconies; some odd large spaces near lobby. [$] *Rooms from: $259* ✉ *1801 Collins Ave., South Beach* ☎ *305/704–3668* 🌐 *www.shelborne.com* 🛏 *200 rooms* 🍴 *No meals.*

★ SLS South Beach

$$$$ | RESORT | Housed in a restored 1939 art deco building, the SLS Hotel South Beach exudes beachfront sophistication over a commingling of Latin and Asian inspiration in its common areas, which include headlining restaurants Bazaar by José Andrés, Katsuya South Beach, and Hyde Beach—an 8,000-square-foot masterpiece of pool, beach, and cabanas attracting glitterati and hotties daily. **Pros:** great in-house restaurants; masterful design; fun pool scene. **Cons:** some small rooms; no lobby per se; $40 per night resort fee. [$] *Rooms from: $413* ✉ *1701 Collins Ave., South Beach* ☎ *305/674–1701* 🌐 *www.slshotels.com/southbeach* 🛏 *140 rooms* 🍴 *No meals.*

★ W South Beach

$$$$ | HOTEL | Fun, fresh, and funky, the W South Beach flaunts some of the nicest rooms in South Beach—even the entry category evokes a wow factor—each with its own kitchen and balcony with ocean views. **Pros:** pool scene; giant Hello Kitty fountain; three in-house restaurants and bars. **Cons:** not a classic art deco building; crowded pool area; loud music at pool. [$] *Rooms from: $494* ✉ *2201 Collins Ave., South Beach* ☎ *305/938–3000* 🌐 *www.wsouthbeach.com* 🛏 *248 rooms* 🍴 *No meals.*

Nightlife

★ Blues Bar

BARS/PUBS | A highlight of any Miami art deco pub crawl is sipping classic cocktails over live music at the nifty wooden Blues Bar, one of many elements original to the iconic, circa 1939 National Hotel. The sights and sounds hark back to an era when you'd expect to watch Ginger Rogers and Fred Astaire dancing across the polished terrazzo floor. ⊠ *National Hotel, 1677 Collins Ave., South Beach* ☎ *305/532–2311* ⊕ *www. nationalhotel.com/food/blues.*

Lost Weekend

BARS/PUBS | Play pin ball, pool, or air hockey; chow down on bar grub; and order a few rounds from the full bar (which includes 150 different beer varieties) at this pool hall–resto–dive bar on quaint Española Way. Mingle with an eclectic crowd, from visiting yuppies to local drag queens to celebs on the down-low. It's so South Beach! ⊠ *218 Española Way, South Beach* ☎ *305/672–1707* ⊕ *www. sub-culture.org/lost-weekend-miami.*

Mac's Club Deuce Bar

BARS/PUBS | Smoky, dark, and delightfully unpolished, this complete dive bar is anything but what you'd expect from glitzy South Beach. The circa-1964 pool hall attracts a colorful crowd of clubbers, locals, celebs, and just about anyone else. Locals consider it a top spot for an inexpensive drink and cheap thrills. Visitors love it as a true locals' hangout. ⊠ *222 14th St., at Collins Ave., South Beach* ☎ *305/531–6200* ⊕ *www.macs-clubdeuce.com.*

Nikki Beach Miami Beach

BARS/PUBS | Smack-dab on the beach, the full-service Nikki Beach Club is filled with more suburbanites and tourists than the in crowd but promises plenty of fun nevertheless. The Beach Club is typically a daytime affair, opening at 11 am and closing at 7 pm (though there are often special evening events, namely on Sundays). Visitors can get their food and drink in the tepees, hammocks, and beach beds (expect DJ-led tunes on weekends and rental fees all days). Sunday brunch at the club's restaurant is pretty spectacular with a true South Beach party atmosphere. ⊠ *1 Ocean Dr., South Beach* ☎ *305/538–1111* ⊕ *www. nikkibeach.com.*

Onyx Bar

BARS/PUBS | Experience Villa Casa Casuarina, the 1930s-era oceanfront mansion that once belonged to late fashion designer Gianni Versace by grabbing a drink at this six-seat bar, a conversion of Versace's former kitchen. The drinks are as opulent as you'd expect from the locale, with gold-leafed accessories and over-the-top taste sensations. ⊠ *1116 Ocean Dr., South Beach* ☎ *786/485–2200* ⊕ *www.vmmiamibeach.com.*

★ Palace Bar

BARS/PUBS | South Beach's gay heyday continues at this fierce oceanfront bar where folks gay, straight, and everything in between—everyone's welcome—come to revel in good times, cheap cocktails, and fierce drag performances. On weekdays the bar gets busiest in the early evening, but on weekends it's all about the drag brunch. It's a true showstopper—or car-stopper, shall we say: using Ocean Drive as a stage, drag queens direct oncoming traffic with street-side splits and acrobatic tricks in heels. ⊠ *1052 Ocean Dr., South Beach* ☎ *305/531–7234* ⊕ *www.palacesouth-beach.com.*

★ The Regent Cocktail Club

BARS/PUBS | This classic cocktail bar exudes elegance and timelessness with strong masculine cocktails, dark furnishings, bartenders dressed to the nines, and the sounds of jazz legends in the background. It's a welcome respite from South Beach's more predictable nightlife scene. Despite some staples, many cocktails—each with bespoke ice cubes and garnishes—change daily and are posted on the house blackboard. ⊠ *Gale South Beach, 1690 Collins Ave., South Beach* ☎ *786/975–2555* ⊕ *www. regentcocktailclub.com.*

Rose Bar

BARS/PUBS | Tucked away inside the art deco-imbued Delano South Beach, Rose Bar is a Miami mainstay and consistently delivers some of the beach's best mixology. Embodying Philippe Starck's original, iconic vision and design for the Delano South Beach, the bar features a rose-quartz bar top, velvet wall curtains, and striking chandeliers. ✉ *Delano Hotel, 1685 Collins Ave., South Beach* ☎ *305/674–5752* ⊕ *www.morganshotel-group.com/delano/delano-south-beach.*

Score

DANCE CLUBS | Since the 1990s, Score has been the see-and-be-seen HQ of Miami's gay community, with plenty of global hotties coming from near and far to show off their designer threads and six-pack abs. DJs spin four nights a week but Planeta Macho Latin Tuesday is exceptionally popular, as is the circuit party–style throw-down every Saturday. Dress to impress (and then be ready to go shirtless and show off your abs). ✉ *1437 Washington Ave., South Beach* ☎ *305/535–1111* ⊕ *www.scorebar.net* ☾ *Closed Mon. and Wed.*

Sweet Liberty

BARS/PUBS | This tropical-chic, come-as-you-are cocktail lounge and restaurant has won all kinds of national and local awards for its incredible spirit-forward cocktails and fresh-and-funky vibe. For something extra special, reserve the Bartender's Table, which operates like a chef's table, but here you're in the thick of the bar action, tasting libations. ✉ *237-B 20th St., South Beach* ☎ *305/763–8217* ⊕ *www.mysweetliberty. com.*

Twist

DANCE CLUBS | Twist is a gay institution in South Beach, having been the late-night go-to place for decades, filling to capacity around 2 am after the beach's fly-by-night bars and more established lounges begin to die down (though it's open daily from 1 pm to 5 am). There's never a cover here—not even on holidays or during gay-pride events—and there are a whopping seven different bars and dance floors spread over two levels and patios. ✉ *1057 Washington Ave., South Beach* ☎ *305/538–9478* ⊕ *www.twistsobe.com.*

Villa Azur

WINE BARS—NIGHTLIFE | St. Tropez meets South Beach at this sceney, French res-to-lounge with prolific alfresco seating in a spacious, tree-lined courtyard and personality-driven relaxation areas indoors (replete with swaying chandeliers, white tufted couches, and whimsically accessorized library shelves). Although Veuve Clicquot is a staple among patrons, the tropical-inspired cocktails and the selection from the in-house wine cellar, La Cave d'Azur, also impress. ✉ *309 23rd St., South Beach* ☎ *305/763–8688* ⊕ *www.villaazurmiami.com.*

Watr at the Rooftop

BARS/PUBS | Come 7 pm Miami Beach's premier rooftop opens to the public as a full-service bar, restaurant, and lounge (before that it is exclusive to guests of the 1 Hotel South Beach). Up in the skies, expect tropically inspired drinks like pineapple and mint caipirinhas overlooking the twinkle of city lights, the sleek rooftop pool, and the lapping waves of the Atlantic Ocean. ✉ *1 Hotel South Beach, 2341 Collins Ave., South Beach* ☎ *305/604–6580* ⊕ *www.1hotels. com/south-beach.*

Shopping

★ Alchemist

CLOTHING | This boutique is synonymous with the pinnacle of design and fashion in the Magic City, so naturally it occupies a cutting-edge, glass-encased studio on the fifth floor of Lincoln Road's trendy Herzog and de Meuron–designed parking garage. The price tags skew high yet represent brands known for innovation and edge (like Adaptation, Es Vedra, Jacquemus, and Matsuda). ✉ *1111 Lincoln*

Rd., Carpark Level 5, South Beach ☎ 305/531–4815 ⊕ www.shopalchemist. com.

Collins Avenue

SHOPPING NEIGHBORHOODS | Give your plastic a workout in South Beach shopping at the many high-profile tenants on this densely packed stretch of Collins between 5th and 8th streets, with stores like Steve Madden, The Webster, Ralph Lauren, and Intermix. Sprinkled among the upscale vendors are hair salons, spas, cafés, and such familiar stores as Gap and Sephora. ✉ Collins Ave., South Beach ✦ Between 5th and 8th Sts. ⊕ www.lincolnroadmall.com/shopping/ collins-avenue.

Consign of the Times

CLOTHING | This women's luxury resale specialist dutifully delivers on all promises. Discover a wealth of vintage and consignment items by top designers at pre-owned prices, including Chanel suits, Fendi bags, and Celine and Prada treasures. The shoes and handbag selections are particularly awesome. ✉ 1935 West Ave., South Beach ☎ 305/535–0811 ⊕ www.consignofthetimes.com.

Dog Bar

GIFTS/SOUVENIRS | Just north of Lincoln Road's main drag, this over-the-top pet boutique caters to enthusiastic animal owners with a variety of unique items for the superpampered pet. From luxurious, vegan "leather" designer dog purse/carriers to bling-bling-studded collars to chic poopy bag holders, Miami's "original pet boutique" carries pretty much every pet accessory imaginable. You'll also find plenty of gourmet food and treats as well as a wide variety of fancy toys for dogs, large and small. ✉ 1684 Jefferson Ave., South Beach ☎ 305/532–5654 ⊕ www. dogbar.com.

frankie. miami

CLOTHING | Expect high style and eye-catching garments at this boutique. The studiolike setting matches the highly edited collection of fashionista favorites (previous brands have included Beck & Bridge, Sam & Lavi, Iro, For Love & Lemons, and Loeffers). Co-owner Cheryl Herger also designs her own private-label line especially for frankie. miami. Skirts and dresses with interesting silhouettes, uniquely cut tops, and swimwear almost too good for just the pool are interspersed with easy-chic basics. ✉ 1891 Purdy Ave., South Beach ☎ 786/479–4898 ⊕ www.frankiemiami.com.

Jessie

CLOTHING | A massive roster of established and young designer brands makes this one-stop boutique of clothing, swimwear, shoes, and accessories a favorite among those in the know. New daily arrivals draw from the latest celebrity looks and include designs by Alexis, Alice + Olivia, Chaser, Mara Hoffman, Karina Grimaldi, Rag & Bone, and many more. ✉ 1708 Alton Rd., South Beach ☎ 305/604–7980 ⊕ www.jessieboutique. com.

★ Lincoln Road Mall

SHOPPING NEIGHBORHOODS | The eight-block-long pedestrian mall between Alton Road and Washington Avenue is home to more than 100 shops, art galleries, restaurants and cafés, and the renovated Colony Theatre. A see-and-be-seen theme is underscored by outdoor seating at every restaurant, where tourists and locals lounge and discuss the people (and pet) parade passing by. Due to high rents, you are more likely to see big corporate stores like Armani, H&M, and Victoria's Secret than original boutiques. Nevertheless, a few emporiums and stores with unique personalities, like Alchemist and Books & Books, remain, along with a number of top-notch restaurants like Juvia and Chotto Matte. ✉ Lincoln Rd., South Beach ✦ Between Alton Rd. and Washington Ave. ⊕ www. lincolnroadmall.com.

★ Romero Britto Fine Art Gallery

ANTIQUES/COLLECTIBLES | Though exhibited throughout galleries and museums in more than 100 countries, the vibrant, pop art creations by Brazilian artist Romero Britto have become most synonymous with Miami's playful spirit. His flagship gallery showcases original paintings and limited-edition sculptures for sale. Collectibles, fine art prints, and his signature interpretations in collaboration with some of America's most iconic characters and brands, including Disney and Coco-Cola, can be found at the Britto Concept store down the street at 532 Lincoln Road. ⊠ *1102 Lincoln Rd., South Beach* ☎ *305/531–8821* ⊕ *www.britto.com.*

★ The Webster South Beach

CLOTHING | Occupying an entire circa-1939 art deco building, The Webster's flagship (and original) location is a tri-level, 20,000-square-foot, one-stop shop for fashionistas. This retail sanctuary carries ready-to-wear fashions by more than 100 top designers, plus in-store exclusive shirts, candles, books, and random trendy items you might need for your South Beach experience—a kind of haute Urban Outfitters for grown-ups. ⊠ *1220 Collins Ave., South Beach* ☎ *305/674–7899* ⊕ *www.thewebster.us.*

Activities

Art Deco District Walking Tour

TOUR—SPORTS | FAMILY | Operated by the Miami Design Preservation League, this is a 90-minute guided walking tour that departs from the league's welcome center at Ocean Drive and 10th Street. It starts at 10:30 am daily, with an extra tour at 6:30 pm Thursday. Alternatively, you can go at your own pace with the league's self-guided iPod audio tour, which also takes roughly an hour and a half. ⊠ *1001 Ocean Dr., South Beach* ☎ *305/763–8026* ⊕ *www.mdpl.org* 🖅 *$25 guided tour, $20 self-guided audio tour.*

★ Miami Beach Bicycle Center

BICYCLING | If you don't want to opt for the hassle of CitiBike or if you want wheels with some style on South Beach, rent a bike from this shop near Ocean Drive. They have all types of two-wheelers, from E-bikes to Carbon Road bikes and Fat Sand bikes, available by the hour, day, or week (and easily booked online). Prices are cheapest for single-speed beach cruisers at $5 per hour, $18 per day, or $80 for the week. All bike rentals include locks, helmets, and baskets. ⊠ *746 5th St., South Beach* ☎ *305/674–0150* ⊕ *www.bikemiamibeach.com.*

★ South Beach Dive and Surf

SCUBA DIVING | Dedicated to all things ocean, this PADI five-star dive shop offers multiple diving and snorkeling trips weekly as well as surfboard, paddleboard, and skateboard sales, rentals, and lessons. From a Discover Scuba course (for noncertified divers) to wreck and reef dives and even shark diving in Jupiter, tours here run the gamut. The dive shop itself is located in the heart of South Beach, but boats depart from marinas in Miami Beach and Key Largo, in the Florida Keys. ⊠ *850 Washington Ave., South Beach* ☎ *305/531–6110* ⊕ *www. southbeachdivers.com.*

Mid-Beach

Where does South Beach end and Mid-Beach begin? North of 23rd Street, Collins Avenue curves its way to 44th Street, where it takes a sharp left turn after running into the Soho House Miami and then the Fontainebleau resort. The area between these two points—and up until 63rd Street—is officially Mid-Beach. The area has been experiencing a renaissance since the $1 billion re-debut of the Fontainebleau resort in 2008. Investors have followed suit with other major projects to revive the Mid-Beach area. Most recently, Argentinean developer Alan Faena completed the neighborhood's latest $1 billion-plus mission: to restore the historic buildings along Collins Avenue from 32nd to 36th streets, creating new hotels, condos, and cultural institutions to collectively become the Miami Beach Faena District. And the results have been nothing short of amazing.

🍴 Restaurants

⭐ Cecconi's Miami Beach

$$$$ | ITALIAN | The wait for a table at this outpost of the iconic Italian restaurant is just as long as for its counterparts in West Hollywood and London. Expect heavy portions of atmosphere: It's a real scene of who's who and who's eating what, cast in a seductive, vintage-chic setting across the courtyard of the Soho Beach House Miami. **Known for:** light and succulent fish carpaccios; truffle pizza; beautiful lighting. $ *Average main: $35 ⊠ Soho Beach House Miami, 4385 Collins Ave., Mid-Beach ☎ 786/507–7902 ⊕ www.cecconismiamibeach.com.*

The Forge

$$$$ | STEAKHOUSE | Antiques, gilt-framed paintings, a chandelier from the Paris Opera House, and Tiffany stained-glass windows from New York's Trinity Church are the fitting background for some of Miami's best cuts. The tried-and-true menu also includes colossal shrimp cocktail, whole branzino, and the famous chocolate soufflé. **Known for:** expansive enomatic wine system; dramatic interiors; bone-in filet mignon. $ *Average main: $45 ⊠ 432 Arthur Godfrey Rd., Mid-Beach ☎ 305/538–8533 ⊕ www.theforge.com ⊘ No lunch.*

⭐ Hakkasan Miami

$$$$ | CANTONESE | This stateside sibling of the Michelin-star London restaurant brings the haute-Chinese-food movement to South Florida, adding Pan-Asian flair to even quite simple and authentic Cantonese recipes, and producing an entire menu that can be classified as blow-your-mind delicious. Superb eats notwithstanding, another reason to experience Hakkasan is that it's arguably the sexiest, best-looking restaurant on Miami Beach. **Known for:** dim sum perfected; roasted silver cod with champagne and honey; high-design interiors including teak walls. $ *Average main: $52 ⊠ Fontainebleau Miami Beach, 4441 Collins Ave., 4th fl., Mid-Beach ☎ 786/276–1388 after 4 pm, 877/326–7412 before 4 pm ⊕ www.hakkasan.com/locations/hakkasan-miami ⊘ No lunch weekdays.*

Malibu Farm

$$ | MODERN AMERICAN | Organic and locally sourced farm-to-table food is the focus at this airy beachfront restaurant, an outpost of the California location. Note that it's located at Eden Roc Miami Beach, but you don't have to be a hotel guest to enjoy the seafood, pizza, steak, and refreshing cocktails. **Known for:** views of the Atlantic; whole fish; fresh-pressed juices. $ *Average main: $20 ⊠ 4525 Collins Ave., Mid-Beach ☎ 305/674–5579 ⊕ www.edenrochotelmiami.com.*

⭐ Matador

$$$ | SPANISH | In one of Miami's most captivating and seductive settings, this headline restaurant by celebrity-chef Jean-Georges Vongerichten fuses Spanish, Caribbean, and Latin American gastronomy while focusing on local products, resulting in a diverse collection of small and large plates. Indulge in tropically inspired plates like avocado pizza; Florida Keys shrimp in "Agua Diablo;" and grilled Florida black-grouper tacos. **Known for:** "Light & Bright" beach-conscious options; the epic pineapple elixir cocktail served in a massive copper pineapple; stunning terrace for outdoor dining. $ *Average main: $29 ⊠ The Miami Beach EDITION, 2901 Collins Ave., Mid-Beach ☎ 786/257–4600 ⊕ www.matadorroom.com.*

Hotels

The stretch of Miami Beach called Mid-Beach is undergoing a renaissance, as formerly run-down hotels are renovated and new hotels and condos are built. Most locals—and visitors—even prefer it to South Beach nowadays.

Circa 39 Hotel

$$ | **HOTEL** | Located in the heart of Mid-Beach, this stylish yet affordable boutique hotel houses 97 tropical-inspired rooms and a swimming pool and sundeck complete with cabanas and umbrella-shaded chaises that invite all-day lounging. **Pros:** lounge areas in the Wunder Garden; beach chairs provided; art deco fireplace. **Cons:** not on the beach side of Collins Avenue; bathrooms have showers only; no spa. [$] *Rooms from: $299* ✉ *3900 Collins Ave., Mid-Beach* ☎ *305/538–4900* 🌐 *www.circa39.com* 🛏 *97 rooms* 🍴 *No meals.*

★ **The Confidante**

$$$ | **RESORT** | Part of Hyatt's Unbound Collection, this hotel in Miami's burgeoning Mid-Beach district is a beachfront classic art deco building reinvented by Martin Brudnizki to channel a colorful, modern incarnation of 1950s Florida glamour, packed with all the trappings one would covet in a Miami beachfront experience. **Pros:** highly photogenic pool area; complimentary fitness classes; Hyatt points accepted for stays. **Cons:** day passes sometimes sold to nonguests; entry-level rooms are on the small side; dark hallways. [$] *Rooms from: $369* ✉ *4041 Collins Ave., Mid-Beach* ☎ *304/424–1234* 🌐 *www.theconfidantehotel.com* 🛏 *363 rooms* 🍴 *No meals.*

Eden Roc Miami Beach

$$$ | **RESORT** | This grand 1950s hotel designed by Morris Lapidus is a lesson in old-school glamour meets modern-day swagger after hundreds of millions in renovations and expansions over the past decade (including the addition of the hotel-within-a-hotel concept Nobu Hotel at Eden Roc). **Pros:** on-site Nobu and Malibu Farm restaurants; great pools; revival of golden age glamour. **Cons:** expensive parking; $35 charge for mini-refrigerator; some small bathrooms. [$] *Rooms from: $330* ✉ *4525 Collins Ave., Mid-Beach* ☎ *786/801–6886* 🌐 *www.edenrochotelmiami.com* 🛏 *345 rooms* 🍴 *No meals.*

★ **Faena Hotel Miami Beach**

$$$$ | **RESORT** | Hotelier Alan Faena delivers on the high expectations of his Miami debut with the jaw-dropping, larger-than-life principal hotel within his billion-dollar Faena Arts District in Miami Beach. **Pros:** incredible design; excellent service; spectacular beach club. **Cons:** pricey; construction in neighborhood; dark hallways. [$] *Rooms from: $609* ✉ *3201 Collins Ave., Mid-Beach* ☎ *305/535–4697* 🌐 *www.faena.com/miami-beach* 🛏 *169 rooms* 🍴 *No meals.*

★ **Fontainebleau Miami Beach**

$$$$ | **RESORT** | **FAMILY** | Vegas meets art deco at Miami's largest hotel, which has more than 1,500 rooms (in four separate towers, almost half of which are suites), 12 renowned restaurants and lounges, LIV nightclub, several pools with cabana islands, a state-of-the-art fitness center, and a 40,000-square-foot spa. **Pros:** expansive pool and beach areas; historic allure; great nightlife. **Cons:** lots of nonguests visiting grounds; massive size; loud, weekend parties outside. [$] *Rooms from: $449* ✉ *4441 Collins Ave., Mid-Beach* ☎ *305/535–3283, 800/548–8886* 🌐 *www.fontainebleau.com* 🛏 *1504 rooms* 🍴 *No meals.*

★ **The Miami Beach EDITION**

$$$$ | **RESORT** | At this reinvention of the 1955 landmark Seville Hotel by hospitality duo Ian Schrager and Marriott, historic glamour parallels modern relaxation from the palm-fringed marble lobby to the beachy guest rooms. **Pros:** excellent spa; hanging gardens in the alfresco area; great beachfront service. **Cons:** a bit pretentious; open bathroom setup in select rooms offers little privacy;

near a particularly rocky part of Miami Beach. [$] *Rooms from: $559* ✉ *2901 Collins Ave., Mid-Beach* ☎ *786/257–4500* 🌐 *www.editionhotels.com/miami-beach* 🛏 *294 rooms* 🍴 *No meals.*

The Palms Hotel & Spa
$$ | HOTEL | If you're seeking a relaxed property away from the noise but close to both Mid-Beach and South Beach nightlife, you'll find an exceptional beach, an easy pace, and beautiful gardens with soaring palm trees and inviting hammocks here, with rooms as fabulous as the grounds. **Pros:** thatched chickee huts; direct beach access; beach yoga. **Cons:** standard rooms do not have balconies (but suites do); room decor a bit tired; not as "cool" as neighboring hotels. [$] *Rooms from: $296* ✉ *3025 Collins Ave., Mid-Beach* ☎ *305/534–0505, 800/550–0505* 🌐 *www.thepalmshotel.com* 🛏 *251 rooms* 🍴 *No meals.*

Soho Beach House
$$$$ | HOTEL | The Soho Beach House is a throwback to swanky vibes of bygone decades, bedazzled in faded color palates, maritime setting, and circa-1930s avant-garde furnishings, luring both somebodies and wannabes to indulge in the amenity-rich, retro-chic rooms as long as they follow stringent house rules (no photos, no mobile phones, no suits, and one guest only). **Pros:** two pools; fabulous restaurant; full spa. **Cons:** members have priority for rooms; lots of pretentious patrons; house rules are a bit much. [$] *Rooms from: $570* ✉ *4385 Collins Ave., Mid-Beach* ☎ *786/507–7900* 🌐 *www.sohobeachhouse.com* 🛏 *49 rooms* 🍴 *No meals.*

Nightlife

★ Basement Miami
GATHERING PLACES | This DJ-fueled, underground adult playground, below the Miami Beach EDITION hotel, features a micro version of the famed Studio 54, a four-lane bowling alley, and a very small ice skating rink. The 2,000-square-foot rink might be too tiny for Olympic-quality skaters, but it's a priceless visit if only for the memory of how you skated on your Miami Beach vacation. ✉ *The Miami Beach EDITION, 2901 Collins Ave., Mid-Beach* ☎ *786/257–4600* 🌐 *www.basementmiami.com.*

★ The Broken Shaker
BARS/PUBS | Popular with the cool crowd, this indoor-outdoor craft cocktail joint lures in droves to revel in creative mixology and fabulous people-watching. Everything here is perfectly Instagrammable, from the daring and beautifully presented drinks to the vintage-chic surrounds. It's no wonder the venue has been awarded national titles such as America's Best Bar. ✉ *Freehand Miami, 2727 Indian Creek Dr., Mid-Beach* ☎ *305/531–2727* 🌐 *www.freehandhotels.com/miami/broken-shaker.*

★ LIV
DANCE CLUBS | It's not hard to see why LIV often makes lists of the world's best clubs—if you can get in, that is (LIV is notorious for lengthy lines, so don't arrive fashionably late). Past the velvet ropes, the dance palladium impresses with its lavish decor, well-dressed international crowd, sensational light-and-sound system, and seductive bi-level club experience. **■ TIP→ Men beware: groups of guys entering LIV are often coerced into insanely priced bottle service.** ✉ *Fontainebleau Miami Beach, 4441 Collins Ave., Mid-Beach* ☎ *305/674–4680 for table reservations* 🌐 *www.livnightclub.com.*

Fisher and Belle Islands

A private island community near the southern tip of South Beach, Fisher Island is accessible only by the island's ferry service. The island is predominantly residential with a few hotel rooms on offer at Fisher Island Club Hotel and Resort. Belle Island is a small island connected to both the mainland and Miami Beach by road. It is a mile north of South Beach and just west over the Venetian Causeway.

Hotels

Fisher Island Hotel and Resort
$$$$ | **RESORT** | An exclusive private island, just south of Miami Beach but accessible only by ferry, Fisher Island houses an upscale residential community that includes a small inventory of overnight accommodations, including opulent cottages, villas, and junior suites, which surround the island's original 1920s-era Vanderbilt mansion. **Pros:** great private beaches; never crowded; varied on-island dining choices. **Cons:** not the warmest fellow guests; pretentious people; limited cell phone service. $ *Rooms from: $1,300* ⊠ *1 Fisher Island Dr., Fisher Island* ☎ *305/535–6000* ⊕ *www.fisherislandclub.com* ⤳ *60 rooms* ◯ *No meals.*

The Standard Spa, Miami Beach
$$ | **RESORT** | An extension of André Balazs's trendy and hip—yet budget-conscious—brand, this shabby-chic boutique spa hotel is a mile from South Beach on an island just over the Venetian Causeway and boasts one of South Florida's most renowned spas, trendiest bars, and hottest pool scenes. **Pros:** free bike and kayak rentals; swank pool scene; great spa. **Cons:** slight trek to South Beach; small rooms with no views; nonguests visiting property spa and restaurants. $ *Rooms from: $224* ⊠ *40 Island Ave., Belle Isle* ☎ *305/673–1717* ⊕ *www.standardhotels.com/miami/properties/miami-beach* ⤳ *105 rooms* ◯ *No meals.*

Nightlife

The Lido Bayside Grill
BARS/PUBS | By day, the colorful and chic waterfront alfresco restaurant is an idyllic place to kick back, sip cocktails, and watch bay-side boats and poolside hotties go by. In the evening, lights braided

into the surrounding trees illuminate the terrace, sparking a seductive atmosphere. On weekdays from 4 to 7, the bar offers a locals-frequented happy hour. ⊠ *The Standard Spa, Miami Beach, 40 Island Ave., Belle Isle* ☎ *786/245–0880* ⊕ *www.standardhotels.com.*

North Beach

Though often referred to collectively as North Beach, there are several neighborhoods above Mid-Beach before reaching the Dade-Broward border. In Miami Beach proper, nearing the 63rd Street mark on Collins Avenue, Mid-Beach gives way to what is officially North Beach (until 87th Street), followed by Surfside (up until 95th Street).

Hotels

★ Carillon Miami Wellness Resort
$$$$ | **RESORT** | Formerly Canyon Ranch Miami, the Carillon Miami Wellness Resort carries the art deco building's original name but the physical and mental well-being motif of its predecessor—a 150-all-suites beachfront hotel, defined by a 70,000-square-foot wellness spa, including a rock-climbing wall, 54 treatment rooms, and 30 exercise classes daily. **Pros:** directly on the beach; spacious suites (minimum 720 square feet); incredible spa treatments. **Cons:** far from nightlife; rooms could be a bit more stylish; day visitors at spa and gym. $ *Rooms from: $495* ⊠ *6801 Collins Ave., North Beach* ☎ *866/800–3858* ⊕ *www.carillonhotel.com* ⤳ *150 suites* ◯ *No meals.*

Bal Harbour

At 96th Street the town of Bal Harbour takes over Collins Avenue from Miami Beach. Bal Harbour is famous for its outdoor high-end shops, and if you take your shopping seriously, you may want to spend some considerable time in this area. The town runs a mere 10 blocks to the north before the bridge to another barrier island. After crossing the bridge, you'll first come to Haulover Beach Park, which is still technically in the village of Bal Harbour.

Beaches

★ Haulover Beach Park

BEACH—SIGHT | This popular clothing-optional beach is embraced by naturists of all ages, shapes, and sizes; there are even sections primarily frequented by families, singles, and gays. Nevertheless, Haulover has more claims to fame than its casual attitude toward swimwear—it's also the best beach in the area for bodyboarding and surfing, as it gets what passes for impressive swells in these parts. Once you park in the North Lot, you'll walk through a short tunnel covered with trees and natural habitat until you emerge on the unpretentious beach, where nudity is rarely met by gawkers. There are volleyball nets, and plenty of beach chair and umbrella rentals to protect your birthday suit from too much exposure—to the sun, that is. The sections of beach requiring swimwear are popular, too, given the park's ample parking and relaxed atmosphere. Lifeguards stand watch. More-active types might want to check out the kite rentals, or charter-fishing excursions. **Amenities:** food and drink; lifeguards; parking (fee); showers; toilets. **Best for:** nudists; surfing; swimming; walking. ✉ *10800 Collins Ave., North Beach* ✣ *North of Bal Harbour* ☎ *305/947–3525* 🌐 *www.miamidade.gov/parks/haulover.asp* 🎫 *Parking $5 per vehicle weekdays, $7 weekends.*

Restaurants

Carpaccio Restaurant

$$$$ | **MODERN ITALIAN** | As expected for its ritzy location, this upscale restaurant matches its high-fashion neighbors: waiters don bow ties and coattails, even for lunch hours, yet are approachable in their knowledge and attentiveness. Practically everything on the menu jumps out, though the handmade mozzarella antipasti, clam linguine, and namesake beef carpaccio are signature dishes, and an extensive list of wines from Italy, California, and other worldly regions perfectly complements a meal here. **Known for:** myriad carpaccios; ladies who lunch; well-heeled crowd. $ *Average main: $31* ✉ *Bal Harbour Shops, 9700 Collins Ave., Bal Harbour* ☎ *305/867–7777* 🌐 *www.carpaccioatbalharbour.com.*

Le Zoo

$$$$ | **FRENCH** | Restaurateur Stephen Starr imports a bona fide Parisian brasserie to the swanky Bal Harbour shops—inclusive of vintage decorations, furnishings, and an entire bar, all of which were shipped directly from France. Expect classics perfected, such as onion soup gratiné, steak frites and moules frites, and seafood *plateaux* (towers); a few delicious deviations like the escargots in hazelnut butter (rather than garlic butter); and plenty of excellent people-watching. **Known for:** Parisian flair; seafood towers; outdoor seating. $ *Average main: $42* ✉ *Bal Harbour Shops, 9700 Collins Ave., No. 135, North Beach* ☎ *305/602–9663* 🌐 *www.lezoo.com.*

★ Makoto

$$$$ | **JAPANESE** | Stephen Starr's Japanese headliner, executed by celebrity-chef and master of Edomae-style sushi Makoto Okuwa, offers two menus: one devoted solely to sushi, sashimi, and maki, the other to Japanese cold and hot dishes. Look forward to hyperfresh raw dishes, tempuras, meats, and vegetables grilled over Japanese charcoal (*robata*), rice and noodle dishes, and a variety of steaks and fish inspired by the Land of the Rising Sun. **Known for:** superfresh sushi; artistic presentation; well-dressed crowd. $ *Average main: $34* ✉ *Bal*

Harbour Shops, 9700 Collins Ave., Bal Harbour ☎ *305/864–8600* 🌐 *www.mako-to-restaurant.com.*

Hotels

The Ritz-Carlton Bal Harbour, Miami
$$$$ | RESORT | FAMILY | In one of South Florida's poshest neighborhoods, this property exudes contemporary beachfront luxury design with decadent mahogany-floor guest rooms featuring large terraces with panoramic views of the water and city, over-the-top bathrooms with 10-foot floor-to-ceiling windows, and LCD TVs built into the bathroom mirrors. **Pros:** proximity to Bal Harbour Shops; bathroom's soaking tubs have ocean views; great contemporary-art collection. **Cons:** narrow beach is a bit disappointing; quiet area; small lobby. [$] *Rooms from: $518* ✉ *10295 Collins Ave., Bal Harbour* ☎ *305/455–5400* 🌐 *www.ritzcarlton.com/en/hotels/miami/bal-harbour* 🛏 *187 rooms* 🍴 *No meals.*

★ **The St. Regis Bal Harbour Resort**
$$$$ | RESORT | This posh resort (which cost over $1 billion to build) embodies the next level of ultraglamour and haute living along Miami's North Beach. **Pros:** beachfront setting; Sunday rosé brunch; large apartment-sized rooms. **Cons:** limited lounge space around main pool; limited privacy on balconies; high price tag. [$] *Rooms from: $1,029* ✉ *9703 Collins Ave., Bal Harbour* ☎ *305/993–3300* 🌐 *www.stregisbalharbour.com* 🛏 *216 rooms* 🍴 *No meals.*

Shopping

★ **Bal Harbour Shops**
SHOPPING CENTERS/MALLS | Beverly Hills meets the South Florida sun at this swank collection of 100 high-end shops, boutiques, and department stores, which currently holds the title as the country's greatest revenue-earner per square foot. The open-air enclave includes Florida's largest Saks Fifth Avenue; an 8,100-square-foot, two-story flagship Salvatore Ferragamo store; and stores by Alexander McQueen, Valentino, and local juggernaut The Webster. Restaurants and cafés, in tropical garden settings, overflow with style-conscious diners. A $400 million expansion is currently under way to add 340,387 square feet of retail, including a Barneys New York flagship store and a Freds at Barneys restaurant. ✉ *9700 Collins Ave., Bal Harbour* ☎ *305/866–0311* 🌐 *www.balharbourshops.com.*

100% Capri
CLOTHING | This shop is one of only two stores by this Italian brand in the United States (the other is in Palm Beach). The collection is all pure linen (including the shopping bags). Designer Antonio Aiello sources and produces all pieces in Capri for an exciting interpretation that takes its wearers to exotic beach locales style-wise—and quite literally, given its clientele. You'll find clothing for women, men, and children, and even home goods with curated glass accessories brought over from Italy. ✉ *Bal Harbour Shops, 9700 Collins Ave., No. 236, Bal Harbour* ☎ *305/866–4117* 🌐 *www.100capri.com/en.*

★ **The Webster Bal Harbour**
CLOTHING | Complementing its sister store in South Beach, The Webster Bal Harbour houses high-level fashions aplenty for both men and women. Nearly every great contemporary luxury designer is represented (Chanel, Céline, Valentino, Givenchy, Proenza Schouler, Stella McCartney, etc.) as well as emerging runway darlings. Fashionably impatient? The store can snag ready-to-wear pieces from the latest shows. It also carries exclusive pieces, a real feat considering its influential mall neighbors, including a continuous flow of capsule collections in collaboration with the likes of Calvin Klein, Marc Jacobs, and Anthony Vaccarello, to name a few. ✉ *Bal Habour Shops, 9700 Collins Ave., No. 204,*

Bal Harbour ☎ 305/868–6544 ⊕ www.
thewebster.us/stores/bal-harbour.

Sunny Isles Beach

Beyond Haulover Beach (and on the same barrier island) is the town of Sunny Isles Beach. Once over the bridge, Collins Avenue bypasses several dozen street numbers, picking up again in the 150s; that's when you know you've arrived in the town of Sunny Isles Beach—an appealing, calm, and predominantly upscale choice for families looking for a beautiful beach, and where Russian may be heard as often as English. There's no nightlife to speak of in Sunny Isles, and yet the half-dozen mega-luxurious skyscraper hotels that have sprung up here in the past decade have created a niche-resort town from the demolished ashes of much older, affordable hotels.

 Restaurants

AQ Chop House by Il Mulino
$$$$ | MODERN ITALIAN | This romantic Italian steak house commingles premium steaks and seafood with classic Italian favorites (and offers an excellent sushi menu, to boot). Consider starting with the grilled octopus, followed by the short rib ravioli, and then a buttery, 12-oz. filet mignon and washing it all down with artisanal cocktails like the AQ Smoked Negroni or the Black Cherry Old Fashioned. **Known for:** tequila-infused Spicy Passion cocktail; chophouse meatball appetizer; Caesar salad. Ⓢ Average main: $41 ✉ Acqualina Resort & Spa on the Beach, 17875 Collins Ave., Sunny Isles Beach ☎ 305/466–9191 ⊕ www.acqualin-aresort.com/dining/aq-chop-house.

Il Mulino New York—Sunny Isles Beach
$$$$ | ITALIAN | For decades Il Mulino New York has ranked among the top Italian restaurants in Gotham, so it's no surprise that this Miami outpost is similarly good. Start your food coma with

the complimentary starters—fresh cuts of Parmesan cheese, four types of fresh bread, garlicky bruschetta, and spicy, fried zucchini whet the palate—and then move on to antipasti like calamari fritti followed by ever-changing risottos and other classic Italian dishes perfected. **Known for:** seafood risotto; excellent service; intimate setting. Ⓢ Average main: $45 ✉ Acqualina Resort & Spa on the Beach, 17875 Collins Ave., Sunny Isles Beach ☎ 305/466–9191 ⊕ www.ilmulino.com/miami.

Hotels

★ **Acqualina Resort & Spa on the Beach**
$$$$ | RESORT | FAMILY | The grand dame of Sunny Isles Beach continues to raise the bar for Miami beachfront luxury, delivering a fantasy of modern Mediterranean opulence, with sumptuously appointed, striking gray- and silver-accented interiors and expansive facilities. **Pros:** excellent beach; in-room check-in; huge spa. **Cons:** no nightlife near hotel; hotel's towering height shades the beach by early afternoon; construction next door. Ⓢ Rooms from: $846 ✉ 17875 Collins Ave., Sunny Isles Beach ☎ 305/918–8000 ⊕ www.acqualinaresort.com ⇆ 98 rooms ⓘⓞⓘ No meals.

North Miami Beach

Don't let the name fool you. North Miami Beach actually isn't on the beach, but its southeastern end does abut Biscayne Bay. Beyond the popular Oleta River State Park on the bay, the city offers little in terms of touristic appeal.

Beaches

Oleta River State Park
BEACH—SIGHT | FAMILY | Tucked away in North Miami Beach, this urban park is a ready-made family getaway. Nature lovers will find it easy to embrace the 1,128

Did You Know?

Aventura Mall is one of the biggest shopping malls in Miami with more than 300 stores and 50 eateries.

acres of subtropical beauty along Biscayne Bay. Swim in the calm bay waters and bicycle, canoe, kayak, and bask among egrets, manatees, bald eagles, and fiddler crabs. Dozens of picnic tables, along with 10 covered pavilions, dot the stunning natural habitat, which was restored with red mangroves to revitalize the ecosystem and draw endangered birds, like the roseate spoonbill. There's a playground for tots, a mangrove island accessible only by boat, 15 miles of mountain-bike trails, a half-mile exercise track, concessions, and outdoor showers. **Amenities:** food and drink; parking (fee); showers; toilets; water sports. **Best for:** solitude; sunrise; sunset; walking. ⊠ *3400 N.E. 163rd St., North Miami Beach* ☎ *305/919–1844* ⊕ *www.floridastateparks.org/park/Oleta-River* ⊠ *$6 per vehicle; $2 per pedestrian.*

North Miami

This suburban city, north of Miami proper, is comprised predominantly of older homes in its western reaches—many derelict—but also some snazzy rebuilds in the sections around Biscayne Bay and U.S. 1. Several strip malls and restaurants line U.S. 1.

Aventura

West of Sunny Isles Beach and on the mainland are the high-rises of Aventura. This city is the heart and soul of South Florida's Jewish community as well as Miami's growing Russian community (along with Sunny Isles Beach). It is known for its high-end shopping opportunities, from the mega Aventura Mall to smaller boutiques in eclectic strip malls.

🍴 Restaurants

Bourbon Steak
$$$$ | STEAKHOUSE | Michael Mina's longstanding South Florida steak house is renowned for its seductive design, sophisticated clientele, outstanding wine list, phenomenal service, and, of course, exceptional food. Dinner begins with a skillet of fresh potato focaccia and flavor-dusted french fries as preludes to entrées like the Maine lobster potpie (with truffle cream) and any of the dozen varieties of butter-poached, wood-grilled steaks (from hormone-free prime cuts to American Wagyu). **Known for:** duck-fat fries with dipping sauces; perfectly cooked steaks; floor-to-ceiling glass wine cellar. Ⓢ *Average main: $65* ⊠ *JW Marriott Miami Turnberry Resort & Spa, 19999 W. Country Club Dr., Aventura* ☎ *786/279–6600* ⊕ *www.michaelmina.net.*

Novecento Aventura
$$$ | MODERN ARGENTINE | FAMILY | At this lively Argentine bistro, empanadas, *picadas* (sharing platters of small bites), sizzling steaks (including a grilled beef tenderloin in a Malbec demi-glace), and homemade pastas (a nod to Argentina's Italian heritage) headline the menu. The dim lighting, seductive atmosphere, and early-19th-century black-and-white imagery recall a bona fide Buenos Aires bistro, helping patrons forget that they are, in fact, in suburban Aventura. **Known for:** homemade empanadas; great wine list; simply grilled meats from the parilla. Ⓢ *Average main: $24* ⊠ *Town Center Aventura, 18831 N. Biscayne Blvd., Aventura* ☎ *305/466–0900* ⊕ *www.novecento.com.*

🛏 Hotels

JW Marriott Turnberry Miami Resort and Spa
$$$$ | RESORT | FAMILY | After a head-to-toe makeover and expansion throughout 2018, golfers and families are once again

flocking to this 300-acre tropical resort, now flaunting 625 jumbo-size rooms and suites (including 325 in the new 16-story Orchid Tower) and even more world-class amenities, including 36 holes of championship golf, prolific tennis courts, an on-site waterpark, the three-story âme Spa & Wellness Collective, and two renowned restaurants—Michael Mina's Bourbon Steak and Corsair restaurant. **Pros:** completely reimagined in 2018; free shuttle to Aventura Mall; situated between Miami and Fort Lauderdale. **Cons:** not on the beach; in residential area; $37 per day resort fee. [$] *Rooms from: $529* ✉ *19999 W. Country Club Dr., Aventura* ☎ *305/932–6200* 🌐 *www.jwturnberry.com* 🛏 *625 rooms* 🍴 *No meals.*

Shopping

★ Aventura Mall

SHOPPING CENTERS/MALLS | This three-story megamall offers the ultimate in South Florida retail therapy and houses many global top performers including the most lucrative outposts of several U.S. chain stores, a supersize Nordstrom and Bloomingdale's, and 300 other shops like a two-story flagship Louis Vuitton, Façonnable, and Fendi, which together create the third-largest mall in the United States. Consider it a one-stop, shop-'til-you-drop retail mecca for locals, out-of-towners, and—frequently—celebrities. ✉ *19501 Biscayne Blvd., Aventura* ☎ *305/935–1110* 🌐 *www.aventuramall.com.*

Activities

Miami Dolphins

FOOTBALL | The Miami Dolphins have one of the largest average attendance figures in the NFL. Come see the team that completed the NFL's only perfect season (circa 1972), ending in a Super Bowl win of Super Bowl VII. They also then won Super Bowl VIII. Home games are September through January at Hard Rock Stadium, which was upgraded to the tune of $350 million between 2015 and 2016 to become a more modern stadium. ✉ *Hard Rock Stadium, 2269 N.W. 199 St., Miami Gardens* ☎ *888/346–7849* 🌐 *www.miamidolphins.com.*

Chapter 4

THE EVERGLADES

4

Updated by
Galena Mosovich

👁 **Sights**
★★★★★

🍴 **Restaurants**
★★☆☆☆

🛏 **Hotels**
★★☆☆☆

🛍 **Shopping**
★☆☆☆☆

🍸 **Nightlife**
★☆☆☆☆

WELCOME TO
THE EVERGLADES

TOP REASONS TO GO

★ **Serious fishing:** Cast for some of the world's most aggressive game fish—600 species in all—in the Everglades' backwaters.

★ **Abundant birdlife:** Check hundreds of birds off your list, including—if you're lucky—the rare Everglades snail kite.

★ **Cool kayaking:** Do a half-day trip in Big Cypress National Preserve or grab a paddle for the ultimate 99-mile Wilderness Waterway.

★ **Swamp cuisine:** Want to chow down on alligator tail or frogs' legs? Or how about swamp cabbage, made from hearts of palm? Better yet, try stone crabs fresh from the traps.

★ **Gator spotting:** This is ground zero for alligator viewing in the United States, and odds are you'll leave having spotted your quota.

The southern third of the Florida peninsula is largely taken up by protected government land that includes Everglades National Park, Big Cypress National Preserve, and Biscayne National Park. Miami sits to the northeast, with Naples and Marco Island to the northwest. Land access to Everglades National Park is primarily by two roads. The park's main road traverses the southern Everglades from the gateway towns of Homestead and Florida City to the outpost of Flamingo on Florida Bay. To the north, Tamiami Trail (U.S. 41) cuts through the Everglades from Greater Miami on the east coast or from Naples on the west coast to the western park entrance near Everglades City at Route 29.

Gulf of Mexico

1 Everglades National Park. Alligators, Florida panthers, black bears, manatees, dolphins, bald eagles, and roseate spoonbills call this vast habitat home.

2 Biscayne National Park. Mostly underwater, this is where the string of coral reefs and islands that form the Florida Keys starts.

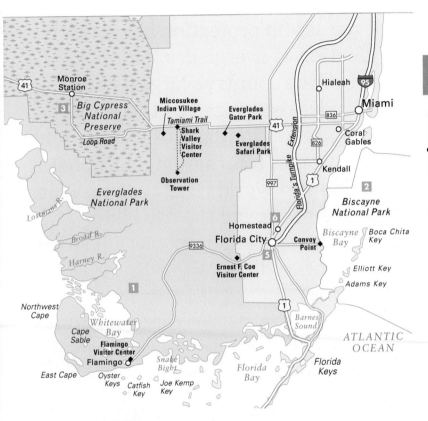

3 Big Cypress National Preserve. Neighbor to Everglades National Park, it's an outdoor lover's paradise.

4 Everglades City. In this small swamp town, the Ten Thousand Islands and fresh seafood await.

5 Florida City. The last suburb of Miami before reaching the Florida Keys, Florida City is home to Everglades National Park.

6 Homestead. A historic district is surrounded by a mix of modern living and farmland, including an exotic-fruit winery.

7 Tamiami Trail. This 100-year-old road is the path to Old Florida's wildest areas.

More than 1.5 million acres of South Florida's 4.3 million acres of subtropical, watery wilderness were given national park status and protection in 1947 with the creation of Everglades National Park. It's one of the country's largest national parks and is recognized by the world community as a Wetland of International Importance, an International Biosphere Reserve, and a World Heritage site. Visit if you want to spend the day biking, hiking, or boating in deep, raw wilderness with lots of wildlife.

To the east of Everglades National Park, Biscayne National Park brings forth a pristine and magical side of Florida. It's the nation's largest marine park and the largest national park boasting living coral reefs within the continental United States. A small portion of the park's 172,000 acres includes mainland coast and outlying islands, but 95 percent remains submerged. Of particular interest are the mangroves and their tangled masses of stiltlike roots that thicken shorelines. These "walking trees," as some locals call them, have curved prop roots arching down from trunks and aerial roots that drop from branches. The roots of these trees filter salt from water and create a coastal nursery that sustains marine life. You can see Miami's high-rise buildings from many of Biscayne's 44 islands, but the park is virtually undeveloped and large enough for escaping everything that Miami and the Upper Keys have become. To truly disconnect, grab scuba-diving or snorkeling gear and lose yourself in the wonders of the coral reefs.

On the northern edge of Everglades National Park lies Big Cypress National Preserve, one of South Florida's least developed watersheds. Established by Congress in 1974 to protect the Everglades, it comprises extensive tracts of prairie, marsh, pinelands, forested swamps and sloughs. Hunting is allowed, as is off-roading. Stop at the Oasis Visitor Center's boardwalk to see the alligators lounging underneath, and then drive Loop Road for a backwoods experience. If time and desire for watery adventure permits, kayak or canoe the Turner River.

Surrounding the parks and preserve are communities where you'll find useful outfitters: Everglades City, Florida City, and Homestead.

Planning

When to Go

Winter is the best, and busiest, time to visit the Everglades. Temperatures and mosquito activity are more tolerable, while low water levels concentrate the resident wildlife, and migratory birds settle in for the season. In late spring the weather turns hot and rainy, and tours and facilities are less crowded. Migratory birds depart, and you must look harder to see wildlife. Summer brings intense sun and afternoon rainstorms. Water levels rise and mosquitoes abound, making outdoor activity virtually unbearable, unless you protect yourself with netting. (Insect repellent is a necessity any time of year.)

Getting Here and Around

Miami International Airport (MIA) is 34 miles from Homestead and 47 miles from the eastern access to Everglades National Park. ⇨ *For MIA airline information, see the Travel Smart chapter.* Shuttles run between MIA and Homestead. Southwest Florida International Airport (RSW), in Fort Myers, a little over an hour's drive from Everglades City, is the closest major airport to the Everglades' western entrance.

Hotels

Accommodations near the parks range from inexpensive to moderate and offer off-season rates in summer, when rampant mosquito populations discourage spending time outdoors, especially at dusk. If you're devoting several days to exploring the east side of the Everglades, stay in park campgrounds; reasonably priced chain motels and RV parks about 11 miles away in Homestead and Florida City; in the Florida Keys; or in the Greater Miami–Fort Lauderdale area. Lodging and campgrounds are plentiful on the Gulf Coast (in Everglades City, Marco Island and Naples; the latter features upscale accommodations).

Restaurants

Dining in the Everglades area is dominated by mom-and-pop spots serving hearty home-style food, and small eateries specializing in fresh local fare such as alligator, fish, stone crab, frogs' legs, and Florida lobster. Native American–inspired restaurants serve these local favorites as well as catfish, Indian fry bread (a flour-and-water flatbread), and pumpkin bread. A flourishing Hispanic population around Homestead means authentic and inexpensive Latin cuisine, with an emphasis on Cuban and Mexican dishes. Restaurants in Everglades City, especially those along the river, specialize in fresh (often just hours out of the water) seafood including particularly succulent, sustainable stone crab. These mostly rustic places are ultracasual and often closed from late summer to fall. For finer dining, head for Marco Island or Naples.

Hotel and restaurant reviews have been shortened. For full information, visit Fodors.com.

What It Costs			
$	$$	$$$	$$$$
RESTAURANTS			
under $15	$15–$20	$21–$30	over $30
HOTELS			
under $200	$200–$300	$301–$400	over $400

Continued on page 121

THE FLORIDA
EVERGLADES

by Lynne Helm

Alternately described as elixir of life or swampland muck, the Florida Everglades is one of a kind—a 50-mi-wide "river of grass" that spreads across hundreds of thousands of acres. It moves at varying speeds depending on rainfall and other variables, sloping south from the Kissimmee River and Lake Okeechobee to estuaries of Biscayne Bay, Florida Bay, and the Ten Thousand Islands.

Today, apart from sheltering some 70 species on America's endangered list, the Everglades also embraces more than 7 million residents, 50 million annual tourists, 400,000 acres of sugarcane, and the world's largest concentration of golf courses.

Demands on the land threaten the Everglades' finely balanced ecosystem. Irrigation canals for agriculture and roadways disrupt natural water flow. Drainage for development leaves wildlife scurrying for new territory. Water runoff, laced with fertilizers, promotes unnatural growth of swamp vegetation. What remains is a miracle of sorts, given decades of these destructive forces.

Creation of the Everglades required unique conditions. South Florida's geology, linked with its warm, wet subtropical climate, is the perfect mix for a marshland ecosystem. Layers of porous, permeable limestone create water-bearing rock, soil, and aquifers, which in turn affects climate, weather, and hydrology.

This rock beneath the Everglades reflects Florida's geologic history—its crust was once part of the African region. Some scientists theorize that continental shifting merged North America with Africa, and then continental rifting later pulled North America away from the African continent but took part of northwest Africa with it—the part that is today's Florida. The Earth's tectonic plates continued to migrate, eventually placing Florida at its current location as a land mass jutting out into the ocean, with the Everglades at its tip.

EXPERIENCING THE ECOSYSTEMS

Eight distinct habitats exist within Everglades National Park, Big Cypress National Preserve, and Biscayne National Park.

ECOSYSTEMS	EASY WAY	MORE ACTIVE WAY
COASTAL PRAIRIE: An arid region of salt-tolerant vegetation lies between the tidal mud flats of Florida Bay and dry land. **Best place to see it: The Coastal Prairie Trail**	Take a guided boat tour of Florida Bay, leaving from Flamingo Marina.	Hike the Coastal Prairie Trail from Eco Pond to Clubhouse Beach.
CYPRESS: Capable of surviving in standing water, cypress trees often form dense clusters called "cypress domes" in natural water-filled depressions. **Best place to see it: Big Cypress National Preserve**	Drive U.S. 41 (also known as Tamiami Trail—pronounced Tammy-Amee), which cuts across Southern Florida, from Naples to Miami.	Hike (or drive) the scenic Loop Road, which begins off Tamiami Trail, running from the Loop Road Education Center to Monroe Station.
FRESH WATER MARL PRAIRIE: Bordering deeper sloughs are large prairies with marl (clay and calcium carbonate) sediments on limestone. Gators like to use their toothy snouts to dig holes in prairie mud. **Best place to see it: Pahayokee Overlook**	Drive there from the Ernest F. Coe Visitor Center.	Take a guided tour, either through the park service or from permitted, licensed guides. You also can set up camp at Long Pine Key.
FRESH WATER SLOUGH AND HARDWOOD HAMMOCK: Shark River Slough and Taylor Slough are the Everglades' two sloughs, or marshy rivers. Due to slight elevation amid sloughs, dense stands of hardwood trees appear as teardrop-shaped islands. **Best place to see it: The Observation Tower**	Take a two-hour guided tram tour from the Shark Valley Visitor Center to the tower and back.	Walk or bike (rentals available) the route to the tower via the tram road and (walkers only) Bobcat Boardwalk trail and Otter Cave Hammock Trail.
MANGROVE: Spread over South Florida's coastal channels and waterways, mangrove thrives where Everglades fresh water mixes with salt water. **Best place to see it: The Wilderness Waterway**	Picnic at the area near Long Pine Key, which is surrounded by mangrove, or take a water tour at Biscayne National Park.	Boat your way along the 99-mi Wilderness Waterway. It's six hours by motorized boat, seven days by canoe.
MARINE AND ESTUARINE: Corals, sponges, mollusks, seagrass, and algae thrive in the Florida Bay, where the fresh waters of the Everglades meet the salty seas. **Best place to see it: Florida Bay**	Take a boat tour from the Flamingo Visitor Center marina.	Canoe or kayak on White Water Bay along the Wilderness Waterway Canoe Trail.
PINELAND: A dominant plant in dry, rugged terrain, the Everglades' diverse pinelands consist of slash pine forest, saw palmettos, and more than 200 tropical plant varieties. **Best place to see it: Long Pine Key trails**	Drive to Long Pine Key, about 6 mi off the main road from Ernest F. Coe Visitor Center.	Hike or bike the 28 mi of Long Pine Key trails.

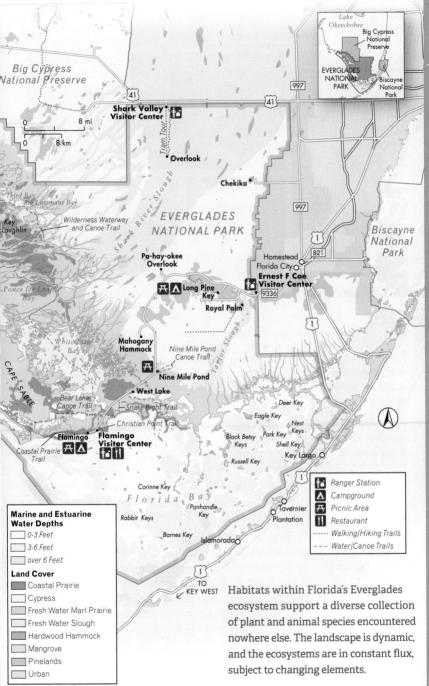

Marine and Estuarine Water Depths
- 0-3 Feet
- 3-6 Feet
- over 6 Feet

Land Cover
- Coastal Prairie
- Cypress
- Fresh Water Marl Prairie
- Fresh Water Slough
- Hardwood Hammock
- Mangrove
- Pinelands
- Urban

Ranger Station
Campground
Picnic Area
Restaurant
Walking/Hiking Trails
Water/Canoe Trails

Habitats within Florida's Everglades ecosystem support a diverse collection of plant and animal species encountered nowhere else. The landscape is dynamic, and the ecosystems are in constant flux, subject to changing elements.

FLORA

❶ CABBAGE PALM

It's virtually impossible to visit the Everglades and not see a cabbage palm, Florida's official state tree. The cabbage palm (or sabal palm), graces assorted ecosystems and grows well in swamps.
Best place to see them: At Loxahatchee National Wildlife Refuge (embracing the northern part of the Everglades, along Alligator Alley), throughout Everglades National Park, and at Big Cypress National Preserve.

❷ SAWGRASS

With spiny, serrated leaf blades resembling saws, sawgrass inspired the term "river of grass" for the Everglades.
Best place to see them: Both Shark Valley and Pahayokee Overlook provide terrific vantage points for gazing over sawgrass prairie; you also can get an eyeful of sawgrass when crossing Alligator Alley, even when doing so at top speeds.

❸ MAHOGANY

Hardwood hammocks of the Everglades live in areas that rarely flood because of the slight elevation of the sloughs, where they're typically found.
Best place to see them: Everglades National Park's Mahogany Hammock Trail (which has a boardwalk leading to the nation's largest living mahogany tree).

❹ MANGROVE

Mangrove forest ecosystems provide both food and protected nursery areas for fish, shellfish, and crustaceans.
Best place to see them: Along Biscayne National Park shoreline, at Big Cypress National Preserve, and within Everglades National Park, especially around the Caple Sable area.

❺ GUMBO LIMBO

Sometimes called "tourist trees" because of peeling reddish bark (not unlike sunburns).
Best place to see them: Everglades National Park's Gumbo Limbo Trail and assorted spots throughout the expansive Everglades.

FAUNA

❶ AMERICAN ALLIGATOR
In all likelihood, on your visit to the Everglades you'll see at least a gator or two. These carnivorous creatures can be found throughout the Everglades swampy wetlands.
Best place to see them: Loxahatchee National Wildlife Refuge (also sheltering the endangered Everglades snail kite) and within Everglades National Park at Shark Valley or Anhinga Trail. Sometimes (logically enough) gators hang out along Alligator Alley, basking in early morning or late-afternoon sun along four-lane I–75.

❷ AMERICAN CROCODILE
Crocs gravitate to fresh or brackish water, subsisting on birds, fish, snails, frogs, and small mammals.
Best place to see them: Within Everglades National Park, Big Cypress National Preserve, and protected grounds in or around Billie Swamp Safari.

❸ EASTERN CORAL SNAKE
This venomous snake burrows in underbrush, preying on lizards, frogs, and smaller snakes.
Best place to see them: Snakes typically shy away from people, but try Snake Bight or Eco Pond near Flamingo, where birds are also prevalent.

❹ FLORIDA PANTHER
Struggling for survival amid loss of habitat, these shy, tan-colored cats now number around 100, up from lows of near 30.
Best place to see them: Protected grounds of Billie Swamp Safari sometimes provide sightings during tours. Signage on roadway linking Tamiami Trail and Alligator Alley warns of panther crossings, but sightings are rare.

❺ GREEN TREE FROG
Typically bright green with white or yellow stripes, these nocturnal creatures thrive in swamps and brackish water.
Best place to see them: Within Everglades National Park, especially in or near water.

● =Extremely Common ● =Very Common ● =Somewhat Common ● =Rare

BIRDS

❶ ANHINGA

The lack of oil glands for waterproofing feathers helps this bird to dive as well as chase and spear fish with its pointed beak. The Anhinga is also often called a "water turkey" because of its long tail, or a "snake bird" because of its long neck.

Best place to see them: The Anhinga Trail, which also is known for attracting other wildlife to drink during especially dry winters.

❷ BLUE-WINGED TEAL

Although it's predominantly brown and gray, this bird's powder-blue wing patch becomes visible in flight. Next to the mallard, the blue-winged teal is North America's second most abundant duck, and thrives particularly well in the Everglades.

Best place to see them: Near ponds and marshy areas of Everglades National Park or Big Cypress National Preserve.

❸ GREAT BLUE HERON

This bird has a varied palate and enjoys feasting on everything from frogs, snakes, and mice to shrimp, aquatic insects, and sometimes even other birds! The all-white version, which at one time was considered a separate species, is quite common to the Everglades.

Best place to see them: Loxahatchee National Wildlife Refuge or Shark Valley in Everglades National Park.

❹ GREAT EGRET

Once decimated by plume hunters, these monogamous, long-legged white birds with S-shaped necks feed in wetlands, nest in trees, and hang out in colonies that often include heron or other egret species.

Best place to see them: Throughout Everglades National Park, along Alligator Alley, and sometimes even on the fringes of Greater Fort Lauderdale.

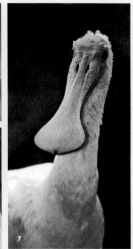

❺ GREATER FLAMINGO

Flocking together and using long legs and webbed feet to stir shallow waters and mud flats, color comes a couple of years after hatching from ingesting shrimplike crustaceans along with fish, fly larvae, and plankton.

Best place to see them: Try Snake Bight or Eco Pond, near Flamingo Marina.

❻ OSPREY

Making a big comeback from chemical pollutant endangerment, ospreys (sometimes confused with bald eagles) are distinguished by black eyestripes down their faces. Gripping pads on feet with curved claws help them pluck fish from water.

Best place to see them: Look near water, where they're fishing for lunch in the shallow areas. Try the coasts, bays, and ponds of Everglades National Park. They also gravitate to trees You can usually spot them from the Gulf Coast Visitor Center, or you can observe them via boating in the Ten Thousand Islands.

❼ ROSEATE SPOONBILL

These gregarious pink-and-white birds gravitate toward mangroves, feeding on fish, insects, amphibians, and some plants. They have long, spoonlike bills, and their feathers can have a touch of red and yellow. These birds appear in the Everglades year-round.

Best place to see them: Sandy Key, southwest of Flamingo, is a spoonbill nocturnal roosting spot, but at sunrise these colorful birds head out over Eco Pond to favored day hangouts throughout Everglades National Park.

❽ WOOD STORK

Recognizable by featherless heads and prominent bills, these birds submerge in water to scoop up hapless fish. They are most common in the early spring and often easiest to spot in the morning.

Best place to see them: Amid the Ten Thousand Island areas, Nine Mile Pond, Mrazek Pond, and in the mangroves at Paurotis Pond.

● =Extremely Common ● =Very Common ● =Somewhat Common ● =Rare

THE STORY OF THE EVERGLADES

Dreams of draining southern Florida took hold in the early 1800s, expanding in the early 1900s to convert large tracts from wetlands to agricultural acreage. By the 1920s, towns like Fort Lauderdale and Miami boomed, and the sugar industry—which came to be known as "Big Sugar"—established its first sugar mills. In 1947 Everglades National Park opened as a refuge for wildlife.

Meanwhile, the sugar industry grew. In its infancy, about 175,000 tons of raw sugar per year was produced from fields totaling about 50,000 acres. But once the U.S. embargo stopped sugar imports from Cuba in 1960 and laws restricting acreage were lifted, Big Sugar took off. Less than five years later, the industry produced 572,000 tons of sugar and occupied nearly a quarter of a million acres.

Fast-forward to 2008, to what was hailed as the biggest conservation deal in U.S. history since the creation of the national parks. A trailblazing restoration strategy hinged on creating a water flow-way between Lake Okeechobee and the Everglades by buying up and flooding 187,000 acres of land. The country's largest producers of cane sugar agreed to sell the necessary 187,000 acres to the state of Florida for $1.75 billion. Environmentalists cheered.

But within months, news broke of a scaled-back land acquisition plan: $1.34 billion to buy 180,000 acres. By spring 2009, the restoration plan had shrunk to $536,000 to buy 73,000 acres. With the purchase still in limbo, critics claim the state might overpay for acreage appraised at pre-recession values and proponents fear dwindling revenues may derail the plan altogether.

The Big Sugar land deal is part of a larger effort to preserve the Everglades. In 2010, two separate lawsuits charged the state, along with the United States Environmental Protection Agency, with stalling Everglades cleanup that was supposed to begin in 2006. "Glacial delay" is how one judge put it. The state must reduce phosphorus levels in water that flows to the Everglades or face fines and sanctions for violating the federal Clean Water Act. The fate of the Everglades remains in the balance.

War on Pythons

The nonnative Burmese python population has flourished in the Everglades for a couple of decades, likely since Hurricane Andrew. Studies show that pythons dramatically reduce prey for native predators and this contributes to the decline of this delicate habitat. The dangerous constrictors are literally squeezing the life out of Everglades.

The South Florida Water Management District (SFWMD) incentivizes select members of the community to locate and remove invasive Burmese pythons in Miami-Dade, Broward, Collier, and Palm Beach counties. In other words, SFWMD is hand-picking hunters to locate and eliminate these apex predators for money. In 2018 the state-sponsored program eliminated more than 1,000 pythons after just 14 months—a huge success for Team Everglades.

The state's war on destructive and invasive species will likely continue, in increasingly creative and aggressive ways, to protect the wildlife of the Everglades. —Galena Mosovich

Everglades National Park

45 miles southwest of Miami International Airport.

If you're heading across the southern portion of Florida on U.S. 41, from Miami to Naples, you'll breeze right through the Everglades. This mostly two-lane road, also known as Tamiami Trail, skirts the edge of Everglades National Park and cuts across the Big Cypress National Preserve. You'll also be near the park if you're en route from Miami to the Florida Keys on U.S. 1, which cuts through Homestead and Florida City—communities east of the main park entrance. Basically, if you're in South Florida, you can't escape at least fringes of the Everglades. With tourist strongholds like Miami, Naples, and the Florida Keys so close, travelers from all over the world typically make day trips to the park.

Everglades National Park has three main entry points: the park headquarters at Ernest F. Coe Visitor Center, southwest of Homestead and Florida City; the Shark Valley area, accessed by Tamiami Trail (U.S. 41); and the Gulf Coast Visitor Center, south of Everglades City to the west and closest to Naples.

Explore on your own or participate in ranger-led hikes, bicycle or bird-watching tours, and canoe trips. The variety of these excursions is greatest from mid-December through April, and some adventures (canoe trips, for instance) typically aren't offered in the sweltering summer months. Among the more popular activities are the Anhinga Amble, a 50-minute walk around the Taylor Slough (departs from the Royal Palm Visitor Center), and the Early Bird Special, a 90-minute walk centered on birdlife (departs from Flamingo Visitor Center). Check with the respective visitor centers for details.

PARK ESSENTIALS

Admission Fees The fee is $25 per vehicle; $20 per motorcycle; and $8 per pedestrian or cyclist. Payable online or at the gates, admission is good for seven consecutive days at all park entrances. Annual passes are $40.

Admission Hours Open daily, year-round. Both the main entrance near Florida City and Homestead and the Gulf Coast entrance are open 24/7. The Shark Valley entrance is open 8:30 a.m. to 6 p.m.

Ernest F. Coe Visitor Center to Flamingo Visitor Center

About 50 miles southwest of Miami.

The most utilized entrance to Everglades National Park is southwest of Homestead and Florida City. If you're traveling from Miami, take State Road 836/Dolphin Expressway West to State Road 826/Palmetto Expressway South to the Homestead Extension of Florida's Turnpike, U.S. 1, and Krome Avenue (State Road 997). Once you're in Homestead, go right (west) from U.S. 1 or Krome Avenue onto Palm Drive (State Road 9336/S.W. 344th Street) and follow signage to the park entrance.

This road runs 38 miles from the Ernest F. Coe Visitor Center to the Florida Bay at Flamingo, the southernmost headquarters of Everglades National Park. On the way it crosses a section of the park's eight distinct ecosystems: hardwood hammock, freshwater prairie, pinelands, freshwater slough, cypress, coastal prairie, mangrove, and marine-estuarine. Highlights include a dwarf cypress forest, the transition zone between sawgrass and mangrove forest, and a wealth of wading birds at Mrazek and Coot Bay ponds, where you can observe them feeding early in the morning or later in the afternoon. Flamingo sightings here are extremely rare. Boardwalks, looped trails, several short spurs, and observation platforms help you stay dry. You can stop along the way to walk several short trails (each takes about 30 minutes): the wheelchair-accessible Anhinga Trail, which cuts through sawgrass marsh and allows you to see lots of wildlife (be on the lookout for alligators and the trail's namesake waterbirds: anhingas); the junglelike yet also wheelchair-accessible Gumbo-Limbo Trail; the Pinelands Trail,

where you can see the park's limestone bedrock; the Pahayokee Overlook Trail, ending at an observation tower; and the Mahogany Hammock Trail, with its dense growth. ■TIP➔ **Before heading out on the trails, inquire about insect and weather conditions. Stocking up on bug repellent, sunscreen, and water is always a good idea. Even on sunny days, it's smart to bring rain gear.**

Sights

To explore this section of the park, follow Palm Drive (State Road 9336) from the main park entrance to Flamingo Visitor Center; you'll find plenty of opportunities to stop along the way and assorted activities to pursue in the Flamingo area. Other than campgrounds, there are no lodging options within the national park.

Ernest F. Coe Visitor Center

ARTS VENUE | FAMILY | Get your park map here, 365 days a year, but don't just grab and go; this visitor center's interactive exhibits and films are well worth your time. The 15-minute film *River of Life,* updated frequently, provides a succinct park overview. A movie on hurricanes and a 35-minute wildlife film for children are available upon request. Learn about the Great Water Debate, the saga of how draining swampland for residential and agricultural development cuts off water-supply routes for precious wetlands in the ecosystem. Artists in Residence in Everglades' (AIRIE) Nest Gallery is also located at the visitor center. You'll also find a schedule of daily ranger-led activities, mainly walks and talks; information on the popular Nike missile site tour (harking back to the Cuban missile crisis era); and details about canoe rentals and boat tours at Flamingo. The visitor center is outside park gates, so you can stop in without paying park admission (and use the restrooms). Due to the remoteness of this location, visitors arriving via ride-sharing services (Uber, Lyft) should plan for return transportation before starting their adventure. There's no public transportation to this site. ✉ *40001 State Rd. 9336, Homestead* ☎ *305/242–7700* ⊠ *Free.*

Flamingo Visitor Center

BODY OF WATER | **FAMILY** | At the southernmost point of the park's main road to the Flamingo community, you'll find a visitor center, marina store (with beverages, snacks and a gift shop), public boat ramp, and campground with nearby hiking and nature trails. This is where you'll go for backcountry permits. Despite the name, you probably won't find any flamingos here. To try to get a glimpse of the flamboyant pink birds with toothpick legs, check out Snake Bight Trail, starting about 5 miles from the Flamingo outpost. But they are a rare sight indeed. Visitors can pitch tents or bring RVs to the campground, where amenities include solar-heated showers and electricity for RV sites. Be sure to make a reservation during winter, and note that during the summer wet season, portions of the campgrounds are closed due to flooding. ✉ *1 Flamingo Lodge Hwy., Homestead* ☎ *239/695–2945* ⊕ *www.nps.gov/ever/planyourvisit/flamdirections.htm.*

Flamingo Visitor Center

BODY OF WATER | **FAMILY** | Check the schedule here for visitor center hours as it's staffed intermittently depending on the season. If you're famished and didn't pack your own picnic, the center's Marina Store sells nonperishable food, drinks, ice, and other supplies. Mosquito repellent will be your favorite accessory here. Many of the additional amenities are closed due to long-standing hurricane damage. ✉ *Flamingo Visitor Center, 1 Flamingo Lodge Hwy., Homestead* ☎ *239/695–2945, 239/695–3101 Main number, 305/501–2852 Canoe, kayak, and bicycle rentals, 855/708–2207 Campground reservations* ⊕ *www.nps.gov/ever/planyourvisit/flamdirections.htm.*

Picnic Spots

Worthwhile spots to pull over for a picnic are **Paurotis Pond,** 24 miles from the main park entrance near Homestead (the actual pond is closed during nesting season) and **Nine Mile Pond,** less than 30 miles from the main visitor center.

Royal Palm Information Station and Bookstore

INFO CENTER | **FAMILY** | Ideal for when there's limited time to experience the Everglades, this small center with a bookstore features ranger-led walks and talks. Visitors can also access the park's Pine Island Trails (Anhinga Trail, Gumbo Limbo Trail, Lone Pine Key Trails, Pineland Trail, Pahayokee Overlook, and Mahogany Hammock Trail) from Royal Palm. Two ranger-led programs, The Anhinga Amble (a 50-minute stroll brings you close to alligators, wading birds, and other wildlife) and Glades Glimpse (a 20-minute talk in the shade), are offered every day, year-round, including the summer months. As always, arm yourself with insect repellent. ✉ *Everglades National Park* ✛ *A little over a mile away from Ernest F. Coe Visitor Center* ☎ *305/242–7237* ⊕ *www.nps.gov/ever/planyourvisit/royal-palm.htm.*

Activities

BIRD-WATCHING

Some of the park region's best birding is in Everglades National Park, especially the Flamingo area.

CANOEING AND KAYAKING

The 99-mile inland **Wilderness Trail** between Flamingo and Everglades City is open to motorboats as well as canoes, although, depending on water levels, powerboats may have trouble navigating above Whitewater Bay. Flat-water canoeing and kayaking are best in winter, when temperatures are moderate, rainfall diminishes, and mosquitoes back off—a little, anyway. This activity is for the experienced and adventurous; most paddlers take eight days to complete the trail. But you can also do a day trip. The Flamingo area has well-marked water trails, but be sure to tell someone where you're going and when you expect to return. Getting lost is easy, and spending the night without proper gear can be unpleasant, if not dangerous. A company known as Guest Services, Inc. is the authorized concessioner for Flamingo, and they handle all reservations and rentals. ⊕ *flamingoeverglades.com*

Gulf Coast Visitor Center Entrance

To reach the park's western gateway, take U.S./Highway 41 (Tamiami Trail) west from Miami for about 90 miles, turn left (south) onto State Road 29, and travel another 3 miles through Everglades City to the Gulf Coast Ranger Station. From Naples on the Gulf Coast, take U.S./Highway 41 east for 37 miles, and turn right onto State Road 29.

Gulf Coast Visitor Center
BODY OF WATER | FAMILY | The best place to start exploring Everglades National Park's watery western side is at this visitor center just south of Everglades City (5 miles south of U.S./Highway 41/Tamiami Trail), where rangers can give you the park lowdown and provide you with informational brochures and backcountry permits. A temporary Visitor Contact Station is in place until necessary repairs can be made to the Gulf Coast Visitor Center that was destroyed by Hurricane Irma in 2017. The Gulf Coast Visitor Center serves as the gateway for exploring the Ten Thousand Islands, a maze of mangrove islands and waterways that extends to Flamingo and Florida Bay and

Everglades Birding

The Tropical Audubon Society is where South Florida's most enthusiastic birders flock together to conserve local ecosystems while ensuring birds and their habitats are safe. This chapter of the National Audobon Society is extremely active year-round, and its birding field trips are fun and educational. Visit the website for the calendar of events and other valuable birding resources. ⊕ *www.tropicalaudubon.org.*

are accessible only by boat in this region. Naturalist-led boat trips are handled by Everglades National Park Boat Tours, the concessioner that also rents canoes and kayaks. ⊠ *815 Oyster Bar Ln., Everglades City* ☎ *239/695–3311* ⊕ *www.nps.gov/ever/planyourvisit/gcdirections.htm.*

🏃 Activities

Everglades National Park Boat Tours
TOUR—SPORTS | FAMILY | This authorized concessioner frequently runs 90-minute trips through the Ten Thousand Islands National Wildlife Refuge. Adventure seekers often see dolphins, manatees, bald eagles, and roseate spoonbills in the saltwater portion of the Everglades. Mangrove wilderness tours on smaller boats (up to six passengers) embark on shorter trips through the swampy, brackish areas. This is the best option to see alligators, bobcats, mangrove fox squirrels, and birds, including the mangrove cuckoo. ⊠ *Gulf Coast Visitor Center, 905 S. Copeland Ave., Everglades City* ☎ *239/695–2591* ⊕ *www.evergladesnationalparkboattoursgulfcoast.com/index.php* 🚤 *Tours from $37.10 for Ten Thousand Islands Tour.*

★ Everglades Adventures

TOUR—SPORTS | This established, year-round source for guided Everglades paddling tours and canoe and kayak rentals is located at the Ivey House Inn in Everglades City. Shuttles will deliver you to major launching areas like Turner River, where you'll meet the small group of adventure seekers on your excursion. Highlights include bird and gator sightings, mangrove forests, and spectacular sunsets, depending on the time of your tour. Every tour is led by a certified naturalist and spans about three to four hours. Longer adventures include equipment rental, guide, and meals. ⊠ *The Ivey House & Everglades Adventures, 107 Camellia St. E., Everglades City* ☎ *877/567–0679, 239/695-3299 International* ⊕ *iveyhouse.com/everglades-adventures* ⊠ *Canoe rentals from $30 per day; kayak rentals from $50 per day.*

Shark Valley Visitor Center

23½ miles west of Florida's Turnpike, off Tamiami Trail. Approximately an hour west of Miami.

You won't see sharks at Shark Valley. The name originates from the Shark River, also known as the River of Grass, that flows through the area. Several species of shark swim up this river from the coast (about 45 miles south of Shark Valley) to give birth, though not at this particular spot. Young sharks (called pups) are vulnerable to predators, but they're able to gain strength in waters of the slough before heading out to sea.

The Shark Valley entrance to Everglades National Park is on U.S./Highway 41 (Tamiami Trail), 25 miles west of Florida's Turnpike or 39 miles east of State Road 29.

Good Reads

- *The Everglades: River of Grass.* This 1947 classic by conservationist Marjory Stoneman Douglas is a must-read.

- *Everglades.* Jean Craighead George illustrates the park's natural history in a children's book.

- *Everglades: The Park Story.* Wildlife biologist William B. Robertson Jr. presents the park's flora, fauna, and history.

- *Swamplandia!* This story of a family's gator-wrestling theme park near Everglades City brings readers into the swamp.

◉ Sights

To cover the most ground, hop aboard a two-hour tram tour with a naturalist guide. It stops halfway for a trip to the top of the 45-foot-tall Shark Valley Observation Tower via a sloping ramp.

Prefer to do the trail on foot? It takes nerve to walk the 15-mile loop in Shark Valley, because in the winter months alligators sunbathe along the road. Most, however, do move out of the way when they see you coming.

You also can ride a bicycle (the folks who operate the tram tours rent well-used bikes daily from 8:30 am to 4 pm for $9 per hour with helmets available). Near the bike-rental area, a short boardwalk trail meanders through sawgrass, and another courses through a tropical hardwood hammock.

Shark Valley Observation Tower

NATIONAL/STATE PARK | **FAMILY** | At the halfway point of the Shark Valley loop or tram tour, you can pause to navigate the Observation Tower, which is the highest accessible point in Everglades National

Much skill is required to navigate boats through the shallow, muddy waters of the Everglades.

Park. The viewing platform of this tower, first built in 1984, is nearly 50 feet from the ground. Once there, you'll find the River of Grass in all its glory, sprawling out as far as the eye can see. Observe waterbirds as well as alligators, and maybe even river otters crossing the road. The tower has a wheelchair-accessible ramp to the top. If you don't want to take the tram from the Shark Valley Visitor Center, you can either hike or bike in, but private cars are not allowed. ✉ *Shark Valley Tram Tours, 36000 S.W. 8th St., Miami* ⊕ *www.sharkvalleytramtours.com.*

Shark Valley Visitor Center

INFO CENTER | **FAMILY** | Inside a relatively modern white building is the Shark Valley Visitor Center. Go here for educational displays, a park video, and informational brochures. Books and other goods, such as hats, sunscreen, insect repellent, postcards are available, along with access to restrooms. Park rangers are also available, ready for your questions. ✉ *36000 S.W. 8th St., Miami* ✛ *23½ miles west of Florida's Turnpike, off*

Tamiami Trail ☎ *305/221–8776* ⊕ *www. nps.gov/ever/planyourvisit/svdirections. htm.*

Activities

Buffalo Tiger Airboat Rides

BOATING | **FAMILY** | A former chief of Florida's Miccosukee tribe—Buffalo Tiger, who died in January 2015 at the age of 94—founded this Shark Valley tour operation, and his spirit carries on. Savvy guides narrate the trip to an old Miccosukee Indian camp on the north side of Tamiami Trail from the Native American perspective. Don't worry about airboat noise, they shut off the engines three times during informative talks and photo opportunities. The standard tours are 45 minutes, and longer private tours are available. Reservations are not required for standard tours, and credit cards are now accepted at this outpost, but it's cheaper to purchase online in advance. ✉ *29701 S.W. 8th St., West Miami-Dade* ☎ *305/559–5250* ⊕ *www.buffalotigers-flevergladesairboattours.com/home.*

html ✉ *Standard tours from $24.75 per person. Private tours from $200 per group of 4.*

Shark Valley Bicycle Rentals
BICYCLING | FAMILY | You can gaze at gators while exercising on a bike rented from the Shark Valley Visitor Center (from the same authorized concessioner that operates the tram tours). Bike 15 miles of paved, level roadway (no hills or holes) to the Observation Tower and back while keeping an eye on the roadside reptile show. The single-speed bikes come with baskets and helmets, along with child seats for kids under 35 pounds. The fleet also includes a few 20-inch junior models. You'll need a driver's license or other ID for a deposit. Arm yourself with water, insect repellent, and sunscreen. ✉ *Shark Valley Visitor Center, 36000 S.W. 8th St., Shark Valley* ☎ *305/221–8455* ⊕ *www.sharkvalleytramtours.com/everglades-bicycle-tours* ✉ *Bike rentals from $9/hour.*

Shark Valley Tram Tours
TOUR—SPORTS | FAMILY | Starting at the Shark Valley Visitor Center, these popular two-hour, narrated tours on bio-diesel trams follow a 15-mile loop into the interior, stopping at a wheelchair-accessible observation tower. Bring your own water. Reservations are recommended December through April. ✉ *Shark Valley Visitor Center, 36000 S.W. 8th St., Miami* ☎ *305/221–8455* ⊕ *www.sharkvalleytramtours.com* ✉ *$25 for adults.*

Big Cypress National Preserve

Through the early 1960s, the world's largest cypress-logging operation prospered in Big Cypress Swamp until nearly all the trees were cut down. With the downfall of the industry, government entities began buying parcels of land, and now more than 729,000 acres of the swamp are included in this national preserve. *Big*

The Everglades with Kids

Although kids of all ages can enjoy the park, those six and older typically get the most out of the experience. Consider how much you as a supervising adult will enjoy keeping tabs on your little ones around so much water and so many teeth. Predators including alligators abound. Plus, some children are frightened by raw wilderness. Many of the tour/rentals have age restrictions.

refers to the swamp, which juts into the north edge of Everglades National Park like a puzzle piece. Its size and location make Big Cypress an important link in the region's hydrological system, where rainwater flows through the preserve then south into the park, and eventually into Florida Bay. Its pattern of wet prairies, ponds, marshes, sloughs, and strands is a natural wildlife sanctuary, and thanks to a policy of balanced land use—"use without abuse"—the watery wilderness is devoted to recreation as well as to research and preservation. Bald cypress trees that may look dead are actually dormant, with green needles springing to life in the spring. The preserve allows—in limited areas—hiking, hunting, and off-road vehicles (airboat, swamp buggy, four-wheel drive) by permit. Compared to Everglades National Park, the preserve is less developed and hosts fewer visitors, and that makes it ideal for naturalists, birders, and hikers.

Several scenic drives branch out from Tamiami Trail; a few lead to camping areas and roadside picnic spots. Aside from the Oasis Visitor Center, a popular springboard for viewing alligators, the newer Big Cypress Swamp Welcome Center features a platform for watching manatees. Both centers, along Tamiami Trail between Miami and Naples, feature a top-notch 25-minute film on Big Cypress.

PARK ESSENTIALS

Admission Fees It's free to visit the preserve.

Admission Hours The park is open 24/7, year-round. The Oasis Visitor Center and the Welcome Center are closed on December 25.

CONTACTS Big Cypress National Preserve. ☎ *239/695–2000* ⊕ *www.nps.gov/bicy/index.htm.*

Sights

Big Cypress Swamp Welcome Center

INFO CENTER | **FAMILY** | The newer Big Cypress Swamp Welcome Center on the preserve's western side has abundant information and educational features, as well as restrooms, picnic facilities, and a 70-seat auditorium. An outdoor breezeway showcases an interactive Big Cypress watershed exhibit, illustrating Florida's water flow. It's a convenient place to stop when crossing from either coast. ■TIP→ **Love manatees? The boardwalk overlooking the canal behind the welcome center can be a good spot for viewing the intriguing mammals. (Legend has it that they were once mistaken for mermaids by thirsty or love-starved sailors.)** ✉ *33000 Tamiami Trail E, Ochopee* ☎ *239/695–4757* ⊕ *www.nps.gov/bicy/planyourvisit/basicinfo.htm* ▵ *Free.*

Big Cypress Gallery

ARTS VENUE | **FAMILY** | Clyde Butcher's Big Cypress Gallery is a wonderful spot for finding a postcard, calendar, or a more serious piece of art. Butcher, a big guy with an even bigger beard, is known for his stunning photography of landscapes and his knowledge of the 'glades. His ability to capture its magnetism through a large-format lens is unrivaled. Even if you can't afford his larger-scale stuff,

you're warmly welcome to gaze at everything in the gallery. Out back, Butcher and his wife, Niki, also rent a bungalow ($295 per night, October–April) and a cottage ($350 per night, year-round). ■TIP→ **Look into Butcher's private eco and photo swamp tours. After all, "to know the swamp, you have to get into the swamp,"** he says. ✉ *52388 Tamiami Trail, Ochopee* ☎ *239/695–2428* ⊕ *clydebutcher.com/galleries.*

Oasis Visitor Center

INFO CENTER | **FAMILY** | The big attraction at the Oasis Visitor Center, on the east side of Big Cypress Preserve, is the observation deck for viewing fish, birds and other wildlife, such as gators. The native plants in a small butterfly garden attract winged wonders. Inside the visitor center, you'll find an exhibition gallery, the Florida National Parks association bookshop, and a theater showing an informative 25-minute film on the swamplands. (Leashed pets are allowed but not on the boardwalk deck.) The off-road vehicle permit office is also located at the Oasis Visitor Center. ✉ *52105 Tamiami Trail E, Ochopee* ☎ *239/695–1201* ⊕ *www.nps.gov/bicy/planyourvisit/oasis-visitor-center.htm* ▵ *Free.*

Ochopee Post Office

BUILDING | **FAMILY** | The smallest post office in the United States is a former shed for irrigation pipes on the Tamiami Trail. Blink and you'll risk missing it. You can support this quaint and historical outpost by purchasing a postcard of the little shack and mailing it off to a history buff. You can also mail packages and buy money orders here. ✉ *United States Postal Service, 38000 Tamiami Trail E, Ochopee* ☎ *800/275–8777* ⊘ *Closed Sun.*

 Restaurants

Joanie's Blue Crab Cafe

$$ | **SEAFOOD** | **FAMILY** | West of the nation's tiniest post office, you'll find this red barn of a place dishing out catfish, frogs' legs, gator, grouper, burgers, salads, and (no surprise here) an abundance of soft-shell crabs, crab cakes, and she-crab soup. Entrées are reasonably priced, and peanut butter pie makes for a solid finish. **Known for:** fresh seafood; live music; beer and wine only. ⓢ *Average main: $15* ✉ *39395 Tamiami Trail E, Ochopee* ✛ *Less than a mile west of Ochopee Post Office* ☎ *239/695–2682* ⊕ *www.joaniesblue-crabcafe.com* ⊗ *Hours of operation vary seasonally; call to confirm.*

🏃 Activities

There are three types of trails—walking (including part of the extensive Florida National Scenic Trail), canoeing, and bicycling. All three trail types are easily accessed from the Tamiami Trail near the preserve visitor center, and one board-walk trail departs from the center. Canoe and bike equipment can be rented from outfitters in Everglades City, 24 miles west, and Naples, 40 miles west.

Hikers can tackle the Florida National Scenic Trail, which begins in the preserve and is divided into segments of 6½ to 28 miles each. Two 5-mile trails, Concho Billy and Fire Prairie, can be accessed off Turner River Road, a few miles east. Turner River Road and Birdon Road form a 17-mile gravel loop drive that's excellent for birding. Bear Island has about 32 miles of scenic, flat, looped trails that are ideal for bicycling. Most trails are hard-packed lime rock, but a few miles are gravel. Cyclists share the road with off-road vehicles, most plentiful from mid-November through December.

To see the best variety of wildlife from your vehicle, follow 26-mile Loop Road, south of U.S. 41 and west of Shark Valley, where alligators, raccoons, and soft-shell turtles crawl around beside the gravel road, often swooped upon by swallowtail kites and brown-shouldered hawks. Stop at H. P. Williams Roadside Park, west of the Oasis, and walk along the boardwalk to spy gators, turtles, and garfish in the river waters.

RANGER PROGRAMS

From the Oasis Visitor Center you can get in on the seasonal ranger-led or self-guided activities, such as campfire and wild-life talks, hikes, slough slogs, and canoe excursions. The 8-mile Turner River Canoe Trail begins nearby and crosses through Everglades National Park before ending in Chokoloskee Bay, near Everglades City. Rangers lead four-hour canoe trips and two-hour swamp walks in season; call for days and times. Bring shoes and long pants for swamp walks and be prepared to wade at least knee-deep in water. Ranger program reservations are accepted up to 14 days in advance. The programs are free to the public.

Biscayne National Park

Occupying 172,000 acres along the southern portion of Biscayne Bay, south of Miami and north of the Florida Keys, Biscayne National Park is 95 percent submerged, its terrain ranges from 4 feet above sea level to 60 feet below. Contained within are four distinct zones, or ecosystems: Biscayne Bay, undeveloped upper Florida Keys, coral reefs, and coastal mangrove forest. Mangroves line the shores of the mainland much like they do elsewhere along South Florida's protected waters. Biscayne Bay serves as a lobster sanctuary and a nursery for fish, sponges, crabs, and other sea life. Manatees and sea turtles frequent its warm, shallow waters. The park hosts legions of boaters and landlubbers (novices) gazing in awe across the bay.

GETTING HERE

To reach Biscayne National Park from south of Homestead, take U.S. Highway and turn right on S.W. 344th Street (Palm Drive, the last light before the Florida Turnpike entrance). After about 4 miles, the road curves to the north near the

Did You Know?

The Everglades is home to four types of mangroves: white, black, red, and buttonwood. The red mangrove plant (*Rhizophora mangle*), shown here in Biscayne National Park, has tall, arching roots and a high tolerance for salt.

Homestead Speedway. Turn right on S.W. 328th Street (North Canal Drive) heading east. Continue for 4 miles to the end of the road. The park entrance is on the left just before the entrance to Homestead Bayfront Marina. From the north, take Florida Turnpike south to Exit 6 (Speedway Boulevard). Turn left from exit ramp and continue south to S.W. 328th Street (North Canal Drive). Turn left on 328th Street and continue for 4 miles to the end of the road. The park entrance is on the left just before the entrance to Homestead Bayfront Marina.

PARK ESSENTIALS

Admission Fees There's no fee to enter Biscayne National Park, and you don't pay a fee to access the islands, but there's a $25 overnight camping fee for each stay at Elliott Key or Boca Chita Key. A solid selection of authorized park concessioners charge for day trips to the coral reefs and islands.

Admission Hours The park is open daily, year-round.

CONTACTS Biscayne National Park. ⊠ 9700 S.W. 328th St., Sir Lancelot Jones Way, Homestead ☎ 305/230–1144 ⊕ www.nps.gov/bisc/index.htm.

 Sights

Biscayne is a hub for boating, diving, snorkeling, canoeing, birding, and, to some extent (if you have a private boat), camping. Elliott Key is the best place to hike; two trails tunnel through the island's tropical hardwood hammock.

Biscayne's corals range from soft, flagellant fans, plumes, and whips found chiefly in shallow patch reefs to the hard brain corals, elkhorn, and staghorn forms that can withstand depths and heavier shoreline wave action.

To the east, about 8 miles off the coast, 44 tiny keys stretch 18 nautical miles north to south, and are reached only by boat. No mainland commercial transportation operates to the islands, and only a handful are accessible: Elliott, Boca Chita, Adams, and Sands Keys (between Elliott and Boca Chita). The rest are wildlife refuges or have rocky shores or waters too shallow for boats. December through April, when the mosquito population is less aggressive, is the best time to explore. Bring insect repellent, sunscreen, and water.

Adams Key

ISLAND | FAMILY | A stone's throw from the western tip of Elliott Key and 9 miles southeast of Convoy Point, Adams Key is open for day use. It was once the site of the Cocolobo Club, a retreat known for hosting Presidents Harding, Hoover, Johnson, and Nixon, as well as other famous and infamous characters. Hurricane Andrew blew away what remained of club facilities in 1992. The island has picnic areas with grills, restrooms, dockage, and a short trail running along the shore through a hardwood hammock. Rangers live on-island. Access is by private boat, with no pets or overnight docking allowed. ⊠ Biscayne National Park ⊕ www.nps.gov/bisc/planyourvisit/adamskey.htm.

Boca Chita Key

HISTORIC SITE | FAMILY | Ten miles northeast of Convoy Point and about 12 miles south of the Cape Florida Lighthouse on Key Biscayne, this island once was owned by the late Mark C. Honeywell, former president of Honeywell Company. It's on the National Register of Historic Places for its 10 historic structures and is the most visited island in the park. A half-mile hiking trail curves around the island's south side. Climb the 65-foot-high ornamental lighthouse (by ranger tour only) for a panoramic view of Miami, or check out the cannon from the HMS Fowey. There's no freshwater, access is by private boat only, and no pets are allowed. Only portable toilets are on-site, with no sinks or showers. A $25 fee for overnight docking (6 pm to 6 am) covers a campsite. ⊠ *Biscayne National Park* ⊕ *www.nps.gov/bisc/planyourvisit/boca-chita.htm.*

★ Dante Fascell Visitor Center

ARTS VENUE | FAMILY | Step out onto the wide veranda to soak up views of mangroves and Biscayne Bay at this Convoy Point visitor center. Inside, artistic vignettes and on-request videos, including the 11-minute *Spectrum of Life*, explore the park's four ecosystems, while the Touch Table gives both kids and adults a feel for bones, feathers, and coral. Facilities include the park's art gallery, canoe and tour concession, restrooms with showers, a ranger information area, gift shop with books, and vending machines. Various ranger programs take place daily during busy fall and winter seasons. Rangers give informal tours on Boca Chita Key, but these must be arranged in advance. A short trail and boardwalk lead to a jetty, and there are picnic tables and grills. This is the only area of the park accessible without a boat. You can snorkel from shore, but the water is shallow, with sea grass and a mud bottom. ⊠ *9700 S.W. 328th St., Sir Lancelot Jones Way, Homestead* ☎ *305/230–1144* ⊕ *www.nps.gov/bisc/index.htm* ⊠ *Free.*

Elliott Key

ISLAND | FAMILY | The largest of the islands, 9 miles east of Convoy Point, Elliott Key has a mile-long hiking trail on the bay side at the north end of the campground. Another trail called Spite Highway runs approximately 6 miles down the center of the island. Boaters may dock at any of 36 slips; the fee for staying overnight includes use of a tent area for up to six people in two tents. Facilities include restrooms, picnic tables, fresh drinking water, cold (occasionally lukewarm) showers, grills, and a campground. Leashed pets are allowed in developed areas only, not on trails. A 30-foot-wide sandy shoreline about a mile north of the harbor on the west (bay) side of the key is the only one in the national park, and boaters like to anchor off here to swim. You can fish (check on license requirements) from the maintenance dock south of the harbor or from the shoreline outside of the swimming area. The beach, fun for families, is for day use only; it has picnic areas and a short trail that cuts through the hammock. Mosquitoes are always present. ⊠ *Biscayne National Park* ⊠ *$25 overnight docking fee for campers.*

Biscayne National Park in One Day ◉

Most visitors come to snorkel or dive. Divers should plan to spend the morning on the water and the afternoon exploring the visitor center. The opposite is true for snorkelers, as snorkel trips (and one-tank shallow-dive trips) depart in the afternoon. If you want to hike, turn to the trails at Elliott Key—just be sure to apply insect repellent (and sunscreen, too, no matter what time of year).

🏃 Activities

BIRD-WATCHING

More than 170 species of birds have been identified in and around the park. Expect to see flocks of brown pelicans patrolling the bay—suddenly rising, then plunging beak first to capture prey in the water. White ibis probe exposed mudflats for small fish and crustaceans. Although all the keys are excellent for birding, Jones Lagoon (south of Adams Key, between Old Rhodes Key and Totten Key) is outstanding. It's approachable only by nonmotorized craft.

DIVING AND SNORKELING

Diving is great year-round, but it's best in the summer, when calmer winds and seas result in clearer waters. Living tropical coral reefs are the highlight here; some are the size of a table, others are as large as a football field. Glass-bottom-boat rides, when operating, showcase this underwater wonderland, but you really should get in the water to fully appreciate it.

A diverse population of colorful fish—angelfish, gobies, grunts, parrot fish, pork fish, wrasses, and many more—hang out in the reefs. Shipwrecks from the 18th century are evidence of the area's international maritime heritage, and a Maritime Heritage Trail has been developed to link six of the major shipwrecks and underwater cultural sites, including the Fowey Rocks Lighthouse, built in 1878. Sites, including a 19th-century wooden sailing vessel, have been plotted with GPS coordinates and marked with mooring buoys.

Everglades City

36 miles southeast of Naples and 85 miles west of Miami.

Aside from a chain gas station or two, Everglades City retains its Old Florida authenticity. High-rises (other than an observation tower named for pioneer Ernest Hamilton) are nowhere to be found along this western gateway to Everglades National Park. Everglades City was developed in the late 19th century by Barron Collier, a wealthy advertising entrepreneur, who built it as a company town to house workers for his numerous projects, including construction of the Tamiami Trail. It grew and prospered until the Depression and World War II. Today the ramshackle town attracts adventure seekers heading to the park for the thrill of canoeing, fishing, and birdwatching. Airboat tours, though popular, are

banned within the park because of the environmental damage they cause to the mangroves. The Everglades Seafood Festival, launched in 1970 and held the first full weekend of February, draws huge crowds for delights from the sea, music, and craft displays. At quieter times dining choices center on a handful of rustic eateries focused on seafood. The town is small, fishing-oriented, and unhurried, making it excellent for boating, bicycling, or just strolling around. You can pedal along the waterfront on a 2-mile strand out to Chokoloskee Island.

VISITOR INFORMATION

CONTACTS Everglades Area Chamber of Commerce Welcome Center. ⊠ *32016 Tamiami Trail E* ☎ *239/695–3941.*

 Sights

Collier-Seminole State Park. At Collier-Seminole State Park, opportunities to try biking, birding, hiking, camping, and canoeing in Everglades territory are plentiful. This makes the 7,000-plus-acre park a prime introduction to the elusive mangrove swampland. The campground was recently renovated and sites come complete with electricity, water, a grill, and a picnic table. Leashed pets are allowed. Alternatively, there are "primitive" campsites accessible by foot or canoe. Of historical interest, a Seminole War blockhouse has been recreated to hold the interpretative center, and one of the "walking dredges"—a towering black machine invented to carve the Tamiami Trail out of the muck—stands silent on the grounds. Kayaks and canoes can be launched into the Blackwater River here. Bring your own, or rent a canoe from the park. The Friends of Collier-Seminole State Park offers guided canoe trips from December to March; reservations are recommended. ⊠ *20200 Tamiami Trail E, Naples* ☎ *239/394–3397* ⊕ *www.floridastateparks.org/parks-and-trails/collier-seminole-state-park* ☞ *$5 per vehicle; $4 for*

Native plants along the Turner River Canoe Trail hem in paddlers on both sides, and alligators lurk nearby.

solo driver; $2 for pedestrians or bikers; camping starts at $22 per night.

Fakahatchee Strand Preserve State Park.
The 2,000-foot-long boardwalk at Big Cypress Bend takes visitors fairly quickly through this swamp forest, providing an opportunity to see rare plants, nesting eagles, and Florida's largest swath of coexisting native royal palms—unique to Fakahatchee Strand—with bald cypress under the forest canopy. Fakahatchee Strand is also considered the orchid and bromeliad capital of the continent with 44 native orchids and 14 native bromeliads, many blooming most extravagantly in hotter months. It's particularly famed for ghost orchids (as seen in Susan Orlean's novel *The Orchid Thief*) that are visible on guided hikes. On your quest for ghost orchids, keep an eye out for white-tailed deer, black bears, bobcats, and the Florida panther. For park nature on parade, take the 6-mile stretch of the Janes Scenic Drive (between the visitor's center and East Main) that's still open to traffic; the rest of the drive is open only to hikers and bikers now. ⊠ *137 Coastline Dr., Copeland* ☎ *239/695–4593* ⊕ *www. floridastateparks.org/parks-and-trails/faka-hatchee-strand-preserve-state-park* ⊠ *$3 per vehicle. $2 per person for bicyclists and pedestrians.*

Museum of the Everglades
BUILDING | FAMILY | At this Collier County museum, you can learn about early Native Americans, pioneers, entrepreneurs, and anglers who played pivotal roles in southwest Florida development. Exhibits of artifacts and photographs, as well as a short film chronicle, detail the tremendous feat of building the Tamiami Trail across mosquito-ridden, gator-infested Everglades wetlands. Permanent displays and monthly shows rotate works by local and regional artists in the Pauline Reeves Gallery. The small museum is housed in the 1927 Laundry Building, which was once used for washing linens from the Rod & Gun Club and the Everglades Inn until it closed during World War II. ⊠ *105 W. Broadway*

☎ *239/695–0008* 🌐 *www.evergladesmuseum.org* 🎟 *Free.*

Restaurants

City Seafood

$$ | **SEAFOOD** | **FAMILY** | Gems from the sea are delivered fresh from the owners' boats to this rustic haven. Enjoy breakfast, lunch, or an early dinner inside, or sit outdoors to watch pelicans, gulls, tarpon, manatees, and the occasional gator play off the dock on the Barron River. **Known for:** sustainable stone crab in season; waterfront hangout; wrapping and shipping fresh seafood. [$] *Average main: $15* ✉ *702 Begonia St.* ☎ *239/695–4700* 🌐 *www.cityseafood1.com.*

Havana Café

$$ | **CUBAN** | Cuban and Caribbean specialties are a welcome alternative to the typical seafood houses in the Everglades City area. This cheery eatery—3 miles south of Everglades City on Chokoloskee Island—has a dozen or so tables inside, and more seating on the porch amid plenty of greenery. Jump-start your day with *café con leche* and a pressed-egg sandwich, or try a Havana omelet. **Known for:** good café con leche for breakfast; Caribbean-style seafood dishes; Cuban specialties. [$] *Average main: $18* ✉ *191 Smallwood Dr., Chokoloskee* ☎ *239/695–2214* 🌐 *havanacafeoftheeverglades.com* 🕐 *Closed Apr.–Oct.*

Triad Seafood Market and Café

$$ | **SEAFOOD** | **FAMILY** | Along the Barron River, seafood houses, fishing boats, and crab traps populate one shoreline, while mangroves line the other. Some seafood houses added picnic tables and eventually grew into restaurants like the family-owned Triad Seafood Market & Café. **Known for:** coveted grouper sandwiches; screened porch for dining; all-you-can-eat stone crab feasts. [$] *Average main: $15* ✉ *401 W. School Dr.* ☎ *239/695–0722* 🌐 *www.triadseafoodmarketcafe.com.*

Hotels

★ **The Ivey House and Everglades Adventures**

$ | **B&B/INN** | What was once a boardinghouse built for crews working on the Tamiami Trail in 1928 is now the top spot to stay in town for adventurers on assorted budgets. **Pros:** bed-and-breakfast style; charming; affordable. **Cons:** not on water; some small rooms; no pets. [$] *Rooms from: $179* ✉ *107 Camellia St. E* ☎ *877/567–0679, 239/695–3299 International* 🌐 *iveyhouse.com* 🛏 *18 rooms* 🍴 *Breakfast.*

Activities

Wings Aero Tours

FLYING/SKYDIVING/SOARING | Wings' flightseeing tours of the Ten Thousand Islands National Wildlife Refuge, Fakahatchee Strand State Preserve, Big Cypress National Preserve, Everglades National Park, and Everglades City are available seasonally, November to May. Hop aboard an Alaskan bush plane to see sawgrass prairies, Native American shell mounds, alligators, manatees, dolphins, and wading birds from above. Captains provide passengers with headsets to keep you informed about the sights below. Flight tours can also be booked to see Marco Island and Key West, among other hot spots. ✉ *Everglades Airpark, 650 E.C. Airpark Rd.* ☎ *239/695–3296* 🌐 *www.wingsaerotours.com* 🎟 *From $150 per adult or $50 each for 3–4 adults.*

BOATING AND CANOEING

On the Gulf Coast, be sure to explore the nooks, crannies, and mangrove islands of Chokoloskee Bay and Ten Thousand Islands National Wildlife Refuge, as well as the rivers near Everglades City. The Turner River Canoe Trail, popular and populated even on Christmas as a pleasant day trip with almost guaranteed bird and alligator sightings, passes through mangrove tunnels, dwarf cypress, coastal prairie, and freshwater slough ecosystems of Everglades National Park and Big Cypress National Preserve.

Florida City

2 miles southwest of Homestead on U.S. 1.

Florida's Turnpike ends in Florida City, the southernmost town of Miami-Dade County's mainland. This is the point where thousands of vehicles spill onto U.S. 1 and eventually west to Everglades National Park, east to Biscayne National Park, or south to the Florida Keys. As the last outpost before 18 miles of mangroves and water, this stretch of U.S. 1 is lined with fast-food eateries, service stations, hotels, bars, dive shops, and restaurants. Hotel rates increase significantly during NASCAR races at the nearby Homestead-Miami Speedway. Like Homestead, Florida City is rooted in agriculture, with expanses of farmland west of Krome Avenue and a huge farmers' market that ships produce nationwide.

GETTING HERE AND AROUND

SuperShuttle
This 24-hour service runs air-conditioned vans between Miami International Aiport (MIA) and PortMiami or wherever you'd like to go in the Miami-Dade County area; pickup is outside baggage claim. ✉ *Miami* ☎ *305/871–2000* 🌐 *miamisuper-shuttle.com.*

Sights

Tropical Everglades Visitor Center
INFO CENTER | Managed by the nonprofit Tropical Everglades Visitor Association, this pastel-pink information center with teal signage offers abundant printed material plus tips from volunteer experts on exploring South Florida, especially Homestead, Florida City, and the Florida Keys. ✉ *160 U.S. 1* ☎ *305/245–9180* 🌐 *www.tropicaleverglades.com/index.php.*

Restaurants

Capri Restaurant
$$ | **ITALIAN** | **FAMILY** | This family-owned enterprise has been a magnet for affordable Italian-American classics since 1958. Eat pasta, crunchy-crust pizza, steak, prime rib, and a multitude of locally inspired desserts amid redbrick walls in the classic Capri dining room. **Known for:** affordable specials; family-friendly environment; full bar. [$] *Average main: $20* ✉ *935 N. Krome Ave.* ☎ *305/247–1542* 🌐 *www.dinecapri.com* 🕒 *Dinner only on Sat. Closed Sun.*

Farmers' Market Restaurant
$ | **SEAFOOD** | This quaint eatery is inside the farmers' market on the edge of town, and it's big on serving fresh vegetables and seafood. A family of anglers runs the place, so fish and shellfish are only hours from the ocean. **Known for:** early hours for breakfast; seafood-centric menu; using fresh produce from the market. [$] *Average main: $13* ✉ *300 S. Krome Ave., Ste. 17* ☎ *305/242–0008.*

Rosita's Mexican Restaurant
$ | **MEXICAN** | This delightful hole-in-the-wall Mexican spot boasts authenticity you can't get at the Tex-Mex chains. Breakfast, lunch, and dinner entrées, served all day, range from Mexican eggs, enchiladas, and taco salad to stewed beef and fried pork chops. **Known for:** authentic Mexican cuisine; a brisk takeout business; breakfast served all day. [$] *Average main: $11* ✉ *199 W. Palm Dr., Homestead* ☎ *305/246–3114.*

Hotels

Best Western Gateway to the Keys
$ | **HOTEL** | For easy access to Everglades and Biscayne National Parks, as well as the Keys, you'll be well situated at this relatively modern, two-story motel

close to Florida's Turnpike. **Pros:** conveniently located; free Wi-Fi and breakfast; attractive poolscape. **Cons:** traffic noise; books up fast in high season; no pets. $ *Rooms from: $120* ⊠ *411 S. Krome Ave.* ☎ *305/246–5100* ☞ *114 rooms* ⑩ *Breakfast* ☞ *A credit card with CHIP is required at check-in.*

Fairway Inn

$ | **HOTEL** | With a waterfall pool, this two-story motel has some of the area's lowest rates, and it's close to the Tropical Everglades Visitor Association, so you'll have easy access to tourism brochures and other information. **Pros:** affordable; conveniently located; nice pool. **Cons:** plain, small rooms; no pets allowed; dated decor. $ *Rooms from: $75* ⊠ *100 S.E. First Ave.* ☎ *305/248–4202, 888/340–4734 International* ⊕ *www.fairwayinnfl. com* ☞ *160 rooms* ⑩ *Breakfast.*

Travelodge by Wyndham

$ | **HOTEL** | This affordable hotel is close to Florida's Turnpike, Everglades and Biscayne National Parks, and Homestead-Miami Speedway. **Pros:** conveniently located; nice pool; complimentary breakfast. **Cons:** busy location; some small rooms; no pets allowed. $ *Rooms from: $70* ⊠ *409 S.E. First Ave.* ☎ *305/482–1961, 877/257–2297 International* ⊕ *www.wyndhamhotels.com* ☞ *88 rooms* ⑩ *Breakfast.*

🛍 Shopping

Robert Is Here Fruit Stand and Farm

FOOD/CANDY | **FAMILY** | This historic fruit stand and farm sells more than 100 types of jams, jellies, honeys, and salad dressings along with farm-fresh veggies, juices, fabulous fresh-fruit milk shakes (try the papaya Key lime or guanabana), and dozens of tropical fruits. The list of rare finds includes carambola, lychee, egg fruit, monstera, sapodilla, dragonfruit, genipa, sugar apple, and tamarind. It all started as a tiny roadside stand back in 1960, when a pint-sized Robert

sat at this spot hawking his father's bumper cucumber crop. Now with years of success and his own book (*Robert Is Here: Looking East for a Lifetime*), Robert remains on the scene daily with wife and kids; they ship nationwide and donate regularly to less fortunate families. An assortment of animals out back—goats, iguanas, and emus—along with a splash pool adds to the fun. Picnic tables, benches, and a waterfall with a koi pond provide serenity. Robert Is Here is open 8 am till 7 pm. ⊠ *19200 S.W. 344th St., Homestead* ☎ *305/246–1592* ⊕ *www. robertishere.com.*

Homestead

40 miles southwest of Miami.

Homestead has established itself as a destination for tropical agritourism and ecotourism. At the confluence of Miami and the Keys, as well as Everglades and Biscayne National Parks, the area has the added dimension of shopping centers, residential development, hotel chains, and the Homestead-Miami Speedway. The historic downtown is a preservation-driven Main Street. Krome Avenue is lined with restaurants, an arts complex, antiques shops, and low-budget accommodations. West of Krome Avenue, miles of fields grow fresh fruits and vegetables. Some are harvested commercially, and others beckon with "U-pick" signs. Stands selling farm-fresh produce and nurseries that grow and sell orchids and tropical plants abound. In addition to its agricultural legacy, the town has an eclectic flavor, attributable to its population mix: descendants of pioneer Crackers, Hispanic growers and farm workers, professionals escaping the Miami mania, and retirees.

Sights

Coral Castle Museum

BUILDING | FAMILY | Driven by unrequited love, Latvian immigrant Ed Leedskalnin (1887–1951) fashioned this attraction along Dixie Highway in the early 1900s out of massive slabs of coral rock, a feat he likened to building the pyramids. You can learn how he populated his fantasy world on his property with an imaginary wife and three children, studied astronomy, and created a simple home and elaborate courtyard without formal engineering education and with mostly handmade tools. Highlights of this National Register of Historic Places site, originally named Rock Gate, include a working sundial, a banquet table shaped like Florida, and other quirky coral sculptures. Fun fact: Billy Idol wrote, recorded, and shot the video for his song "Sweet Sixteen" on the grounds of Coral Castle as a tribute to Ed. Candidly, among locals, it's known as a tourist trap. ⊠ *28655 S. Dixie Hwy., Miami* ☎ *305/248–6345* ⊕ *coralcastle. com* 🎫 *$18.*

★ Fruit & Spice Park

GARDEN | FAMILY | You won't find this kind of botanical garden anywhere else in the United States. The tropical climate here helps it produce more than 500 varieties of fruit, nuts, and spices, as well as 75 varieties of bananas and 160 types of mango. The 37-acre park in Homestead's Redland historic agricultural district offers guided tram tours with experts several times a day, so visitors can make the most of their time on the property. You'll learn if what you're picking up off the ground to eat is, in fact, edible, and why some specimens may seem out of place for their designated region. You can sample fresh fruit at the gift shop, which also stocks canned and dried fruits plus cookbooks. The Mango Café is open for lunch daily and serves mango salsa, smoothies, and shakes along with salads, wraps, sandwiches, and its signature Mango Passion Cheesecake. Picnic in the garden at provided tables or on your own blankets. ⊠ *24801 S.W. 187th Ave.* ☎ *305/247–5727* ⊕ *www.fruitandspice-park.com* 🎫 *$8.*

Schnebly Redland's Winery and Brewery

STORE/MALL | Homestead's fruit bounty is transformed into wine at this flourishing enterprise that started producing wines with lychee, mango, guava, and others as a way to eliminate waste from family groves each year. Over the course of a few decades, the Schnebly's tropical winery expanded to include a tasting room, a full-service restaurant, a lush plaza picnic area landscaped in coral rock, tropical plants, and waterfalls—plus a chickee hut inspired by the Seminole Indians. It's also home to popular beer brand Miami Brewing Company. ⊠ *30205 S.W. 217th Ave.* ☎ *305/242–1224* ⊕ *www.schnebly-winery.com* 🎫 *Weekend tours $8 per person* ⊗ *Redlander Restaurant closed Mon.–Wed.*

Restaurants

Royal Palm Grill and Deli

$ | AMERICAN | FAMILY | You may have a déjà vu moment if you drive down Krome Avenue, where two Royal Palm Grills are just a hop-skip away from each other. This popular "breakfast all day, every day" enterprise has two locations, only a few blocks apart, to accommodate a steady stream of customers coming into the retro haven for everything from omelets and pancakes to biscuits and gravy, plus salads, steaks, and seafood. (Royal Palm's second location is at 436 N. **Known for:** opens early; breakfast all day; retro decor and vibe. 🅢 *Average main: $10* ⊠ *806 N. Krome Ave.* ☎ *305/246–5701* ⊕ *royalpalmhomestead.com.*

Shiver's BBQ

$$ | BARBECUE | FAMILY | Piggin' out since the 1950s, Shiver's BBQ is celebrated near and far for its slowly smoked pork, beef, and chicken in assorted forms of barbecue from baby back ribs to briskets.

Are baby alligators more to your liking than their parents? You can pet one at Gator Park.

Be forewarned as you settle in at the communal tables, this spot is no place to cut calories. **Known for:** hickory-smoked barbecue; baby back ribs; takeout service. [$] *Average main: $19* ✉ *28001 S. Dixie Hwy.* ☎ *305/248–2272* 🌐 *shiversbq.com.*

Suvi Thai & Sushi Homestead

$$ | **ASIAN FUSION** | **FAMILY** | For fresh and light Asian fare near the Everglades, you can find Thai and Japanese favorites—from pad Thai and curries to traditional raw and cooked sushi rolls—at Suvi Thai & Sushi. If you want to go big here, try the sautéed Royal Thai Lobster or keep it simple with the Homestead Spicy Roll. **Known for:** lunch specials; family-friendly atmosphere; Asian favorites. [$] *Average main: $20* ✉ *250 N. Homestead Blvd.* ☎ *305/247–3500* 🌐 *suvimiami.com.*

White Lion Cafe

$$ | **AMERICAN** | Although the antique shop within White Lion Cafe's cottage is now history, this 45-seat comfort-food haven, with a full bar, remains embellished with reminders of the past. From a 1950s-era wooden wall phone to a metal icebox and a Coca-Cola machine, you'll also find a mounted jackalope watching over a wide list of specials (Homestead crab cakes, burgers, fried chicken, and meatloaf). **Known for:** comfort food; lively bar scene; kitschy decor. [$] *Average main: $18* ✉ *146 N.W. 7th St.* ☎ *305/248–1076* 🌐 *www.whitelioncafe.com* ⏲ *Closed Sun. and Mon.*

Hotels

The Hotel Redland

$ | **HOTEL** | Of downtown Homestead's smattering of mom-and-pop lodges, this historic inn is by far the most desirable. **Pros:** historic charm; conveniently located; excellent dining. **Cons:** traffic noise; small rooms; potentially haunted; dated website. [$] *Rooms from: $150* ✉ *5 S. Flagler Ave.* ☎ *305/246–1904* 🌐 *www.cityhallbistromartinibar.com* 🛏 *13 rooms* 🍴 *No meals.*

🏃 Activities

Homestead Bayfront Park

WATER SPORTS | FAMILY | Boaters, anglers, and beachgoers give unending praise to this recreational area adjacent to Biscayne National Park and the Florida Keys Marine Sanctuary. There's a natural atoll pool and beach, all within close proximity to coral reefs. The Herbert Hoover Marina can accommodate vessels up to 50 feet; it has a ramp, dock, bait-and-tackle shop, fuel station, ice station, and dry storage. The park also has a tropical restaurant called La Playa Grill, a playground, and a picnic pavilion with grills, showers, and restrooms. ✉ *Homestead Bayfront Park, 9698 S.W. 328th St.* ☎ *305/230–3033* ⊕ *www.miamidade.gov/parks/homestead-bayfront.asp* ⊠ *$7 per car on weekends; $5 per car on weekdays.*

Homestead-Miami Speedway

AUTO RACING | FAMILY | Buzzing more than 300 days a year, the 600-acre speedway hosts racing, manufacturer testing, car-club events, driving schools, and ride-along programs. The motorsports facility has 65,000 grandstand seats, club seating, and two tracks—a 2.21-mile road course and a 1.5-mile oval. A packed schedule includes NASCAR events like Ford Championship Weekend. Parking includes space for 30,000 vehicles. ✉ *One Ralph Sanchez Speedway Blvd.* ☎ *305/230–5000, 866/409–7223 Ticket office* ⊕ *www.homesteadmiamispeedway.com.*

Tamiami Trail

U.S. 41, between Naples and Miami.

There's a long stretch of U.S. 41 (originally known as the Tamiami Trail) that traverses the Everglades, Big Cypress National Preserve, and Fakahatchee Strand Preserve State Park, while connecting Florida's west coast to Miami. The road was conceived in 1915 to link Miami to Fort Myers and Tampa, but when it finally became a reality in 1928, it cut through the Everglades and altered the natural flow of water as well as the lives of the Miccosukee Indians who were trying mightily to make a living fishing, hunting, farming, and frogging here. The landscape is surprisingly varied, changing from hardwood hammocks to pinelands, then abruptly to tall cypress trees dripping with Spanish moss and back to sawgrass marsh. Slow down to take in the scenery and you'll likely be rewarded with glimpses of alligators sunning themselves along the banks of roadside canals and hundreds of water-birds, especially in winter. The man-made portion of the landscape includes Native American villages, chickee huts, and airboats parked at roadside enterprises. Between Miami and Naples the road goes by several names, including Tamiami Trail, U.S. 41, Ninth Street in Naples, and, at the Miami end, Southwest 8th Street/Calle Ocho. ■**TIP→ Businesses along the trail estimate distance based on how far they are from Naples or the outskirts of Miami (from Krome Avenue or Florida's Turnpike).**

Sights

Everglades Safari Park

AMUSEMENT PARK/WATER PARK | FAMILY | A perennial favorite with tour operators, this family-run park has been in business since 1968 on a wild plot of land just 15 miles from overdeveloped West Miami. It has an arena for alligator wrestling shows with seating for up to 300 people. Before and after the show, get a closer look at both American alligators and American crocodiles on Gator Island, follow a jungle trail, walk through a small wildlife museum, or board an airboat for a 40-minute ride on the River of Grass (fee is included in park admission). The park also has a restaurant, a gift shop, and an observation platform overlooking the the lush vegetation in the surrounding

Everglades. Smaller, private airboats can be chartered for tours lasting 40 minutes to two hours. Check online for discounts and count on free parking. ✉ *26700 S.W. 8th St., Miami* ☎ *305/226–6923* ⊕ *www. evergladessafaripark.com* 🍴 *$28.*

Gator Park

AMUSEMENT PARK/WATER PARK | FAMILY | At Gator Park, you can really get to know alligators, and even touch a baby gator during the park's wildlife show. You can also meet turtles, macaws, and peacocks. Native snakes also reside nearby, including the Blackpine, Brooks Kingsnake, Florida Kingsnake, and Red Ratsnake. The park, open rain or shine, also provides educational airboat tours through the River of Grass, as well as a gift shop and restaurant serving swamp fare like burgers, gator tail, and sausage. Tickets include admission, a group airboat ride, and an alligator wrestling show. Private tours are available. ✉ *24050 S.W. Eighth St., Miami* ☎ *305/559–2255, 800/559–2205 International* ⊕ *gatorpark. com* 🍴 *$19.99 online ($24.99 at the gate).*

Miccosukee Indian Village Museum

ARTS VENUE | FAMILY | Showcasing the skills and lifestyle of the Miccosukee Tribe of Florida, this cultural center offers craft demonstrations and insight into interaction with alligators. Narrated 30-minute airboat rides take you into the wilderness where natives hid after the Seminole Wars and Indian Removal Act of the mid-1800s. In modern times, many of the Miccosukee have relocated to this village on Tamiami Trail, but most still maintain their hammock farming and hunting camps. The museum shows two films on tribal culture and displays chickee hut structures and artifacts. Guided tours run throughout the day, and a gift shop stocks dolls, apparel, silver jewelry, beadwork, and other handicrafts. ✉ *Mile Marker 36, U.S. 41, Miami* ☎ *305/552–8365* ⊕ *www.miccosukee. com/indian-village-c/museum* 🍴 *Village entry $15; airboat rides $20.*

Crocs or Gators?

You can tell you're looking at a crocodile, not an alligator, if you can see its lower teeth sticking up over the upper lip when those powerful jaws are shut. Gators are much darker in color—a grayish black—compared with the lighter tan shades of crocodiles. Alligator snouts form a U-shape and are also much wider than their long, thin crocodilian counterparts (V-shape). South Florida is the only place in the world where the two coexist in the wild.

Restaurants

The Pit Bar-B-Q

$$ | BARBECUE | FAMILY | This old-fashioned roadside eatery on Tamiami Trail near Krome Avenue was opened in 1965 by the late Tommy Little, who wanted to provide easy access to cold drinks and rib-sticking fare for folks heading to and from the Everglades. Now spiffed up, the backwoods heritage vision remains a popular, affordable family option for lunch and dinner. **Known for:** huge pork sandwiches; Latin specialties; family-friendly atmosphere. 💲 *Average main: $15* ✉ *16400 S.W. 8th St., Miami* ☎ *305/226–2272* ⊕ *thepitbarbq.com/site.*

🛏 Hotels

Miccosukee Resort & Gaming

$ | RESORT | Like an oasis on the horizon of endless sawgrass, this nine-story resort on the edge of the Everglades can't help but attract attention—even if you're not a fan of 24-hour gaming action. **Pros:** casino; relatively modern; golf course. **Cons:** smoke-filled lobby; limited parking; stark contrast to its surroundings. 💲 *Rooms* *from: $169* ⊠ *500 S.W. 177th Ave., Miami* ☎ *305/222–4600, 877/242–6464 International* ⊕ *www.miccosukee.com/resort* ⤴ *302 rooms* ❍❘ *No meals.*

Activities

BOAT TOURS

Many Everglades-area tours operate only in season, roughly November through April.

Coopertown Airboat Tours

TOUR—SPORTS | FAMILY | Coopertown is the oldest airboat operator in the Everglades. The nearly 75-year-old business, which is attached to a restaurant with the same name, offers 35- to 40-minute tours that take you 9 miles into the fragile ecosystem to see hammocks and alligator holes, red-shouldered hawks, and turtles. You can also book longer private charters with the company. ⊠ *22700 S.W. 8th St., Miami* ☎ *305/226–6048* ⊕ *coopertownairboats.com* ⤴ *From $23.*

Everglades Alligator Farm

TOUR—SPORTS | FAMILY | More than 2,000 alligators live within the Everglades Alligator Farm. It's the oldest of its kind in South Florida and offers animal experiences, encounters, and airboat rides. Some are by reservation only, so check the website for details. It's a working farm—home of the late 14-foot "Grandpa" gator (now mounted for display)—and feedings for 500 hungry gators are at noon and 3 pm. ⊠ *40351 S.W. 192nd Ave., Homestead* ☎ *305/247–2628* ⊕ *www.everglades.com* ⤴ *From $19.50 per person.*

Wooten's Everglades Airboat Tours

BOATING | FAMILY | This classic Florida roadside attraction is known as a one-stop-shop for Everglades adventures. They offer airboat tours through the Everglades, swamp buggy rides through the Big Cypress Swamp, educational sessions in the animal sanctuary, and live alligator shows. Some packages include an airboat ride, swamp buggy adventure, and sanctuary access. Rates change frequently, so check the website for individual prices and combo packages. ⊠ *32330 Tamiami Trail E, Ochopee* ☎ *239/695–2781, 800/282–2781 International* ⊕ *www.wootenseverglades.com* ⤴ *Tours from $32.50; combo packages from $59.99; alligator show from $9.*

Chapter 5

THE FLORIDA KEYS

Updated by
Jill Martin

👁 Sights	🍴 Restaurants	🛏 Hotels	🛍 Shopping	🍸 Nightlife
★★★★☆	★★★☆☆	★★★☆☆	★★★☆☆	★★★☆☆

WELCOME TO THE FLORIDA KEYS

TOP REASONS TO GO

★ **John Pennekamp Coral Reef State Park:** A perfect introduction to the Florida Keys, this nature reserve offers snorkeling, diving, camping, and kayaking. An underwater highlight is the massive Christ of the Deep statue.

★ **Viewing the Underwater World:** Whether you scuba dive, snorkel, or ride a glass-bottom boat, don't miss gazing at the coral reef and its colorful denizens.

★ **Sunset at Mallory Square:** Sure, it's touristy, but just once while you're here, you've got to witness the circuslike atmosphere of this nightly celebration.

★ **Duval crawl:** Shop, eat, drink, repeat. Key West's Duval Street and the nearby streets make a good day's worth of window-shopping and people-watching.

★ **Getting on the water:** From angling for trophy-size fish to zipping out to the Dry Tortugas, a boat trip is in your future. It's really the whole point of the Keys.

1 Key Largo. The first Key reachable by car, it's a prime spot for diving and snorkeling.

2 Islamorada. Sportfishing in deep offshore waters and backcountry reigns.

3 Duck Key. Come for a beautiful marina resort and boating.

4 Grassy Key. Known for natural wonders like Curry Hammock State Park.

5 Marathon. Most activity in the Middle Keys revolves around this bustling town.

6 Bahia Honda Key. One of the top beaches in Florida, with fine sand and clear water.

7 Big Pine Key. Laid-back community that's home to an impressive wildlife refuge.

8 Little Torch Key. A good jumping off point for divers headed to Looe Key Reef.

9 Key West. The ultimate in Keys craziness, this party town is for the open-minded.

10 Dry Tortugas National Park. Take a day trip to snorkel at these islands off Key West.

0   10 mi

0   10 km

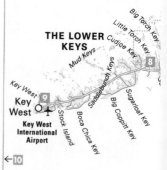

THE LOWER KEYS

Big Torch Key

Little Torch Key

Cudjoe Key

Mud Keys

Saddlebunch Keys

8

Key West

Key West

Key West International Airport

Stock Island

Boca Chica Key

Sugarloaf Key

Big Coppitt Key

9

← 10

SEAFOOD IN THE FLORIDA KEYS

Fish. It's what's for dinner in the Florida Keys. The Keys' runway between the Gulf of Mexico or Florida Bay and Atlantic warm waters means fish of many fin. Restaurants take full advantage by serving it fresh, whether you caught it or a local fisherman did.

Menus at colorful waterfront shacks such as **Snapper's** (⌀ *139 Seaside Ave., Key Largo* ☎ *305/852–5956*) in Key Largo and **Half Shell Raw Bar** (⌀ *231 Margaret St., Key West* ☎ *305/294–7496*) range from basic raw, broiled, grilled, or blackened fish to some Bahamian and New Orleans–style interpretations. Other seafood houses dress up their fish in creative styles, such as **Pierre's** (⌀ *MM 81.5 BS, Islamorada* ☎ *305/664–3225* ⊕ *www. pierres-restaurant.com*) hogfish meunière, or yellow-tail snapper with pear-ricotta pasta at **Café Marquesa** (⌀ *600 Fleming St., Key West* ☎ *305/292–1244* ⊕ *www. marquesa.com*). Try a Keys-style breakfast of "grits and grunts"—fried fish and grits—at the **Stuffed Pig** (⌀ *3520 Overseas Hwy., Marathon* ☎ *305/743–4059*).

BUILT-IN FISH

You know it's fresh when you see a fish market as soon as you open the restaurant door. It happens frequently in the Keys. You can even peruse the seafood showcases and pick the fish you want.

Many of the Keys' best restaurants are found in marina complexes, where the fishermen bring their catches straight from the sea. Try those in **Stock Island** (north of Key West) and at **Keys Fisheries Market & Marina** (⌀ *MM 49 BS, end of 35th St., Marathon* ☎ *305/743–4353, 866/743–4353*).

CONCH

One of the tastiest legacies of the Keys' Bahamian heritage (and most mispronounced), conch (pronounced *konk*) shows up on nearly every menu in some shape or form. It's so prevalent in local diets that natives refer to themselves as Conchs. Conch fritters are the most popular culinary manifestations, followed by cracked (pounded, breaded, and fried) conch, and conch salad, a ceviche-style refresher. Since the harvesting of queen conch is now illegal, most of the islands' conch comes from the Bahamas.

FLORIDA LOBSTER

Where are the claws? Stop looking for them: Florida spiny lobsters don't have them. The sweet tail meat, however, makes up for the loss. Divers harvest these crustaceans from late July through March. Check with local dive shops on restrictions, and then get ready for a fresh feast. Restaurants serve them broiled with drawn butter or in dishes such as lobster Benedict, lobster spring rolls, lobster Reuben, and lobster tacos.

GROUPER

Once central to Florida's trademark seafood dish—fried grouper sandwich—its populations have been overfished in recent years, meaning that the state has exerted more control over bag

regulations and occasionally closes grouper fishing on a temporary basis during the winter season. Some restaurants have gone antigrouper to try to bring back the abundance, but most grab it when they can. Black grouper is the most highly prized variety.

STONE CRAB

In season October 15 through May 15, it gets its name from its rock-hard shell. Fishermen take only one claw, which can regenerate in a sustainable manner. Connoisseurs prefer them chilled with tangy mustard sauce. Some restaurants give you a choice of hot claws and drawn butter, but this means the meat will be cooked twice, because it's usually boiled or steamed as soon as it's taken from its crab trap.

YELLOWTAIL SNAPPER

The preferred species of snappers, it's more plentiful in the Keys than in any other Florida waters. As pretty as it is tasty, its mild, sweet, and delicate meat lends itself to any number of preparations, and it's available pretty much year-round. Chefs top it with everything from key lime beurre blanc to mango chutney. **Ballyhoo's** in Key Largo (⊠ *MM 97.8, in median* ☎ *305/852–0822*) serves it 10 different ways.

Your Keys experience begins on your 18-mile drive south on "The Stretch," a portion of U.S. 1 with a specially colored blue median that takes you from Florida City to Key Largo. The real magic begins at mile marker 113, where the Florida Keys Scenic Highway begins. As the only All-American Road in Florida, it is a destination unto itself, one that crosses 42 bridges over water, including the Seven Mile Bridge—with its stunning vistas—and ends in Key West. Look for crocodiles, alligators, and bald eagles along the way.

Key West has a Mardi Gras mood with Fantasy Festival, a Hemingway look-alike contest, and the occasional threat to secede from the Union. It's an island whose eclectic natives, known as "Conchs," mingle well with visitors (of the spring-break variety as well as those seeking to escape reality for a while) on this scenic, sometimes raucous 4x2-mile island paradise.

Although life elsewhere in the island chain isn't near as offbeat, it is as diverse. Overflowing bursts of bougainvillea, shimmering waters, and mangrove-lined islands can be admired throughout. The one thing most visitors don't admire much in the Keys are their beaches. They're not many, and they're not what you'd expect. The reason? The coral reef. It breaks up the waves and prevents

sand from being dumped on the shores. That's why the beaches are mostly rough sand, as it's crushed coral. Think of it as a trade-off: the Keys have the only living coral reef in the United States, but that reef prevents miles of shimmering sands from ever arriving.

In season, a river of traffic gushes southwest on this highway. But that doesn't mean you can't enjoy the ride as you cruise along the islands. Gaze over the silvery blue-and-green Atlantic and its living coral reef, with Florida Bay, the Gulf of Mexico, and the backcountry on your right (the Keys extend southwest from the mainland). At a few points the ocean and gulf are as much as 10 miles apart; in most places, however, they're from 1 to 4 miles apart, and on the narrowest landfill islands they're separated only by the road.

While the views can be mesmerizing, to appreciate the Keys you need to get off the highway, especially in more developed regions like Key Largo, Islamorada, and Marathon. Once you do, rent a boat, anchor, and then fish, swim, or marvel at the sun, sea, and sky. Or visit one of the many sandbars, which are popular places to float the day away. Ocean side, dive or snorkel spectacular coral reefs or pursue grouper, blue marlin, mahimahi, and other deepwater game fish. Along Florida Bay's coastline, kayak to secluded islands through mangrove forests, or seek out the bonefish, snapper, snook, and tarpon that lurk in the shallow grass flats and mangrove roots of the backcountry.

MAJOR REGIONS
As the doorstep to the islands' coral reefs and blithe spirit, **the Upper Keys** introduce all that's sporting and sea-oriented about the Keys. They stretch from Key Largo, 56 miles south of Miami International Airport, to the Long Key Channel (MM 105–65). Centered on the town of Marathon, **the Middle Keys** hold most of the chain's historic and natural attractions outside of Key West. They go from Conch (pronounced *konk*) Key through Marathon to the south side of the Seven Mile Bridge, including Pigeon Key (MM 65–40). The Middle Keys make a fitting transition from the Upper Keys to the Lower Keys not only geographically but also mentally. Crossing Seven Mile Bridge prepares you for the slow pace and don't-give-a-damn attitude you'll find a little farther down the highway. Pressure drops another notch when you reach **the Lower Keys**, the most laid-back part of the region, where key-deer viewing and fishing reign supreme. The Lower Keys go from Little Duck Key west through Big Coppitt Key (MM 40–9). Finally, **Key West** lies 150 miles from Miami and encompasses MM 9–0.

Planning

When to Go

In high season, from mid-December through mid-April, traffic is inevitably heavy. From November to mid-December, crowds are thinner, the weather is superlative, and hotels and shops drastically reduce their prices. Summer is a second high season, especially among families, Europeans, bargain-seekers, and lobster divers.

Florida is rightly called the Sunshine State, but it could also be dubbed the "Humidity State." From June through September, 90% humidity levels are not uncommon. Thankfully, the weather in the Keys is more moderate than in mainland Florida. Temperatures can be 10°F cooler during the summer and up to 10°F warmer during the winter. The Keys also get substantially less rain than mainland Florida, mostly in quick downpours on summer afternoons. In hurricane season, June through November, the Keys get their fair share of warnings; pay heed, and evacuate earlier rather than later, when flights and automobile traffic get backed up.

Getting Here and Around

AIR TRAVEL
About 760,000 passengers use Key West International Airport (EYW) each year; its most recent renovation includes a beach where travelers can catch their last blast of rays after clearing security. Because direct flights to Key West are few, many prefer flying into Miami International Airport (MIA) or Fort Lauderdale–Hollywood International Airport (FLL) and driving the 110-mile Overseas Highway (aka U.S. 1).

BOAT AND FERRY TRAVEL

Key West Express operates air-conditioned ferries between the Key West Terminal (Caroline and Grinnell streets) and Marco Island and Fort Myers Beach. The trip takes at least four hours each way and costs $95 one way, from $125 round-trip (a $3 convenience fee is added to all online bookings). Ferries depart from Fort Myers Beach at 8:30 am and from Key West at 6 pm. The Marco Island ferry departs at 8:30 am (the return trip leaves Key West at 5 pm). A photo ID is required for each passenger. Advance reservations are recommended.

Boaters can travel to and through the Keys either along the Intracoastal Waterway (5-foot draft limitation) through Card, Barnes, and Blackwater sounds and into Florida Bay, or along the deeper Atlantic Ocean route through Hawk Channel, a buoyed passage. Refer to NOAA Nautical Charts Nos. 11451, 11445, and 11441. The Keys are full of marinas that welcome transient visitors, but they don't have enough slips for everyone. Make reservations in advance, and ask about channel and dockage depth—many marinas are quite shallow.

CONTACT Key West Express. ✉ *100 Grinnell St., Key West* ☎ *239/463–5733* ⊕ *www.keywestexpress.net.*

BUS TRAVEL

Keys Transportation provides private airport transfers to any destination in the Keys from either MIA or FLL. Prices start at $49 per person for transportation to Key Largo and get more expensive as you move south. Call or email for a price quote.

Greyhound Lines runs a special Keys shuttle twice a day (times depend on the day of the week) from Miami International Airport (departing from Concourse E, lower level) and stops throughout the Keys. Fares run from around $25 for Key Largo (✉ *MM 99.6*) or Islamorada (✉ *Burger King, MM 82*) to around $45

for Key West (✉ *3535 S. Roosevelt, Key West International Airport*).

Keys Shuttle runs scheduled service six times a day in 15-passenger vans between Miami and Fort Lauderdale airports and Key West with stops throughout the Keys for $60 to $90 per person sharing rides.

SuperShuttle charges $191 for up to two passengers for trips to the Upper Keys; to go farther, you must book an entire 11-person van, which costs $402. For a trip to the airport, place your request 24 hours in advance.

CONTACTS Greyhound. ☎ *800/231–2222* ⊕ *www.greyhound.com.* **Keys Shuttle.** ✉ *1333 Overseas Hwy., Marathon* ☎ *888/765–9997* ⊕ *www.keysshuttle. com* **Keys Transportation.** ☎ *305/395–0299* ⊕ *www.keystransportation.com.* **SuperShuttle.** ☎ *800/258–3826* ⊕ *www. supershuttle.com.*

CAR TRAVEL

By car, from Miami International Airport, follow signs to Coral Gables and Key West, which puts you on LeJeune Road, then Route 836 west. Take the Homestead Extension of Florida's Turnpike south (toll road), which ends at Florida City and connects to the Overseas Highway (U.S. 1). Tolls from the airport run approximately $3. Payment is collected via Sun- Pass, a prepaid toll program, or with Toll-By-Plate, a system that photographs each vehicle's license plate and mails a monthly bill for tolls, plus a $2.50 administrative fee, to the vehicle's registered owner.

Vacationers traveling in their own cars can obtain a mini-SunPass sticker via mail before their trip for $4.99 and receive the cost back in toll credits and discounts. The pass also is available at many major Florida retailers and turnpike service plazas. It works on all Florida toll roads and many bridges. For details on purchasing a mini-Sun-Pass, call or visit the website.

For visitors renting cars in Florida, most major rental companies have programs allowing customers to use the Toll-By-Plate system. Tolls, plus varying service fees, are automatically charged to the credit card used to rent the vehicle (along with a hefty service charge in most cases). For details, including pricing options at participating rental-car agencies, check the program website. Under no circumstances should motorists attempt to stop in high-speed electronic tolling lanes. Travelers can contact Florida's Turnpike Enterprise for more information about the all-electronic tolling on Florida's Turnpike.

The alternative from Florida City is Card Sound Road (Route 905A), which has a (cash-only) bridge toll of $1. SunPass isn't accepted. Continue to the only stop sign and turn right on Route 905, which rejoins the Overseas Highway 31 miles south of Florida City.

Except in Key West, a car is essential for visiting the Keys.

CONTACTS Florida's Turnpike Enterprise. ☎ 800/749–7453 ⊕ www.floridasturnpike. com. **SunPass.** ☎ 888/865–5352 ⊕ www. sunpass.com.

The Mile Marker System

Getting lost in the Keys is almost impossible once you understand the unique address system. Many addresses are simply given as a mile marker (MM) number. The markers are small, green, rectangular signs along the side of the Overseas Highway (U.S. 1). They begin with MM 126, 1 mile south of Florida City, and end with MM 0, in Key West. Keys residents use the abbreviation BS for the bay side of Overseas Highway and OS for the ocean side. From Marathon to Key West, residents may refer to the bay side as the gulf side.

Hotels

Throughout the Keys, the types of accommodations are remarkably varied, from 1950s-style motels to cozy inns to luxurious resorts. Most are on or near the ocean, so water sports are popular. Key West's lodging portfolio includes historic cottages, restored Conch houses, and large resorts. Some larger properties throughout the Keys charge a mandatory daily resort fee, which can cover equipment rental, fitness-center use, and other services. You can expect another 12.5% (or more) in state and county taxes. Some guesthouses and inns don't welcome children, and many don't permit smoking.

Restaurants

Seafood rules in the Keys, which is full of chef-owned restaurants with not-too-fancy food. Many restaurants serve cuisine that reflects the proximity of the Bahamas and Caribbean (you'll see the term "Floribbean" on many menus). Tropical fruits figure prominently—especially on the beverage side of the menu. Florida spiny lobster should be local and fresh from August to March, and stone crabs from mid-October to mid-May. And don't dare leave the islands without sampling conch, be it in a fritter or in ceviche. Keep an eye out for authentic key lime pie—yellow custard in a graham-cracker crust. If it's green, just say "no." Note: Particularly in Key West and particularly during spring break, the more affordable and casual restaurants can get loud and downright rowdy, with young visitors often more interested in drinking than eating. Live music contributes to the decibel levels. If you're more of the quiet, intimate-dining type, avoid such overly exuberant scenes by eating early or choosing a restaurant where the bar isn't the main focus.

Hotel and restaurant reviews have been shortened. For full information, visit Fodors.com.

What It Costs

	$	$$	$$$	$$$$
RESTAURANTS				
	under $15	$15–$20	$21–$30	over $30
HOTELS				
	under $200	$200–$300	$301–$400	over $400

Visitor Information

There are several separate tourism offices in the Florida Keys, and you can use Visit Florida's website (⊕ *www.visit-florida.com*) for general information and referrals to local agencies. *See individual chapters for local visitor information centers.*

In addition to traditional tourist information, many divers will be interested in the Florida Keys National Marine Sanctuary, which has its headquarters in Key West and has another office in Key Largo.

CONTACT Florida Keys National Marine Sanctuary. ⊠ *MM 95.23 BS* ☎ *305/809-4700* ⊕ *floridakeys.noaa.gov.*

Key Largo

56 miles south of Miami International Airport.

The first of the Upper Keys reachable by car, 30-mile-long Key Largo is the largest island in the chain. Key Largo—named Cayo Largo ("Long Key") by the Spanish—makes a great introduction to the region. This is the gateway to the Keys, and an evening of fresh seafood and views of the sunset on the water will get you in the right state of mind.

The history of Largo reads much like that of the rest of the Keys: a succession of native people, pirates, wreckers, and developers. The first settlement on Key Largo was named Planter, back in the days of pineapple, and later, key lime plantations. For a time it was a convenient shipping port, but when the railroad arrived Planter died on the vine. Today three communities—North Key Largo and Key Largo as well as the separately incorporated city of Tavernier—make up the whole of Key Largo.

What's there to do on Key Largo besides gaze at the sunset? Not much if you're not into diving or snorkeling. Nobody comes to Key Largo without visiting John Pennekamp Coral Reef State Park, one of the jewels of the state park system. Water-sports enthusiasts head to the adjacent Key Largo National Marine Sanctuary, which encompasses about 190 square miles of coral reefs, sea-grass beds, and mangrove estuaries. If you've never tried diving, Key Largo is the perfect place to learn. Dozens of companies will be more than happy to show you the ropes.

Fishing is the other big draw, and world records are broken regularly in the waters around the Upper Keys. There are plenty of charter companies to help you find the big ones and teach you how to hook the elusive bonefish, sometimes known as the ghost fish.

On land, Key Largo provides all the conveniences of a major resort town, including restaurants that will cook your catch or prepare their own creations with inimitable style. You'll notice that some unusual specialties pop up on the menu, such as cracked conch, spiny lobster, and stone crab. Don't pass up a chance to try the local delicacies, especially the key lime pie.

Most businesses are lined up along U.S. 1, the four-lane highway that runs down the middle of the island. Cars whiz past at all hours—something to remember when you're booking a room. Most lodgings are on the highway, so you'll want to be as far back as possible. At MM 95, look for the mural painted in 2011 to commemorate the 100th anniversary of the railroad to the Keys.

GETTING HERE AND AROUND
Key Largo is 56 miles south of Miami International Airport, with its mile markers ranging from 106 to 91. The island runs northeast–southwest, with the Overseas Highway, divided by a median most of the way, running down the center. If the highway is your only glimpse of the island, you're likely to feel barraged by its tacky commercial side. Make a point of driving Route 905 in North Key Largo and down side streets to get a better feel for it.

VISITOR INFORMATION
In addition to traditional tourist information, many divers will be interested in the Florida Keys National Marine Sanctuary, which has an office in Key Largo.

CONTACTS Florida Keys National Marine Sanctuary. ⊠ *MM 95.23 BS* ☎ *305/809–4700* ⊕ *floridakeys.noaa.gov.* **Key Largo Chamber of Commerce.** ⊠ *MM 106 BS, 10600 Overseas Hwy.* ☎ *305/451–4747, 800/822–1088* ⊕ *www.keylargochamber. org.*

 ## Sights

Dagny Johnson Key Largo Hammock Botanical State Park
LOCAL INTEREST | FAMILY | American crocodiles, mangrove cuckoos, white-crowned pigeons, Schaus swallowtail butterflies, mahogany mistletoe, wild cotton, and 100 other rare critters and plants inhabit these 2,400 acres, sandwiched between Crocodile Lake National Wildlife Refuge and the waters of Pennekamp Coral Reef State Park. The park is also a user-friendly place to explore the largest remaining stand of the vast West Indian tropical hardwood hammock and mangrove wetland that once covered most of the Keys. Interpretive signs describe many of the tropical tree species along a wide, 1-mile, paved road (2 miles round-trip) that invites walking and biking. A new, unpaved, extended loop trail can add 1–2 miles to your walk. There are also more than 6 additional miles of nature trails, most of which are accessible to both bikes and wheelchairs with a permit, easily obtainable from John Pennekamp State Park. Pets are welcome if on a leash no longer than 6 feet. You'll also find restrooms, information kiosks, and picnic tables. ■ TIP→ **Rangers recommend not visiting when it's raining as the trees can drip poisonous sap.** ⊠ *Rte. 905 OS, ½ mile north of Overseas Hwy., North Key Largo* ☎ *305/451–1202* ⊕ *www. floridastateparks.org/parks-and-trails/ dagny-johnson-key-largo-hammock-bo-tanical-state-park* ☞ *$2.50 (exact change needed for the honor box).*

Dolphins Plus Bayside
ZOO | FAMILY | This educational program begins with a get-acquainted session beneath a tiki hut. After that, you slip into the water for some frolicking with your new dolphin pals. Options range from a shallow-water swim to a hands-on structured swim with a dolphin. You can also spend the day shadowing a trainer—it's $350 for a half day or a hefty $630 for a full day. ⊠ *MM 101.9 BS, 101900 Overseas Hwy.* ☎ *305/451–4060, 866/860–7946* ⊕ *www.dolphinsplus. com* ☞ *$10 admission only; interactive programs from $150.*

Dolphins Plus Marine Mammal Responder
COLLEGE | FAMILY | This nonprofit focuses on marine mammal conservation, and you can help it by participating in one of the educational offerings. One popular option is the Splash and Wade, a shallow-water program that begins with a one-hour briefing, after which you enter the water up to your waist to interact with the dolphins. Prefer to stay mostly dry? Opt to paint with a dolphin, or get a

dolphin "kiss." For tactile interaction (fin tows, for example), sign up for the Interactive Swim, which is more expensive. ✉ *MM 99, 31 Corrine Pl.* ☎ *305/453–4321* 🌐 *www.dpmmr.org* 🎟 *Programs from $125.*

Florida Keys Wild Bird Center

COLLEGE | **FAMILY** | Have a nose-to-beak encounter with ospreys, hawks, herons, and other unreleasable birds at this bird rehabilitation center. The birds live in spacious screened enclosures along a boardwalk running through some of the best waterfront real estate in the Keys. Rehabilitated birds are set free, but about 30 have become permanent residents. Free birds—especially pelicans and egrets—come to visit every day for a free lunch from the center's staff. A short nature trail runs into the mangrove forest (bring bug spray May to October). Be sure to visit its interactive education center about 1½ miles south. ✉ *MM 93.6 BS, 93600 Overseas Hwy., Tavernier* ☎ *305/852–4486* 🌐 *www.keepthemflying.org* 🎟 *Free, donations accepted.*

Jacobs Aquatic Center

CITY PARK | **FAMILY** | Take the plunge at one of three swimming pools: an eight-lane, 25-meter lap pool with two diving boards; a 3- to 4-foot-deep pool accessible to people with mobility challenges; and an interactive children's play pool with a waterslide, pirate ship, waterfall, and sloping zero entry instead of steps. Because so few of the motels in Key Largo have pools, it remains a popular destination for visiting families. ✉ *Key Largo Community Park, 320 Laguna Ave., at St. Croix Pl.* ☎ *305/453–7946* 🌐 *www.jacobsaquaticcenter.org* 🎟 *$12 ($2 discount weekdays).*

Beaches

★ **John Pennekamp Coral Reef State Park**

BEACH—SIGHT | **FAMILY** | This state park is on everyone's list for easy access to the best diving and snorkeling in Florida. The underwater treasure encompasses 78 nautical square miles of coral reefs and sea-grass beds. It lies adjacent to the Florida Keys National Marine Sanctuary, which contains 40 of the 52 species of coral in the Atlantic Reef System and nearly 600 varieties of fish, from the colorful parrotfish to the demure cocoa damselfish. Whatever you do, get in the water. Snorkeling and diving trips ($30 and $75, respectively; equipment extra) and glass-bottom-boat rides to the reef ($24) are available, weather permitting. One of the most popular snorkel trips is to see *Christ of the Deep,* the 2-ton underwater statue of Jesus. The park also has nature trails, two man-made beaches, picnic shelters, a snack bar, and a campground. **Amenities:** food and drink; parking (fee); showers; toilets; water sports. **Best for:** snorkeling; swimming. ✉ *MM 102.5 OS, 102601 Overseas Hwy.* ☎ *305/451–1202 for park, 305/451–6300 for excursions* 🌐 *pennekamppark.com* 🎟 *$4 for 1 person in vehicle, $8 for 2–8 people, $2 for pedestrians and cyclists or extra people (plus a 50¢ per-person county surcharge).*

Restaurants

Alabama Jack's

$ | **SEAFOOD** | Calories be damned—the conch fritters here are heaven on a plate. Don't expect the traditional, golf-ball-size spheres of dough; these are unusual, mountainous, free-form creations of fried, loaded-with-flavor perfection. **Known for:** heavenly conch fritters; unique setting; live music. [$] *Average main: $11* ✉ *58000 Card Sound Rd.* ☎ *305/248–8741.*

★ **Buzzard's Roost Grill and Pub**

$$$ | **SEAFOOD** | The views are nice at this waterfront restaurant, but the food is what gets your attention. Burgers, fish tacos, and seafood baskets are lunch faves. **Known for:** marina views; daily chef's specials; Sunday brunch with live steel drums. [$] *Average main: $21*

✉ *Garden Cove Marina, 21 Garden Cove Dr.* ☎ *305/453–3746* 🌐 *www.buzzardsroostkeylargo.com.*

Chad's Deli & Bakery

$ | AMERICAN | It's a deli! It's a bakery! It's a pasta place! It's also where the locals go. **Known for:** homemade soups and chowders; eight varieties of supersized homemade cookies; huge portions. [$] *Average main: $10* ✉ *MM 92.3 BS, 92330 Overseas Hwy., Tavernier* ☎ *305/853–5566* 🌐 *www.chadsdeli.com.*

The Fish House

$$$ | SEAFOOD | Restaurants not on the water have to produce the highest-quality food to survive in the Keys. Try fish Matecumbe style—baked with tomatoes, capers, olive oil, and lemon juice, or the buttery pan sautéed. **Known for:** smoked fish chunks and dip; excellent key lime pie; fresh-as-can-be seafood served fast. [$] *Average main: $21* ✉ *MM 102.4 OS, 102341 Overseas Hwy.* ☎ *305/451–4665* 🌐 *www.fishhouse.com* 🕒 *Closed Sept.*

Harriette's Restaurant

$ | AMERICAN | If you're looking for comfort food—like melt-in-your-mouth biscuits the size of a salad plate or old-fashioned hotcakes with sausage or bacon—try this refreshing throwback for a hearty breakfast. At lunch, Harriette's shines in the burger department, and all the soups—from garlic tomato to chili—are homemade. **Known for:** always a wait but worth it; best muffins in Key Largo; tight dining space. [$] *Average main: $8* ✉ *MM 95.7 BS, 95710 Overseas Hwy.* ☎ *305/852–8689* 🕒 *No dinner* ☞ *American Express not accepted.*

Jimmy Johnson's Big Chill

$$ | SEAFOOD | Owned by former NFL coach Jimmy Johnson, this waterfront establishment offers three entertaining experiences: the best sports bar in the Upper Keys; a main restaurant with all-glass dining room and a waterfront deck; and an enormous outdoor tiki bar with entertainment seven nights a week. There's even a pool and cabanas where (for an entrance fee) you can spend the day sunning. **Known for:** the place to watch a game; fantastic bay views; brick oven chicken wings with rosemary. [$] *Average main: $20* ✉ *MM 104 BS, 104000 Overseas Hwy.* ☎ *305/453–9066* 🌐 *www.jjsbigchill.com.*

Key Largo Conch House

$$ | AMERICAN | This family-owned restaurant in a Victorian-style home tucked into the trees is worth seeking out. Seven varieties of Benedicts, including conch, are brunch favorites, while lunch and dinner menus highlight local seafood like lionfish (when available) and yellowtail snapper. **Known for:** shrimp and grits; all-season outside dining; seafood tacos. [$] *Average main: $16* ✉ *MM 100.2, 100211 Overseas Hwy.* ☎ *305/453–4844* 🌐 *www.keylargoconchhouse.com.*

Mrs. Mac's Kitchen

$$ | SEAFOOD | FAMILY | Locals pack the counters and booths at this tiny eatery where license plates decorate the walls, to dine on everything from blackened prime rib to crab cakes. Every night is themed including Meatloaf Monday, Italian Wednesday, and Seafood Sensation (offered Friday and Saturday). **Known for:** a second location a half mile south with a full liquor bar; champagne breakfast; being a stop on the Florida Keys Food Tour. [$] *Average main: $17* ✉ *MM 99.4 BS, 99336 Overseas Hwy.* ☎ *305/451–3722, 305/451–6227* 🌐 *www.mrsmacskitchen.com* 🕒 *Closed Sun.*

Sal's Ballyhoo's

$$$ | SEAFOOD | Occupying a 1930s Conch house with outdoor seating right alongside U.S. 1 under the sea-grape trees, this local favorite is all about the fish: yellowtail snapper, tuna, and mahimahi. Choose your favorite, then choose your preparation, such as the Hemingway, with a Parmesan crust, crabmeat, and key lime butter. **Known for:** spicy corn muffins; fish and fried-tomato sandwich; grilled avocado appetizer. [$] *Average* *main: $24* ✉ *MM 97.8 median, 97800 Overseas Hwy.* ☎ *305/852–0822* ⊕ *www. ballyhoosrestaurant.com.*

Snapper's

$$ | SEAFOOD | In a lively, mangrove-ringed, waterfront setting, Snapper's has live music, Sunday brunch (including a build-your-own Bloody Mary bar), killer rum drinks, and seating alongside the fishing dock. "You hook 'em, we cook 'em" is the motto here—but you have to clean your own fish—and dinner is $14 for a single diner, $15 per person family-style meal with a mix of preparations when you provide the fish. **Known for:** grouper Oscar-style; fun and happening vibe; local crowd. Ⓢ *Average main: $17* ✉ *MM 94.5 OS, 139 Seaside Ave.* ☎ *305/852–5956* ⊕ *www.snapperskeylargo.com.*

Sundowners

$$$ | AMERICAN | If it's a clear night and you can snag a reservation, this restaurant will treat you to a sherbet-hue sunset over Florida Bay. The food is also excellent: try the key lime seafood, a happy combo of sautéed shrimp, lobster, and crabmeat swimming in a tangy sauce spiked with Tabasco served over penne or rice. **Known for:** prime rib every Wednesday and Friday; Friday-night fish fry; choose your fish, choose your preparation. Ⓢ *Average main: $29* ✉ *MM 104 BS, 103900 Overseas Hwy.* ☎ *305/451–4502* ⊕ *sundownerskeylargo.com.*

Hotels

Azul del Mar

$$ | B&B/INN | The dock points the way to many beautiful sunsets at this no-smoking, adults-only boutique hotel, which Karol Marsden (an ad exec) and her husband, Dominic (a travel photographer), have transformed from a run-down mom-and-pop place into a waterfront gem. **Pros:** quality bed linens and towels; good location; sophisticated design. **Cons:** small beach; high prices; minimum stays during holidays. Ⓢ *Rooms from: $299*

✉ *MM 104.3 BS, 104300 Overseas Hwy.* ☎ *305/451–0337, 888/253–2985* ⊕ *www. azulkeylargo.com* ⇆ *6 units* ⦿ *No meals.*

★ Baker's Cay Resort Key Largo, Curio Collection by Hilton

$$$ | RESORT | FAMILY | Nestled within a "hardwood hammock" (localese for uplands habitat where hardwood trees such as live oak grow) near the southern border of Everglades National Park, this sparkling new, sprawling 13-acre resort is not to be missed. **Pros:** you never have to leave the resort; pretty pools with waterfalls; 21-slip marina for all your boating needs. **Cons:** some rooms overlook the parking lot; pools near the highway; expensive per-night resort fee. Ⓢ *Rooms from: $399* ✉ *MM 97 BS, 97000 Overseas Hwy.* ☎ *305/852–5553, 888/871–3437* ⊕ *www.keylargoresort. com* ⇆ *200 rooms* ⦿ *No meals.*

Coconut Bay Resort & Bay Harbor Lodge

$ | RESORT | Some 200 feet of waterfront is the main attraction at these side-by-side sister properties that offer a choice between smaller rooms and larger separate cottages. **Pros:** temperature-controlled pool; owner Peg's homemade, amazing scones; free use of kayaks, paddleboat, and paddleboards. **Cons:** a bit dated; small sea-walled sand beach; bring your own charcoal for the barbecue grills. Ⓢ *Rooms from: $195* ✉ *MM 97.7 BS, 97702 Overseas Hwy.* ☎ *305/852–1625, 800/385–0986* ⊕ *www. bayharborkeylargo.com* ⇆ *21 units* ⦿ *Free Breakfast.*

Coconut Palm Inn

$$ | B&B/INN | You'd never find this waterfront haven unless someone told you it was there, as it's tucked into a residential neighborhood beneath towering palms and native gumbo limbos. **Pros:** secluded and quiet; 100% smoke-free resort; sophisticated feel. **Cons:** front desk closes early each evening; no access to ice machine when staff leave; breakfast is ho-hum. Ⓢ *Rooms from: $299* ✉ *MM 92 BS, 198 Harborview Dr., via Jo-Jean Way* *off Overseas Hwy., Tavernier ☎ 305/852–3017 🌐 www.coconutpalminn.com 🛏 20 rooms 🍴 Free Breakfast.*

MB Resort at Key Largo

$$ | B&B/INN | With its sherbet-hue rooms and plantation-style furnishings, these tropical-style units range in size from simple lodge rooms to luxury two-bedroom suites. **Pros:** luxurious rooms; 10% discount to Snapper's restaurant next door; discounted ecotours from the dock. **Cons:** no beach; some find the music from next door bothersome; office closes at 8 pm. [$] *Rooms from: $269* ✉ *MM 94.5 OS, 147 Seaside Ave.* ☎ *305/852–6200, 800/401–0057* 🌐 *www.mbatkeylargo.com* 🛏 *14 rooms* 🍴 *Free Breakfast.*

★ **Kona Kai Resort, Gallery & Botanic Gardens**

$$ | RESORT | Brilliantly colored bougainvillea, coconut palm, and guava trees—and a botanical garden of other rare species—make this 2-acre adult hideaway one of the prettiest places to stay in the Keys. **Pros:** friendly staff; free use of sports equipment; spa-like pool area. **Cons:** expensive; some rooms are very close together. [$] *Rooms from: $299* ✉ *MM 97.8 BS, 97802 Overseas Hwy.* ☎ *305/852–7200, 800/365–7829* 🌐 *www.konakairesort.com* 🛏 *13 rooms* 🍴 *Free Breakfast.*

Marriott's Key Largo Bay Beach Resort

$$$ | RESORT | FAMILY | This 17-acre bay-side resort has plenty of diversions, from diving to a day spa. **Pros:** lots of activities; free covered parking; dive shop on property; free Wi-Fi. **Cons:** rooms facing highway can be noisy; thin walls; starting to show wear. [$] *Rooms from: $359* ✉ *MM 103.8 BS, 103800 Overseas Hwy.* ☎ *305/453–0000, 866/849–3753* 🌐 *www.marriottkeylargo.com* 🛏 *153 rooms* 🍴 *No meals.*

The Pelican

$ | HOTEL | This 1950s throwback is reminiscent of the days when parents packed the kids into the station wagon and headed to no-frills seaside motels, complete with old-fashioned fishing off the dock. **Pros:** free use of kayaks and a canoe; well-maintained dock; reasonable rates. **Cons:** some rooms are small; basic accommodations and amenities; road noise with some units. [$] *Rooms from: $159* ✉ *MM 99.3, 99340 Overseas Hwy.* ☎ *305/451–3576, 877/451–3576* 🌐 *www.hungrypelican.com* 🛏 *21 units* 🍴 *Free Breakfast.*

★ **Playa Largo Resort and Spa, Autograph Collection**

$$$ | RESORT | At this luxurious 14-acre bay-front retreat, you'll find one of the nicest beaches in the Keys, as well as water sports galore, bocce, tennis, basketball, and a fitness center with inspiring pool views. **Pros:** comfortable rooms, most with balconies; excellent service; Playa Largo Kids Club. **Cons:** $41.93 per night resort fee; minimum stays may be required; luxury will cost you. [$] *Rooms from: $399* ✉ *97450 Overseas Hwy.* ☎ *305/853–1001* 🌐 *playalargoresort.com* 🛏 *178 units* 🍴 *No meals* 💳 *No credit cards.*

Popp's Motel

$ | HOTEL | Stylized metal herons mark the entrance to this 67-year-old family-run motel. **Pros:** great beach; intimate feel; full kitchen in each unit. **Cons:** limited amenities; minimum stays in season; limited dock space. [$] *Rooms from: $149* ✉ *MM 95.5 BS, 95500 Overseas Hwy.* ☎ *305/852–5201, 877/852–5201* 🌐 *www.poppsmotel.com* 🛏 *9 units* 🍴 *No meals.*

Seafarer Resort and Beach

$ | HOTEL | FAMILY | If you're looking for modern and updated, this very basic, budget lodging isn't for you—this place is all about staying on the water for a song. **Pros:** kitchen units available; complimentary kayak use; cheap rates. **Cons:** can hear road noise in some rooms; some complaints about cleanliness. [$] *Rooms from: $149* ✉ *MM 97.6 BS, 97684 Overseas Hwy.* ☎ *305/852–5349* 🌐 *www.*

seafarerkeylargo.com ➔ 15 units ⏀ *Free Breakfast*.

Nightlife

The semiweekly *Keynoter* (Wednesday and Saturday), weekly *Reporter* (Thursday), and Friday through Sunday editions of the *Miami Herald* are the best sources of information on entertainment and nightlife. Daiquiri bars, tiki huts, and seaside shacks pretty well summarize Key Largo's bar scene.

Breezers Tiki Bar & Grille

BARS/PUBS | Mingle with locals over cocktails and catch amazing sunsets from the comfort of an enclosed, air-conditioned bar. Floor-to-ceiling doors can be opened on cool days and closed on hot days. It's located at Marriott's Key Largo Bay Beach Resort. ✉ *Marriott's Key Largo Bay Beach Resort, 103800 Overseas Hwy.* ☎ *305/453–0000*.

Caribbean Club

BARS/PUBS | Walls plastered with Bogart memorabilia remind customers that the classic 1948 Bogart–Bacall flick *Key Largo* has a connection with this worn watering hole. Although no food is served and the floors are bare concrete, this landmark draws boaters, curious visitors, and local barflies to its humble bar stools and pool tables. But the real magic is around back, where you can grab a seat on the deck and catch a postcard-perfect sunset. Live music draws revelers Thursday through Sunday. ✉ *MM 104 BS, 104080 Overseas Hwy.* ☎ *305/451–4466* ⊕ *caribbeanclubkl. com*.

Shopping

For the most part, shopping is sporadic in Key Largo, with a couple of shopping centers and fewer galleries than you find on the other big islands. If you're looking to buy scuba or snorkel equipment, you'll have plenty of choices.

★ **Key Largo Chocolates**

FOOD/CANDY | **FAMILY** | Specializing in key lime truffles made with quality Belgian chocolate, this is the only chocolate factory in the Florida Keys. But you'll find much more than just the finest white-, milk-, and dark-chocolate truffles; try the cupcakes, ice cream, and famous "chocodiles." The salted turtles, a fan favorite, are worth every calorie. Chocolate classes are also available for kids and adults, and a small gift area showcases local art, jewelry, hot sauces, and other goodies. Look for the bright-green-and-pink building. ✉ *MM 100 BS, 100471 Overseas Hwy.* ☎ *305/453–6613* ⊕ *www. keylargochocolates.com*.

Key Lime Products

LOCAL SPECIALTIES | Go into olfactory overload—you'll find yourself sniffing every single bar of soap and scented candle inside this key lime treasure trove. Take home some key lime juice (supereasy pie-making directions are right on the bottle), marmalade, candies, sauces, even key lime shampoo. Outside, you'll find a huge selection of wood carvings, pottery, unique patio furniture, and artwork. The fresh fish sandwiches and conch fritters served at the on-site Key Lime Cafe are alone worth the stop. ✉ *MM 95.2 BS, 95231 Overseas Hwy.* ☎ *305/853–0378, 800/870–1780* ⊕ *www. keylimeproducts.com*.

Randy's Florida Keys Gift Co.

GIFTS/SOUVENIRS | Since 1989, Randy's has been *the* place for unique gifts. Owner Randy and his wife Lisa aren't only fantastic at stocking the store with a plethora of items, they're also well respected in the community for their generosity and dedication. Stop in and say hello, then browse the aisles and loaded shelves filled with key lime candles, books, wood carvings, jewelry, clothing, T-shirts, and eclectic, tropical decor items. This friendly shop prides itself on carrying wares from local craftsmen, and there's something for every budget. ✉ *102421* *s Hwy.* ✛ *On U.S. 1, next to the Sandal Factory Outlet* ☎ *305/453–9229* ⊕ *www.keysmermaid.com.*

Shell World
GIFTS/SOUVENIRS | You can find lots of shops in the Keys that sell cheesy souvenirs—snow globes, alligator hats, and shell-encrusted anything. This is the granddaddy of them all. But this sprawling building in the median of Overseas Highway contains much more than the usual tourist trinkets—you'll find high-end clothing, jewelry, housewares, artwork, and a wide selection of keepsakes, from delightfully tacky to tasteful. ⊠ *MM 97.5, 97600 Overseas Hwy.* ☎ *305/852–8245, 888/398–6233* ⊕ *www.shellworldflkeys. com.*

 Activities

BOATING
Everglades Eco-Tours
BOATING | FAMILY | For over 30 years, Captain Sterling has operated Everglades and Florida Bay ecology tours and more expensive sunset cruises. With his expert guidance, you can see dolphins, manatees, and birds from the casual comfort of his pontoon boat, equipped with PVC chairs. Bring your own food and drinks; each tour has a maximum of six people. ⊠ *Sundowners Restaurant, MM 104 BS , 103900 Overseas Hwy.* ☎ *305/853–5161, 888/224–6044* ⊕ *www.captainsterling. com* ☞ *From $59.*

M.V. *Key Largo Princess*
BOATING | FAMILY | Two-hour glass-bottom-boat trips and more expensive sunset cruises on a luxury 70-foot motor yacht with a 280-square-foot glass viewing area depart from the Holiday Inn docks three times a day. ■TIP➔ **Purchase tickets online to save big.** ⊠ *Holiday Inn, MM 100 OS, 99701 Overseas Hwy.* ☎ *305/451–4655, 877/648–8129* ⊕ *www. keylargoprincess.com* ☞ *$30.*

CANOEING AND KAYAKING
Sea kayaking continues to gain popularity in the Keys. You can paddle for a few hours or the whole day, on your own or with a guide. Some outfitters even offer overnight trips. The **Florida Keys Overseas Paddling Trail,** part of a statewide system, runs from Key Largo to Key West. You can paddle the entire distance, 110 miles on the Atlantic side, which takes 9 to 10 days. The trail also runs the chain's length on the bay side, which is a longer route.

Coral Reef Park Co.
CANOEING/ROWING/SKULLING | At John Pennekamp Coral Reef State Park, this operator has a fleet of canoes and kayaks for gliding around the 2½-mile mangrove trail or along the coast. Powerboat rentals are also available. ⊠ *MM 102.5 OS, 102601 Overseas Hwy.* ☎ *305/451–6300* ⊕ *www.pennekamppark.com* ☞ *Rentals from $20 per hr.*

Florida Bay Outfitters
CANOEING/ROWING/SKULLING | Rent canoes, sea kayaks, or Hobie Eclipses (the newest craze) from this company, which sets up self-guided trips on the Florida Keys Paddling Trail, helps with trip planning, and matches equipment to your skill level. It also runs myriad guided tours around Key Largo. Take a full-moon paddle or a one- to seven-day kayak tour to the Everglades, Lignumvitae Key, or Indian Key. ⊠ *MM 104 BS, 104050 Overseas Hwy.* ☎ *305/451–3018* ⊕ *www. paddlefloridakeys.com* ☞ *From $15.*

FISHING
Private charters and big "head" boats (so named because they charge "by the head") are great for anglers who don't have their own vessel.

Sailors Choice
FISHING | Fishing excursions depart twice daily (half-day trips are cash only), but the company also does private charters. The 65-foot boat leaves from the Holiday Inn docks. Rods, bait, and license are included. ⊠ *Holiday Inn Resort & Marina,*

MM 100 OS, 99701 Overseas Hwy.
☎ 305/451–1802, 305/451–0041 ⊕ www.
sailorschoicefishingboat.com ⊠ From
$45.

SCUBA DIVING AND SNORKELING

Much of what makes the Upper Keys a
singular dive destination is variety. Places
like Molasses Reef, which begins 3 feet
below the surface and descends to 55
feet, have something for everyone from
novice snorkelers to experienced divers.
The *Spiegel Grove*, a 510-foot vessel, lies
in 130 feet of water, but its upper regions
are only 60 feet below the surface. On
rough days, Key Largo Undersea Park's
Emerald Lagoon is a popular spot. Expect
to pay about $80 to $85 for a two-tank,
two-site dive trip with tanks and weights,
or $35 to $40 for a two-site snorkel
outing. Get big discounts by booking
multiple trips.

Amy Slate's Amoray Dive Resort

SCUBA DIVING | This outfit makes diving
easy. Stroll down to the full-service dive
shop (PADI, TDI, and BSAC certified),
then onto a 45-foot catamaran. Certifi-
cation courses are also offered. ⊠ *MM
104.2 BS, 104250 Overseas Hwy.*
☎ 305/451–3595, 800/426–6729 ⊕ www.
amoray.com ⊠ From $85.

Conch Republic Divers

SCUBA DIVING | Book diving instruction as
well as scuba and snorkeling tours of all
the wrecks and reefs of the Upper Keys.
Two-location dives are the standard,
and you'll pay an extra $20 for tank and
weights. ⊠ *MM 90.8 BS, 90800 Overseas Hwy.* ☎ 305/852–1655, 800/274–
3483 ⊕ www.conchrepublicdivers.com
⊠ From $80.

Coral Reef Park Co.

SCUBA DIVING | At John Pennekamp Coral
Reef State Park, this company gives
3½-hour scuba and 2½-hour snorkeling
tours of the park. In addition to the great
location and the dependability it's also
suited for water adventurers of all levels.
⊠ *MM 102.5 OS, 102601 Overseas Hwy.*

☎ 305/451–6300 ⊕ www.[...]
park.com ⊠ From $30.

Horizon Divers

SCUBA DIVING | The company h[...]
tomized diving and snorkeling t[...]
depart daily aboard a 45-foot cata[...]an.
⊠ *105800 Overseas Hwy.* ☎ *305/453–
3535, 800/984–3483 ⊕ www.horizondiv-
ers.com ⊠ From $50 for snorkeling, from
$85 for diving.*

Island Ventures

SCUBA DIVING | If you like dry, British
humor and no crowds, this is the opera-
tor for you. It specializes in small groups
for snorkeling or dive trips, no more than
10 people per boat. Scuba trips are two
tanks, two locations, and include tanks
and weights; ride-alongs pay just $35.
Choose morning or afternoon. ⊠ *Jules
Undersea Lodge, 51 Shoreland Dr.*
☎ 305/451–4957 ⊕ www.islandventure.
com ⊠ Snorkel trips $45, diving $85.

Rainbow Reef Dive Center

SCUBA DIVING | The PADI five-star facility
has been around since 1975 and offers
day and night dives, a range of courses,
and dive-lodging packages. Two-tank reef
dives include tank and weight rental.
There are also organized snorkeling trips
with equipment. Two locations to choose
from. ⊠ *MM 100 OS, 522 Caribbean Dr.*
☎ 305/451–1113, 800/451–1113 ⊕ www.
oceandivers.com ⊠ Snorkel trips from
$35, diving from $80.

★ Quiescence Diving Services

SCUBA DIVING | This operator sets itself
apart in two ways: it limits groups to six
to ensure personal attention and offers
both two-dive day and night dives, as
well as twilight dives when sea creatures
are most active. There are also organized
snorkeling excursions. ⊠ *MM 103.5 BS,
103680 Overseas Hwy.* ☎ 305/451–2440
⊕ www.quiescence.com ⊠ Snorkel trips
$55, diving from $89.

Islamorada's warm waters attract large fish and the anglers and charter captains who want to catch them.

Islamorada

Islamorada is between MM 90.5 and 70.

Early settlers named this key after their schooner, *Island Home,* but to make it sound more romantic they translated it into Spanish: *Isla Morada.* The Chamber of Commerce prefers to use its literal translation, "Purple Island," which refers either to a purple-shelled snail that once inhabited these shores or to the brilliantly colored orchids and bougainvilleas.

Early maps show Islamorada as encompassing only Upper Matecumbe Key. But the incorporated "Village of Islands" is made up of a string of islands that the Overseas Highway crosses, including Plantation Key, Windley Key, Upper Matecumbe Key, Lower Matecumbe Key, Craig Key, and Fiesta Key. In addition, two state-park islands accessible only by boat—Indian Key and Lignumvitae Key—belong to the group.

Islamorada (locals pronounce it "*eye-*la-mor-*ah-*da") is one of the world's top fishing destinations. For nearly 100 years, seasoned anglers have fished these clear, warm waters teeming with trophy-worthy fish. There are numerous options for those in search of the big ones, including chartering a boat with its own crew or heading out on a vessel rented from one of the plethora of marinas along this 20-mile stretch of the Overseas Highway. More than 150 back-country guides and 400 offshore captains are at your service.

GETTING HERE AND AROUND
Most visitors arrive in Islamorada by car. If you're flying in to Miami International Airport or Key West International Airport, you can easily rent a car (reserve in advance) to make the drive.

TOURS
CONTACT Florida Keys Food Tours.
☎ *305/393–9183* ⊕ *www.flkeysfoodtours. com.*

VISITOR INFORMATION
CONTACT Islamorada Chamber of Commerce & Visitors Center. ✉ *MM 87.1 BS, 87100 Overseas Hwy.* ☎ *305/664–4503, 800/322–5397* ⊕ *www.islamoradachamber.com.*

 Sights

Florida Keys Memorial / Hurricane Monument
MEMORIAL | On Monday, September 2, 1935, more than 400 people perished when the most intense hurricane to make landfall in the United States swept through this area of the Keys. Two years later, the Florida Keys Memorial was dedicated in their honor. Native coral rock, known as keystone, covers the 18-foot obelisk monument that marks the remains of more than 300 storm victims. A sculpted plaque of bending palms and waves graces the front (although many are bothered that the palms are bending in the wrong direction). In 1995, the memorial was placed on the National Register of Historic Places. ✉ *MM 81.8, in front of the public library, 81831 Old State Hwy. 4A, Upper Matecumbe Key* ⊹ *Just south of the Cheeca Lodge entrance* ➠ *Free.*

History of Diving Museum
MUSEUM | Adding to the region's reputation for world-class diving, this museum plunges into the history of man's thirst for undersea exploration. Among its 13 galleries of interactive and other interesting displays are a submarine and helmet re-created from the film *20,000 Leagues Under the Sea.* Vintage U.S. Navy equipment, diving helmets from around the world, and early scuba gear explore 4,000 years of diving history. For the grand finale, spend $3 for a mouthpiece and sing your favorite tune at the helium bar. There are extended hours (until 6:45 pm) on the third Wednesday of every month. ✉ *MM 83 BS, 82990 Overseas Hwy.,* *Upper Matecumbe Key* ☎ *305/664–9737* ⊕ *www.divingmuseum.org* ➠ *$12.*

Robbie's Marina
MARINA | FAMILY | Huge, prehistoric-looking denizens of the not-so-deep, silver-sided tarpon congregate around the docks at this marina on Lower Matecumbe Key. Children—and lots of adults—pay $4 for a bucket of sardines to feed them and $2.25 each for dock admission. Spend some time hanging out at this authentic Keys community, where you can grab a bite to eat indoors or out, shop at a slew of artisans' booths, or charter a boat, kayak, or other watercraft. ✉ *MM 77.5 BS, 77522 Overseas Hwy., Lower Matecumbe Key* ☎ *305/664–8070, 877/664–8498* ⊕ *www.robbies.com* ➠ *Dock access $1.*

Theater of the Sea
ZOO | FAMILY | The second-oldest marine-mammal center in the world doesn't attempt to compete with more modern, more expensive parks. Even so, it's among the better attractions north of Key West, especially if you have kids in tow. In addition to marine-life exhibits and shows, you can make reservations for up-close-and-personal encounters like a swim with a dolphin or sea lion, or stingray and turtle feedings (which include general admission; reservations required). These are popular, so reserve in advance. Ride a "bottomless" boat to see what's below the waves and take a guided tour of the marine-life exhibits. Nonstop animal shows highlight conservation issues. You can stop for lunch at the grill, shop in the extensive gift shop, or sunbathe and swim at the private beach. This could easily be an all-day attraction. ✉ *MM 84.5 OS, 84721 Overseas Hwy., Windley Key* ☎ *305/664–2431* ⊕ *www.theaterofthesea.com* ➠ *$35.95; interaction programs $45–$199.*

🍴 Restaurants

★ Chef Michael's

$$$ | **SEAFOOD** | This local favorite—whose motto is "Peace. Love. Hogfish."—has been making big waves since its opening in 2011 with chef Michael Ledwith at the helm. Seafood is selected fresh daily, then elegantly prepared with a splash of tropical flair. **Known for:** watermelon mint sangria; fresh catch "Juliette" with shrimp and scallops; intimate tropical dining. [$] *Average main: $30* ✉ *MM 81.7, 81671 Overseas Hwy., Upper Matecumbe Key* ☎ *305/664–0640* 🌐 *www.foodtotalkabout.com* 🕒 *No lunch Mon.–Sat.*

Green Turtle Inn

$$$ | **SEAFOOD** | This circa-1947 landmark inn and its vintage neon sign is a slice of Florida Keys history. Period photographs decorate the wood-paneled walls. **Known for:** excellent conch chowder; a piece of Florida Keys history; huge homemade sticky buns. [$] *Average main: $24* ✉ *MM 81.2 OS, 81219 Overseas Hwy., Upper Matecumbe Key* ☎ *305/664–2006* 🌐 *www.greenturtlekeys.com* 🕒 *Closed Mon.*

Hungry Tarpon

$$ | **SEAFOOD** | As part of the colorful, bustling Old Florida scene at Robbie's Marina, you know that the seafood here is fresh and top quality. The extensive menu seems as if it's bigger than the dining space, which consists of a few tables and counter seating indoors, plus tables out back under the mangrove trees. **Known for:** insanely good Bloody Marys with a beefstick straw; heart-of-the-action location; biscuits and gravy. [$] *Average main: $19* ✉ *MM 77.5 BS, 77522 Overseas Hwy., Lower Matecumbe Key* ☎ *305/664–0535* 🌐 *www.hungrytarpon.com.*

Islamorada Fish Company

$$ | **SEAFOOD** | **FAMILY** | When a restaurant is owned by Bass Pro Shops, you know the seafood should be as fresh as you can get it. The restaurant, housed in an open-air, oversize tiki hut on Florida Bay, is the quintessential Keys experience, with menu highlights that include cracked conch beaten 'til tender and fried crispy, and fresh catch Portofino blackened perfectly and topped with Key West shrimp and a brandied lobster sauce. **Known for:** tourist hot spot; great views; afternoon fish and shark feedings in its private lagoon. [$] *Average main: $18* ✉ *MM 81.5 BS, 81532 Overseas Hwy., Windley Key* ☎ *305/664–9271* 🌐 *restaurants.basspro.com/fishcompany/Islamorada.*

Kaiyo Grill & Sushi

$$$$ | **JAPANESE** | The decor—an inviting setting that includes colorful abstract mosaics and upholstered banquettes—almost steals the show, but the food is equally interesting. The menu, a fusion of East and West, offers sushi rolls that combine local ingredients with traditional Japanese tastes. **Known for:** drunken scallops; showstopping decor; dessert cupcakes that look like sushi. [$] *Average main: $35* ✉ *MM 81.5 OS, 81701 Overseas Hwy., Upper Matecumbe Key* ☎ *305/664–5556* 🕒 *Closed Sun. and Mon. No lunch.*

Lorelei Restaurant & Cabana Bar

$$ | **AMERICAN** | While local anglers gather here for breakfast, lunch and dinner bring a mix of islanders and visitors for straightforward food and front-row seats to the sunset. Live music seven nights a week ensures a lively nighttime scene, and the menu staves off inebriation with burgers, barbecued baby back ribs, and Parmesan-crusted snapper. **Known for:** amazing sunset views; you catch it, they'll cook it; excellent tuna nachos. [$] *Average main: $15* ✉ *MM 82 BS, 81924 Overseas Hwy., Upper Matecumbe Key* ☎ *305/664–2692* 🌐 *www.loreleicabanabar.com.*

Marker 88

$$$$ | **SEAFOOD** | A few yards from Florida Bay, on one of the Keys only natural beaches, this popular seafood restaurant

has large picture windows that offer great sunset views, but most choose to dine outside on the sand. Chef Bobby Stoky serves such irresistible entrées as onion-crusted mahimahi and house-smoked sea-salt-and-black-pepper-encrusted rib eye. **Known for:** a gathering place for locals and visitors; fantastic fresh fish sandwich; extensive wine list. $ *Average main: $34* ⊠ *MM 88 BS, 88000 Overseas Hwy., Plantation Key* ☎ *305/852–9315* ⊕ *www.marker88.info.*

Morada Bay Beach Café

$$$ | ECLECTIC | FAMILY | This bay-front restaurant wins high marks for its surprisingly stellar cuisine, tables in the sand, and tiki torches that bathe the evening in romance. Seafood takes center stage, but you can always get roasted organic chicken or prime rib. **Known for:** feet-in-the-sand dining; full-moon parties; intoxicating sunset views. $ *Average main: $27* ⊠ *MM 81 BS, 81600 Overseas Hwy., Upper Matecumbe Key* ☎ *305/664–0604* ⊕ *www.moradabay.com.*

★ Pierre's

$$$$ | FRENCH | One of the Keys' most elegant restaurants, Pierre's marries colonial style with modern food trends and lets you taste the world from its romantic verandas. French chocolate, Australian lamb, Hawaiian fish, Florida lobster—whatever is fresh and in season will be masterfully prepared and beautifully served. **Known for:** romantic spot for that special night out; seasonally changing menu; full-moon parties. $ *Average main: $43* ⊠ *MM 81.5 BS, 81600 Overseas Hwy., Upper Matecumbe Key* ☎ *305/664–3225* ⊕ *www.moradabay.com* ⊘ *No lunch.*

Hotels

Amara Cay Resort

$$ | RESORT | Simple yet chic, Islamorada's newest resort is an oceanfront gem. **Pros:** free shuttle to local attractions; free use of kayaks, bikes, paddleboards; oceanfront zero-entry pool. **Cons:** pricey $30 daily resort fee; living areas of rooms lack seating. $ *Rooms from: $299* ⊠ *MM 80 OS, 80001 Overseas Hwy.* ☎ *305/664–0073* ⊕ *www.amaracayresort.com* ⊅ *110 rooms* ⦿ *No meals.*

★ Casa Morada

$$$$ | B&B/INN | This relic from the 1950s has been restyled into a suave, design-forward, all-suites property with outdoor showers and Jacuzzis in some of the suites. **Pros:** private island connected by footbridge; adults only; complimentary use of bikes, kayaks, paddleboards, and snorkel gear. **Cons:** dinner off property; beach is small and inconsequential; minimum two-night stay on weekends. $ *Rooms from: $400* ⊠ *MM 82 BS, 136 Madeira Rd., Upper Matecumbe Key* ☎ *305/664–0044, 888/881–3030* ⊕ *www.casamorada.com* ⊅ *16 suites* ⦿ *Free Breakfast.*

★ Cheeca Lodge & Spa

$$$$ | RESORT | While Cheeca's 27 acres took a beating during Hurricane Irma, the grounds are looking better every month, and this legendary resort still packs in more amenities than any other we can think of. **Pros:** everything you need in on-site; new designer rooms; water-sports center on property. **Cons:** expensive rates; expensive resort fee; very busy. $ *Rooms from: $410* ⊠ *MM 82 OS, 81801 Overseas Hwy., Upper Matecumbe Key* ☎ *305/664–4651, 800/327–2888* ⊕ *www.cheeca.com* ⊅ *123 rooms* ⦿ *No meals.*

Drop Anchor Resort and Marina

$$ | HOTEL | Immaculately maintained, this place has the feel of an old friend's beach house, even though it's been completely redone since Hurricane Irma blew through town. **Pros:** bright and colorful; very clean; laid-back charm. **Cons:** noise from the highway; beach is for fishing not swimming; simplicity isn't for everyone. $ *Rooms from: $200* ⊠ *MM 85 OS, 84959 Overseas Hwy., Windley Key* ☎ *305/664–4863, 888/664–4863* ⊕ *www.*

dropanchorresort.com 🛏 *18 suites* 🍴 *No meals.*

The Islander Resort

$$ | **RESORT** | Guests here get to choose between a self-sufficient town home on the bay side or an oceanfront resort with on-site restaurants and oodles of amenities. **Pros:** spacious rooms; nice kitchens; eye-popping views. **Cons:** pricey; ocean side not open till January 2019; no dining at bay-side location. [$] *Rooms from: $300* ✉ *MM 82.1 OS, 82200 Overseas Hwy., Upper Matecumbe Key* ☎ *305/664–0082* 🌐 *www.islanderfloridakeys.com* 🛏 *25 town homes at the bay-side property* 🍴 *No meals.*

★ **The Moorings Village**

$$$$ | **HOTEL** | This tropical retreat is everything you imagine when you envision the laid-back Keys—from hammocks swaying between towering trees to manicured sand lapped by aqua-green waves. **Pros:** romantic setting; good dining options with room-charging privileges; beautiful views. **Cons:** no room service; $25 daily resort fee for activities; must cross the highway to walk or drive to its restaurants. [$] *Rooms from: $800* ✉ *MM 81.6 OS, 123 Beach Rd., Upper Matecumbe Key* ☎ *305/664–4708* 🌐 *www.themooringsvillage.com* 🛏 *17 cottages* 🍴 *No meals.*

Postcard Inn Beach Resort & Marina at Holiday Isle

$$ | **RESORT** | After an $11 million renovation that encompassed updating everything from the rooms to the public spaces, this iconic property (formerly known as the Holiday Isle Beach Resort) has found new life. **Pros:** large private beach; heated pools; on-site restaurants including Ciao Hound Italian Kitchen & Bar. **Cons:** rooms near tiki bar are noisy; minimum stay required during peak times; rooms without an oceanfront view overlook a parking lot. [$] *Rooms from: $267* ✉ *MM 84 OS, 84001 Overseas Hwy., Plantation Key* ☎ *305/664–2321* 🌐 *www.holidayisle.com* 🛏 *145 rooms* 🍴 *No meals.*

Ragged Edge Resort

$$ | **HOTEL** | **FAMILY** | Nicely tucked away in a residential area at the ocean's edge, this family-owned hotel draws returning guests who'd rather fish off the dock and grill up dinner than loll around on Egyptian cotton sheets. **Pros:** oceanfront setting; boat docks and ramp; cheap rates for Islamorada. **Cons:** dated decor; off the beaten path; not within walking distance to anything. [$] *Rooms from: $209* ✉ *MM 86.5 OS, 243 Treasure Harbor Rd., Plantation Key* ☎ *305/852–5389, 800/436–2023* 🌐 *www.ragged-edge.com* 🛏 *10 units* 🍴 *No meals.*

Shopping

Art galleries, upscale gift shops, and the mammoth World Wide Sportsman (if you want to look the part of a local fisherman, you must wear a shirt from here) make up the variety and superior style of Islamorada shopping.

Banyan Tree Garden and Boutique

HOUSEHOLD ITEMS/FURNITURE | Stroll and shop among the colorful orchids and lush plants at this outdoor garden and indoor boutique known for its tropical splendor, unique gifts, and free-spirited clothing. There is nothing quite like it in the area. ✉ *MM 81.2 OS, 81197 Overseas Hwy., Upper Matecumbe Key* ☎ *305/664–3433* 🌐 *www.banyantreeboutique.com.*

Casa Mar Village

SHOPPING CENTERS/MALLS | Change is good, and in this case, it's fantastic. What was once a row of worn-down buildings is now a merry blend of gift shops and galleries with the added bonus of a place selling fresh-roasted coffee. By day, these colorful shops glisten at their canal-front location; by nightfall, they're lit up like a lovely Christmas town. The offerings include What The Fish Rolls & More restaurant; Casa Mar Seafood fish market; and Paddle The Florida Keys,

Kayak ready to be used on the beach in the Florida Keys

where you can rent paddleboards and kayaks. ☒ *MM 90 OS, 90775 Old Hwy., Upper Matecumbe Key* ⊕ *www.casamar-village.com.*

Rain Barrel Artisan Village

CRAFTS | This is a natural and unhurried shopping showplace. Set in a tropical garden of shady trees, native shrubs, and orchids, the crafts village has shops selling the work of local and national artists as well as resident artists who sell work from their own studios. Take a selfie with "Betsy," the giant Florida lobster, roadside. ☒ *MM 86.7 BS, 86700 Overseas Hwy., Plantation Key* ☏ *305/852–3084.*

Redbone Gallery

CRAFTS | This gallery stocks hand-stitched clothing, giftware, and jewelry, in addition to works of art by watercolorists C. D. Clarke, Christine Black, and Julie Joyce; and painters David Hall, Steven Left, Tim Borski, and Jorge Martinez. Proceeds benefit cystic fibrosis research. Find them in the Morada Way Arts and Cultural District. ☒ *MM 81.5 OS, 200*

Morada Way, Upper Matecumbe Key ☏ *305/664–2002* ⊕ *www.redbone.org.*

World Wide Sportsman

SPORTING GOODS | This two-level retail center sells upscale and everyday fishing equipment, resort clothing, sportfishing art, and other gifts. When you're tired of shopping, relax at the Zane Grey Long Key Lounge, located on the second level—but not before you step up and into *Pilar,* a replica of Hemingway's boat. ☒ *MM 81.5 BS, 81576 Overseas Hwy., Upper Matecumbe Key* ☏ *305/664–4615, 800/327–2880.*

Activities

BOATING

Keys Boat Rental

BOATING | You can rent both fishing and deck boats here (from 18 to 29 feet) by the day or the week. Free local delivery with seven-day rentals from each of its locations is available. ☒ *MM 85.9 BS and 99.7 OS, 85920 Overseas Hwy., Upper Matecumbe Key* ☏ *305/664–9404,*

877/453–9463 ⊕ www.keysboatrental.
com ✉ Rentals from $240 per day.

Early Bird Fishing Charters

FISHING | Captain Ross knows these
waters well and he'll hook you up with
whatever is in season—mahimahi,
sailfish, tuna, and wahoo, to name a
few—while you cruise on a comfy and
stylish 43-foot custom Willis charter boat.
The salon is air-conditioned for those hot
summer days, and everything but booze
and food is included. ⊠ Bud and Mary's
Marina, MM 79.8 OS, 79851 Overseas
Hwy. ☎ 305/942–3618 ⊕ www.fishearly-
bird.com ✉ 4 hrs $850; 6 hrs $1,100; 8
hrs $1,300.

Nauti-Limo

BOATING | Captain Joe Fox has converted
the design of a 1983 pink Caddy stretch
limo into a less-than-luxurious but certainly curious watercraft. The seaworthy
hybrid—complete with wheels—can sail
with the top down if you're in the mood.
Only in the Keys! One-hour and longer
tours are available. New to the fleet is a
40-foot pirate ship, complete with plastic
swords, that can hold about 14 people,
available for two-hour rides. ⊠ Lorelei
Restaurant & Yacht Club, MM 82 BS,
96 Madeira Rd., Upper Matecumbe Key
☎ 305/942–3793 ⊕ www.nautilimo.com
✉ From $90.

Robbie's Boat Rentals

BOATING | This full-service company will
even give you a crash course on how
not to crash your boat. The rental fleet
includes an 18-foot skiff with a 90-horse-
power outboard to a 21-foot deck boat
with a 130-horsepower engine. Robbie's
also rents snorkeling gear (there's good
snorkeling nearby) and sells bait, drinks,
and snacks. Want to hire a guide who
knows the local waters and where the
fish lurk? Robbie's offers offshore-fishing
trips, patch-reef trips, and party-boat fishing. Backcountry flats trips are a specialty. ⊠ MM 77.5 BS, 77522 Overseas Hwy.,
Lower Matecumbe Key ☎ 305/664–9814,

877/664–8498 ⊕ www.robbies.com
✉ From $185 per day.

FISHING

Here in the self-proclaimed "Sportfishing
Capital of the World," sailfish is the prime
catch in the winter and mahimahi in
the summer. Buchanan Bank just south
of Islamorada is a good spot to try for
tarpon in the spring. Blackfin tuna and
amberjack are generally plentiful in the
area, too. ■TIP→ The Hump at Islamorada ranks highest among anglers' favorite
fishing spots in Florida (declared Florida
Monthly magazine's best for seven years in
a row) due to the incredible offshore marine
life.

Captain Ted Wilson

FISHING | Go into the backcountry for
bonefish, tarpon, redfish, snook, and
shark aboard a 17-foot boat that accom-
modates up to three anglers. Choose
half-day (four hours), three-quarter-day
(six hours), or full-day (eight hours) trips,
or evening tarpon fishing excursions.
Rates are for one or two anglers. There's
a $75 charge for an additional person.
⊠ Bud N' Mary's Marina, MM 79.9 OS,
79851 Overseas Hwy., Upper Matecumbe Key ☎ 305/942–5224 ⊕ www.
captaintedwilson.com ✉ Half-day and
evening trips from $450.

Florida Keys Fly Fish

FISHING | Like other top fly-fishing and
light-tackle guides, Captain Geoff Colmes
helps his clients land trophy fish in the
waters around the Keys, from Islamorada to Flamingo in the Everglades.
⊠ 105 Palm La., Upper Matecumbe Key
☎ 305/393–1245 ⊕ www.floridakeysfly-
fish.com ✉ From $550.

Florida Keys Outfitters

FISHING | Long before fly-fishing became
popular, Sandy Moret was fishing the
Keys for bonefish, tarpon, and redfish.
Now he attracts anglers from around
the world on a quest for the big catch.
His weekend fly-fishing classes include
classroom instruction, equipment, and

Did You Know?

The coral making up the Barrier Reef is living and provides an ecosystem for small marine creatures. Bumping against or touching the coral can kill these creatures as well as damage the reef itself.

daily lunch. Guided fishing trips can be done for a half day or full day. Packages combining fishing and accommodations at Islander Resort are available. ⊠ *Green Turtle, MM 81.2, 81219 Overseas Hwy., Upper Matecumbe Key* ☎ *305/664–5423* ⊕ *www.floridakeysoutfitters.com* ⌦ *Half-day trips from $550.*

Miss Islamorada

FISHING | This 65-foot party boat offers full-day trips. Bring your lunch or buy one from the dockside deli. ⊠ *Bud N' Mary's Marina, MM 79.8 OS, 79851 Overseas Hwy., Upper Matecumbe Key* ☎ *305/664–2461, 800/742–7945* ⊕ *www.budnmarys.com* ⌦ *$70.*

SCUBA DIVING AND SNORKELING

San Pedro Underwater Archaeological Preserve State Park

SCUBA DIVING | About 1¼ nautical miles south of Indian Key is the San Pedro Underwater Archaeological Preserve State Park, which includes the remains of a Spanish treasure-fleet ship that sank in 1733. The state of Florida protects the site for divers; no spearfishing or souvenir collecting is allowed. Seven replica cannons and a plaque enhance what basically amounts to a 90-foot-long pile of ballast stones. Resting in only 18 feet of water, its ruins are visible to snorkelers as well as divers and attract a colorful array of fish. ⊠ *MM 85.5 OS* ☎ *305/664–2540* ⊕ *www.floridastateparks.org/parks-and-trails/san-pedro-underwater-archaeological-preserve-state-park.*

Florida Keys Dive Center

SCUBA DIVING | Dive from John Pennekamp Coral Reef State Park to Alligator Reef with this outfitter. The center has two 46-foot Coast Guard–approved dive boats, offers scuba training, and is one of the few Keys dive centers to offer nitrox and trimix (mixed-gas) diving. ⊠ *MM 90.5 OS, 90451 Overseas Hwy., Plantation Key* ☎ *305/852–4599, 800/433–8946* ⊕ *www.floridakeysdivectr.com* ⌦ *Snorkeling from $38, diving from $84.*

Islamorada Dive Center

SCUBA DIVING | This one-stop dive shop has a resort, pool, restaurant, lessons, and twice-daily dive and snorkel trips and the newest fleet in the Keys. You can take a day trip with a two-tank dive or a one-tank night trip with their equipment or yours. Snorkel and spearfishing trips are also available. ⊠ *MM 84 OS, 84001 Overseas Hwy., Windley Key* ☎ *305/664–3483, 800/327–7070* ⊕ *www.islamoradadivecenter.com* ⌦ *Snorkel trips from $45, diving from $85.*

WATER SPORTS

The Kayak Shack

WATER SPORTS | You can rent kayaks for trips to Indian (about 20 minutes one-way) and Lignumvitae (about 45 minutes one-way) keys, two favorite destinations for paddlers. Kayaks can be rented for a half day (and you'll need plenty of time to explore those mangrove canopies). The company also offers guided two-hour Jet Ski tours, including a snorkel trip to Indian Key or backcountry ecotours. It also rents stand-up paddleboards, including instruction, and canoes. ⊠ *Robbie's Marina, MM 77.5 BS, 77522 Overseas Hwy., Lower Matecumbe Key* ☎ *305/664–4878* ⊕ *www.kayakthefloridakeys.com* ⌦ *From $40 for single, $55 for double; guided trips from $45.*

Duck Key

MM 61.

Duck Key holds one of the region's nicest marina resorts, Hawks Cay, plus a boating-oriented residential community.

🍴 Restaurants

Sixty-One Prime

$$$$ | **AMERICAN** | This fine-dining restaurant in Hawks Cay Resort serves steaks and seafood in an elegant setting. Chefs work with local farmers and fishermen to find what's fresh and in season, then

Did You Know?

Dolphins in Florida are predominantly of the Atlantic bottlenose variety. These playful and smart creatures love to leap out of the water and synchronize their movements with others. By swimming next to boats, dolphins can conserve energy.

create a menu that will wow your palate (and your wallet). **Known for:** naturally raised certified Black Angus beef; nightly changing menu; attentive service. $ *Average main: $36 ⊠ Hawks Cay Resort, 61 Hawks Cay Blvd. ☎ 305/743–7000, 888/432–2242 ⊕ www.hawkscay.com* ⦵ *No lunch.*

 Hotels

★ **Hawks Cay Resort**
$$$ | RESORT | FAMILY | The 60-acre, Caribbean-style retreat with a full-service spa and two restaurants has plenty to keep the kids occupied (and adults happy). **Pros:** huge rooms; restful spa; full-service marina and dive shop. **Cons:** no real beach; far from Marathon's attractions; tram gets busy so either wait or walk far. $ *Rooms from: $315 ⊠ MM 61 OS, 61 Hawks Cay Blvd. ☎ 305/743–7000, 888/432–2242 ⊕ www.hawkscay.com* ⇨ *431 units* ⦿ *No meals.*

Grassy Key

MM 60–57.

Local lore has it that this sleepy little key was named not for its vegetation—mostly native trees and shrubs—but for an early settler by the name of Grassy. A few families operating small fishing camps and roadside motels primarily inhabit the key. There's no marked definition between it and Marathon, so it feels sort of like a suburb of its much larger neighbor to the south. Grassy Key's sights tend toward the natural, including a worthwhile dolphin attraction and a small state park.

GETTING HERE AND AROUND
Most visitors arriving by air drive to this destination either from Miami International Airport or Key West International Airport. Rental cars are readily available at both, and in the long run, are the most convenient means of transportation for getting here and touring around the Keys.

 Sights

Curry Hammock State Park
NATIONAL/STATE PARK | Looking for a slice of the Keys that's far removed from tiki bars? On the ocean and bay sides of Overseas Highway are 260 acres of upland hammock, wetlands, and mangroves. On the bay side, there's a trail through thick hardwoods to a rocky shoreline. The ocean side is more developed, with a sandy beach, a clean bathhouse, picnic tables, a playground, grills, and a 28-site campground, each with electric and water. Locals consider the paddling trails under canopies of arching mangroves one of the best kayaking spots in the Keys. Manatees frequent the area, and it's a great spot for bird-watching. Herons, egrets, ibis, plovers, and sanderlings are commonly spotted. Raptors are often seen in the park, especially during migration periods. ⊠ *MM 57 OS, 56200 Overseas Hwy., Little Crawl Key ☎ 305/289–2690 ⊕ www. floridastateparks.org/parks-and-trails/ curry-hammock-state-park* $ *$4.50 for 1 person, $6 for 2, $0.50 per additional person* ⇨ *Campsites are $43 per night.*

Dolphin Research Center
ZOO | FAMILY | The 1963 movie *Flipper* popularized the notion of humans interacting with dolphins, and Milton Santini, the film's creator, also opened this center, which is home to a colony of dolphins and sea lions. The nonprofit center has educational sessions and programs that allow you to greet the dolphins from dry land or play with them in their watery habitat. You can even paint a T-shirt with a dolphin—you pick the paint, the dolphin "designs" your shirt. The center also offers five-day programs for children and adults with disabilities. ⊠ *MM 59 BS, 58901 Overseas Hwy. ☎ 305/289–1121 information, 305/289–0002 reservations* ⊕ *www.dolphins.org* ⤳ *$28.*

Restaurants

Hideaway Café

$$$ | AMERICAN | It's easy to miss this café tucked between Grassy Key and Marathon, but when you find it (upstairs at Rainbow Bend Resort), you'll discover a favorite of locals who appreciate a well-planned menu, lovely ocean view, and quiet evening away from the crowds. For starters, dig into escargots à la Edison (sautéed with vegetables, pepper, cognac, and cream) before feasting on several specialties, such as a rarely found chateaubriand for one, or the seafood medley combining the catch of the day with scallops and shrimp. **Known for:** seclusion and quiet; amazing escargot; hand-cut steaks and fresh fish. $ *Average main: $30* ⊠ *Rainbow Bend Resort, MM 58 OS, 57784 Overseas Hwy.* ☎ *305/289–1554* ⊕ *www.hideawaycafe. com* ☾ *No lunch.*

Marathon

MM 53–47.5.

New Englanders founded this former fishing village in the early 1800s. The community on Vaca Key subsequently served as a base for pirates, salvagers (also known as "wreckers"), spongers, and, later, Bahamian farmers who eked out a living growing cotton and other crops. More Bahamians arrived in the hope of finding work building the railroad. According to local lore, Marathon was renamed when a worker commented that it was a marathon task to position the tracks across the 6-mile-long island.

During the building of the railroad, Marathon developed a reputation for lawlessness that rivaled that of the Old West. It is said that to keep the rowdy workers from descending on Key West for their off-hours endeavors, residents would send boatloads of liquor up to Marathon.

Needless to say, things have quieted down considerably since then.

Still, Marathon is a bustling town, at least compared to other communities in the Keys. As it leaves something to be desired in the charm department, Marathon may not be your first choice of places to stay, but water-sports types will find plenty to enjoy, and its historic and natural attractions merit a visit. Surprisingly good dining options abound, so you'll definitely want to stop for a bite even if you're just passing through on the way to Key West.

Throughout the year, Marathon hosts fishing tournaments (practically monthly), a huge seafood festival in March, and lighted boat parades around the holidays.

GETTING HERE AND AROUND

SuperShuttle charges $102 per passenger for trips from Miami International Airport to the Upper Keys. To go farther into the Keys, you must book an entire 11-person van, which costs about $280 to Marathon. For a trip to the airport, place your request 24 hours in advance. *See Getting Here and Around: Bus Travel.*

VISITOR INFORMATION

CONTACT Greater Marathon Chamber of Commerce and Visitor Center. ⊠ *MM 53.5 BS, 12222 Overseas Hwy.* ☎ *305/743–5417, 800/262–7284* ⊕ *www.florida-keysmarathon.com.*

◉ Sights

Crane Point Museum, Nature Center, and Historic Site

MUSEUM | FAMILY | Tucked away from the highway behind a stand of trees, Crane Point—part of a 63-acre tract that contains the last-known undisturbed thatch-palm hammock—is delightfully undeveloped. This multiuse facility includes the **Museum of Natural History of the Florida Keys,** which has displays about local wildlife, a seashell exhibit, and a marine-life display that makes you feel like you're at the bottom of the sea. Kids love the replica 17th-century galleon and pirate dress-up room where they can play, and the re-created **Cracker House** filled with insects, sea-turtle exhibits, and children's activities. On the 1-mile indigenous loop trail, visit the **Laura Quinn Wild Bird Center** and the remnants of a Bahamian village, site of the restored **George Adderly House.** It is the oldest surviving example of Bahamian tabby (a concretelike material created from sand and seashells) construction outside Key West. A boardwalk crosses wetlands, rivers, and mangroves before ending at Adderly Village. From November to Easter, docent-led tours are available; bring good walking shoes and bug repellent during warm weather. ✉ *MM 50.5 BS, 5550 Overseas Hwy.* ☎ *305/743–9100* ⊕ *www.cranepoint.net* 🎟 *$14.95.*

Florida Keys Aquarium Encounters
LOCAL INTEREST | FAMILY | This isn't your typical large-city aquarium. It's more hands-on and personal, and it's all outdoors with several tiki huts to house the encounters and provide shade as you explore, rain or shine; plan to spend at least two to three hours here. You'll find a 200,000-gallon aquarium and plenty of marine encounters (extra cost), as well as guided tours, viewing areas, and a predator tank. The Coral Reef encounter ($95 snorkel, $130 regulator) lets you dive in a reef environment without hearing the theme from *Jaws* in your head (although you can see several sharks on the other side of the glass). Touch tanks are great for all ages and even have unique critters like slipper lobsters. Hungry? The on-site Eagle Ray Cafe serves up wings, fish tacos, salads, burgers, and more. Note that general admission is required, even if you're signed up for a marine encounter. ✉ *MM 53 BS, 11710 Overseas Hwy.* ☎ *305/407–3262* ⊕ *www.floridakeysaquariumencounters.com* 🎟 *$20.*

Pigeon Key
HISTORIC SITE | There's much to like about this 5-acre island under the Old Seven Mile Bridge. You might even recognize it from a season finale of the TV show *The Amazing Race.* You can reach it via a ferry that departs from their new gift shop location, a trailer at mile marker 47.5. Once there, tour the island on your own or join a guided tour to explore the buildings that formed the early-20th-century work camp for the Overseas Railroad that linked the mainland to Key West in 1912. Later the island became a fish camp, a state park, and then government-administration headquarters. Exhibits in a small museum recall the history of the Keys, the railroad, and railroad baron Henry M. Flagler. The ferry ride with tour lasts two hours; visitors can self-tour and catch the ferry back in a half hour. ■ TIP→ **Bring your own snorkel gear and dive flag and you can snorkel right from the shore.** Pack a picnic lunch, too. ✉ *MM 47.5 BS, between the Marriott and Hyatt Place, 2010 Overseas Hwy., Pigeon Key* ☎ *305/743–5999* ⊕ *pigeonkey.net* 🎟 *$12.*

Seven Mile Bridge
BRIDGE/TUNNEL | This is one of the most photographed images in the Keys. Actually measuring slightly less than 7 miles, it connects the Middle and Lower Keys and is believed to be the world's longest segmental bridge. It has 39 expansion joints separating its various concrete sections. Each April runners gather in Marathon for the annual Seven Mile Bridge Run. The expanse running parallel to Seven Mile Bridge is what remains of the **Old Seven Mile Bridge,** an engineering and architectural marvel in its day that's now on the National Register of Historic Places. Once proclaimed the Eighth Wonder of the World, it rested on a record 546 concrete piers. No cars are allowed on the old bridge today. ✉ *Marathon.*

The Turtle Hospital
COLLEGE | FAMILY | More than 100 injured sea turtles check in here every year. The

90-minute guided tours take you into recovery and surgical areas at the world's only state-certified veterinary hospital for sea turtles. In the "hospital bed" tanks, you can see recovering patients and others that are permanent residents due to their injuries. After the tour, you can feed some of the residents. Call ahead—space is limited and tours are sometimes canceled due to medical emergencies. The turtle ambulance out front makes for a memorable souvenir photo. ✉ *MM 48.5 BS, 2396 Overseas Hwy.* ☎ *305/743–2552* 🌐 *www.turtlehospital.org* 🎟 *$25.*

Beaches

Sombrero Beach

BEACH—SIGHT | **FAMILY** | No doubt one of the best beaches in the Keys, here you'll find pleasant, shaded picnic areas that overlook a coconut palm–lined grassy stretch and the Atlantic Ocean. Roped-off areas allow swimmers, boaters, and windsurfers to share the narrow cove. Facilities include barbecue grills, a large playground, a pier, a volleyball court, and a paved, lighted bike path off Overseas Highway. Sunday afternoons draw lots of local families toting coolers. The park is accessible for those with disabilities and allows leashed pets. Turn east at the traffic light in Marathon and follow signs to the end. **Amenities:** showers; toilets. **Best for:** swimming; windsurfing. ✉ *MM 50 OS, Sombrero Beach Rd.* ☎ *305/743–0033* 🎟 *Free.*

Restaurants

Fish Tales Market and Eatery

$ | **SEAFOOD** | This no-frills, roadside eatery has a loyal local following, an unfussy ambience, a couple of outside picnic tables, and friendly service. Signature dishes include snapper on grilled rye with coleslaw and melted Muenster cheese, a fried fish burrito, George's crab cake, and tomato-based conch chowder. **Known for:** luscious lobster bisque; fresh and affordable seafood and meat market; affordable dinner specials. [$] *Average main: $10* ✉ *MM 52.5 OS, 11711 Overseas Hwy.* ☎ *305/743–9196, 888/662–4822* 🕒 *Closed Sun. No dinner Sat.*

Key Colony Inn

$$ | **ITALIAN** | The inviting aroma of an Italian kitchen pervades this family-owned favorite known for its Sunday brunch, served November through April. For lunch there are fish and steak entrées served with fries, salad, and bread in addition to Italian specialties. **Known for:** friendly and attentive service; Italian specialties; Sunday brunch. [$] *Average main: $20* ✉ *MM 54 OS, 700 W. Ocean Dr., Key Colony Beach* ☎ *305/743–0100* 🌐 *www.kcinn.com.*

Keys Fisheries Market & Marina

$$ | **SEAFOOD** | **FAMILY** | You can't miss the enormous tiki bar on stilts, but the walk-up window on the ground floor is the heart of this warehouse turned restaurant. A huge lobster Reuben served on thick slices of toasted bread is the signature dish, and the adults-only upstairs tiki bar offers a sushi and raw bar for eat-in only. **Known for:** seafood market; marina views; fish-food dispensers (25¢) so you can feed the tarpon. [$] *Average main: $16* ✉ *MM 49 BS, 3390 Gulfview Ave., at the end of 35th St.* ✥ *Turn onto 35th St. from Overseas Hwy.* ☎ *305/743–4353, 866/743–4353* 🌐 *www.keysfisheries.com.*

★ Lazy Days South

$$$ | **SEAFOOD** | Tucked into Marathon Marina a half mile north of the Seven Mile Bridge, this restaurant offers views just as spectacular as its highly lauded food. A spin-off of an Islamorada favorite, here you'll find a wide range of daily offerings from fried or sautéed conch and a coconut-fried fish du jour sandwich to seafood pastas and beef tips over rice. **Known for:** water views; delicious seafood entrées; hook and cook. [$] *Average main: $22* ✉ *MM 47.3 OS, 725 11th St.* ☎ *305/289–0839* 🌐 *www.new.lazy-dayssouth.com.*

The Stuffed Pig

$ | **DINER** | With only nine tables and a counter inside, this breakfast-and-lunch place is always hopping. The kitchen whips up daily lunch specials like seafood platters or pulled pork with hand-cut fries, but the all-day breakfast is the main draw. **Known for:** pig's breakfast special; daily lunch specials; large portions. [$] *Average main: $9* ✉ *MM 49 BS, 3520 Overseas Hwy.* ☎ *305/743–4059* 🌐 *www.thestuffedpig.com* 💳 *No credit cards* 🕒 *No dinner.*

Sunset Grille & Raw Bar

$$$ | **SEAFOOD** | Treat yourself to a seafood lunch or dinner at this vaulted tiki hut at the foot of the Seven Mile Bridge. For lunch, try the Voodoo grouper sandwich topped with mango-guava mayo (and wear your swimsuit if you want to take a dip in the pool afterward). **Known for:** weekend pool parties and barbecues; pricey dinner specials; a swimming pool for patrons. [$] *Average main: $22* ✉ *MM 47 OS, 7 Knights Key Blvd.* ☎ *305/396–7235* 🌐 *www.sunsetgrille7milebridge.com.*

Hotels

Glunz Ocean Beach Hotel & Resort

$$ | **RENTAL** | The Glunz family got it right when they purchased this former time-share property and put a whole lot of love into renovating it to its full ocean-front potential. **Pros:** no resort fees, ever; nice private beach; excellent free Wi-Fi. **Cons:** small elevator; no interior corridors; not cheap. [$] *Rooms from: $300* ✉ *MM 53.5 OS, 351 E. Ocean Dr., Key Colony Beach* ☎ *305/289–0525* 🌐 *www.GlunzOceanBeachHotel.com* 🛏 *46 units* 🍴 *No meals.*

★ **Tranquility Bay**

$$$$ | **RESORT** | **FAMILY** | Ralph Lauren could have designed the rooms at this stylish, luxurious resort on a nice beach. **Pros:** secluded setting; tiki bar on the beach; main pool is nice and big. **Cons:** a bit sterile; no privacy on balconies; cramped building layout. [$] *Rooms from: $425* ✉ *MM 48.5 BS, 2600 Overseas Hwy.* ☎ *305/289–0888, 866/643–5397* 🌐 *www.tranquilitybay.com* 🛏 *102 rooms* 🍴 *No meals.*

Activities

BIKING

Tooling around on two wheels is a good way to see Marathon. There's easy cycling on a 1-mile off-road path that connects to the 2 miles of the Old Seven Mile Bridge leading to Pigeon Key.

Bike Marathon Bike Rentals

BICYCLING | "Have bikes, will deliver" could be the motto of this company, which gets beach cruisers to your hotel door, including a helmet, basket, and lock. It also rents kayaks. There's no physical location, but services are available Monday through Saturday 9–4 and Sunday 9–2. ✉ *Marathon* ☎ *305/743–3204* 🌐 *www.bikemarathonbikerentals.com* 🎟 *$45 per wk.*

BOATING

Sail, motor, or paddle: whatever your choice of modes, boating is what the Keys is all about. Brave the Atlantic waves and reefs or explore the back-country islands on the gulf side. If you don't have a lot of boating and chart-reading experience, it's a good idea to tap into local knowledge on a charter.

Captain Pip's

BOATING | This operator rents 18- to 24-foot outboards as well as snorkeling gear. Ask about multiday deals, or try one of the accommodation packages and walk right from your bay-front room to your boat. ✉ *MM 47.5 BS, 1410 Overseas Hwy.* ☎ *305/743–4403, 800/707–1692* 🌐 *www.captainpips.com* 🎟 *Rentals from $199 per day.*

Fish'n Fun

BOATING | Get out on the water on 19- to 26-foot powerboats. Rentals can be for a half or full day. The company also offers free delivery in the Middle Keys. ☒ Duck Key Marina, MM 61 OS, 1149 Greenbriar Rd. ☎ 305/743–2275, 800/471–3440 ⊕ www.fishnfunrentals.com ☜ From $175.

FISHING

For recreational anglers, the deepwater fishing is superb in both bay and ocean. Marathon West Hump, one good spot, has depths ranging from 500 to more than 1,000 feet. Locals fish from a half dozen bridges, including Long Key Bridge, the Old Seven Mile Bridge, and both ends of Tom's Harbor. Barracuda, bonefish, and tarpon all frequent local waters. Party boats and private charters are available.

Marathon Lady

FISHING | Morning, afternoon, and night, fish for mahimahi, grouper, and other tasty catch aboard this 73-footer, which departs on half-day excursions from the Vaca Cut Bridge (MM 53), north of Marathon. Join the crew for night fishing ($55) from 6:30 to midnight from Memorial Day to Labor Day; it's especially beautiful on a full-moon night. ☒ MM 53 OS, 11711 Overseas Hwy., at 117th St. ☎ 305/743–5580 ⊕ www.marathonlady.net ☜ From $45.

Sea Dog Charters

FISHING | Captain Jim Purcell, a deep-sea specialist for ESPN's The American Outdoorsman, provides one of the best values in Keys fishing. Next to the Seven Mile Grill, his company offers half- and full-day offshore, reef and wreck, and backcountry fishing trips, as well as fishing and snorkeling trips aboard 30- to 37-foot boats. The per-person cost for a half-day trip is the same regardless of whether your group fills the boat, and includes bait, light tackle, ice, coolers, and fishing licenses. If you prefer an all-day private charter on a 37-foot boat, he offers those, too, for up to six people. A fuel surcharge may apply. ☒ MM 47.5 BS,

1248 Overseas Hwy. ☎ 305/743–8255 ⊕ www.seadogcharters.net ☜ From $60.

SCUBA DIVING AND SNORKELING

Local dive operations take you to Sombrero Reef and Lighthouse, the most popular down-under destination in these parts. For a shallow dive and some lobster nabbing, Coffins Patch, off Key Colony Beach, is a good choice. A number of wrecks such as Thunderbolt serve as artificial reefs. Many operations out of this area will also take you to Looe Key Reef.

Hall's Diving Center & Career Institute

SCUBA DIVING | The institute has been training divers for more than 40 years. Along with conventional twice-a-day snorkel and two-tank dive trips to the reefs at Sombrero Lighthouse and wrecks like the Thunderbolt, the company has more unusual offerings like rebreather, photography, and nitrox courses. ☒ MM 48.5 BS, 1994 Overseas Hwy. ☎ 305/743–5929, 800/331–4255 ⊕ www.hallsdiving.com ☜ From $45.

Spirit Snorkeling

SCUBA DIVING | Join regularly scheduled snorkeling excursions to Sombrero Reef and Lighthouse Reef on this company's comfortable catamaran. It also offers sunset cruises and private charters. ☒ MM 47.5 BS, 1410 Overseas Hwy., Slip No. 1 ☎ 305/289–0614 ⊕ www.captainpips. com ☜ From $30.

Tildens Scuba Center

SCUBA DIVING | Since the mid-1980s, Tildens Scuba Center has been providing lessons, tours, gear rental, and daily snorkel, scuba, and Snuba adventures. Look for the huge, colorful angelfish sculpture outside the building. ☒ MM 49.5 BS, 4650 Overseas Hwy. ☎ 305/743–7255, 888/728–2235 ☜ From $60 for snorkel trips; from $70 for dive trips.

Did You Know?

An old railroad bridge connected Bahia Honda Key with Key West until a hurricane destroyed it in 1935. The bridge is no longer in operation, yet it's standing, barely. Falling debris prevents snorkeling or exploring below, but it makes for pretty photos, especially at sunrise and sunset.

Bahia Honda Key

MM 38.5–36.

All of Bahia Honda Key is devoted to its eponymous state park, which keeps it in a pristine state. Besides the park's outdoor activities, it offers an up-close view of the original railroad bridge.

Sights

⭐ Bahia Honda State Park

NATIONAL/STATE PARK | **FAMILY** | Most first-time visitors to the region are dismayed by the lack of beaches—but then they discover Bahia Honda Key. The 524-acre park sprawls across both sides of the highway, giving it 2½ miles of fabulous sandy coastline. The snorkeling isn't bad, either; there's underwater life (soft coral, queen conchs, random little fish) just a few hundred feet offshore. Seasonal ranger-led nature programs take place at or depart from the Sand and Sea Nature Center. There are rental cabins, a campground, snack bar, gift shop, 19-slip marina, nature center, and facilities for renting kayaks and arranging snorkeling tours. Get a panoramic view of the island from what's left of the railroad—the Bahia Honda Bridge. ✉ *MM 37 OS, 36850 Overseas Hwy.* ☎ *305/872–2353* ⊕ *www.floridastateparks.org/park/Bahia-Honda* 🎟 *$4.50 for single-occupant vehicle, $8 for vehicle with 2–8 people, plus $0.50 per person up to 8.*

Beaches

Sandspur Beach

BEACH—SIGHT | Bahia Honda Key State Beach contains three beaches in all—on both the Atlantic Ocean and the Gulf of Mexico. Scheduled to reopen in June 2019 after being devastated by Hurricane Irma, Sandspur Beach, the largest, is regularly declared the best beach in the Florida Keys, and you'll be hard-pressed to argue. The sand is baby-powder soft, and the aqua water is warm, clear, and shallow. With their mild currents, the beaches are great for swimming, even with small fry. **Amenities:** food and drink; showers; toilets; water sports. **Best for:** snorkeling; swimming. ✉ *MM 37 OS, 36850 Overseas Hwy.* ☎ *305/872–2353* ⊕ *www.floridastateparks.org/park/Bahia-Honda* 🎟 *$4.50 for single-occupant vehicle, $9 for vehicle with 2–8 people.*

Hotels

Bahia Honda State Park Cabins

$ | **RENTAL** | Elsewhere you'd pay big bucks for the wonderful water views available at these cabins on Florida Bay. Each of three cabins has two, two-bedroom units with a full kitchen and bath and air-conditioning (but no television, radio, or phone). **Pros:** great bay-front views; beachfront camping; affordable rates. **Cons:** books up fast; area can be buggy. 🅢 *Rooms from: $163* ✉ *MM 37 OS, 36850 Overseas Hwy.* ☎ *305/872–2353, 800/326–3521* ⊕ *www.reserveamerica.com* 🛏 *6 cabins* 🍽 *No meals.*

Activities

Bahia Honda Dive Shop

SCUBA DIVING | The concessionaire at Bahia Honda State Park manages a 19-slip marina; rents wet suits, snorkel equipment, and corrective masks; and operates twice-daily offshore-reef snorkel trips. Park visitors looking for other fun can rent kayaks and beach chairs. ✉ *MM 37 OS, 36850 Overseas Hwy.* ☎ *305/872–3210* ⊕ *www.bahiahondapark.com* ☞ *Kayak rentals from $10 per hr; snorkel tours from $30.*

Big Pine Key

MM 32–30.

Welcome to the Keys' most natural holdout, where wildlife refuges protect rare and endangered animals. Here you have left behind the commercialism of the Upper Keys for an authentic back-country atmosphere. How could things get more casual than Key Largo, you might wonder? Find out by exiting U.S. 1 to explore the habitat of the charmingly diminutive Key deer or cast a line from No Name Bridge. Tours explore the expansive waters of National Key Deer Refuge and Great White Heron National Wildlife Refuge, one of the first such refuges in the country. Along with Key West National Wildlife Refuge, it encompasses more than 200,000 acres of water and more than 8,000 acres of land on 49 small islands. Besides its namesake bird, the Great White Heron National Wildlife Refuge provides habitat for uncounted species of birds and three species of sea turtles. It is the only U.S. breeding site for the endangered hawksbill turtle.

GETTING HERE AND AROUND
Most people rent a car to get to Big Pine Key so they can also explore Key West and other parts of the chain.

VISITOR INFORMATION
CONTACT Big Pine and the Lower Keys Chamber of Commerce. ⊠ *31020 Overseas Hwy.* ☎ *305/872–2411, 800/872–3722* ⊕ *www.lowerkeyschamber.com.*

◉ Sights

National Key Deer Refuge
NATURE PRESERVE | This 84,824-acre refuge was established in 1957 to protect the dwindling population of the Key deer, one of more than 22 animals and plants federally classified as endangered or threatened, including five that are found nowhere else on Earth. The Key deer, which stands about 30 inches at the shoulders and is a subspecies of the Virginia white-tailed deer, once roamed throughout the Lower and Middle Keys, but hunting, destruction of their habitat, and a growing human population caused their numbers to decline to 27 by 1957. The deer have made a comeback,

increasing their numbers to approximately 750. The best place to see Key deer in the refuge is at the end of Key Deer Boulevard and on No Name Key, a sparsely populated island just east of Big Pine Key. Mornings and evenings are the best time to spot them. Deer may turn up along the road at any time of day, so drive slowly. They wander into nearby yards to nibble tender grass and bougainvillea blossom, but locals do not appreciate tourists driving into their neighborhoods after them. Feeding them is against the law and puts them in danger.

A quarry left over from railroad days, the **Blue Hole** is the largest body of freshwater in the Keys. From the observation platform and nearby walking trail, you might see the resident alligator, turtles, and other wildlife. There are two well-marked trails, recently revamped: the Jack Watson Nature Trail (0.6 mile), named after an environmentalist and the refuge's first warden; and the Fred Mannillo Nature Trail (0.2 mile), one of the most wheelchair-accessible places to see an unspoiled pine-rockland forest and wetlands. The visitor center has exhibits on Keys biology and ecology. The refuge also provides information on the Key West National Wildlife Refuge and the Great White Heron National Wildlife Refuge. Accessible only by water, both are popular with kayak outfitters. ⊠ *Visitor Center–Headquarters, Big Pine Shopping Center, MM 30.5 BS, 28950 Watson Blvd.* ☎ *305/872–2239* ⊕ *www.fws.gov/ nationalkeydeer* ⊠ *Free* ⊙ *Visitor center closed Sun. and Mon.*

Restaurants

Good Food Conspiracy
$ | VEGETARIAN | Like good wine, this small natural-foods eatery and market surrenders its pleasures a little at a time. Step inside to the aroma of brewing coffee, and then pick up the scent of fresh strawberries or carrots blending into a

smoothie, the green aroma of wheatgrass juice, followed by the earthy odor of hummus. **Known for:** vegetarian and vegan dishes; sandwiches and smoothies; organic items. $ *Average main: $10* ✉ *MM 30.2 OS, 30150 Overseas Hwy.* ☎ *305/872–3945* ⊕ *www.goodfoodconspiracy.com* ✪ *No dinner Sun.*

No Name Pub

$$ | AMERICAN | This no-frills honky-tonk has been around since 1936, delighting inveterate locals and intrepid vacationers who come for the excellent pizza, cold beer, and *interesting* companionship. The decor, such as it is, amounts to the autographed dollar bills that cover every inch of the place. **Known for:** shrimp pizza and fish sandwich; local and tourist favorite; decor of dollar bills. $ *Average main: $15* ✉ *MM 30 BS, 30813 Watson Blvd.* ⊹ *From U.S. 1, turn west on Wilder Rd., left on South St., right on Ave. B, right on Watson Blvd.* ☎ *305/872–9115* ⊕ *www. nonamepub.com.*

Hotels

Big Pine Key Fishing Lodge

$ | HOTEL | There's a congenial atmosphere at this lively, family-owned lodge-campground-marina—a happy mix of tent campers (who have the fabulous waterfront real estate), RVers (who look pretty permanent), and motel dwellers who like to mingle at the rooftop pool and challenge each other to a game of poker. **Pros:** local fishing crowd; nice pool; great price. **Cons:** RV park is too close to motel; deer will eat your food if you're camping; trees and trails recovering from Hurricane Irma. $ *Rooms from: $134* ✉ *MM 33 OS, 33000 Overseas Hwy.* ☎ *305/872–2351* ⊕ *www.bpkfl.com* ➪ *16 rooms* ☉ *No meals* ☞ *To protect Key deer, no dogs allowed.*

Deer Run Bed & Breakfast

$$$ | B&B/INN | Although Hurricane Irma came ashore here in 2017, the owners of Deer Run have made lemonade from Irma's lemons with a new raised addition that sits adjacent to the main building and houses three guest rooms, all with ocean views, cathedral ceilings, king beds, private baths, small porches, and calming decor. **Pros:** quiet neighborhood; vegan, organic breakfasts; complimentary use of bikes, kayaks, beach towels, and state park passes. **Cons:** major deforestation and loss of mangroves from hurricane; a little hard to find; may be too secluded for some. $ *Rooms from: $375* ✉ *MM 33 OS, 1997 Long Beach Dr.* ☎ *305/872–2015* ⊕ *www. deerrunfloridabb.com* ➪ *4 rooms* ☉ *Free Breakfast.*

Activities

BIKING

A good 10 miles of paved roads run from MM 30.3 BS, along Wilder Road, across the bridge to No Name Key, and along Key Deer Boulevard into the National Key Deer Refuge. Along the way you might see some Key deer. Stay off the trails that lead into wetlands, where fat tires can damage the environment.

Big Pine Bicycle Center

BICYCLING | Owner Marty Baird is an avid cyclist and enjoys sharing his knowledge of great places to ride. He's also skilled at selecting the right bike for the journey, and he knows his repairs, too. His old-fashioned single-speed, fat-tire cruisers rent by the half or full day. Helmets, baskets, and locks are included. ✉ *MM 30.9 BS, 31 County Rd.* ☎ *305/872–0130* ⊕ *www.bigpinebikes.com* 🎟 *From $10.*

FISHING

Cast from No Name Key Bridge or hire a charter to take you into backcountry or deep waters for fishing year-round.

Captain Hook's Looe Key Reef Adventures and Strike Zone Charters

BOATING | Glass-bottom-boat excursions venture into the backcountry and Atlantic Ocean. The five-hour Out Island Excursion and Picnic emphasizes nature and Keys history; besides close encounters with birds, sea life, and vegetation, there's a fish cookout on an island. Snorkel and fishing equipment, food, and drinks are included. This is one of the few nature outings in the Keys with wheelchair access. Deep-sea charter rates for up to six people can be arranged for a half or full day. It also offers flats fishing in the Gulf of Mexico. Dive excursions head to the wreck of the 110-foot *Adolphus Busch,* and scuba and snorkel trips to Looe Key Reef, prime scuba and snorkeling territory, aboard glass-bottom boats. ✉ *MM 29.6 BS, 29675 Overseas Hwy.* ☎ *305/872–9863, 800/654–9560* 🌐 *www.captainhooks.com* 🎟 *From $38.*

KAYAKING

There's nothing like the vast expanse of pristine waters and mangrove islands preserved by national refuges from here to Key West. The mazelike terrain can be confusing, so it's wise to hire a guide at least the first time out.

Big Pine Kayak Adventures
KAYAKING | There's no excuse to skip a water adventure with this convenient kayak rental service, which delivers them to your lodging or anywhere between Seven Mile Bridge and Stock Island. The company, headed by *The Florida Keys Paddling Guide* author Bill Keogh, will rent you a kayak and then ferry you—called taxi-yakking—to remote islands with clear instructions on how to paddle back on your own. Rentals are by the half day or full day. Three-hour group kayak tours are the cheapest option and explore the mangrove forests of Great White Heron and Key Deer National Wildlife Refuges. More expensive four-hour custom tours transport you to exquisite backcountry areas teeming with wildlife. Kayak fishing charters are also popular. Paddleboard ecotours, rentals, and yoga are available. ✉ *Old Wooden Bridge Fishing Camp, 1791 Bogie Dr.* ✣ *From MM 30, turn right at traffic light, continue on Wilder Rd. toward No Name Key; the fishing camp is just before the bridge with a big yellow kayak on the sign out front* ☎ *305/872–7474* 🌐 *www.keyskayaktours.com* 🎟 *From $50.*

Little Torch Key

MM 29–10.

Little Torch Key and its neighbor islands, Ramrod Key and Summerland Key, are good jumping-off points for divers headed for Looe Key Reef. The islands also serve as a refuge for those who want to make forays into Key West but not stay in the thick of things.

The undeveloped backcountry at your door makes Little Torch Key an ideal location for fishing and kayaking. Nearby **Ramrod Key,** which also caters to divers bound for Looe Key, derives its name from a ship that wrecked on nearby reefs in the early 1800s.

🍴 Restaurants

Baby's Coffee
$ | **AMERICAN** | The aroma of rich, roasting coffee beans arrests you at the door of "the Southernmost Coffee Roaster in America." Buy beans by the pound or coffee by the cup, along with sandwiches and sweets. **Known for:** best coffee in the Keys; gluten-free, vegan, and vegetarian specialty foods; excellent service. [$] *Average main: $8* ✉ *MM 15 OS, 3180 Overseas Hwy.* ☎ *305/744–9866, 800/523–2326* 🌐 *www.babyscoffee.com.*

Geiger Key Smokehouse Bar & Grill
$$ | **AMERICAN** | There's a strong hint of the Old Keys at this ocean-side marina restaurant, where local fisherman stop for breakfast before heading out to catch the big one, and everyone shows up on Sunday for the barbecue from 4 to 9. "On the backside of paradise," as the sign says, its tiki structures overlook quiet mangroves at an RV park marina. **Known for:** Sunday barbecue; casual atmosphere

on the water; conch fritters loaded with conch. [$] *Average main: $16* ✉ *MM 10, 5 Geiger Key Rd., off Boca Chica Rd., Bay Point* ☎ *305/296–3553, 305/294–1230* 🌐 *www.geigerkeymarina.com.*

Mangrove Mama's Restaurant
$$ | SEAFOOD | This could be the prototype for a Keys restaurant, given its shanty appearance, lattice trim, and roving sort of indoor-outdoor floor plan. Then there's the seafood, from the ubiquitous fish sandwich (fried, grilled, broiled, or blackened) to lobster Reubens, crab cakes, and coconut shrimp. **Known for:** pizza; award-winning conch chowder; slow service. [$] *Average main: $20* ✉ *MM 20 BS, Sugarloaf Key* ☎ *305/745–3030* 🌐 *www.mangrovemamasrestaurant.com.*

★ **My New Joint**
$ | AMERICAN | Atop the famed Square Grouper restaurant is a secret spot that locals love and smart travelers seek out for its tapas and well-stocked bar. Sit at a high-top table or on a sofa, and savor made-from-scratch small plates you won't soon forget, like salted carmel puffs or chicken lollipops. **Known for:** craft cocktails and 170 types of beer; cheese or chocolate fondue; raw bar. [$] *Average main: $13* ✉ *22658 Overseas Hwy., 2nd fl. of Square Grouper restaurant, Sugarloaf Key* ☎ *305/745–8880* 🌐 *www.mynewjoint420lounge.com* 🕓 *Closed Sun. and Mon.*

★ **Square Grouper**
$$$ | SEAFOOD | In an unassuming warehouse-looking building on U.S. 1, chef-owner Lynn Bell is creating seafood magic. For starters, try the flash-fried conch with wasabi drizzle or homemade smoked-fish dip. **Known for:** everything made fresh, in-house; long lines in season; outstanding seafood. [$] *Average main: $25* ✉ *MM 22.5 OS* ☎ *305/745–8880* 🌐 *www.squaregrouperbarandgrill.com* 🕓 *Closed Sun.; Mon. May–Dec.; and Sept.*

Hotels

★ **Little Palm Island Resort & Spa**
$$$$ | RESORT | This ultra-luxurious tropical retreat set on a private island was devastated by Hurricane Irma but is scheduled to reopen in late 2019—check the website for updates. **Pros:** secluded setting; heavenly spa; easy wildlife viewing. **Cons:** expensive; might be too quiet for some; accessible only by boat or seaplane. [$] *Rooms from: $1,590* ✉ *MM 28.5 OS, 28500 Overseas Hwy.* ☎ *305/872–2524, 800/343–8567* 🌐 *www.littlepalmisland.com* 🛏 *30 suites* 🍴 *Some meals* ☞ *No one under age 16 allowed on island.*

Looe Key Reef Resort & Center
$ | HOTEL | If your Keys vacation is all about diving, you won't mind the no-frills, basic motel rooms with dated furniture at this scuba-obsessed operation because it's the closest place to stay to the stellar reef. **Pros:** guests get discounts on dive and snorkel trips; inexpensive rates; casual Keys atmosphere. **Cons:** some reports of uncleanliness; unheated pool; close to the road. [$] *Rooms from: $115* ✉ *MM 27.5 OS, 27340 Overseas Hwy., Ramrod Key* ☎ *305/872–2215, 877/816–3483* 🌐 *www.diveflakeys.com* 🛏 *24 rooms* 🍴 *No meals.*

Parmer's Resort
$ | HOTEL | Almost every room at this budget-friendly option has a view of South Pine Channel, with the lovely curl of Big Pine Key in the foreground. **Pros:** bright rooms; pretty setting; good value. **Cons:** a bit out of the way; housekeeping costs extra; little shade around the pool. [$] *Rooms from: $159* ✉ *MM 28.7 BS, 565 Barry Ave.* ☎ *305/872–2157* 🌐 *www.parmersresort.com* 🛏 *47 units* 🍴 *Free Breakfast.*

🏃 Activities

SCUBA DIVING AND SNORKELING

This is the closest you can get on land to Looe Key Reef, and that's where local dive operators love to head.

In 1744 the HMS *Looe,* a British warship, ran aground and sank on one of the most beautiful coral reefs in the Keys. Today the key owes its name to the ill-fated ship. The 5.3-square-nautical-mile reef, part of the **Florida Keys National Marine Sanctuary,** has strands of elkhorn coral on its eastern margin, purple sea fans, and abundant sponges and sea urchins. On its seaward side, it drops almost vertically 50 to 90 feet. In its midst, **Shipwreck Trail** plots the location of nine historic wreck sites in 14 to 120 feet of water. Buoys mark the sites, and underwater signs tell the history of each site and what marine life to expect. Snorkelers and divers will find the sanctuary a quiet place to observe reef life—except in July, when the annual Underwater Music Festival pays homage to Looe Key's beauty and promotes reef awareness with six hours of music broadcast via underwater speakers. Dive shops, charters, and private boats transport about 500 divers and snorkelers to hear the spectacle, which includes classical, jazz, New Age, and Caribbean music, as well as a little Jimmy Buffett. There are even underwater Elvis impersonators.

Looe Key Reef Resort & Dive Center

SCUBA DIVING | This center, the closest dive shop to Looe Key Reef, offers two affordable trips daily, at 8 am and 12:45 pm (for divers, snorkelers, or bubble watchers). The maximum depth is 30 feet, so snorkelers and divers go on the same boat. Call to check for availability for wreck and night dives. The dive boat, a 45-foot catamaran, is docked at the full-service Looe Key Reef Resort. ⊠ *Looe Key Reef Resort, MM 27.5 OS, 27340 Overseas Hwy., Ramrod Key*
☎ *305/872–2215, 877/816–3483* ⊕ *www. diveflakeys.com* 🏷 *From $40.*

WATER SPORTS

★ Reelax Charters

BOATING | For a guided tour, join Captain Andrea Paulson of Reelax Charters, who takes you to remote locations by boat, then hops in a kayak for a tour like no other. Charters carry up to six people at $85 per person and can include snorkeling and beaching on a secluded island in the Keys backcountry. ⊠ *Sugarloaf Marina, MM 17 BS, 17015 Overseas Hwy., Sugarloaf Key* ☎ *305/304–1392* ⊕ *www.keyskayaking.com* 🏷 *From $255 per boat.*

Sugarloaf Marina

BOATING | Rates for one-person kayaks are based on an hourly or daily rental. Two-person kayaks are also available. Delivery is free for rentals of three days or more. The folks at the marina can also hook you up with an outfitter for a day of offshore or backcountry fishing. There's also a well-stocked ship store. ⊠ *MM 17 BS, 17015 Overseas Hwy., Sugarloaf Key* ☎ *305/745–3135* ⊕ *www.sugarloafkeymarina.com* 🏷 *From $15 per hr.*

Key West

Situated 150 miles from Miami, 90 miles from Havana, and an immeasurable distance from sanity, this end-of-the-line community has never been like anywhere else. Even after it was connected to the rest of the country—by the railroad in 1912 and by the highway in 1938—it maintained a strong sense of detachment. The United States acquired Key West from Spain in 1821, along with the rest of Florida. The Spanish had named the island Cayo Hueso, or Bone Key, after the Native American skeletons they found on its shores. In 1823, President James Monroe sent Commodore David S. Porter to chase pirates away. For three decades, the primary industry in Key

West was wrecking—rescuing people and salvaging cargo from ships that foundered on the nearby reefs. According to some reports, when pickings were lean the wreckers hung out lights to lure ships aground. Their business declined after 1849, when the federal government began building lighthouses.

In 1845, the army began construction on Fort Taylor, which kept Key West on the Union side during the Civil War. After the fighting ended, an influx of Cubans unhappy with Spain's rule brought the cigar industry here. Fishing, shrimping, and sponge gathering became important industries, as did pineapple canning. Throughout much of the 19th century and into the 20th, Key West was Florida's wealthiest city per capita. But in 1929, the local economy began to unravel. Cigar making moved to Tampa, Hawaii dominated the pineapple industry, and the sponges succumbed to blight. Then the Depression hit, and within a few years half the population was on relief.

Tourism began to revive Key West, but that came to a halt when a hurricane knocked out the railroad bridge in 1935. To help the tourism industry recover from that crushing blow, the government offered incentives for islanders to turn their charming homes—many of them built by shipwrights— into guesthouses and inns. That wise foresight has left the town with more than 100 such lodgings, a hallmark of Key West vacationing today. In the 1950s, the discovery of "pink gold" in the Dry Tortugas boosted the economy of the entire region. Catching Key West shrimp required a fleet of up to 500 boats and flooded local restaurants with some of the sweetest shrimp alive. The town's artistic community found inspiration in the colorful fishing boats.

Key West reflects a diverse population: Conchs (natives, many of whom trace their ancestry to the Bahamas), freshwater Conchs (longtime residents who migrated from somewhere else years ago), Hispanics (primarily Cuban immigrants), recent refugees from the urban sprawl of mainland Florida, military personnel, and an assortment of vagabonds, drifters, and dropouts in search of refuge. The island was once a gay vacation hot spot, and it remains a decidedly gay-friendly destination. Some of the once-renowned gay guesthouses, however, no longer cater to an exclusively gay clientele. Key Westers pride themselves on their tolerance of all peoples, all sexual orientations, and even all animals. Most restaurants allow pets, and it's not surprising to see stray cats, dogs, and even chickens roaming freely through the dining rooms. The chicken issue is one that government officials periodically try to bring to an end, but the colorful fowl continue to strut and crow, particularly in the vicinity of Old Town's Bahamian Village.

As a tourist destination, Key West has a lot to sell—an average temperature of 79°F, 19th-century architecture, and a laid-back lifestyle. Yet much has been lost to those eager for a buck. Duval Street is starting to resemble a shopping mall with name-brand storefronts, garish T-shirt shops, and tattoo shops with sidewalk views of the inked action. Cruise ships dwarf the town's skyline and fill the streets with day-trippers gawking at the hippies with dogs in their bike baskets, gay couples walking down the street holding hands, and the oddball lot of locals, some of whom bark louder than the dogs.

GETTING HERE AND AROUND
AIR TRAVEL
You can fly directly to Key West on a limited number of flights, most of which connect at other Florida airports. But a lot of folks fly into Miami or Fort Lauderdale and drive down or take the bus.

BOAT TRAVEL
Key West Express operates air-conditioned ferries between the Key West Terminal (Caroline and Grinnell Streets) and

Marco Island, and Fort Myers Beach. The trip from Fort Myers Beach takes at least four hours each way and costs $95 one way, $155 round-trip. Ferries depart from Fort Myers Beach at 8:30 am and from Key West at 6 pm. The Miami and Marco Island ferry costs $95 one way and $155 round-trip, and departs at 8:30 am. A photo ID is required for each passenger. Advance reservations are recommended and can save money.

BUS AND SHUTTLE TRAVEL TO KEY WEST

Greyhound Lines runs a special Keys Shuttle up to twice a day (depending on the day of the week) from Miami International Airport (departing from Concourse E, lower level) that stops throughout the Keys. Fares run about $45 (web fare) to $57 for Key West. Keys Shuttle runs scheduled service three times a day in 15-passenger vans between Miami Airport and Key West with stops throughout the Keys for $70 to $90 per person. SuperShuttle charges $102 per passenger for trips from Miami International Airport to the Upper Keys. To go farther into the Keys, you must book an entire 11-person van, which costs about $350 to Key West. You need to place your request for transportation back to the airport 24 hours in advance. Uber is also available throughout the Keys and from the airport. *For detailed information on these services, see Getting Here and Around: Bus Travel*

BUS TRAVEL AROUND KEY WEST

Between mile markers 4 and 0, Key West is the one place in the Keys where you could conceivably do without a car, especially if you plan on staying around Old Town. If you've driven the 106 miles down the chain, you're probably ready to abandon your car in the hotel parking lot anyway. Trolleys, buses, bikes, scooters, and feet are more suitable alternatives. When your feet tire, catch a rickshaw-style pedicab ride, which will run you about $1.50 a minute. But to explore the beaches, New Town, and Stock Island, you'll need a car or taxi.

The City of Key West Department of Transportation has six color-coded bus routes traversing the island from 5:30 am to 11:30 pm. Stops have signs with the international bus symbol. Schedules are available on buses and at hotels, visitor centers, shops, and online. The fare is $2 one way.

VISITOR INFORMATION

CONTACTS Greater Key West Chamber of Commerce. ⊠ *510 Greene St., 1st fl.* ☎ *305/294–2587, 800/527–8539* ⊕ *www. keywestchamber.org.*

TOURS

Conch Tour Train

BUS TOURS | The Conch Tour Train is a 90-minute narrated tour of Key West, traveling 14 miles through Old Town and around the island. Board at Mallory Square or Angela Street and Duval Street depot every half hour from 9 to 4:30. Discount tickets are available online. ⊠ *Key West* ☎ *305/294–5161, 888/916–8687* ⊕ *www.conchtourtrain.com* ⊠ *$31.45.*

Historic Florida Keys Foundation

WALKING TOURS | In addition to publishing several good guides on Key West, the foundation conducts tours of the City Cemetery on Tuesday and Thursday at 9:30 am. ⊠ *Old City Hall, 510 Greene St.* ☎ *305/292–6718* ⊕ *www.historicflorida-keys.org* ⊠ *$15.*

Key West Promotions

WALKING TOURS | If you're not entirely a do-it-yourselfer, Key West Promotions offers a variety of pub tours, from the famous Duval Crawl to a chilling, haunted, and "spirited" adventure. ⊠ *424 Greene St.* ☎ *305/294–7170* ⊕ *www. keywestwalkingtours.com.*

Lloyd's Original Tropical Bike Tour

BICYCLE TOURS | Explore the natural, noncommercial side of Key West at a leisurely pace, stopping on backstreets and in backyards of private homes to sample

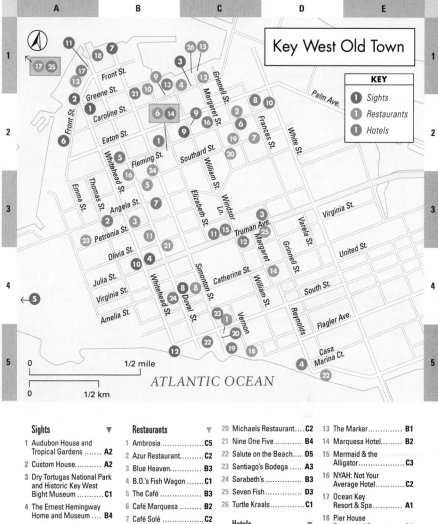

Key West Old Town

KEY

- 🔵 Sights
- 🔵 Restaurants
- 🔵 Hotels

ATLANTIC OCEAN

0 _____ 1/2 mile

0 _____ 1/2 km

native fruits and view indigenous plants and trees with a 45-year Key West veteran. The behind-the-scenes tours run two hours and include a bike rental. ⌧ *Moped Hospital, Truman Ave. and Simonton St.* ☎ *305/304–4700* ⊕ *www.lloydstropical-biketour.com* 🖃 *$49.*

Old Town Trolley
BUS TOURS | **FAMILY** | Old Town Trolley operates trolley-style buses, departing from Mallory Square every 30 minutes from 9 to 4:30, for 90-minute narrated tours of Key West. The smaller trolleys go places the larger Conch Tour Train won't fit and you can ride a second consecutive day for only $15. You may disembark at any of 13 stops and reboard a later trolley. You can save nearly $4 by booking online. It also offers package deals with Old Town attractions. ⌧ *1 Whitehead St.* ☎ *305/296–6688, 855/623–8289* ⊕ *www.trolleytours.com* 🖃 *$38.80.*

Sights

OLD TOWN
The heart of Key West, the historic Old Town area runs from White Street to the waterfront. Beginning in 1822, wharves, warehouses, chandleries, ship-repair facilities, and eventually, in 1891, the U.S. Custom House, sprang up around the deep harbor to accommodate the navy's large ships and other sailing vessels. Wreckers, merchants, and sea captains built lavish houses near the bustling waterfront. A remarkable number of these fine Victorian and pre-Victorian structures have been restored to their original grandeur and now serve as homes, guesthouses, shops, restaurants, and museums. These, along with the dwellings of famous writers, artists, and politicians who've come to Key West over the past 175 years, are among the area's approximately 3,000 historic structures. Old Town also has the city's finest restaurants and hotels, lively street life, and popular nightspots.

The Sunblock Ban

In order to protect the only living coral barrier reef in the continental United States, Key West will ban the sale of sunscreens with two harmful chemicals known to negatively impact marine life and cause coral bleaching: oxybenzone and octinoxate. The ban takes effect in 2021.

Audubon House and Tropical Gardens
GARDEN | If you've ever seen an engraving by ornithologist John James Audubon, you'll understand why his name is synonymous with birds. See his works in this three-story house, which was built in the 1840s for Captain John Geiger and filled with period furniture. It now commemorates Audubon's 1832 stop in Key West while he was traveling through Florida to study birds. After an introduction by a docent, you can do a self-guided tour of the house and gardens. An art gallery sells lithographs of the artist's famed portraits. ⌧ *205 Whitehead St.* ☎ *305/294–2116, 877/294–2470* ⊕ *www.audubonhouse.com* 🖃 *$14.*

★ Custom House
HISTORIC SITE | When Key West was designated a U.S. port of entry in the early 1820s, a customhouse was established. Salvaged cargoes from ships wrecked on the reefs were brought here, setting the stage for Key West to become—for a time—the richest city in Florida. The imposing redbrick-and-terra-cotta Richardsonian Romanesque–style building reopened as a museum and art gallery in 1999. Smaller galleries have long-term and changing exhibits about the history of Key West, including a Hemingway room and a permanent Henry Flagler exhibit that commemorates the arrival of Flagler's railroad to Key West in 1912.

See the typewriter Hemingway used at his home office in Key West. He lived here from 1931 to 1942.

✉ *281 Front St.* ☎ *305/295–6616* ⊕ *www. kwahs.com* ✉ *$10.*

Dry Tortugas National Park and Historic Key West Bight Museum

HISTORIC SITE | FAMILY | If you can't see Ft. Jefferson in the Dry Tortugas in person, this is the next best thing. Opened in 2013 by the national park's official ferry commissioner, this free attraction located in Key West's historic seaport has an impressive (1:87) scale model of the fort; life-size figures including the fort's most famous prisoner, Dr. Samuel Mudd; and even a junior ranger station for the little ones with hands-on educational fun. The exhibits are housed in a historic site as well, the old Thompson Fish House, where local fisherman would bring their daily catch for processing. History lingers on within these walls, but to get a whiff of the sea and days gone past, you'll have to walk the docks out front. ✉ *240 Margaret St.* ☎ *305/294–7009* ⊕ *www. drytortugas.com* ✉ *Free.*

★ The Ernest Hemingway Home and Museum

HOUSE | Amusing anecdotes spice up the guided tours of Ernest Hemingway's home, built in 1801 by the town's most successful wrecker. While living here between 1931 and 1942, Hemingway wrote about 70% of his life's work, including classics like *For Whom the Bell Tolls*. Few of his belongings remain aside from some books, and there's little about his actual work, but photographs help you visualize his day-to-day life. The famous six-toed descendants of Hemingway's cats—many named for actors, artists, authors, and even a hurricane—have free rein of the property. Tours begin every 10 minutes and take 30 minutes; then you're free to explore on your own. Be sure to find out why there is a urinal in the garden! ✉ *907 Whitehead St.* ☎ *305/294–1136* ⊕ *www.hemingway-home.com* ✉ *$14.*

Fort Zachary Taylor Historic State Park

BEACH—SIGHT | Construction of the fort began in 1845 but was halted during the

Hemingway Was Here

In a town where Pulitzer Prize–winning writers are almost as common as coconuts, Ernest Hemingway stands out. Many bars and restaurants around the island claim that he ate or drank there.

Hemingway came to Key West in 1928 at the urging of writer John Dos Passos and rented a house with his second wife, Pauline Pfeiffer. They spent winters in the Keys and summers in Europe and Wyoming, occasionally taking African safaris. Along the way, they had two sons, Patrick and Gregory. In 1931, Pauline's wealthy uncle Gus gave the couple the house at 907 Whitehead Street. Now known as the Ernest Hemingway Home & Museum, it's Key West's number one tourist attraction. Renovations included the addition of a pool and a tropical garden.

In 1935, when the visitor bureau included the house in a tourist brochure, Hemingway promptly built the brick wall that surrounds it today. He wrote of the visitor bureau's offense in a 1935 essay for *Esquire*, saying, "The house at present occupied by your correspondent is listed as number eighteen in a compilation of the forty-eight things for a tourist to see in Key West. So there will be no difficulty in a tourist finding it or any other of the sights of the city, a

map has been prepared by the local F.E.R.A. authorities to be presented to each arriving visitor. This is all very flattering to the easily bloated ego of your correspondent but very hard on production."

During his time in Key West, Hemingway penned some of his most important works, including *A Farewell to Arms, To Have and Have Not, Green Hills of Africa*, and *Death in the Afternoon*. His rigorous schedule consisted of writing almost every morning in his second-story studio above the pool, then promptly descending the stairs at midday. By afternoon and evening he was ready for drinking, fishing, swimming, boxing, and hanging around with the boys.

One close friend was Joe Russell, a craggy fisherman and owner of the rugged bar Sloppy Joe's, originally at 428 Greene Street but now at 201 Duval Street. Russell was the only one in town who would cash Hemingway's $1,000 royalty check. Russell and Charles Thompson introduced Hemingway to deep-sea fishing, which became fodder for his writing.

Hemingway stayed in Key West for 11 years before leaving Pauline for his third wife. Pauline and the boys stayed on in the house, which sold in 1951 for $80,000, 10 times its original cost.

Civil War. Even though Florida seceded from the Union, Yankee forces used the fort as a base to block Confederate shipping. More than 1,500 Confederate vessels were detained in Key West's harbor. The fort, finally completed in 1866, was also used in the Spanish-American War. Take a 30-minute guided walking tour of the redbrick fort, a National Historic Landmark, at noon and 2, or self-guided tour anytime between 8 and 5. In February a celebration called Civil War Heritage Days includes costumed reenactments and demonstrations. From mid-January to mid-April the park serves as an open-air gallery for pieces created for Sculpture Key West. One of its most popular features is its man-made beach, a rest

Divers examine the intentionally scuttled 327-foot former U.S. Coast Guard cutter *Duane* in 120 feet of water off Key Largo.

stop for migrating birds in the spring and fall; there are also picnic areas, hiking and biking trails, and a kayak launch. ✉ *Southard St., at end of street, through Truman Annex* ☎ *305/292–6713* ⊕ *www. floridastateparks.org/park/Fort-Taylor* 🎫 *$4 for single-occupant vehicles, $6 for 2–8 people in a vehicle, plus a 50¢ per person county surcharge.*

Harry S. Truman Little White House Museum
HOUSE | Renovations to this circa-1890 landmark have restored the home and gardens to the Truman era, down to the wallpaper pattern. A free photographic review of visiting dignitaries and presidents—John F. Kennedy, Jimmy Carter, and Bill Clinton are among the chief executives who passed through here—is on display in the back of the gift shop. Engaging 45-minute tours begin every 20 minutes until 4:30. They start with an excellent 10-minute video on the history of the property and Truman's visits. On the grounds of **Truman Annex,** a 103-acre former military parade grounds and barracks, the home served as a

"winter White House" for presidents Truman, Eisenhower, and Kennedy. Entry is cheaper when purchased in advance online; tickets bought on-site add sales tax. ■**TIP→ The house tour does require climbing steps. Visitors can do a free self-guided botanical tour of the grounds with a brochure from the museum store.** ✉ *111 Front St.* ☎ *305/294–9911* ⊕ *www. trumanlittlewhitehouse.com* 🎫 *$21.45.*

Historic Seaport at Key West Bight
HISTORIC SITE | What was once a funky— in some places even seedy—part of town is a 20-acre historic restoration of businesses, including waterfront restaurants, open-air bars, museums, clothing stores, and water-sports concessions. It's all linked by the 2-mile waterfront **Harborwalk,** which runs between Front and Grinnell Streets, passing big ships, schooners, sunset cruises, fishing charters, and glass-bottom boats. This is where the locals go for great music and good drinks. ✉ *100 Grinnell St.* ⊕ *www. keywesthistoricseaport.com.*

The Conch Republic

Beginning in the 1970s, pot smuggling became a source of income for islanders who knew how to dodge detection in the maze of waterways in the Keys. In 1982, the U.S. Border Patrol threw a roadblock across the Overseas Highway just south of Florida City to catch drug runners and undocumented aliens. Traffic backed up for miles as Border Patrol agents searched vehicles and demanded that the occupants prove U.S. citizenship.

Officials in Key West, outraged at being treated like foreigners by the federal government, staged a protest and formed their own "nation," the so-called Conch Republic. They hoisted a flag and distributed mock border passes, visas, and Conch currency. The embarrassed Border Patrol dismantled its roadblock, and now an annual festival recalls the city's victory.

The Key West Butterfly and Nature Conservatory

GARDEN | FAMILY | This air-conditioned refuge for butterflies, birds, and the human spirit gladdens the soul with hundreds of colorful wings—more than 45 species of butterflies alone—in a lovely glass-encased bubble. Waterfalls, artistic benches, paved pathways, birds, and lush, flowering vegetation elevate this above most butterfly attractions. The gift shop and gallery are worth a visit on their own. ⊠ *1316 Duval St.* ☎ *305/296–2988, 800/839–4647* ⊕ *www.keywestbutterfly. com* ⊠ *$12.*

Key West Library

LIBRARY | Check out the pretty palm garden next to the Key West Library at 700 Fleming Street, just off Duval. This leafy, outdoor reading area, with shaded benches, is the perfect place to escape the frenzy and crowds of downtown Key West. There's free Internet access in the library, too. ⊠ *700 Fleming St.* ☎ *305/292–3595* ⊕ *www.keyslibraries. org* ☉ *Closed Sun.*

Key West Lighthouse Museum and Keeper's Quarters

LIGHTHOUSE | For the best view in town, climb the 88 steps to the top of this 1847 lighthouse. The 92-foot structure has a Fresnel lens, which was installed in the 1860s at a cost of $1 million. The keeper lived in the adjacent 1887 clapboard house, which now exhibits vintage photographs, ship models, nautical charts, and artifacts from all along Key West's reefs. A kids' room is stocked with books and toys. ⊠ *938 Whitehead St.* ☎ *305/294–0012* ⊕ *www.kwahs.com* ⊠ *$10.*

Mallory Square and Pier

LOCAL INTEREST | For cruise-ship passengers, this is the disembarkation point for an attack on Key West. For practically every visitor, it's the requisite venue for a nightly sunset celebration that includes street performers—human statues, sword swallowers, tightrope walkers, musicians, and more—plus craft vendors, conch-fritter fryers, and other regulars who defy classification. With all the activity, don't forget to watch the main show: a dazzling tropical sunset. ⊠ *Mallory Sq.*

The Southernmost Point

HISTORIC SITE | Possibly the most photographed site in Key West (even though the actual geographic southernmost point in the continental United States lies across the bay on a naval base, where you see a satellite dish), this is a must-see. Have your picture taken next to the big striped buoy that's been marking the southernmost point in the continental United States since 1983. A plaque next to it honors Cubans who lost their lives trying to escape to America, and other signs tell Key West history. ⊠ *Whitehead and South Sts.*

NEW TOWN

The Overseas Highway splits as it enters Key West, the two forks rejoining to encircle New Town, the area east of White Street to Cow Key Channel. The southern fork runs along the shore as South Roosevelt Boulevard (Route A1A) and skirts Key West International Airport, while the northern fork runs along the north shore as North Roosevelt Boulevard and turns into Truman Avenue once it hits Old Town. Part of New Town was created with dredged fill. The island would have continued growing this way had the Army Corps of Engineers not determined in the early 1970s that it was detrimental to the nearby reef.

Fort East Martello Museum & Gardens

MUSEUM | This redbrick Civil War fort never saw a lick of action during the war. Today it serves as a museum, with historical exhibits about the 19th and 20th centuries. Among the latter are relics of the USS *Maine,* cigar factory and ship-wrecking exhibits, and the citadel tower you can climb to the top. The museum, operated by the Key West Art and Historical Society, also has a collection of Stanley Papio's "junk art" sculptures inside and out, and a gallery of Cuban folk artist Mario Sanchez's chiseled and painted wooden carvings of historic Key West street scenes. ⊠ *3501 S. Roosevelt Blvd.* ☎ *305/296–3913* ⊕ *www.kwahs.com* ⊠ *$10.*

Key West Tropical Forest & Botanical Garden

LOCAL INTEREST | Established in 1935, this unique habitat is the only frost-free botanical garden in the continental United States. You won't see fancy topiaries and exotic plants, but you'll see a unique ecosystem that naturally occurs in this area and the Caribbean. There are paved walkways that take you past butterfly gardens, mangroves, Cuban palms, lots of birds like herons and ibis, and ponds where you can spy turtles and fish. It's a nice respite from the sidewalks and shops, and offers a natural slice of Keys paradise. ⊠ *5210 College Rd.* ☎ *305/296–1504* ⊕ *www.kwbgs.org* ⊠ *$7.*

Beaches

OLD TOWN

Dog Beach

BEACH—SIGHT | Next to Louie's Backyard restaurant, this tiny beach—the only one in Key West where dogs are allowed unleashed—has a shore that's a mix of sand and rocks. **Amenities:** none. **Best for:** walking. ⊠ *Vernon and Waddell Sts.* ⊠ *Free.*

Fort Zachary Taylor Beach

BEACH—SIGHT | **FAMILY** | The park's beach is the best and safest place to swim in Key West. There's an adjoining picnic area with barbecue grills and shade trees, a snack bar, and rental equipment, including snorkeling gear. A café serves sandwiches and other munchies. Water shoes are recommended since the bottom is rocky here. **Amenities:** food and drink; showers; toilets; water sports. **Best for:** snorkeling; swimming. ⊠ *End of Southard St., through Truman Annex* ☎ *305/292–6713* ⊕ *www.fortzacharytaylor.com* ⊠ *$4 for single-occupant vehicles, $6 for 2–8 people, plus $0.50 per person county surcharge.*

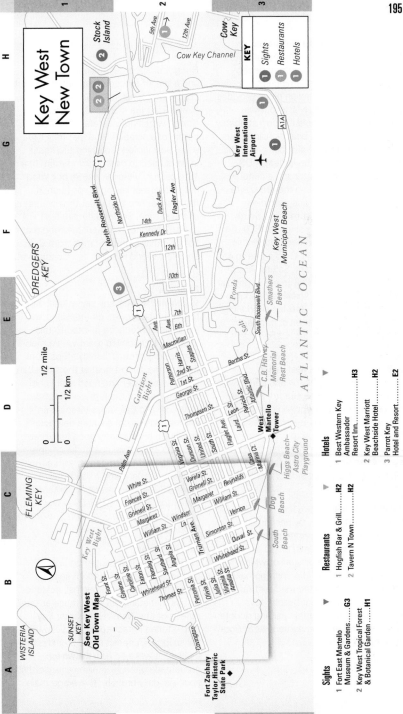

Key West New Town

KEY
- Sights
- Restaurants
- Hotels

Sights ▶
1 Fort East Martello Museum & Gardens **G3**
2 Key West Tropical Forest & Botanical Garden **H1**

Restaurants ▶
1 Hogfish Bar & Grill **H2**
2 Tavern N Town **H2**

Hotels ▶
1 Best Western Key Ambassador Resort Inn **H3**
2 Key West Marriott Beachside Hotel **H2**
3 Parrot Key Hotel and Resort **E2**

Higgs Beach–Astro City Playground
BEACH—SIGHT | **FAMILY** | This Monroe County park with its groomed pebbly sand is a popular sunbathing spot. A nearby grove of Australian pines provides shade, and the West Martello Tower provides shelter should a storm suddenly sweep in. Kayak and beach-chair rentals are available, as is a volleyball net. The beach also has the largest AIDS memorial in the country and a cultural exhibit commemorating the grave site of 295 enslaved Africans who died after being rescued from three South America–bound slave ships in 1860. An athletic trail with 10 fitness stations is also available. Hungry? Grab a bite to eat at the on-site restaurant, Salute. Across the street, **Astro City Playground** is popular with young children. **Amenities:** parking; toilets; water sports. **Best for:** snorkeling; swimming. ✉ *Atlantic Blvd. between White and Reynolds Sts.* 🎟 *Free.*

NEW TOWN

C. B. Harvey Memorial Rest Beach
BEACH—SIGHT | This beach and park were named after Cornelius Bradford Harvey, former Key West mayor and commissioner. Adjacent to Higgs Beach, it has half a dozen picnic areas across the street, dunes, a pier, and a wheelchair and bike path. **Amenities:** none. **Best for:** walking. ✉ *Atlantic Blvd., east side of White St. Pier* 🎟 *Free.*

Smathers Beach
BEACH—SIGHT | This wide beach has nearly 1 mile of nice white sand, plus beautiful coconut palms, picnic areas, and volleyball courts, all of which make it popular with the spring-break crowd. Trucks along the road rent rafts, windsurfers, and other beach "toys." **Amenities:** food and drink; parking; toilets; water sports. **Best for:** partiers. ✉ *S. Roosevelt Blvd.* 🎟 *Free.*

🍴 Restaurants

Bring your appetite, a sense of daring, and a lack of preconceived notions about propriety. A meal in Key West can mean overlooking the crazies along Duval Street, watching roosters and pigeons battle for a scrap of food that may have escaped your fork, relishing the finest in what used to be the dining room of a 19th-century Victorian home, or gazing out at boats jockeying for position in the marina. And that's just the diversity of the setting. Seafood dominates local menus, but the treatment afforded that fish or crustacean can range from Cuban and New World to Asian and Continental.

OLD TOWN

Ambrosia
$$ | **JAPANESE** | Ask any savvy local where to get the best sushi on the island and you'll undoubtedly be pointed to this bright and airy dining room with a modern indoor waterfall literally steps from the Atlantic. Grab a seat at the sushi bar and watch owner and head sushi chef Masa (albeit not the famous chef from New York and Las Vegas) prepare an impressive array of sashimi delicacies. **Known for:** consistently good fish; great tempura and teriyaki bento lunch specials; the Ambrosia special, with a mix of sashimi, sushi, and rolls. [$] *Average main: $20* ✉ *Santa Maria Resort, 1401 Simonton St.* ☎ *305/293–0304* 🌐 *www.ambrosiasushi.com* 🕒 *Closed 2 wks after Labor Day. No lunch weekends.*

Azur Restaurant
$$$ | **ECLECTIC** | In a contemporary setting with indoor and outdoor seating, welcoming staff serve original, eclectic dishes that stand out from those at the hordes of Key West restaurants. Key lime–stuffed French toast and yellowtail snapper Benedict make breakfast a pleasant wake-up call. **Known for:** homemade gnocchi; a nice variety of fish specials; daily brunch. [$] *Average main:*

$26 ✉ 425 Grinnell St. ☎ 305/292–2987 🌐 www.azurkeywest.com.

Blue Heaven

$$$ | CARIBBEAN | The outdoor dining area here is often referred to as "the quintessential Keys experience," and it's hard to argue. There's much to like about this historic Caribbean-style restaurant where Hemingway refereed boxing matches and customers cheered for cockfights. **Known for:** shrimp and grits; lobster Benedict with key lime hollandaise; the wait for a table and lack of parking. [$] *Average main: $24 ✉ 729 Thomas St. ☎ 305/296–8666 🌐 www.blueheavenkw.com ⏲ Closed after Labor Day for 6 wks.*

★ **B.O.'s Fish Wagon**

$$ | SEAFOOD | What started out as a fish house on wheels appears to have broken down on the corner of Caroline and William streets and is today the cornerstone for one of Key West's junkyard-chic dining institutions. Step up to the window and order a grouper sandwich fried or grilled and topped with key lime sauce. **Known for:** lots of Key West charm; Friday-night jam sessions; all seating on picnic tables in the yard. [$] *Average main: $18 ✉ 801 Caroline St. ☎ 305/294–9272 🌐 bosfishwagon.com.*

The Café

$ | VEGETARIAN | You don't have to be a vegetarian to love this new-age café decorated with bright artwork and a corrugated-tin-fronted counter. Local favorites include homemade soup, veggie sandwiches and burgers (order them with a side of sweet-potato fries), grilled portobello mushroom salad, seafood, vegan specialties, stir-fry dinners, and grilled veggie pizzas. **Known for:** vegan options; homemade sangria; weekend brunch. [$] *Average main: $11 ✉ 509 Southard St. ☎ 305/296–5515 🌐 www.thecafekw.com.*

★ **Café Marquesa**

$$$ | EUROPEAN | You'll find seven or more inspired entrées on a changing menu each night, including anything from yellowtail snapper to seared duck breast. End your meal on a sweet note with chocolate pot de crème and homemade ice cream—there's also a fine selection of wines and custom martinis. **Known for:** relaxed but elegant setting; good wine and martini lists; desserts worth ordering. [$] *Average main: $30 ✉ 600 Fleming St. ☎ 305/292–1244 🌐 www.marquesa.com ⏲ No lunch.*

Café Solé

$$$ | FRENCH | This little corner of France hides behind a high wall in a residential neighborhood. Inside, French training intertwines with local ingredients, creating delicious takes on classics, including a must-try conch carpaccio and some of the best bouillabaisse that you'll find outside Marseilles. **Known for:** hogfish in several different preparations; intimate, romantic atmosphere; award-winning key lime pie. [$] *Average main: $28 ✉ 1029 Southard St. ☎ 305/294–0230 🌐 www.cafesole.com.*

Camille's Restaurant

$$$ | MODERN AMERICAN | FAMILY | Break out the stretchy pants because everything on the menu at this affordable hot spot not only sounds scrumptious, it is. Start your day with a shrimp, lobster, or crab-cake Benedict—the latter was voted best in the Florida Keys. **Known for:** popularity with both locals and tourists; fresh seafood daily; BOGO menu from 3 pm to closing daily. [$] *Average main: $21 ✉ 1202 Simonton St., at Catherine St. ☎ 305/296–4811.*

Coffee Plantation

$ | BAKERY | Get your morning (or afternoon) buzz, and hook up to the Internet in the comfort of a homelike setting in a circa-1890 Conch house. Sit inside or out and munch on sandwiches, wraps, and pastries, and sip a hot or cold espresso beverage. **Known for:** tropical macchiatos; Almond Joy lattes; homemade quiche of the day. [$] *Average main: $3 ✉ 713 Caroline St. ☎ 305/295–9808 🌐 www.*

coffeeplantationkeywest.com ⏲ *Closed Sun.*

Conch Republic Seafood Company

$$$ | **SEAFOOD** | **FAMILY** | Because of its location where the fast ferry docks, Conch Republic does a brisk business. It's huge, open-air, on the water, and the menu is ambitious, offering more than just standard seafood fare. **Known for:** "Royal Reds" peel-and-eat shrimp; no reservations; live music most nights. [$] *Average main: $25* ✉ *631 Greene St., at Elizabeth St.* ☎ *305/294–4403* 🌐 *www.conchrepublicseafood.com.*

Croissants de France

$ | **FRENCH** | Pop into the bakery for something sinfully sweet or spend some time people-watching at the sidewalk café next door. You can get breakfast or lunch at the café, and the bakery is open late. **Known for:** gluten-free buckwheat crepes; popularity with both locals and visitors; great coffee and croissants. [$] *Average main: $14* ✉ *816 Duval St.* ☎ *305/294–2624* 🌐 *www.croissantsdefrance.com.*

Dante's Key West Restaurant and Pool Bar

$$ | **SEAFOOD** | With the motto "Come be an aquaholic," Dante's is as unique as Key West itself. Sun loungers, tiki bars, and tables with umbrellas and chairs surround a large free-form swimming pool. **Known for:** food and drink minimum at some key tables; popular happy hour; "Hook and Cook" (bring your fresh catch and they cook it for you). [$] *Average main: $18* ✉ *Conch Harbor Marina, 951 Caroline St.* ☎ *305/423–2001* 🌐 *www.danteskeywest.com.*

El Meson de Pepe

$$ | **CUBAN** | If you want a taste of the island's Cuban heritage, this is the place to dine alfresco or in the dining room on refined Cuban classics. Begin with a megasize mojito while you browse the expansive menu offering *tostones rellenos* (green plantains with different traditional fillings), ceviche, and more. **Known for:** authentic plantain chips; Latin band during the nightly sunset celebration; touristy atmosphere. [$] *Average main: $19* ✉ *Mallory Sq., 410 Wall St.* ☎ *305/295–2620* 🌐 *www.elmesondepepe.com.*

El Siboney

$ | **CUBAN** | Dining at this family-style restaurant is like going to Mom's for Sunday dinner—if your mother is Cuban. The dining room is noisy, and the food is traditional *cubano*. To make a good thing even better, the prices are very reasonable and the homemade sangria is *muy bueno*. **Known for:** memorable paella and traditional dishes; wine and beer only; cheaper than more touristy options close to Duval. [$] *Average main: $11* ✉ *900 Catherine St.* ☎ *305/296–4184* 🌐 *www.elsiboneyrestaurant.com.*

Half Shell Raw Bar

$$ | **SEAFOOD** | **FAMILY** | Smack-dab on the docks, this legendary institution gets its name from the oysters, clams, and peel-and-eat shrimp that are a departure point for its seafood-based diet. It's not clever recipes or fine dining (or even air-conditioning) that packs 'em in; it's fried fish, po'boy sandwiches, and seafood combos. **Known for:** daily happy hour with food and drink deals; few non-seafood options; good people-watching spot. [$] *Average main: $16* ✉ *Lands End Village at Historic Seaport, 231 Margaret St.* ☎ *305/294–7496* 🌐 *www.halfshellrawbar.com.*

Jimmy Buffett's Margaritaville Cafe

$$ | **AMERICAN** | If you must have your cheeseburger in paradise, it may as well be here. The first of Buffett's line of chain eateries, it belongs here more than anywhere else, but quite frankly it's more about the name, music, and attitude (and margaritas) than the food. **Known for:** pricey Caribbean bar food; good and spicy conch chowder; raucous party atmosphere almost all the time. [$] *Average main: $18* ✉ *500 Duval St.* ☎ *305/292–1435* 🌐 *www.margaritaville.com.*

Latitudes

$$$ | ECLECTIC | For a special treat, take the short boat ride to lovely Sunset Key for lunch or dinner on the beach. Creativity and quality ingredients combine for dishes that are bound to impress as much as the setting, like the fish tacos with chipotle aioli. **Known for:** amazing sunset views; sophisticated atmosphere and expensive food; lobster bisque. $ *Average main: $28* ⊠ *Sunset Key Guest Cottages, 245 Front St.* ☎ *305/292–5300, 888/477–7786* ⊕ *www.sunsetkeycottages.com/latitudes-key-west* ☞ *Reservations are required to catch the ferry: no reservation, no ride.*

Louie's Backyard

$$$$ | ECLECTIC | Feast your eyes on a steal-your-breath-away view and beautifully presented dishes prepared by executive chef Doug Shook. Once you get over sticker shock on the seasonally changing menu, settle in on the outside deck and enjoy dishes like cracked conch with mango chutney, lamb chops with sun-dried tomato relish, and tamarind-glazed duck breast. **Known for:** fresh, pricey seafood and steaks; affordable lunch menu; late night drinks at Afterdeck Bar, directly on the water. $ *Average main: $36* ⊠ *700 Waddell Ave.* ☎ *305/294–1061* ⊕ *www.louiesbackyard. com* ⊗ *Closed Labor Day–mid-Sept. Café closed Sun. and Mon.*

Mangia Mangia

$$ | ITALIAN | This longtime favorite serves large portions of homemade pastas that can be matched with any of the homemade sauces. Tables are arranged in a brick garden hung with twinkling lights and in a cozy, casual dining room in an old house. **Known for:** extensive wine list with a nice range of prices; gluten-free and organic pastas; outdoor seating in the garden. $ *Average main: $18* ⊠ *900 Southard St.* ☎ *305/294–2469* ⊕ *www. mangia-mangia.com* ⊗ *No lunch.*

Michaels Restaurant

$$$$ | AMERICAN | White tablecloths, subdued lighting, and romantic music give Michaels the feel of an urban eatery, while garden seating reminds you that you are in the Keys. Chef-owner Michael Wilson flies in prime rib, cowboy steaks, and rib eyes from Allen Brothers in Chicago, which has supplied top-ranked steak houses for more than a century. **Known for:** elegant, romantic atmosphere; small plates available until 7:30 Sunday–Thursday; steak and seafood. $ *Average main: $32* ⊠ *532 Margaret St.* ☎ *305/295–1300* ⊕ *www.michaelskeywest.com* ⊗ *No lunch.*

Nine One Five

$$$$ | ECLECTIC | Twinkling lights draped along the lower- and upper-level outdoor porches of a 100-year-old Victorian home set an unstuffy and comfortable stage here. If you like to sample and sip, you'll appreciate the variety of smaller-plate selections and wines by the glass. **Known for:** fun place to people-watch; intimate and inviting atmosphere; light jazz during dinner. $ *Average main: $32* ⊠ *915 Duval St.* ☎ *305/296–0669* ⊕ *www.915duval. com* ⊗ *No lunch Mon. and Tues.*

Salute on the Beach

$$$ | ITALIAN | Sister restaurant to Blue Heaven, this colorful establishment sits on Higgs Beach, giving it one of the island's best lunch views—and a bit of sand and salt spray on a windy day. The intriguing menu is Italian with a Caribbean flair and will not disappoint. **Known for:** amazing water views; casual, inviting atmosphere; pricey slice of key lime pie. $ *Average main: $22* ⊠ *Higgs Beach, 1000 Atlantic Blvd.* ☎ *305/292–1117* ⊕ *www.saluteonthebeach.com.*

★ Santiago's Bodega

$ | TAPAS | Picky palates will be satisfied at this funky, dark, and sensuous tapas restaurant, which is well off the main drag—it's a secret spot for local foodies in the know. Small plates include yellowfin tuna ceviche with hunks of avocado and mango, and filet mignon with creamy Gorgonzola butter. **Known for:** legendary bread pudding; homemade white or red sangria; a favorite with local chefs. Ⓢ *Average main: $14* ✉ *Bahama Village, 207 Petronia St.* ☎ *305/296–7691* ⊕ *www.santiagosbodega.com.*

Sarabeth's
$$ | AMERICAN | Named for the award-winning jam-maker and pastry chef Sarabeth Levine, who runs the kitchen, this restaurant serves all-day breakfast, best enjoyed in the picket-fenced front yard of this circa-1870 synagogue. Lemon ricotta pancakes, pumpkin waffles, and homemade jams make the meal. **Known for:** homemade granola and old-fashioned porridge; daily specials including meat loaf and mac and cheese; orange apricot bread pudding. Ⓢ *Average main: $20* ✉ *530 Simonton St., at Souhard St.* ☎ *305/293–8181* ⊕ *www.sarabethskeywest.com* ☾ *Closed Mon. and Tues.*

Seven Fish
$$$ | SEAFOOD | This local hot spot exudes a casual Key West vibe with an eclectic mix of dishes. The specialty is the local fish of the day (like snapper with creamy Thai curry). **Known for:** fresh seafood; busy spot requiring reservations; amazing foccacia bread. Ⓢ *Average main: $26* ✉ *921 Truman Ave.* ☎ *305/296–2777* ⊕ *www.7fish.com* ☾ *Closed Tues. No lunch.*

Turtle Kraals
$$ | SEAFOOD | FAMILY | Named for the kraals, or corrals, where sea turtles were once kept until they went to the cannery, this place calls to mind the island's history. The menu offers an assortment of marine cuisine that includes seafood enchiladas, mesquite-grilled fish of the day, and mango crab cakes. **Known for:** mesquite-grilled oysters with Parmesan and cilantro; Peruvian-style ceviche; great views of the harbor. Ⓢ *Average main: $16* ✉ *231 Margaret St.* ☎ *305/294–2640* ⊕ *www.turtlekraals.com.*

Hogfish Bar & Grill
$$ | SEAFOOD | It's worth a drive to Stock Island, one of Florida's last surviving working waterfronts, just outside Key West, to indulge in the freshness you'll witness at this down-to-earth spot. Hogfish is the specialty, of course. **Known for:** pricey fish sandwiches; a taste of local life; fried grouper cheeks. Ⓢ *Average main: $17* ✉ *6810 Front St., Stock Island* ☎ *305/293–4041* ⊕ *www.hogfishbar.com.*

Tavern N Town
$$$$ | ECLECTIC | This handsome and warm restaurant has an open kitchen that adds lovely aromas from the wood-fired oven. The dinner menu offers a variety of options, including small plates and full entrées. **Known for:** upscale atmosphere (and prices); popular happy hour; noisy when busy. Ⓢ *Average main: $33* ✉ *Key West Marriott Beachside Resort, 3841 N. Roosevelt Blvd.* ☎ *305/296–8100, 800/546–0885* ⊕ *www.taverntown.com* ☾ *No lunch.*

Hotels

Historic cottages, restored century-old Conch houses, and large resorts are among the offerings in Key West, the majority charging between $100 and $300 a night. In high season, Christmas through Easter, you'll be hard-pressed to find a decent room for less than $200, and most places raise prices considerably during holidays and festivals. Many guesthouses and inns do not welcome children under 16, and most do not permit smoking indoors. Most tariffs include an expanded Continental breakfast and, often, an afternoon glass of wine or snack.

LODGING ALTERNATIVES
The Key West Lodging Association is an umbrella organization for dozens of local properties. Vacation Rentals Key West lists historic cottages, homes, and

condominiums for rent. Rent Key West Vacations specializes in renting vacation homes and condos for a week or longer. Vacation Key West lists all kinds of properties throughout Key West. In addition to these local agencies, 🌐 *airbnb.com* and 🌐 *vrbo.com* have many offerings in Key West.

CONTACTS Lodging Association of Key West and the Florida Keys. ☎ *800/492–1911* 🌐 *www.keywestinns.com* . **Key West Vacations.** ☎ *888/775–3993* 🌐 *www.keywestvacations.com* . **Rent Key West Vacations.** ✉ *1075 Duval St., Suite C11* ☎ *305/294–0990, 800/833–7368* 🌐 *www.rentkeywest.com.* **Vacation Key West.** ✉ *100 Grinnell St., Key West Ferry Terminal* ☎ *305/295–9500, 800/595–5397* 🌐 *www.vacationkw.com.*

OLD TOWN

Ambrosia Key West

$$$ | **B&B/INN** | If you desire personal attention, a casual atmosphere, and a dollop of style, stay at these twin inns spread out on nearly 2 acres. **Pros:** spacious rooms; breakfast served poolside; great location. **Cons:** on-street parking can be tough to come by; a little too spread out; high windows in some rooms let in the early morning light. [$] *Rooms from: $385* ✉ *615, 618, 622 Fleming St.* ☎ *305/296–9838, 800/535–9838* 🌐 *www.ambrosiakeywest.com* 🛏 *20 rooms* 🍴 *Free Breakfast.*

Angelina Guest House

$ | **B&B/INN** | In the heart of Old Town, this adults-only home away from home offers simple, clean, attractively priced accommodations. **Pros:** good value; nice garden; friendly staff. **Cons:** thin walls; basic rooms with no TVs; shared balcony and four of the rooms share a bathroom. [$] *Rooms from: $159* ✉ *302 Angela St.* ☎ *305/294–4480, 888/303–4480* 🌐 *www.angelinaguesthouse.com* 🛏 *13 rooms* 🍴 *Free Breakfast.*

Azul Key West

$$ | **B&B/INN** | The ultramodern—nearly minimalistic—redo of this classic circa-1903 Queen Anne mansion is a break from the sensory overload of Key West's other abundant Victorian guesthouses. **Pros:** lovely building; marble-floored baths; luxurious linens. **Cons:** on a busy street; modern isn't for everyone; two-night minimum stay, five nights in season. [$] *Rooms from: $289* ✉ *907 Truman Ave.* ☎ *305/296–5152, 888/253–2985* 🌐 *www.azulhotels.us* 🛏 *11 rooms* 🍴 *Free Breakfast.*

Casa Marina, A Waldorf-Astoria Resort

$$$ | **RESORT** | **FAMILY** | This luxurious property is on the largest private beach in Key West, and it has the same richly appointed lobby with beamed ceilings, polished pine floor, and original art as it did when it opened on New Year's Eve 1920. **Pros:** hugh beach; on-site dining, bars, and water sports; away from the crowds. **Cons:** long walk to central Old Town; expensive resort fee; spa is across the street in a separate building. [$] *Rooms from: $399* ✉ *1500 Reynolds St.* ☎ *305/296–3535, 866/203–6392* 🌐 *www.casamarinaresort.com* 🛏 *311 rooms* 🍴 *No meals.*

Crowne Plaza La Concha Hotel and Spa

$$$ | **HOTEL** | History and franchises can mix, as this 1920s-vintage hotel proves with its handsome atrium lobby and sleep-conducive rooms. **Pros:** location is everything; good on-site restaurant and wine bar; free Wi-Fi. **Cons:** high-traffic area; rooms are small, bathrooms are smaller; expensive valet-only parking. [$] *Rooms from: $350* ✉ *430 Duval St.* ☎ *305/296–2991* 🌐 *www.laconchakeywest.com* 🛏 *178 rooms* 🍴 *No meals.*

Eden House

$$ | **HOTEL** | From the vintage metal rockers on the streetside porch to the old neon hotel sign in the lobby, this 1920s rambling Key West mainstay hotel is high on character, low on gloss. **Pros:** free parking; hot tub is actually hot;

daily happy hour around the pool. **Cons:** pricey for older rooms; brown towels take getting used to; parking is first-come, first-served. [$] *Rooms from: $225* ✉ *1015 Fleming St.* ☎ *305/296–6868, 800/533–5397* 🌐 *www.edenhouse.com* 🛏 *44 rooms* 🍴 *No meals.*

★ The Gardens Hotel

$$$$ | HOTEL | Built in 1875, this gloriously shaded, well-loved property was a labor of love from the get-go, and it covers a third of a city block in Old Town. **Pros:** luxurious bathrooms; secluded garden seating; free Wi-Fi. **Cons:** hard to get reservations; expensive; nightly secure parking fee. [$] *Rooms from: $415* ✉ *526 Angela St.* ☎ *305/294–2661, 800/526–2664* 🌐 *www.gardenshotel.com* 🛏 *23 rooms* 🍴 *Free Breakfast.*

Heron House

$$ | B&B/INN | Built in the 1850s, rooms at this hotel just off Duval (not to be confused with Heron House Court, although they are sister properties) are outfitted in rattan and tropical watercolors, and bathrooms are updated with a touch of granite. **Pros:** vintage charm; close enough to the action but quiet; friendly staff. **Cons:** early bird gets the hot food at breakfast; furnishings need updating; no designated parking lot. [$] *Rooms from: $229* ✉ *512 Simonton St.* ☎ *305/294–8477, 800/294–1644* 🌐 *www.heronhousehotels.com* 🛏 *23 rooms* 🍴 *Free Breakfast.*

Island City House Hotel

$$$ | B&B/INN | A private garden with brick walkways, tropical plants, and a canopy of palms sets this convivial guesthouse apart from the pack. **Pros:** lush gardens; knowledgeable staff; bike rentals on-site. **Cons:** spotty Wi-Fi service; front desk is staffed only 8 am–8 pm; no parking. [$] *Rooms from: $320* ✉ *411 William St.* ☎ *305/294–5702, 800/634–8230* 🌐 *www.islandcityhouse.com* 🛏 *24 suites* 🍴 *No meals.*

Island House

$$$$ | HOTEL | Geared specifically toward gay men, this hotel features a health club, a video lounge, a café and bar, and rooms in historic digs. **Pros:** lots of privacy; just the place to get that all-over tan; free happy hour for guests. **Cons:** no women allowed; three rooms share a bath; day passes bring visitors of every age, which is a pro or con depending on your mood. [$] *Rooms from: $459* ✉ *1129 Fleming St.* ☎ *305/294–6284, 800/890–6284* 🌐 *www.islandhousekeywest.com* 🛏 *34 rooms* 🍴 *No meals.*

Key Lime Inn

$$ | B&B/INN | This 1854 Grand Bahama–style house on the National Register of Historic Places succeeds by offering amiable service, a great location, and simple rooms with natural-wood furnishings. **Pros:** walking distance to clubs and bars; some rooms have private outdoor spaces; free Wi-Fi. **Cons:** over a mile to the sunset end of Duval Street; pool faces a busy street; $20 daily parking fee. [$] *Rooms from: $259* ✉ *725 Truman Ave.* ☎ *305/294–5229, 800/549–4430* 🌐 *www.keylimeinn.com* 🛏 *37 rooms* 🍴 *Free Breakfast.*

La Pensione

$$ | B&B/INN | Hospitality and period furnishings make this 1891 home, once owned by a cigar executive, a wonderful glimpse into Key West life in the late 19th century. **Pros:** pine-paneled walls; first-come, first-served parking included; some rooms have wraparound porches. **Cons:** street-facing rooms are noisy; rooms do not have TVs; rooms accommodate only two people. [$] *Rooms from: $258* ✉ *809 Truman Ave.* ☎ *305/292–9923, 800/893–1193* 🌐 *www.lapensione.com* 🛏 *9 rooms* 🍴 *Free Breakfast.*

The Marker

$$$ | RESORT | The Marker is one of Key West's newest hotels, and a welcome and luxurious addition to the waterfront in Old Town, with Conch-style architecture and an authentic Keys aesthetic.

Pros: convenient Old Town location; on-site restaurant Cero Bodega; three saltwater pools, including one for adults only. **Cons:** hefty resort and parking fees nightly; "locals welcome" policy means pool loungers can be hard to come by; lots of walking if your room isn't near the amenities. [$] *Rooms from: $400* ✉ *200 William St.* ☎ *305/501–5193* 🌐 *www.themarkerkeywest.com* 🛏 *96 rooms* 🍴 *No meals.*

★ **Marquesa Hotel**

$$$ | **HOTEL** | In a town that prides itself on its laid-back luxury, this complex of four restored 1884 houses stands out. **Pros:** room service; romantic atmosphere; turndown service. **Cons:** street-facing rooms can be noisy; expensive rates; no elevator. [$] *Rooms from: $395* ✉ *600 Fleming St.* ☎ *305/292–1919, 800/869–4631* 🌐 *www.marquesa.com* 🛏 *27 rooms* 🍴 *No meals.*

Mermaid & the Alligator

$$ | **B&B/INN** | An enchanting combination of flora and fauna makes this 1904 Victorian house a welcoming retreat. **Pros:** hot plunge pool; massage pavilion; island-getaway feel. **Cons:** minimum stay required (length depends on season); dark public areas; plastic lawn chairs. [$] *Rooms from: $278* ✉ *729 Truman Ave.* ☎ *305/294–1894, 800/773–1894* 🌐 *www.kwmermaid.com* 🛏 *9 rooms* 🍴 *Free Breakfast.*

NYAH: Not Your Average Hotel

$$$ | **B&B/INN** | From its charming white picket fence, it may look similar to other Victorian-style Key West B&Bs, but that's where the similarities end. **Pros:** central location; perfect for traveling with a group of friends; free daily happy hour. **Cons:** small rooms, even smaller closets; street parking only; no toiletries provided. [$] *Rooms from: $349* ✉ *420 Margaret St.* ☎ *305/296–2131* 🌐 *www.nyahotels.com* 🛏 *36 rooms* 🍴 *Free Breakfast* ☞ *Age 18 and over only.*

★ **Ocean Key Resort & Spa**

$$$$ | **RESORT** | This full resort—relatively rare in Key West—has large, tropical-look rooms with private balconies and excellent amenities, including a pool and bar overlooking Sunset Pier and a Thai-inspired spa. **Pros:** well-trained staff; lively pool scene; fantastic location at the busy end of Duval. **Cons:** daily valet parking and resort fee; too bustling for some; rooms are starting to show their age. [$] *Rooms from: $495* ✉ *Zero Duval St.* ☎ *305/296–7701, 800/328–9815* 🌐 *www.oceankey.com* 🛏 *100 rooms* 🍴 *No meals.*

Pier House Resort and Spa

$$$$ | **RESORT** | This upscale resort, near Mallory Square in the heart of Old Town, offers a wide range of amenities, including a beach and comfortable, traditionally furnished rooms. **Pros:** beautiful beach; free Wi-Fi; nice spa and restaurant. **Cons:** lots of conventions; poolside rooms are small; not really suitable for children under 16. [$] *Rooms from: $470* ✉ *1 Duval St.* ☎ *305/296–4600, 800/327–8340* 🌐 *www.pierhouse.com* 🛏 *145 rooms* 🍴 *No meals.*

The Reach, A Waldorf Astoria Resort

$$$ | **RESORT** | Embracing Key West's only natural beach, this full-service, luxury resort offers sleek rooms, all with balconies and modern amenities as well as reciprocal privileges to its sister Casa Marina resort nearby. **Pros:** removed from Duval hubbub; great sunrise views; pullout sofas in most rooms. **Cons:** expensive resort fee; high rates; some say it lacks the grandeur you'd expect of a Waldorf property. [$] *Rooms from: $399* ✉ *1435 Simonton St.* ☎ *305/296–5000, 888/318–4316* 🌐 *www.reachresort.com* 🛏 *150 rooms* 🍴 *No meals.*

★ **Santa Maria Suites**

$$$$ | **RESORT** | It's odd to call this a hidden gem when it sits on a prominent corner just one block off Duval, but you'd never know what luxury awaits behind its concrete facade, which creates total seclusion from the outside world. **Pros:**

The Holidays Key West Style

On New Year's Eve, Key West celebrates the turning of the calendar page with three separate ceremonies that parody New York's dropping-of-the-ball drama. Here they let fall a 6-foot conch shell from Sloppy Joe's Bar, a pirate wench from the towering mast of a tall ship at the Historic Seaport, and a drag queen (elegantly decked out in a ball gown and riding an oversize red high-heel shoe) at Bourbon Street Pub. You wouldn't expect any less from America's most outrageous city.

Key West is one of the nation's biggest party towns, so the celebrations here take on a colorful hue. In keeping with

Key West's rich maritime heritage, its monthlong Bight Before Christmas begins Thanksgiving Eve at Key West Bight. The Lighted Boat Parade creates a quintessential Florida spectacle with live music and decorated vessels of all shapes and sizes.

Some years, the Tennessee Williams Theatre hosts a Key West version of *The Nutcracker*. In this unorthodox retelling, the heroine sails to a coral reef and is submerged in a diving bell. (What? No sugarplum fairies?) Between Christmas and New Year's Day, the Holiday House and Garden Tour is another yuletide tradition.

amenities galore; front desk concierge services; private parking lot. **Cons:** daily resort fee; poolside units must close curtains for privacy; only two-bedroom units available. $ *Rooms from: $549* ✉ *1401 Simonton St.* ☎ *866/726–8259, 305/296–5678* ⊕ *www.santamariasuites. com* ⇄ *35 suites* ⦿ *No meals.*

Simonton Court

$$$ | B&B/INN | A small world all its own, this adults-only maze of accommodations and four swimming pools makes you feel deliciously sequestered from Key West's crasser side but keeps you close enough to get there on foot. **Pros:** lots of privacy; well-appointed accommodations; friendly staff. **Cons:** minimum stay required in high season; off-street parking $25 nightly; some street noise in basic rooms. $ *Rooms from: $310* ✉ *320 Simonton St.* ☎ *305/294–6386, 800/944–2687* ⊕ *www. simontoncourt.com* ⇄ *29 rooms* ⦿ *Free Breakfast.*

Southernmost Beach Resort

$$$ | HOTEL | Rooms at this hotel on the quiet end of Duval—a 20-minute walk from downtown—are modern and

sophisticated, and it's far enough from the hubub that you can relax but close enough that you can participate if you wish. **Pros:** pool attracts a lively crowd; access to nearby properties and beach; free parking and Wi-Fi. **Cons:** can get crowded around the pool and public areas; expensive nightly resort fee; beach is across the street. $ *Rooms from: $359* ✉ *1319 Duval St.* ☎ *305/296–6577, 800/354–4455* ⊕ *www.southernmost-beachresort.com* ⇄ *118 rooms* ⦿ *No meals.*

Southwinds

$$ | B&B/INN | Operated by the same company as the ultra-high-end Santa Maria Suites, this motel-style property, though still pretty basic, has been modestly upgraded and is a good value-oriented option in pricey Key West. **Pros:** early (2 pm) check-in may be available; clean and spacious rooms; free parking and Wi-Fi. **Cons:** bland decor; small pools; thin walls. $ *Rooms from: $200* ✉ *1321 Simonton St.* ☎ *305/296–2829, 877/879–2362* ⊕ *www.keywestsouthwinds.com* ⇄ *58 rooms* ⦿ *Free Breakfast.*

Sunset Key cottages are right on the water's edge, far away from the action of Old Town.

Speakeasy Inn

$ | **B&B/INN** | During Prohibition, Raul Vasquez made this place popular by smuggling in rum from Cuba; today its reputation is for having reasonably priced rooms within walking distance of the beach. **Pros:** good location; all rooms have kitchenettes; first-come, first-served free parking. **Cons:** no pool; on busy Duval; rooms are fairly basic. *[$] Rooms from: $189 ✉ 1117 Duval St. ☎ 305/296–2680 🌐 www.speakeasyinn.com 🛏 7 suites 🍴 Free Breakfast.*

NEW TOWN

Best Western Key Ambassador Resort Inn

$$ | **HOTEL** | You know what to expect from this chain hotel: well-maintained rooms, predictable service, and competitive prices. **Pros:** big pool area; popular tiki bar serves liquor and food; most rooms have screened-in balconies. **Cons:** roar of airplanes from nearby airport; lacks personality; far from Duval Street. *[$] Rooms from: $300 ✉ 3755 S. Roosevelt Blvd., New Town ☎ 305/296–3500, 800/432–4315 🌐 www.keyambassador.com 🛏 100 rooms 🍴 Free Breakfast.*

Key West Marriott Beachside Hotel

$$$$ | **HOTEL** | **FAMILY** | This hotel vies for convention business with the biggest ballroom in Key West, but it also appeals to families with its spacious condo units decorated with impeccable good taste. **Pros:** private tanning beach; poolside cabanas; complimentary shuttle to Old Town and airport. **Cons:** no swimming at its beach; lots of conventions and conferences; cookie-cutter facade. *[$] Rooms from: $409 ✉ 3841 N. Roosevelt Blvd., New Town ☎ 305/296–8100, 800/546–0885 🌐 www.keywestmarriottbeachside.com 🛏 93 rooms, 93 1-bedroom suites, 10 2-bedroom suites, 26 3-bedroom suites 🍴 No meals.*

Parrot Key Hotel and Resort

$$$ | **HOTEL** | This revamped destination resort feels like an old-fashioned beach community with picket fences and rocking-chair porches. **Pros:** four pools; finely appointed units; access to marina and other facilities at three sister properties

in Marathon. **Cons:** not in walking distance to Old Town; no transportation provided; hefty resort fee. $ *Rooms from: $355* ✉ *2801 N. Roosevelt Blvd., New Town* ☎ *305/809–2200* ⊕ *www.parrotkeyresort.com* ⌨ *222 units* ❍ *No meals.*

★ Sunset Key

$$$$ | **RESORT** | This luxurious private island retreat with its own sandy beach feels completely cut off from the world, yet you're just minutes away from the action: a 10-minute ride from Mallory Square on the 24-hour free ferry. **Pros:** all units have kitchens; roomy verandas; free Wi-Fi. **Cons:** luxury doesn't come cheap; beach shore is rocky; launch runs only every 30 minutes. $ *Rooms from: $780* ✉ *245 Front St.* ☎ *305/292–5300, 888/477–7786* ⊕ *www.sunsetkeycottages.com* ⌨ *40 cottages* ❍ *Free Breakfast.*

Nightlife

Rest up: much of what happens in Key West occurs after dark. Open your mind and take a stroll. Scruffy street performers strum next to dogs in sunglasses. Characters wearing parrots or iguanas try to sell you your photo with their pet. Brawls tumble out the doors of Sloppy Joe's. Drag queens strut across stages in Joan Rivers garb. Tattooed men lick whipped cream off women's body parts. And margaritas flow like a Jimmy Buffett tune.

Capt. Tony's Saloon

BARS/PUBS | When it was the original Sloppy Joe's in the mid-1930s, Hemingway was a regular. Later, a young Jimmy Buffett sang here and made this watering hole famous in his song "Last Mango in Paris." Captain Tony was even voted mayor of Key West. Yes, this place is a beloved landmark. Stop in and take a look at the "hanging tree" that grows through the roof, listen to live music seven nights a week, and play some

pool. ✉ *428 Greene St.* ☎ *305/294–1838* ⊕ *www.capttonyssaloon.com.*

Cowboy Bill's Honky Tonk Saloon

BARS/PUBS | Ride the mechanical bucking bull, listen to live bands croon cry-in-your-beer tunes, and grab some pretty decent chow at the indoor-outdoor spread known as Cowboy Bill's Honky Tonk Saloon. There's live music from Tuesday through Saturday. Wednesday brings— we kid you not—sexy bull riding. ✉ *610½ Duval St.* ☎ *305/295–8219* ⊕ *www.cowboybillskw.com.*

Durty Harry's

BARS/PUBS | This megasize entertainment complex is home to eight different bars and clubs, both indoor and outdoor. Their motto is "Eight Famous Bars, One Awesome Night," and they're right. You'll find pizza, dancing, live music, Rick's Key West, and the infamous Red Garter strip club. ✉ *208 Duval St.* ☎ *305/296–5513* ⊕ *www.ricksbarkeywest.com.*

The Garden of Eden

BARS/PUBS | Perhaps one of Duval's more unusual and intriguing watering holes, The Garden of Eden sits atop the Bull & Whistle saloon and has a clothing-optional policy. Most drinkers are lookie-loos, but some actually bare it all, including the barmaids. ✉ *Bull & Whistle Bar, 224 Duval St.* ☎ *305/396–4565.*

Green Parrot Bar

BARS/PUBS | Pause for a libation in the open air and breathe in the spirit of Key West. Built in 1890 as a grocery store, this property has been many things to many people over the years. It's touted as the oldest bar in Key West and the sometimes-rowdy saloon has locals outnumbering out-of-towners, especially on nights when bands play. ✉ *601 Whitehead St., at Southard St.* ☎ *305/294–6133* ⊕ *www.greenparrot.com.*

Hog's Breath Saloon

BARS/PUBS | Belly up to the bar for a cold mug of the signature Hog's Breath Lager at this infamous joint, a must-stop on the

Sloppy Joe's is one must-stop on most Key West visitors' bar-hop stroll, also known as the Duval Crawl.

Key West bar crawl. Live bands play daily 1 pm–2 am (except when the game's on TV). You never know who'll stop by and perhaps even jump on stage for an impromptu concert (can you say Kenny Chesney?). ⊠ *400 Front St.* ☎ *305/296–4222* ⊕ *www.hogsbreath.com.*

Margaritaville Café

BARS/PUBS | A youngish, touristy crowd mixes with aging Parrot Heads. It's owned by former Key West resident and recording star Jimmy Buffett, who has been known to perform here. The drink of choice is, of course, a margarita, made with Jimmy's own brand of Margaritaville tequila. There's live music nightly, as well as lunch and dinner. ⊠ *500 Duval St.* ☎ *305/292–1435* ⊕ *www.margaritaville-keywest.com.*

Pier House

BARS/PUBS | The party here begins at the Beach Bar with live entertainment daily to celebrate the sunset on the beach, then moves to the funky Chart Room. It's small and odd, but there are free hot dogs and peanuts, and its history is worth learning. ⊠ *1 Duval St.* ☎ *305/296–4600, 800/327–8340* ⊕ *www.pierhouse.com.*

Schooner Wharf Bar

BARS/PUBS | This open-air waterfront bar and grill in the historic seaport district retains its funky Key West charm and hosts live entertainment daily. Its margaritas rank among Key West's best, as does the bar itself, voted Best Local's Bar six years in a row. For great views, head up to the second floor and be sure to order up some fresh seafood and fritters and Dark and Stormy cocktails. ⊠ *202 William St.* ☎ *305/292–3302* ⊕ *www. schoonerwharf.com.*

Sloppy Joe's

BARS/PUBS | There's history and good times at the successor to a famous 1937 speakeasy named for its founder, Captain Joe Russell. Decorated with Hemingway memorabilia and marine flags, the bar is popular with travelers and is full and noisy all the time. A Sloppy Joe's T-shirt is a de rigueur Key West souvenir, and the gift shop sells them like crazy. Grab a seat (if you can) and be entertained by the bands and by the parade of people in constant motion. ✉ *201 Duval St.* ☎ *305/294–5717* ⊕ *www.sloppyjoes. com.*

Two Friends Patio Lounge

BARS/PUBS | Love karaoke? Get it out of your system at Two Friends Patio Lounge, where your performance gets a live Internet feed via the bar's Karaoke Cam. The singing starts at 8:30 pm most nights. The Bloody Marys are famous. ✉ *512 Front St.* ☎ *305/296–3124* ⊕ *www. twofriendskeywest.com.*

Shopping

On these streets, you'll find colorful local art of widely varying quality, key limes made into everything imaginable, and the raunchiest T-shirts in the civilized world. Browsing the boutiques—with frequent pub stops along the way—makes for an entertaining stroll down Duval Street. Cocktails certainly help the appreciation of some goods, such as the figurine of a naked man blowing bubbles out his backside or the swashbuckling pirate costumes that are no longer just for Halloween.

Alan S. Maltz Gallery

ART GALLERIES | The owner, declared the state's official wildlife photographer by the Wildlife Foundation of Florida, captures the state's nature and character in stunning portraits. Spend four figures for large-format images on canvas or save on small prints and closeouts. ✉ *1210 Duval St.* ☎ *305/294–0005* ⊕ *www.alanmaltz. com.*

Art@830

ART GALLERIES | This inviting gallery carries a little bit of everything, from pottery to paintings and jewelry to sculptures. Most outstanding is its selection of glass art, particularly the jellyfish lamps. Take time to admire all that is here. ✉ *830 Caroline St., Historic Seaport* ☎ *305/295–9595* ⊕ *www.art830.com.*

Bahama Village

SHOPPING CENTERS/MALLS | Where to start your shopping adventure? This cluster of spruced-up shops, restaurants, and vendors is responsible for the restoration of the colorful historic district where Bahamians settled in the 19th century. The village lies roughly between Whitehead and Fort streets and Angela and Catherine streets. Hemingway frequented the bars, restaurants, and boxing rings in this part of town. ✉ *Between Whitehead and Fort Sts. and Angela and Catherine Sts.*

Cayo Hueso y Habana

GIFTS/SOUVENIRS | Part museum, part shopping center, this circa-1879 warehouse includes a hand-rolled-cigar shop, one-of-a-kind souvenirs, a Cuban restaurant, and exhibits that tell of the island's Cuban heritage. Outside, a memorial garden pays homage to the island's Cuban ancestors. ✉ *410 Wall St., Mallory Sq.* ☎ *305/293–7260.*

Fairvilla Megastore

SPECIALTY STORES | Don't leave town without a browse through the legendary shop. Although it's not really a clothing store, you'll find an astonishing array of fantasy wear, outlandish costumes (check out the pirate section), as well as other "adult" toys. (Some of the products may make you blush.) ✉ *520 Front St.* ☎ *305/292–0448* ⊕ *www.fairvilla.com.*

Fausto's Food Palace

FOOD/CANDY | Since 1926 Fausto's has been the spot to catch up on the week's gossip and to chill out in summer—it has groceries, organic foods, marvelous wines, a sushi chef on duty 8 am–3 pm, and box lunches and dinners-by-the-pound to go. There are two locations you can shop at in Key West (the other is at 1105 White Street) plus a recently opened online store. ✉ *522 Fleming St.* ☎ *305/296–5663* ⊕ *www.faustos.com.*

Gallery on Greene

ART GALLERIES | This is the largest gallery–exhibition space in Key West and it showcases 37 museum-quality artists. It prides itself on being the leader in the field of representational fine art, painting, sculptures, and reproductions from the Florida Keys and Key West. You can see the love immediately from gallery curator Nancy Frank, who aims to please everyone, from the casual buyer to the established collector. ⊠ *606 Greene St.* ☎ *305/294–1669* ⊕ *www.galleryon-greene.com.*

Gingerbread Square Gallery

ART GALLERIES | The oldest private art gallery in Key West represents local and internationally acclaimed artists on an annually changing basis, in media ranging from paintings to art glass. ⊠ *1207 Duval St.* ☎ *305/296–8900* ⊕ *www.ginger-breadsquaregallery.com.*

★ Kermit's Key West Lime Shoppe

FOOD/CANDY | You'll see Kermit himself standing on the corner every time a trolley passes, pie in hand. Besides pie, his shop carries a multitude of key lime products from barbecue sauce to jelly beans. His prefrozen pies, topped with a special long-lasting whipped cream instead of meringue, travels well. This is a must-stop shop while in Key West. The key lime pie is the best on the island; once you try it frozen on a stick, dipped in chocolate, you may consider quitting your job and moving here. Savor every bite on the outdoor patio-garden area, or come for breakfast or lunch at the on-site café. A smaller second location is on the corner of Duval and Front streets. ⊠ *200 Elizabeth St., Historic Seaport* ☎ *305/296–0806, 800/376–0806* ⊕ *www. keylimeshop.com.*

Key West Island Bookstore

BOOKS/STATIONERY | This home away from home for the large Key West writers' community carries new, used, and rare titles. It specializes in Hemingway, Tennessee Williams, and South Florida mystery writers. ⊠ *513 Fleming St.* ☎ *305/294–2904* ⊕ *www.keywestisland-books.com.*

Key West Pottery

CERAMICS/GLASSWARE | You won't find any painted coconuts here, but you will find a collection of contemporary tropical ceramics. Wife-and-husband owners Kelly Lever and Adam Russell take real pride in this working studio that, in addition to their own creations, features artists from around the country. This is one of the island's few specialty galleries. ⊠ *1203 Duval St.* ☎ *305/900–8303* ⊕ *www. keywestpottery.com.*

Kino Sandals

TEXTILES/SEWING | A pair of Kino sandals was once a public declaration that you'd been to Key West. The attraction? You can watch these inexpensive items being made. The factory has been churning out several styles since 1966. Walk up to the counter, grab a pair, try them on, and lay down some cash. It's that simple. ⊠ *107 Fitzpatrick St.* ☎ *305/294–5044* ⊕ *www. kinosandalfactory.com.*

Lucky Street Gallery

ART GALLERIES | High-end contemporary paintings are the focus at this gallery that has been in business for over 30 years. There are also a few pieces of jewelry by internationally recognized Key West–based artists. Changing exhibits, artist receptions, and special events make this a lively venue. Although the location has changed, the passionate staff remain the same. ⊠ *1204 White St.* ☎ *305/294–3973* ⊕ *www.luckystreetgallery.com.*

Peppers of Key West

FOOD/CANDY | If you like it hot, you'll love this collection of hundreds of sauces, salsas, and sweets guaranteed to heat you up. Take a seat at the tasting bar and see which products light your fire. ⊠ *602 Greene St.* ☎ *305/295–9333, 800/597–2823* ⊕ *www.peppersofkeywest.com.*

Seam Shoppe

TEXTILES/SEWING | Take home a shopping bag full of scarlet hibiscus, fuchsia heliconias, blue parrotfish, and even pink flamingo fabric, selected from the city's widest selection of tropical-print fabrics. ✉ *1113 Truman Ave.* ☎ *305/296–9830* ⊕ *www.tropicalfabricsonline.com.*

 # Activities

Unlike the rest of the region, Key West isn't known primarily for outdoor pursuits. But everyone should devote at least half a day to relaxing on a boat tour, heading out on a fishing expedition, or pursuing some other adventure at sea. The ultimate excursion is a boat or seaplane trip to Dry Tortugas National Park for snorkeling and exploring Ft. Jefferson. Other excursions cater to nature lovers, scuba divers, and snorkelers, and folks who just want to get out in the water and enjoy the scenery and sunset. For those who prefer land-based recreation, biking is the way to go. Hiking is limited, but walking the streets of Old Town provides plenty of exercise.

BIKING

Key West was practically made for bicycles, but don't let that lull you into a false sense of security. Narrow and one-way streets along with car traffic result in several bike accidents a year. Some hotels rent or lend bikes to guests; others will refer you to a nearby shop and reserve a bike for you. Rentals usually start at about $12 a day, but some places also rent by the half day. ■ TIP→ **Lock up; bikes—and porch chairs!—are favorite targets for local thieves.**

A&M Rentals

BICYCLING | Rent beach cruisers with large baskets, scooters, and electric mini-cars. Look for the huge American flag on the roof, or call for free airport, ferry, or cruise-ship pickup. A second location is on South Street. ✉ *523 Truman Ave.* ☎ *305/294–0399* ⊕ *www.amscooterskeywest.com* 🖃 *Bicycles from $15, scooters from $35, electric cars from $139.*

Eaton Bikes

BICYCLING | Tandem, three-wheel, and children's bikes are available in addition to the standard beach cruisers and hybrid bikes. Delivery is free for all Key West rentals. ✉ *830 Eaton St.* ☎ *305/294–8188* ⊕ *www.eatonbikes.com* 🖃 *From $18 per day.*

Moped Hospital

BICYCLING | This outfit supplies balloon-tire bikes with yellow safety baskets for adults and kids, as well as scooters and even double-seater scooters. ✉ *601 Truman Ave.* ☎ *305/296–3344, 866/296–1625* ⊕ *www.mopedhospital.com* 🖃 *Bicycles from $12 per day, scooters from $35 per day.*

BOATING

Key West is surrounded by marinas, so it's easy to find what you're looking for, whether it's sailing with dolphins or paddling in the mangroves. In addition to its popular kayaking trips, Key West Eco-Tours offers sunset sails and private charters *(see Kayaking).*

★ Classic Harbor Line

SAILING | The *Schooner America 2.0* is refined and elegant, and her comfortable seating makes her a favorite when she sails Key West each November–April. Two-hour sunset champagne cruises are an island highlight. Make reservations well in advance. These sailings are popular with locals and visitors. ✉ *202-R Williams St.* ☎ *305/293–7245* ⊕ *www.sail-keywest.com* 🖃 *Day sails from $55, sunset sails from $85.*

Dancing Dolphin Spirit Charters

BOATING | FAMILY | Victoria Impallomeni-Spencer, a wilderness guide and environmental marine science walking encyclopedia, invites up to six nature lovers—especially children—aboard the *Imp II*, a 25-foot Aquasport, for four- and seven-hour ecotours that frequently include encounters with wild dolphins. While island-hopping, you visit underwater gardens and reefs, natural shoreline, and mangrove habitats. For the "Dolphin Day for Humans" tour, you'll be pulled through the water, equipped with mask and snorkel, on a specially designed "dolphin water massage board" that simulates dolphin swimming motions. All equipment is supplied. Captain Victoria is known around these parts as the dolphin whisperer as she's been guiding for over 40 years. ⊠ *MM 5 OS, Murray's Marina, 5710 Overseas Hwy.* ☎ *305/304–7562, 305/745–9901* ⊕ *www.dancingdolphin-spirits.com* 🖃 *From $600.*

FISHING

Any number of local fishing guides can take you to where the big ones are biting, either in the backcountry for snapper and snook or to the deep water for the marlins and shark that lured Hemingway here.

Key West Bait & Tackle

FISHING | Prepare to catch a big one with the live bait, frozen bait, and fishing equipment provided here. They even offer rod and reel rentals (starting at $15 for one day, $5 each additional day). Stop by their on-site Live Bait Lounge where you can sip $3.25 ice-cold beer while telling fish tales. ⊠ *241 Margaret St.* ☎ *305/292–1961* ⊕ *www.keywest-baitandtackle.com.*

Key West Pro Guides

FISHING | This outfitter offers private charters, and you can choose four-, five-, six-, or eight-hour trips. Choose from flats, backcountry, reef, offshore fishing, and even specialty trips to the Dry Tortugas. Whatever your fishing (even spearfishing) pleasure, their captains will hook you up. ⊠ *G–31 Miriam St.* ☎ *866/259–4205* ⊕ *www.keywestproguides.com* 🖃 *From $450.*

GOLF

Key West Golf Club

GOLF | Key West isn't a major golf destination, but there is one course on Stock Island designed by Rees Jones that will downright surprise you with its water challenges and tropical beauty. It's also the only "Caribbean" golf course in the United States, boasting 200 acres of unique Florida foliage and wildlife. Hole 8 is the famous "Mangrove Hole," which will give you stories to tell. It's a 143-yard par 3 that is played completely over a mass of mangroves with their gnarly roots and branches completely intertwined. Bring extra balls and book your tee time early in season. Nike rental clubs are available. ⊠ *6450 E. College Rd.* ☎ *305/294–5232* ⊕ *www.keywestgolf.com* 🖃 *$55–$99* 🏌 *. 18 holes, 6500 yards, par 70.*

KAYAKING

Key West Eco-Tours

KAYAKING | Key West is surrounded by marinas, so it's easy to find a water-based activity or tour, whether it's sailing with dolphins or paddling in the mangroves. These sail-kayak-snorkel excursions take you into backcountry flats and mangrove forests without the crowds. The 4½-hour trip includes a light lunch, equipment, and even dry camera bags. Private sunset sails, backcountry boating adventures, kayak, and paddleboard tours are available, too. ⊠ *Historic Seaport behind Turtle Kraals, 231 Margaret St.* ☎ *305/294–7245* ⊕ *www.keywestecot-ours.com* 🖃 *From $115.*

Lazy Dog

KAYAKING | Take a two-hour backcountry mangrove ecotour or a four-hour guided sea kayak–snorkel tour around the mangrove islands just east of Key West. Costs include transportation, bottled water, a snack, and supplies, including snorkeling gear. Paddleboard tours, PaddleYoga, and PaddleFit classes are also available, as are maps and rentals for self-touring. ⊠ *5114 Overseas Hwy.* ☎ *305/295–9898* ⊕ *www.lazydog.com* 🖃 *From $50.*

SCUBA DIVING AND SNORKELING

The Florida Keys National Marine Sanctuary extends along Key West and beyond to the Dry Tortugas. Key West National Wildlife Refuge further protects the pristine waters. Most divers don't make it this far out in the Keys, but if you're looking for a day of diving as a break from the nonstop party in Old Town, expect to pay about $65 and upward for a two-tank dive. Serious divers can book dive trips to the Dry Tortugas. The USS *Vandenberg* is another popular dive spot, known for its world's-first underwater transformative art exhibit on an artificial reef.

Captain's Corner

SCUBA DIVING | This PADI-certified dive shop has classes in several languages and twice-daily snorkel and dive trips to reefs and wrecks aboard a 60-foot dive boat, the *Sea Eagle*. Use of weights, belts, masks, and fins is included. ⊠ *125 Ann St.* ☎ *305/296–8865* ⊕ *www.captainscorner.com* ⏋ *From $45.*

Dive Key West

SCUBA DIVING | Operating over 40 years, Dive Key West is a full-service dive center that has charters, instruction, gear rental, sales, and repair. You can take either snorkel excursions or scuba trips with this outfit that is dedicated to coral reef education and preservation. ⊠ *3128 N. Roosevelt Blvd.* ☎ *305/296–3823* ⊕ *www.divekeywest.com* ⏋ *Snorkeling from $69, scuba from $95.*

Snuba of Key West

SCUBA DIVING | **FAMILY** | If you've always wanted to dive but never found the time to get certified, Snuba is for you. You can dive safely using a regulator tethered to a floating air tank with a simple orientation. Ride out to the reef on a catamaran, then follow your guide underwater for a one-hour tour of the coral reefs. It's easy and fun. No prior diving or snorkeling experience is necessary, but you must know how to swim and be at least eight years old. The price includes beverages. ⊠ *Garrison Bight Marina, Palm Ave. between Eaton St. and N. Roosevelt Blvd.* ☎ *305/292–4616* ⊕ *www.snubakeywest.com* ⏋ *From $109.*

STAND-UP PADDLEBOARDING

SUP Key West

KAYAKING | This ancient sport from Hawaii involves a surfboard and a paddle and has quickly become a favorite Florida water sport known as SUP (stand-up paddleboarding). SUP Key West gives lessons and morning, afternoon, or sunset tours of the estuaries. What's more, your tour guides are experts (one's even a PhD) in marine biology and ecology. Call ahead to make arrangements. ⊠ *110 Grinnell St.* ☎ *305/240–1426* ⊕ *www.supkeywest. com* ⏋ *From $45.*

Excursion to Dry Tortugas National Park

70 miles southwest of Key West.

The Dry Tortugas lie in the central time zone. Key West Seaplane pilots like to tell their passengers that they land 15 minutes before they take off. If you can't do the time-consuming (and by air, at least, expensive) trip, the national park operates an interpretive center in the Historic Seaport at Old Key West Bight.

GETTING HERE AND AROUND

For now, the ferryboat *Yankee Freedom III* departs from a marina in Old Town and does day trips to Garden Key. Key West Seaplane Adventures has half- and full-day trips to the Dry Tortugas, where you can explore Ft. Jefferson, built in 1846, and snorkel on the beautiful protected reef. Departing from the Key West airport, the flights include soft drinks and snorkel equipment for $265 half day, $465 full day, plus there's a $10 park fee (cash only). If you want to explore the park's other keys, look into renting a boat or hiring a private charter. The Dry Tortugas National Park and Historic Key West Bight Museum at 240 Margaret Street is a way to experience it for free. *See Exploring in Key West.*

Key West Seaplane Adventures

TRANSPORTATION SITE (AIRPORT/BUS/FERRY/TRAIN) | The 35- to 40-minute trip to the Dry Tortugas skims above the trademark windowpane-clear waters of the Florida Keys. The seaplane perspective provides an awesome experience that could result in a stiff neck from craning to look out the window and down from 500 feet above. In the flats that edge Key West, you can spot stingrays, sea turtles, and sharks in the shallow water. In the area dubbed The Quicksands, water plunges to 30-foot depths and sand undulates in dunelike formations. Shipwrecks also festoon these waters; here's where Mel Fisher harvested treasure from the *Atocha* and *Margarita.* His 70-foot work ship, the *Arbutus,* deteriorated and eventually sank at the northern edge of the treasure sites. With its mast poking out above water, it's easy to spot and fun to photograph. From there, the water deepens from emerald hues to shades of deep blue as depths reach 70 feet. Seaplanes of Key West's most popular trip is the half-day option, where you spend about 2½ hours on Garden Key. The seaplanes leave during your stay, so be prepared to carry all of your possessions with you. The morning trip beats the ferries to the island, so you'll have it to yourself until the others arrive. Snorkeling equipment, soft drinks, and birding lists are supplied. ✉ *3471 S. Roosevelt Blvd., Key West* ☎ *305/615–7429* ⊕ *www.keywestseaplanecharters.com* ✈ *From $342.*

Yankee Freedom III

TRANSPORTATION SITE (AIRPORT/BUS/FERRY/TRAIN) | The fast, sleek, 110-foot catamaran *Yankee Freedom III* travels to the Dry Tortugas in 2¼ hours. The time passes quickly on the roomy vessel equipped with four restrooms, three warm freshwater showers, and two bars. Stretch out on two decks that are both air-conditioned, with cushioned seating. There is also an open sundeck with sunny and shaded seating. Continental breakfast and lunch are included. On arrival, a naturalist leads a 45-minute guided tour, which is followed by lunch and a free afternoon for swimming, snorkeling (gear included), and exploring. The vessel is ADA-certified for visitors using wheelchairs. The Dry Tortugas lies in the central time zone. ✉ *Ticket booth, 240 Margaret St., Key West* ☎ *305/294–7009, 800/634–0939* ⊕ *www.drytortugas. com* ✈ *$180; parking $19 in city garage* ☞ *Vessel departs from the Ferry Terminal at 100 Grinnell St. in the Historic Seaport.*

 ## Sights

Dry Tortugas National Park

NATIONAL/STATE PARK | This park, 70 miles off the shores of Key West, consists of seven small islands. Tour the fort; then lay out your blanket on the sunny beach for a picnic before you head out to snorkel on the protected reef. Many people like to camp here ($15 per site for one of eight sites, plus a group site and overflow area; first-come, first-served), but note that there's no freshwater supply and you must carry off whatever you bring onto the island.

The typical visitor from Key West, however, makes it no farther than the waters of Garden Key. Home to 19th-century Ft. Jefferson, it is the destination for seaplane and fast ferry tours out of Key West. With 2½ to 6½ hours to spend on the island, visitors have time to tour the mammoth fort-prison and then cool off with mask and snorkel along the fort's moat wall.

History buffs might remember long-deactivated Ft. Jefferson, the largest brick building in the western hemisphere, as the prison that held Dr. Samuel Mudd, who unwittingly set John Wilkes Booth's leg after the assassination of Abraham Lincoln. Three other men were also held there for complicity in the assassination. Original construction on the fort began in 1846 and continued for 30 years, but was never completed because the invention of the rifled cannon made it obsolete.

That's when it became a Civil War prison and later a wildlife refuge. In 1935 President Franklin Roosevelt declared it a national monument for its historic and natural value.

The brick fort acts as a gigantic, almost 16-acre reef. Around its moat walls, coral grows and schools of snapper, grouper, and wrasses hang out. To reach the offshore coral heads requires about 15 minutes of swimming over sea-grass beds. The reef formations blaze with the color and majesty of brain coral, swaying sea fans, and flitting tropical fish. It takes a bit of energy to swim the distance, but the water depth pretty much measures under 7 feet all the way, allowing for sandy spots to stop and rest. (Standing in sea-grass meadows and on coral is detrimental to marine life.)

Serious snorkelers and divers head out farther offshore to epic formations, including Palmata Patch, one of the few surviving concentrations of elkhorn coral in the Keys. Day-trippers congregate on the sandy beach to relax in the sun and enjoy picnics. Overnight tent campers have use of restroom facilities and achieve a total getaway from noise, lights, and civilization in general. Remember that no matter how you get here, the park's $15 admission fee must be paid in cash.

The park has signposted a self-guided tour that takes about 45 minutes. You should budget more time if you're into photography, because the scenic shots are hard to pass up. Ranger-guided tours are also available at certain times. Check in at the visitor center for a schedule. The small office also shows an orientation video, sells books and other educational materials, and, most importantly, provides a blast of air-conditioning on hot days.

Birders in the know bring binoculars to watch some 100,000 nesting sooty terns at their only U.S. nesting site, Bush Key, adjacent to Garden Key. Noddy terns also nest in the spring. During winter migrations, birds fill the airspace so thickly they literally fall from the sky to make their pit stops, birders say. Nearly 300 species have been spotted in the park's seven islands, including frigate birds, boobies, cormorants, and broad-winged hawks. Bush Key is closed to foot traffic during nesting season, January through September. ⊠ *Key West* ⊕ *www.nps.gov/drto* ▧ *$15.*

FORT LAUDERDALE

6

Updated by
Galena Mosovich

⊙ Sights	🍴 Restaurants	🛏 Hotels	⊝ Shopping	⍟ Nightlife
★★★★☆	★★★★☆	★★★★☆	★★★☆☆	★★★☆☆

WELCOME TO FORT LAUDERDALE

TOP REASONS TO GO

★ **Blue waves:** The cerulean waters of the Atlantic Ocean hugging Broward County's entire coast form a 23-mile stretch of picturesque beaches between Miami-Dade and Palm Beach counties.

★ **Inland waterways:** More than 300 miles of inland waterways, including downtown Fort Lauderdale's historic New River and Intracoastal, create what's known as the "Venice of America."

★ **Everglades adventures:** The untamed landscape of the Everglades—home to alligators, crocodiles, colorful birds, and other elusive wildlife—is a short trip from beachfront luxury.

★ **Emerging arts scene:** Experience the local contemporary art scene as it grows into a major force in the region.

★ **Cruise gateway:** A dozen supermodern terminals serve about 4 million cruisers and ferry guests a year at Port Everglades, one of the busiest cruise ports in the country.

Along Florida's Gold Coast, Fort Lauderdale and Broward County present a delightful middle ground between the posh Palm Beaches and the extravagance of Miami. From downtown Fort Lauderdale, it's about a four-hour drive to Orlando or Key West, but Broward's allure is undeniable. From oceanside to inland, the county's sprawling geography encompasses 31 communities with a resident population of 1.9 million.

1 Downtown and Las Olas. The eclectic hub of town is known for its arts and nightlife scenes and is complemented by Las Olas Boulevard's boutiques, sidewalk cafés, and restaurants.

2 Fort Lauderdale Beach. Fort Lauderdale's 23 miles of sparkling beaches are lined with restaurants and hotels.

3 Intracoastal and Inland Fort Lauderdale. Even if you're not on the beach, you're likely still near the water: waterways and canals that weave through town are big among the boating community.

4 Wilton Manors and Oakland Park. Wilton Manors is a progressive area with independent shops and nightlife venues.

5 Western Suburbs and Beyond. The suburbs are just as bustling, if not more, than the city center, but out west you're essentially on the edge of the Everglades.

6 Lauderdale-by-the-Sea. North of Fort Lauderdale on State Road A1A, old-school seaside charm draws families and cost-conscious travelers to a more low-rise, low-key beach alternative to Fort Lauderdale.

7 Pompano Beach. Explore shipwrecks and coral reefs on a scuba diving adventure off the shore of this beach town, just north of Lauderdale-by-the-Sea.

8 Hollywood. From the beachside Broadwalk to historic Young Circle (now ArtsPark), this South Broward destination provides grit and good times in a laid-back manner.

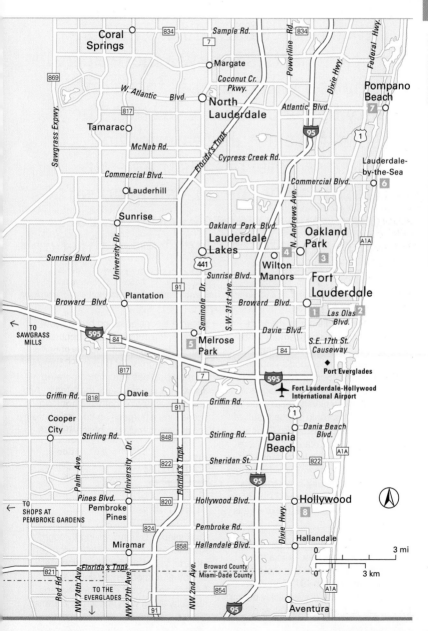

Coral Springs
834
7
Sample Rd.
834
Powerline Rd.
Dixie Hwy.
Federal Hwy.

Margate

869
W. Atlantic Blvd.
Coconut Cr. Pkwy.
North Lauderdale
Pompano Beach
7
Atlantic Blvd.
95
1

817
Tamarac

McNab Rd.
Cypress Creek Rd.
Florida's Tnpk.

Commercial Blvd.
Lauderhill
Commercial Blvd.
Lauderdale-by-the-Sea
6

Sunrise
Oakland Park Blvd.
Lauderdale Lakes
N. Andrews Ave.
Oakland Park
A1A
3

Sunrise Blvd.
University Dr.
441
Wilton Manors
4
Fort Lauderdale

TO SAWGRASS MILLS
595
84
Broward Blvd.
Plantation
91
Seminole Dr.
S.W. 31st Ave.
Broward Blvd.
Las Olas Blvd.
1
2
Davie Blvd.
Melrose Park
5
S.E. 17th St. Causeway
84
Port Everglades
7
595
Fort Lauderdale-Hollywood International Airport

Griffin Rd.
818
Davie
91
Griffin Rd.
1

Cooper City
Stirling Rd.
848
Stirling Rd.
Dania Beach
Dania Beach Blvd.
A1A
University Dr.
822
Sheridan St.
822
95
Palm Ave.

Pines Blvd.
820
Hollywood Blvd.
Hollywood
8
TO SHOPS AT PEMBROKE GARDENS
Pembroke Pines
824
Dixie Hwy.
Pembroke Rd.

Miramar
858
Hallandale Blvd.
Hallandale
0   3 mi

821
Florida's Tnpk.
Red Rd.
NW 74th Ave.
NW 27th Ave.
NW 2nd Ave.
Broward County
Miami-Dade County
854
0   3 km

TO THE EVERGLADES
91
95
Aventura
A1A

It was only a matter of time before the sun-soaked streets of Fort Lauderdale faced an identity crisis. What was once a hotbed of dive bars, diners, and all-day beach parties is now a more upscale destination with a deeper focus on quality in the pursuit of leisure. The city has more notable eateries and world-class hotel brands than ever, and fortunately, the upscaling doesn't follow Miami's over-the-top lead. Fort Lauderdale is still a place where flip-flops are acceptable, if not encouraged.

Along the Strip and west to the Intracoastal, many of the midcentury-modern boutique properties are trying to preserve the neighborhood's vintage design aesthetic. Somehow Greater Fort Lauderdale gracefully melds disparate eras into nouveau nirvana, seasoned with a lot of sand. This could be the result of its massive territory: Broward County encompasses more than 1,100 square miles of land—ranging from dense residential enclaves to agricultural farms and subtropical wilds. But it's the county's beautiful beaches and some 3,000 hours of sunshine each year that make all this possible.

Fort Lauderdale was named for Major William Lauderdale, who built a fort in 1838 during the Second Seminole War. It was incorporated in 1911 with only 175 residents, but it grew quickly during the Florida boom of the 1920s, and it became a popular spring break destination in the 1960s. Today's population is more than 178,000, and the suburbs continue to grow. Of Broward County's 31 municipalities and unincorporated areas, Fort Lauderdale is the largest. And now showstopping hotels, a hot food scene, and a burgeoning cultural platform accompany the classic beach lifestyle.

Planning

When to Go

Peak season is Thanksgiving through April, when cultural events (performing arts, visual art displays, concerts, and other outdoor entertainment) go full throttle. Expect extreme heat and humidity along with rain in the summer.

Hurricanes come most notably in August and September. Tee times are harder to get on weekends year-round. Regardless of season, remember that Fort Lauderdale sunshine will burn even on a cloudy day.

ANNUAL FESTIVALS AND EVENTS

Fort Lauderdale International Boat Show
(*FLIBS*). The city hosts the world's largest in-water boat show in the fall. FLIBS has been the end-all, be-all of marine envy since 1960, with more than $2 billion in boats, yachts, superyachts, and accessories from every major manufacturer and builder worldwide. The city buzzes with parties to celebrate, while the official show takes place at several locations along the Intracoastal and A1A. Tickets are required. ⊠ *Bahia Mar Yachting Center, 801 Seabreeze Blvd., Beachfront* ☎ *954/463-6762 Informa U.S. Boat Shows* ⊕ *www.flibs.com/en/home. html* ☞ *From $33 per day/per person.*

Fort Lauderdale International Film Festival
(*FLIFF*). Founded in 1986, this annual festival is a celebration of independent cinema, showcasing more than 100 American and international feature, documentary, and short films at various locations across Broward County. Cinema Paradiso in downtown Fort Lauderdale is the base camp. In addition to more than two weeks of screenings, seminars, events, and parties fill the calendar, but don't expect the pomp of a big-city film festival. With that said, the Florida Arts Council refers to FLIFF as the highest-rated film festival in the state of Florida and it's the only film festival in the South to receive four major grants from the Academy of Motion Picture Arts and Sciences. ☎ *954/525-3456* ⊕ *www.fliff.com.*

Seminole Hard Rock Winterfest Boat Parade
Known as "the greatest show on H2O" and the largest one-day spectator event in Florida, the Seminole Hard Rock Winterfest Boat Parade's 12-mile route through Fort Lauderdale's main waterways draws about a million people every

year. The theme and decorations change, as do the participating yachts and superyachts. If you can't make it, you can watch the event live on the the Internet. ☎ *954/767–0686* ⊕ *winterfestparade. com.*

Getting Here and Around

AIR TRAVEL

Fort Lauderdale–Hollywood International Airport (FLL) serves more than 32 million passengers a year with nonstop flights to over 100 U.S. and international cities. FLL is 3 miles south of downtown Fort Lauderdale—just off U.S. 1 (South Federal Highway) between Fort Lauderdale and Hollywood, and near Port Everglades and Fort Lauderdale Beach. Other options include **Miami International Airport (MIA),** which is about 32 miles southwest, and the far less chaotic **Palm Beach International Airport (PBI),** which is about 50 miles north.

AIRPORT INFORMATION Fort Lauderdale–Hollywood International Airport (*FLL*). ☎ *866/435–9355* ⊕ *www.broward. org.* **Miami International Airport** (*MIA*). ☎ *305/876-7000* ⊕ *www.iflymia.com.* **Palm Beach International Airport** (*PBI*). ☎ *561/471–7420* ⊕ *www.pbia.org.*

BUS TRAVEL

Broward County Transit (BCT) operates Bus Route 1 between the airport and its main terminal at Broward Boulevard and Northwest First Avenue in downtown Fort Lauderdale. Service from the airport (Rental Car Center, Stop 7) is every 20 to 30 minutes and begins at 5:29 am on weekdays, 6:04 am Saturday, and 6:44 am Sunday; the last bus leaves the airport at 11:36 pm on weekdays, 11:44 pm Saturday, and 9:44 pm Sunday. The one-way cash fare is $2 (exact change). ■TIP→ **The Northwest First Avenue stop is in a sketchy part of town. Exercise caution there, day or night. Better yet, take an Uber, Lyft, or taxi to and from the airport.** BCT also covers the county on fixed routes to four transfer terminals: Broward Central Terminal, West Regional Terminal, Lauderhill Mall Transfer Facility, and Northeast Transit Center. The fare for an all-day bus pass is $5 (exact change). Service starts around 4:30 am and continues to 12:40 am, except on Sunday.

BUS CONTACTS Broward County Transit (*BCT*). ☎ *954/357–8400* ⊕ *www.broward. org/BCT.*

CAR TRAVEL

Renting a car to get around Broward County is highly recommended. Traditional cabs are unreliable and expensive; ride-hailing apps such as Uber and Lyft are a cheaper, better option. Public transportation is not a realistic option for most travelers, but the Sun Trolley can be sufficient for some visitors who don't need or wish to explore beyond the downtown core and beaches.

By car, access to Broward County from north or south is via Florida's Turnpike, Interstate 95, U.S. 1, or U.S. 441. Interstate 75 (Alligator Alley, requiring a toll despite being part of the nation's interstate-highway system) connects Broward with Florida's west coast and runs parallel to State Road 84 within the county. East–west Interstate 595 runs from westernmost Broward County and connects Interstate 75 with Interstate 95 and U.S. 1, providing easy access to the airport and seaport. State Road A1A, designated a Florida Scenic Highway by the state's Department of Transportation, runs parallel to the beach.

TRAIN TRAVEL

Amtrak provides daily service to Fort Lauderdale and stops in Deerfield Beach and Hollywood.

All three of the region's airports link to Tri-Rail, a commuter train operating daily through Palm Beach, Broward, and Miami-Dade counties.

The modern, privately operated Virgin Trains USA (formerly Brightline) high-speed train service connects downtown Miami, Fort Lauderdale, and West Palm Beach. The trip from downtown Miami to Fort Lauderdale takes about 30 minutes; it's another 30 minutes to West Palm Beach.

CONTACTS Virgin Trains USA (*Formerly Brightline*). ⊕ *www.virgin.com.*

Hotels

A collection of relatively young luxury beachfront hotels—the Atlantic Hotel & Spa, The Conrad, Four Seasons, The Gale, Hilton Fort Lauderdale Beach Resort, the Ritz-Carlton, the W, the Westin—that opened within the last decade are welcoming newcomers to the "Luxe Lauderdale" corridor. These seriously sophisticated places to stay are increasingly popular as smaller retro spots are disappearing. You can also find hotel chains along the Intracoastal Waterway. If you want to be *on* the beach, be sure to ask when booking your room, as many hotels on the inland waterways or on A1A advertise "waterfront" accommodations.

Restaurants

Greater Fort Lauderdale offers one of the best and most diverse dining scenes of any U.S. city its size. There are more than 4,000 eateries in Broward offering everything from new American and South American to Pan-Asian cuisines. Go beyond the basics, and you'll find an endless supply of hidden gems.

Hotel and restaurant reviews have been shortened. For full information, visit Fodors.com.

What It Costs			
$	$$	$$$	$$$$
RESTAURANTS			
under $15	$15–$20	$21–$30	over $30
HOTELS			
under $200	$200–$300	$301–$400	over $400

Fort Lauderdale

Like most of southeast Florida, Fort Lauderdale has long been revitalizing. Despite wariness of overdevelopment, city leaders have allowed a striking number of glittering high-rises and new hotels. Nostalgic locals and frequent visitors fret over the diminishing vision of sailboats bobbing in waters near downtown; however, Fort Lauderdale remains the yachting capital of the world, and the water toys don't seem to be going anywhere. Sharp demographic changes are also altering the face of Greater Fort Lauderdale with increasingly cosmopolitan communities. Young professionals and families are settling into Fort Lauderdale proper, whereas longtime residents are heading north for more space. Downtown Fort Lauderdale's burgeoning arts district, cafés, and nightlife venues continue to the main drag of Las Olas Boulevard, where boutiques and restaurants dot the pedestrian-friendly street. Farther east is the sparkling shoreline. There are myriad neighborhoods to the north and south of Las Olas Boulevard that all offer their own brand of charm.

GETTING HERE AND AROUND

The city's road system suffers from traffic overload. Interstate 595 connects the city and suburbs and provides a direct route to the Fort Lauderdale–Hollywood International Airport and Port Everglades, but lanes slow to a crawl during rush hours. The Intracoastal Waterway is the nautical equivalent of an interstate highway; it provides easy boating access to local hot spots as well as neighboring waterfront communities.

To bounce around for relatively cheap, catch a multicolored Sun Trolley. There are seven routes and each operates on its own schedule. Simply wave at the trolley driver: trolleys will stop for pickups anywhere along their route. Luggage is not allowed, so this isn't a viable option for airport transportation. The most popular routes—Las Olas/Beaches Link—is $1 per ride or $3 for a day pass (cash only); it even connects to the city's train station.

Yellow Cab covers most of Broward County, but it's very expensive. You can book by phone, text, app, or website, and all Yellow Cab vehicles accept major credit cards. The Uber and Lyft ride-sharing services give more attention to the passenger experience and charge cheaper rates, hence their significant presence in the area.

CONTACTS Sun Trolley. ☎ 954/876–5539 ⊕ www.suntrolley.com. **Yellow Cab Broward.** ☎ 954/777–7777 ⊕ www. yellowcabbroward.com.

TOURS

The labyrinthine waterways of Fort Lauderdale are home to thousands of privately owned vessels, but you don't need to be or know a boat owner to play on the water. To fully understand this city of canals (aka the "Venice of America"), you must see it from the water. Kick back on a boat tour or hop on a Water Taxi, Fort Lauderdale's floating trolley.

Carrie B Cruises

BOAT TOURS | Board the *Carrie B,* a 112-foot paddle wheeler, for a 90-minute sightseeing tour of the New River, Intracoastal Waterway, and Port Everglades. Cruises depart at 11 am, 1 pm, and 3 pm daily from October through April; Thursday–Monday between May and September. The cost is $23.95 plus tax. Book ahead online for discounts. ✉ 440

N New River Dr. E ☎ *888/238-9805* ⊕ *www.carriebcruises.com.*

Jungle Queen Riverboats

BOAT TOURS | FAMILY | The kitschy *Jungle Queen* and *River Queen* riverboats cruise through the heart of Fort Lauderdale on the New River. It's an old-school experience that dates back to 1935, when the company launched its tours, and the touristy charm is a big part of the fun. There are several types of sightseeing tours that leave at various times of day—from morning cruises to dinner cruises with entertainment—and prices start at around $25 per person. Check the website for details and availability. ⊠ *Bahia Mar Yachting Center, 801 Seabreeze Blvd.* ☎ *954/462–5596* ⊕ *www.junglequeen. com.*

★ **Water Taxi**

BOAT TOURS | FAMILY | At once a sightseeing tour and a mode of transportation, the Water Taxi is a smart way to experience most of Fort Lauderdale and Hollywood's waterways. There are 15 scheduled stops and on-demand whistle stops and the system has three connected routes: the Fort Lauderdale, the Margaritaville Express, and the Hollywood Local. The Fort Lauderdale and River routes run from around 10 am to 10 pm; the Margaritaville route starts at 9 am and runs every other hour. It's possible to cruise all day while taking in the sights. Captains and crew share fun facts and white lies about the city's history, as well as quirky tales about celebrity homes. A day pass is $28. Download the free Water Taxi Tracker app for accurate arrival times. ⊠ *Fort Lauderdale* ☎ *954/467– 6677* ⊕ *watertaxi.com.*

VISITOR INFORMATION

Greater Fort Lauderdale Convention and Visitors Bureau

(Hello Sunny). ⊠ *101 NE Third Ave., Suite 100* ☎ *954/765–4466* ⊕ *www.sunny.org.*

Downtown and Las Olas

The jewel of downtown is the Arts and Entertainment District, where Broadway shows, ballet, and theater take place at the Broward Center for the Performing Arts on the riverfront. A cluster of cultural entities are within a five-minute walk: the Museum of Discovery and Science, the Fort Lauderdale Historical Society, and the NSU Museum of Art. Restaurants, sidewalk cafés, bars, and nightclubs flourish along Las Olas's downtown extension, and its main presence brings a more upscale atmosphere. Riverwalk ties these two areas together with a 2-mile stretch along the New River's north and south banks, though the commercial success of this section has been tepid. Tropical gardens with benches and interpretive displays line the walk on the north, with boat landings on the south side.

 Sights

★ **Flagler + Arts + Technology Village**
(FATVillage)

ARTS VENUE | FAMILY | Inspired by Miami's Wynwood Arts District, Flagler + Arts + Technology Village (or FATVillage) encompasses several square blocks of a formerly blighted warehouse district in downtown Fort Lauderdale. It's now thriving with a slew of production studios, art studios, loft-style apartments, and a fabulous coffee shop. On the last Saturday of the month (except in December), FATVillage hosts an evening art walk, in which businesses display contemporary artworks by local talent, and where food trucks gather. There are libations, of course, and the warehouse district erupts into a giant, culture-infused street party. Check out one of Fort Lauderdale's coolest coffee shops slash bars, Next Door at C&I Studios. It's nestled inside a creative agency's lofty space. Adorned with antique nods to the literary world, tufted couches, and an eerie 1972

Airstream trailer, Next Door serves the locally made Brew Urban Cafe. After dark, it turns into a cocktail bar with live music, film screenings, and networking. ⊠ *FATVillage, 521 NW First Ave., Downtown* ☎ *954/760–5900* ⊕ *www.fatvillage. com.*

Fort Lauderdale Antique Car Museum

MUSEUM | **FAMILY** | To preseve the history of the Packard, a long-vanished luxury American car company, Arthur O. Stone and his wife, Shirley, set up a foundation and a showroom in downtown Fort Lauderdale. The collection includes about two dozen of the buggy-style Packards (all in pristine and working condition) made in the Midwest from 1909 to 1958. The collection includes everything from grease caps, spark plugs, and gearshift knobs to Texaco Oil signage, plus an enlarged automotive library. There's also a gallery saluting Franklin Delano Roosevelt and his family. ⊠ *Fort Lauderdale Antique Car Museum, 1527 SW First Ave., Downtown* ☎ *954/779–7300* ⊕ *www. antiquecarmuseum.net* ⊠ *$10 minimum donation* ⊘ *By appointment only Sat.; closed Sun.*

Fort Lauderdale Fire and Safety Museum

BUILDING | **FAMILY** | The museum is housed inside the historic building formerly known as Fire Station No. 3, which has been restored to its original Mediterranean beauty (circa 1927). The Sailboat Bend landmark was designed by architect Francis Abreu and retired from active duty in 2004; it now functions on the weekends as a historical, cultural, and educational facility with vintage equipment including a 1942 Chevrolet "Parade" fire engine. Legend has it the fire station is haunted by a young firefighter. ⊠ *1022 W Las Olas Blvd., at SW 11th Ave., Downtown* ☎ *954/763–1005* ⊕ *https://www.fortlauderdalefiremuseum.com* ⊠ *Free; donations appreciated* ⊘ *Closed weekdays.*

Historic Stranahan House Museum

BUILDING | **FAMILY** | The city's oldest surviving structure was once home to businessman Frank Stranahan, who arrived from Ohio in 1892. With his wife, Ivy, the city's first schoolteacher, he befriended and traded with Seminole Indians. In 1901 he built a store that would later become his home after serving as a post office, a general store, and a restaurant. The couple's tale is filled with ups and downs. Their home remains Fort Lauderdale's principal link to its brief history and has been on the National Register of Historic Places since 1973. Guided tours are about an hour long and are offered a few times a day; however, calling ahead for availability is a good idea. Self-guided tours of the museum are not allowed. ⊠ *335 SE Sixth Ave., Downtown* ☎ *954/524–4736* ⊕ *www. stranahanhouse.org* ⊠ *$12* ⊘ *Closed holidays.*

★ Las Olas Boulevard

COMMERCIAL CENTER | **FAMILY** | What Lincoln Road is to South Beach, Las Olas Boulevard is to Fort Lauderdale. Regarded as the heart and soul of Broward County, Las Olas has historically been the premier street for restaurants, art galleries, museums, shopping, dining, and people watching. Lined with high-rises in the downtown area and original boutiques and ethnic eateries along 10 blocks of the main stretch, it's also home to beautiful mansions and traditional Florida homes along the Intracoastal Waterway to the east, which typify the modern-day aesthetic of Fort Lauderdale. The ocean appears beyond the residential swath, and that's where you see that the name "Las Olas" (Spanish for "The Waves") begins to make more sense. It's a pedestrian-friendly thoroughfare, but it's not closed to vehicular traffic at any point. ⊠ *E Las Olas Blvd., Downtown* ⊕ *www.lasolasboulevard.com.*

Museum of Discovery and Science and AutoNation IMAX Theater

COLLEGE | **FAMILY** | There are dozens of interactive exhibits here to entertain children—*and* adults—through the wonders

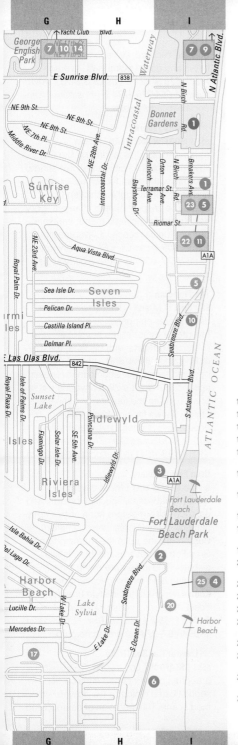

Sights ▼

1 Bonnet House
Museum and Gardens ...I2

2 Flagler + Arts +
Technology Village A3

3 Fort Lauderdale
Antique Car Museum... A8

4 Fort Lauderdale Fire and
Safety Museum A5

5 Historic Stranahan
House Museum B5

6 Las Olas Boulevard..... B5

7 Museum of Discovery and
Science and AutoNation
IMAX Theater A4

8 NSU Museum of Art
Fort Lauderdale A5

Restaurants ▼

1 American Social C5

2 Big City Tavern B5

3 Canyon
Southwest Cafe......... F1

4 Casa D'Angelo
Ristorante................. E1

5 Casablanca Cafe......... I4

6 Coco Asian Bistro
and Bar C9

7 Eduardo de
San Angel............... G1

8 The Floridian D5

9 Gran Forno Bakery D5

10 Kitchenetta G1

11 Lips D1

12 Lobster Bar Sea Grille.. B5

13 Luigi's Coal Oven Pizza. D5

14 Mai-Kai Restaurant and
Polynesian Show G1

15 Old Fort Lauderdale
Breakfast House A4

16 Old Heidelberg
Restaurant............... A9

17 Pelican Landing......... G8

18 Rocco's Tacos and
Tequila Bar D5

19 The Royal Pig Pub B5

20 Sea Level Restaurant and
Ocean Bar................I8

21 Southport Raw Bar..... D8

22 Steak 954 .... I3

23 S3........................... I3

24 Stork's Cafe and
Bakery D1

25 3030 Ocean...............I8

26 Timpano Italian
Chophouse............. B5

27 Tom Jenkins'
Barbecue................ B7

28 Wild Sea Oyster
Bar and Grille C5

Hotels ▼

1 The Atlantic
Resort and Spa............I2

2 B Ocean Resort...........I7

3 Bahia Mar
Fort Lauderdale
Beach Hotel,
a DoubleTree
by Hilton H6

4 Fort Lauderdale Marriott
Harbor Beach
Resort and Spa...........I8

5 Hilton Fort Lauderdale
Beach Resort.............I3

6 Lago Mar
Resort and Club ... H9

7 Pelican Grand Beach
Resort.....................I1

8 Pineapple Point E4

9 Residence Inn
Fort Lauderdale
Intercoastal/
Il Lugano..................I1

10 The Ritz-Carlton,
Fort Lauderdale I4

11 W Fort Lauderdale........I3

of science and Florida's delicate ecosystem. The state-of-the-art 7-D theater takes guests on a virtual tour of aviation technology, while the Ecodiscovery Center comes with an Everglades Airboat Adventure ride, resident otters, and an interactive Florida storm center. The 300-seat AutoNation IMAX theater is part of the complex and shows mainstream and educational films, some in 3-D, on the biggest screen in South Florida with a rare high-tech laser projection system. ✉ *401 SW Second St., Downtown* ☎ *954/467–6637 Museum, 954/463–4629 IMAX* 🌐 *mods.org* 🎟 *Museum $17, IMAX tickets are extra and start at $9 per person.*

★ **NSU Museum of Art Fort Lauderdale**
ARTS VENUE | **FAMILY** | Led by visionary director and chief curator Bonnie Clearwater, the NSU Museum of Art's international exhibition programming ignites downtown Fort Lauderdale. The interior of the 83,000-square-foot modernist building, designed by architect Edward Larrabee Barnes in 1986, holds an impressive permanent collection of more than 7,000 works, including the country's largest collection of paintings by American realist William Glackens, and pivotal works by female and multicultural artists, avant-garde CoBrA artists, and a wide array of Latin American masters. **TIP→ The lobby-level Museum Café is a cool hangout with art-inspired gifts.** ✉ *1 E Las Olas Blvd., Downtown* ☎ *954/525–5500* 🌐 *nsuartmuseum.org* 🎟 *$12* 🕒 *Closed Mon.*

🍴 Restaurants

American Social
$$$ | **MODERN AMERICAN** | In the sports bar desert of South Florida, it's nice to know you can eat well while watching your team. American Social flaunts a seafood-mac-and-cheese skillet, shrimp-pesto flatbread, and a full spectrum of gourmet burgers with sides of parmesan-truffle fries or sweet-potato fries. **Known for:** upscale bar food; live sports on TV; craft beers and good cocktails. [$] *Average main: $25* ✉ *721 E Las Olas Blvd., Downtown* ☎ *954/715-1134* 🌐 *https://americansocialbar.com/las-olas/.*

★ **Big City Tavern**
$$$ | **MODERN AMERICAN** | **FAMILY** | A must-visit Las Olas landmark, Big City Tavern mingles Asian entrées like shrimp pad Thai with Italian four-cheese ravioli and an American grilled-chicken Cobb salad. The crispy flatbread changes every day. **Known for:** eclectic menu; weekend brunch; fun bar scene. [$] *Average main: $26* ✉ *609 E Las Olas Blvd., Downtown* ☎ *954/727–0307* 🌐 *www.bigcitylasolas.com.*

The Floridian
$$ | **DINER** | **FAMILY** | This classic 24-hour diner serves no-nonsense breakfast favorites (no matter the hour) like oversized omelets with biscuits, toast, or English muffins, and a choice of grits or sliced tomatoes. Good hangover eats abound, but don't expect anything exceptional besides the location and the low prices. **Known for:** breakfast anytime; low prices; always open. [$] *Average main: $15* ✉ *1410 E Las Olas Blvd., Downtown* ☎ *954/463–4041* 🌐 *thefloridiandiner.com.*

Gran Forno Bakery
$ | **BAKERY** | **FAMILY** | Most days, the Italian sandwiches, specialty breads, and pastries sell out before noon at this aptly named bakery ("large oven" in Italian). Customers line up in the morning to get Gran Forno's hot artisanal breads like ciabatta (800 loaves are made a day), returning later for the decadent desserts. **Known for:** great Italian-style breads; desserts; strong coffee. [$] *Average main: $14* ✉ *1235 E Las Olas Blvd., Downtown* ☎ *954/467–2244* 🌐 *granforno.com.*

★ **Lobster Bar Sea Grille**
$$$$ | **SEAFOOD** | Lobster Bar Sea Grille brought a much-needed infusion of sophisticated dining to the downtown food scene. The selection of seafood and

fish is solid and ranges from Nova Scotian lobsters to Atlantic char from Iceland. **Known for:** fresh seafood and steaks; sophisticated atmosphere; lively happy hour. $ *Average main: $40* ⊠ *450 E Las Olas Blvd., Downtown* ☎ *954/772–2675* ⊕ *buckheadrestaurants.com/restaurant/lobster-bar-sea-grille-ft-lauderdale.*

★ Luigi's Coal Oven Pizza

$$ | **PIZZA** | **FAMILY** | One of the best little pizza joints in South Florida, Luigi's Coal Oven Pizza has the full gamut of pizzas, phenomenal salads with fresh dressings, classics like eggplant parmigiana, and oven-baked chicken wings. For the Margherita Napoletana, the quality and flavors of the crust, cheese, and sauce are the result of Luigi's century-old recipe from Napoli. **Known for:** traditional Neopolitan-style pizza; intimate dining room; coal-fired oven. $ *Average main: $19* ⊠ *1415 E Las Olas Blvd., Downtown* ☎ *954/522–8888* ⊕ *www.luigiscoalovenpizza.com/index.html.*

★ Old Fort Lauderdale Breakfast House

(*O-B House*)

$$$ | **AMERICAN** | Locals can't get enough of the O-B House's commitment to quality; you'll find only fresh and organic ingredients here. Try cheesy grits, mega-pancakes with real Vermont maple syrup, or the free-range-egg omelets with wild-caught mahimahi. **Known for:** organic ingredients; fun breakfast options; unique renovation of an old post office. $ *Average main: $21* ⊠ *333 Himmarshee St., Downtown* ☎ *954/530–7520* ⊕ *www.o-bhouse.com* ⌖ *No lunch Sun.*

Rocco's Tacos and Tequila Bar

$$ | **MODERN MEXICAN** | With pitchers of margaritas, Rocco's is more of a scene than a restaurant. In fact, Rocco's drink menu is even larger than its sizable food menu. **Known for:** 400 kinds of tequila; fresh guacamole; busy atmosphere. $ *Average main: $19* ⊠ *1313 E Las Olas Blvd., Downtown* ☎ *954/524–9550* ⊕ *www.roccostacos.com.*

The Royal Pig Pub

$$$ | **CAJUN** | This gastropub revels in doling out hefty portions of Cajun comfort food and potent cocktails. It's one of Fort Lauderdale's busiest watering holes. **Known for:** busy bar; barbecue shrimp; weekend brunch. $ *Average main: $24* ⊠ *350 E Las Olas Blvd., Downtown* ☎ *954/617–7447* ⊕ *www.royalpigpub.com.*

Timpano Italian Chophouse

$$$ | **ITALIAN** | Combine the likes of a high-end steakhouse with a typical trattoria, and you've got yourself a successful recipe for an Italian chophouse. Timpano's offerings include fresh pastas, flatbreads, and the full gamut of parmesans, marsalas, and fra diavolos. **Known for:** great salads; steakhouse favorites; live music in the Starlight Lounge. $ *Average main: $25* ⊠ *450 E Las Olas Blvd., Downtown* ☎ *954/462–9119* ⊕ *timpanochophouse.net.*

Wild Sea Oyster Bar and Grille

$$$$ | **SEAFOOD** | In the heart of Las Olas, this oyster bar and grill keeps things simple with a small menu focused on a beautiful raw bar and ever-changing preparations of diverse catches from Florida, Hawaiian, and New England waters. **Known for:** worldly interpretations of seafood; raw bar; extensive wine list. $ *Average main: $43* ⊠ *Riverside Hotel, 620 E Las Olas Blvd., Downtown* ☎ *954/467–2555* ⊕ *www.wildseaonlasolas.com.*

Hotels

Pineapple Point

$$ | **B&B/INN** | Tucked a few blocks behind Las Olas Boulevard in the residential neighborhood of Victoria Park, clothing-optional Pineapple Point is a magnificent maze of posh tropical cottages and dense foliage catering to the gay community and is nationally renowned for its stellar service. **Pros:** superior service; luxurious and tropical setting;

clothing is optional. **Cons:** difficult to find at first; cancellations or changes require 14-day notice; rates can get high during season. [$] *Rooms from: $300* ✉ *315 NE 16th Terr., Downtown* ☎ *954/527–0094, 888/844–7295* 🌐 *www.pineapplepoint.com* 🛏 *25 rooms* 🍴 *Breakfast.*

Nightlife

The majority of Fort Lauderdale nightlife takes place near downtown, beginning on Himmarshee Street (Second Street) and continuing on to the riverfront, and then to Las Olas Boulevard. The downtown area tends to draw a younger demographic somewhere between underage teens and late twenties. On Himmarshee Street, a dozen rowdy bars and clubs, ranging from the seedy to the sophisticated, entice a wide range of partygoers. Toward East Las Olas Boulevard, near the financial towers and boutique shops, upscale bars cater to the yuppie crowd.

★ Laser Wolf
BARS/PUBS | Far from the main drag of Fort Lauderdale's nightlife district, Laser Wolf celebrates the urban grit on the other side of the tracks as an artsy, hipster, craft-beer bar. It's located on the railroad tracks in a cool indoor-outdoor space and might be the most popular bar for locals because of its great drinks, music, and overall vibe. Motto: "No jerks. Yes beer." **TIP→ Drive or Uber it here. It's best not to walk from other bars off Las Olas and Himmarshee due to distance and safety concerns.** ✉ *901 Progresso Dr., No. 101, Downtown* ☎ *954/667–9373* 🌐 *www.laserwolf.bar/home.html.*

ROK: BRG
BARS/PUBS | Downtown Fort Lauderdale loves this personality-driven burger bar and gastropub, as it gives the grown-ups something to enjoy in the teenage-infested nightlife district. The long and narrow venue, adorned with exposed-brick walls and flat-screen TVs, is great for watching sports and for mingling on weekends. Locals come here for the great cocktails and beer selection. The burgers are also locally famous. ✉ *208 SW Second St., Downtown* ☎ *954/525–7656* 🌐 *rokbrgr.com/location/ft-lauderdale.*

Stache, 1920's Drinking Den + Coffee Bar
BARS/PUBS | Inspired by the Roaring Twenties, this speakeasy-style drinking den and nightclub infuses party-hard downtown Fort Lauderdale with some class and pizzazz. Expect awesome craft cocktails, inclusive of bespoke ice cubes for old-school drinks like Manhattans and Sidecars. Late-night on Friday and Saturday anticipate great music and a fun crowd. The 5,000-square-foot bar opens at 7 am on the weekdays to serve coffee. ✉ *109 SW Second Ave., Downtown* ☎ *954/449–1025* 🌐 *stacheftl.com.*

★ Tap 42 Bar and Kitchen
BARS/PUBS | With 42 rotating draft beers from around the U.S., 50-plus bourbons, a few dozen original cocktails (including beer cocktails), and dozens of bottled craft beers, good times await. The drafts adorn a stylish wall constructed of pennies, which creates an interesting trompe l'oeil. The venue attracts large crowds of young professionals for nights of heavy drinking and high-calorie bar eats. ✉ *1411 S Andrews Ave., Downtown* ☎ *954/463–4900* 🌐 *tap42.com/ft-lauderdale.*

Performing Arts

★ Broward Center for the Performing Arts
ARTS CENTERS | **FAMILY** | Fort Lauderdale's 2,700-seat architectural gem offers more than 500 events annually, including Broadway-style musicals, plays, dance, symphony, opera, rock, film, lectures, comedy, and children's theater. The theaters are state-of-the-art and dining venues are available, including the restaurant Marti's New River Bistro and the Intermezzo Lounge. An elevated walkway connects the centerpiece of the

complex to a parking garage across the street. ⊠ *201 SW Fifth Ave., Downtown* ☎ *954/462–0222* ⊕ *www.browardcenter. org.*

Savor Cinema
ARTS-ENTERTAINMENT OVERVIEW | FAMILY | Formerly called Cinema Paradiso, this arthouse theater operates out of a former church south of New River near the county courthouse. The space doubles as headquarters for the Fort Lauderdale International Film Festival (FLIFF), while still playing films year-round. FLIFF's website is the easiest way to see what's playing on any given evening at the cinema. ⊠ *503 SE Sixth St., Downtown* ☎ *954/525–3456* ⊕ *www.fliff.com.*

Shopping

★ **Las Olas Boulevard**
ANTIQUES/COLLECTIBLES | FAMILY | Las Olas Boulevard is the epicenter of Fort Lauderdale's lifestyle. Not only are 50 of the city's best boutiques, dozens of top restaurants, and eclectic art galleries found along this landscaped street, but Las Olas links the growing downtown area with Fort Lauderdale's beautiful beaches. ⊠ *E Las Olas Blvd., Downtown* ☎ *954/258–8382* ⊕ *lasolasboulevard. com.*

Fort Lauderdale Beach

If you want to stop for a bite to eat or a drink before or after visiting Bonnet House, consider **Casablanca Café** (⊠ *3049 Alhambra St.*) or **Steak 954** (⊠ *W Fort Lauderdale, 401 N Fort Lauderdale Beach Blvd.*).

Sights

★ **Bonnet House Museum and Gardens**
BUILDING | FAMILY | This 35-acre subtropical estate endures as a tribute to Old South Florida. Prior to its "modern" history, the grounds had already seen 4,000 years of activity when settler Hugh Taylor Birch purchased the site in 1895. Birch gave it to his daughter Helen as a wedding gift when she married Frederic Bartlett, and the newlyweds built a charming home for a winter residence in 1920. Years after Helen died, Frederic married his second wife, Evelyn, and the artistically gifted couple embarked on a mission to embellish the property with personal touches and surprises that are still evident today. This historic place is a must-see for its architecture, artwork, and horticulture. While admiring the fabulous gardens, look out for playful monkeys swinging from the trees. ⊠ *Bonnet House Museum and Gardens, 900 N Birch Rd., Beachfront* ☎ *954/563–5393* ⊕ *www.bonnethouse.org* ⊴ *$20 for house tours or $10 for gardens only; $4 for tram tour* ☉ *Closed Mon., holidays.*

Beaches

★ **Fort Lauderdale Beach**
BEACH—SIGHT | FAMILY | The same stretch of sand that once welcomed America's wild spring breakers is now miles of beachside sophistication. It remains gloriously open and uncluttered when compared to other major beaches along the Florida coastline; walkways line both sides of the road, and traffic is trimmed to two gently curving northbound lanes. Fort Lauderdale Beach unofficially begins between the B Ocean Resort (formerly the Sheraton Yankee Clipper) and the DoubleTree by Hilton Bahia Mar Resort, starting with the quiet **Fort Lauderdale Beach Park,** where picnic tables and palm trees rule. Going north, a younger crowd gravitates toward the section near Las Olas Boulevard. The beach is actually most crowded from here to **Beach Place,** home of Marriott's vacation rentals and touristy places like Hooters and Fat Tuesday (and a beach-themed CVS). An LGBTQ crew soaks up the sun along **Sebastian Street Beach,** just north of the Ritz-Carlton. Families with children enjoy

hanging out between Seville Street and Vistamar Street, between the Westin Fort Lauderdale Beach and the Atlantic Resort and Spa. High-spirited dive bars dot the Strip and epitomize its "anything goes" attitude. **Amenities:** food and drink; lifeguards; parking (fee). **Best for:** partiers; sunrise; swimming; walking; windsurfing. ✉ *SR A1A, from Holiday Dr. to Sunrise Blvd., Beachfront.*

Harbor Beach

BEACH—SIGHT | **FAMILY** | The posh Harbor Beach community includes Fort Lauderdale's most opulent residences on the Intracoastal Waterway. Due east of this community, a stunning beach has adopted the name of its surroundings. The Harbor Beach section has some of the only private beaches in Fort Lauderdale, and most of this beach belongs to hotels like the Marriott Harbor Beach Resort and the Lago Mar Resort & Club. (To be clear: Only hotel guests have access.) Such status allows the hotels to provide guests with full-service amenities and dining options on their own slices of heaven. **Amenities:** water sports. **Best for:** solitude; swimming; walking. ✉ *S Ocean Ln. and Holiday Dr., Beachfront.*

🍴 Restaurants

Casablanca Cafe

$$$ | **ECLECTIC** | **FAMILY** | The menu at this piano bar and restaurant offers a global hodgepodge of American, Mediterranean, and Asian flavors, with a specific focus on eclectic preparations of Florida fish. The food isn't particularly good, but the atmosphere at this historic home is excellent. **Known for:** dining with ocean views; historic setting in Jova House; popular piano bar. [$] *Average main: $28* ✉ *3049 Alhambra St., Beachfront* ☎ *954/764–3500* 🌐 *www.casablancacafeonline.com.*

★ S3

$$$ | **FUSION** | S3 stands for the fabulous trio of sun, surf, and sand, paying homage to its prime beachfront location. The menu features a variety of Japanese-inspired raw dishes, sushi rolls, and dishes with a New American focus. **Known for:** eclectic Asian and American flavors; solid selection of wine and cocktails; drawing both locals and visitors. [$] *Average main: $29* ✉ *Hilton Fort Lauderdale Beach Resort, 505 N Fort Lauderdale Beach Blvd., Beachfront* 🌐 *s3restaurant.com.*

Sea Level Restaurant and Ocean Bar

$$$ | **SEAFOOD** | **FAMILY** | You have to take the road less traveled to find Sea Level, a haven for fresh seafood. The indoor-outdoor restaurant literally overlooks the ocean from sea level at Marriott's Harbor Beach Resort and Spa, and its seasonal menu wows with daily specials and cocktails featuring ingredients from the chef's organic garden. **Known for:** the freshest seafood; outdoor dining; good cocktail menu. [$] *Average main: $25* ✉ *Fort Lauderdale Marriott Harbor Beach Resort and Spa, 3030 Holiday Dr., Beachfront* ☎ *954/765–3041* 🌐 *www.marriott.com.*

Steak 954

$$$$ | **MODERN AMERICAN** | It's not just the steaks that impress at Stephen Starr's superstar spot inside the W Fort Lauderdale, the seafood selections shine, too. Order as many dishes as possible, like the lobster and crab-coconut ceviche, the red snapper tiradito, and the Colorado lamb chops. **Known for:** high-quality (and expensive) steaks and seafood; outdoor dining; Sunday brunch. [$] *Average main: $55* ✉ *W Fort Lauderdale, 401 N Fort Lauderdale Beach Blvd., Beachfront* ☎ *954/414–8333* 🌐 *steak954.com.*

★ 3030 Ocean

$$$$ | **SEAFOOD** | 3030 Ocean's unpredictable menus are guided by award-winning chef Adrienne Grenier's perfectionist flair. Her interpretation of modern American seafood focuses on balancing complex flavors to enhance her fresh ingredients—without subtracting from their integrity. **Known for:** ever-changing menu;

Fort Lauderdale's picture-perfect beach is designated Blue Wave certified by the Clean Beaches Coalition.

locally sourced seafood; consistently good food. $ *Average main: $45* ✉ *Fort Lauderdale Marriott Harbor Beach Resort and Spa, 3030 Holiday Dr., Beachfront* ☎ *954/765–3030* ⊕ *www.3030ocean. com.*

 Hotels

The Atlantic Resort and Spa

$$$ | **HOTEL** | **FAMILY** | This towering oceanfront hotel has fantastic views of the ocean from its beds (unless, of course, you select a city view). **Pros:** oceanfront property; en suite kitchenettes; pet-friendly. **Cons:** dated decor in the rooms; expensive parking; issues with service. $ *Rooms from: $320* ✉ *601 N Fort Lauderdale Beach Blvd., Beachfront* ☎ *954/516–1720* ⊕ *www.atlantichotelfl. com* 🛏 *104 rooms* ☉ *No meals.*

B Ocean Resort

$$ | **HOTEL** | This iconic riverboat-shaped landmark, once the Yankee Clipper, is chic yet functional, and the unobstructed ocean views and beach access set it apart from neighboring properties. **Pros:** retro mermaid show in swimming pool; proximity to beach; excellent gym. **Cons:** small rooms; low ceilings in lobby; some aspects need a refresh. $ *Rooms from: $200* ✉ *1140 Seabreeze Blvd., Beachfront* ☎ *954/564–1000* ⊕ *www.bhotelsandresorts.com/b-ocean* 🛏 *481 rooms* ☉ *No meals.*

Bahia Mar Fort Lauderdale Beach Hotel, A DoubleTree by Hilton

$$ | **HOTEL** | **FAMILY** | This nicely situated resort has identical rooms in both its marina building and its tower building; however, the latter offers superior views. **Pros:** crosswalk from hotel to beach; on-site yacht center; Water Taxi stop. **Cons:** busy location; small bathrooms; high rates during events. $ *Rooms from: $215* ✉ *801 Seabreeze Blvd., Beachfront* ☎ *954/764–2233* ⊕ *www.bahiamarhotel. com* 🛏 *296 rooms* ☉ *No meals.*

★ Fort Lauderdale Marriott Harbor Beach Resort and Spa

$$$$ | **RESORT** | **FAMILY** | Bill Marriott's personal choice for his annual four-week

family vacation, the Marriott Harbor Beach sits on a quarter-mile of private beach; it shines with the luxe personality of a top-notch island resort. **Pros:** private beachfront; all rooms have balconies; great eateries. **Cons:** Wi-Fi isn't free; expensive parking; large resort feel. [$] *Rooms from: $450* ✉ *3030 Holiday Dr., Beachfront* ☎ *954/525–4000* 🌐 *www.marriott.com* 🛏 *650 rooms* 🍴 *No meals.*

Hilton Fort Lauderdale Beach Resort
$$$ | **HOTEL** | **FAMILY** | This oceanfront sparkler features tasteful, large suites and a fabulous sixth-floor pool deck. **Pros:** fun pool and adults-only lounge; most rooms have balconies; great spa. **Cons:** not pet-friendly; expensive valet parking; beach umbrellas not included in resort fee. [$] *Rooms from: $300* ✉ *505 N Fort Lauderdale Beach Blvd., Beachfront* ☎ *954/414–2222* 🌐 *www3.hilton.com* 🛏 *374 rooms* 🍴 *No meals.*

Lago Mar Resort and Club
$$$ | **RESORT** | **FAMILY** | The sprawling family-friendly Lago Mar retains its sparkle and authentic Florida feel thanks to committed owners. **Pros:** secluded setting; no resort fee; free valet and self-parking. **Cons:** not easy to find; far from restaurants and beach action; dated decor. [$] *Rooms from: $375* ✉ *1700 S Ocean La., Beachfront* ☎ *954/523–6511* 🌐 *lagomar.com* 🛏 *204 rooms* 🍴 *No meals.*

Pelican Grand Beach Resort
$$$ | **RESORT** | **FAMILY** | This bright yellow Key West–style Noble House property fuses a heritage seaside charm with understated luxury. **Pros:** incredible spa; directly on the beach; romantic restaurant. **Cons:** small fitness center; dated room decor; small property. [$] *Rooms from: $350* ✉ *2000 N Ocean Blvd., Beachfront* ☎ *954/568–9431* 🌐 *www.pelicanbeach.com* 🛏 *159 rooms* 🍴 *No meals.*

★ **The Ritz-Carlton, Fort Lauderdale**
$$$$ | **HOTEL** | Twenty-four dramatically tiered, glass-walled stories rise from the sea, forming a resort that's helping to revive a golden age of luxury travel. **Pros:** prime beach location; exceptional service; organic spa treatments. **Cons:** expensive valet parking; cancel at least 14 days in advance or get hit with a two-night penalty; extra-busy poolscape. [$] *Rooms from: $750* ✉ *1 N Fort Lauderdale Beach Blvd., Beachfront* ☎ *954/465–2300* 🌐 *www.ritzcarlton.com/FortLauderdale* 🛏 *192 rooms* 🍴 *No meals.*

W Fort Lauderdale
$$ | **HOTEL** | Fort Lauderdale's trendiest hotel has a glamorous poolscape, übermodern rooms and suites, and dramatic views from every direction. **Pros:** amazing pool; pet-friendly; great restaurant. **Cons:** party atmosphere not for everyone; can be hard to navigate the property; Wi-Fi isn't free. [$] *Rooms from: $300* ✉ *435 N Fort Lauderdale Beach Blvd., Beachfront* ☎ *954/414–8200* 🌐 *www.marriott.com/hotels/travel/fllwh-w-fort-lauderdale* 🛏 *329 rooms* 🍴 *No meals.*

🍸 Nightlife

Given its roots as a beachside party town, it's hard to believe that Fort Lauderdale Beach offers very few options in terms of nightlife. A few dive bars are at opposite ends of the main strip, near Sunrise Boulevard and Route A1A, as well as Las Olas Boulevard and A1A. On the main thoroughfare between Las Olas and Sunrise, a few high-end bars at the beach's showstopping hotels have become popular, namely those at the W Fort Lauderdale.

McSorley's Beach Pub
BARS/PUBS | This modern take on a classic Irish pub offers standard pub fun—from a jukebox to 35 beers on tap—but remains wildly popular thanks to its location right across from Fort Lauderdale Beach. Indeed, it's one of the few places on the beach to get an affordable drink and attracts its fair share of tourists and locals. Upstairs, the pub has a second

lounge that's far clubbier as well as a rooftop terrace. ⊠ *837 N Fort Lauderdale Beach Blvd., Beachfront* ☏ *954/565–4446* ⊕ *www.mcsorleysftl.com.*

The World Famous Parrot Lounge

BARS/PUBS | **FAMILY** | A venerable Fort Lauderdale hangout, this dive bar–sports bar is particularly popular with Philadelphia Eagles fans and folks reminiscing about the big hair and spray tans of '80s Fort Lauderdale (aka its heyday). This place is stuck in the past, but it's got great bartenders, wings, chicken fingers, poppers, and skins. 'Nuff said. ⊠ *911 Sunrise La., Beachfront* ☏ *954/563–1493* ⊕ *www.parrotlounge.com.*

The Wreck Bar

BARS/PUBS | Travel back in time to the '50s at this "under the sea" dive bar and seafood eatery at B Ocean Resort, where huge aquariums and a porthole show off live mermaids, who perform in the pool on Friday and Saturday. ⊠ *B Ocean Resort, 1140 Seabreeze Blvd., Beachfront* ☏ *954/524–5551* ⊕ *www.bhotelsandresorts.com/b-ocean/wreck-bar.*

👜 Shopping

Most of Fort Lauderdale's upscale spas are located within elegant beachfront hotels, yet they remain open to the public. During low season (September and October), top spas offer $99 treatments during the "Spa Chic" promotion (⊕ *www.sunny.org/spachic*).

The Gallery at Beach Place

GIFTS/SOUVENIRS | **FAMILY** | Just north of Las Olas Boulevard on Route A1A, this shopping gallery is attached to the mammoth Marriott's BeachPlace Towers' timeshare property. Retail spaces are occupied by touristy shops that sell everything from sarongs to alligator heads, chain restaurants like Hooter's, bars serving frozen drinks, and a supersized CVS pharmacy, which sells everything you need for the beach. ■ TIP→ **Beach Place has covered parking,**

and usually has plenty of spaces, but you can pinch pennies by using a nearby municipal lot. ⊠ *17 S Fort Lauderdale Beach Blvd., Beachfront* ☏ *954/764-3460* ⊕ *www.galleryatbeachplace.com.*

★ The Ritz-Carlton Spa, Fort Lauderdale

SPA/BEAUTY | The Ritz-Carlton's expansive 8,500-foot hideaway is focused on tranquility and relaxation, from the layout of the treatment rooms to the magical hands of Fort Lauderdale's top therapists. Massage options run the gamut, including Swedish, aromatherapy, hot stone, couples, deep tissue, hydrotherapy, reflexology, Thai, and prenatal. Dermatologist-developed skin-care treatments, anti-cellulite and anti-aging treatments, facials, manicures, and pedicures are also on the menu. Go for the Intuitive Ocean treatment for an intense detoxification with help from the marine mud, seaweed, and sea salt. You'll feel a renewed sense of balance after the body scrub, wrap, and massage. ⊠ *The Ritz-Carlton Spa, Fort Lauderdale, 1 N Fort Lauderdale Beach Blvd., Beachfront* ☏ *954/302–6490* ⊕ *www.ritzcarlton.com/en/hotels/florida/fort-lauderdale/spa.*

Spa Atlantic

SPA/BEAUTY | Spa Atlantic exudes a relaxed glamour and offers perfected core spa services. Many treatments are rooted in Asia, the Middle East, and the Mediterranean. Body treatments include a wide variety of massages, baths, body wraps, and body glows (exfoliation). Other beauty treatments offered include skin-care enhancements, anti-aging treatments, facials, manicures, pedicures, waxing, hair, and makeup. ⊠ *The Atlantic Hotel and Spa, 601 N Fort Lauderdale Beach Blvd., Beachfront* ☏ *954/567–8085* ⊕ *www.atlantichotelfl.com/spa-atlantic.*

Did You Know?

More than 165 miles of canals and waterways earned Fort Lauderdale the nickname "the Venice of America."

Intracoastal and Inland Fort Lauderdale

Beaches

★ Hugh Taylor Birch State Park

BEACH—SIGHT | **FAMILY** | North of the bustling beachfront at Sunrise Boulevard, quieter sands run parallel to Hugh Taylor Birch State Park, an exquisite patch of Old Florida. The 180-acre subtropical oasis forms a barrier island between the Atlantic Ocean and the Intracoastal Waterway—surprisingly close to the urban core. Lush vegetation includes mangroves, and there are lovely nature trails through the hammock system. Visit the Birch House Museum, enjoy a picnic, play volleyball, or grab a canoe, kayak, or stand-up paddleboard. **Amenities:** toilets, water sports. **Best for:** solitude; walking. ✉ *3109 E Sunrise Blvd., Intracoastal and Inland* ☎ *954/564–4521* 🌐 *www.floridastateparks.org/parks-and-trails/hugh-taylor-birch-state-park* 🎫 *$6 for group in vehicle; $4 single driver or motorcycle; $2 per pedestrian or bicyclist.*

Restaurants

Canyon Southwest Cafe

$$$ | **SOUTHWESTERN** | Inside this magical enclave, a Southwestern fusion of Central and South American flavors and a twist of Asian influence is on the menu. Pair the fresh seafood or wild game with a robust selection of tequilas, a few mezcals, or a bottle from the decent wine list. **Known for:** locally sourced ingredients; long waits; large selection of tequilas. [$] *Average main: $28* ✉ *1818 E Sunrise Blvd., Intracoastal and Inland* ✣ *At NE 18th Ave.* ☎ *954/765–1950* 🌐 *www.canyonfl.com* 🕓 *Closed Mon.*

★ Casa D'Angelo Ristorante

$$$$ | **ITALIAN** | Casa D'Angelo is always packed. The Tuscan-style fine-dining restaurant is beloved for its rustic and refined philosophy. **Known for:** everything made from scratch; grilled tiger prawns; extensive wine list. [$] *Average main: $40* ✉ *1201 N Federal Hwy., No. 5A, Intracoastal and Inland* ☎ *954/564–1234* 🌐 *www.casa-d-angelo.com.*

★ Coco Asian Bistro and Bar

$$$ | **ASIAN** | The best of Thai and Japanese cooking unite in an unassuming Fort Lauderdale strip mall. Chef-owner Mike Ponluang's lobster pad Thai and classic curries are the go-to for loyal locals, as are sushi rolls and more traditional Japanese selections. **Known for:** extensive Pan-Asian menu; soothing, elegant atmosphere; good desserts. [$] *Average main: $27* ✉ *Harbor Shops, 1841 Cordova Rd., Intracoastal and Inland* ☎ *954/525–3541* 🌐 *www.cocoasianbistro.com.*

Kitchenetta

$$$ | **ITALIAN** | **FAMILY** | Kitchenetta is a modern trattoria serving gourmet Italian-American favorites in an industrial-chic setting. The best things to come out of this family-owned kitchen include the spaghetti with Neopolitan-style stuffed artichokes (seasonal), gnocchi Gorgonzola, and the wood-fired mushroom pizza. **Known for:** family-sized portions; good pastas; special Sunday supper. [$] *Average main: $25* ✉ *2850 N Federal Hwy., Intracoastal and Inland* ☎ *954/567–3333* 🌐 *www.kitchenetta.com* 🕓 *Closed Mon. No lunch.*

Old Heidelberg Restaurant

$$$ | **GERMAN** | **FAMILY** | Old Heidelberg is like a Bavarian mirage on State Road 84 with a killer list of German specialties and beers on tap. Classics like bratwurst, knockwurst, kielbasa, and spaetzle dovetail nicely with four types of Wiener schnitzel. **Known for:** kitschy decor; huge selection of German imports on tap; extensive menu of German favorites. [$] *Average main: $25* ✉ *900 W State Road 84, Intracoastal and Inland* ☎ *954/463–6747* 🌐 *www.heidelbergfl.com* 🕓 *No lunch weekends.*

Lago Mar Resort and Club in Fort Lauderdale has its own private beach on the Atlantic Ocean.

Pelican Landing

$$ | SEAFOOD | FAMILY | Somehow Pelican Landing has managed to stay under the radar in spite of its high-quality seafood, burgers, and Caribbean dishes. The fish is caught daily, served simply blackened or grilled, and presented with sides. **Known for:** fresh seafood; casual atmosphere; sunset views. [$] *Average main: $19* ✉ *Pier Sixty-Six Hotel & Marina, 2301 SE 17th St., Intracoastal and Inland* ✣ *At end of main dock* ☎ *954/524-3444* 🌐 *www.pelican-landing.com.*

Southport Raw Bar

$$ | SEAFOOD | You can't go wrong at this unpretentious dive where seafood reigns. Feast on raw or steamed clams, raw oysters, and peel-and-eat shrimp. **Known for:** affordable prices; fresh seafood; open late on weekends. [$] *Average main: $19* ✉ *1536 Cordova Rd., Intracoastal and Inland* ☎ *954/525–2526* 🌐 *www.southportrawbar.com.*

Tom Jenkins' Barbecue

$ | BARBECUE | FAMILY | Big portions of dripping barbecue are dispensed at this chill spot for eat-in or take-out. Dinners come with two sides from a list that includes baked beans, collards, and mac and cheese. **Known for:** ample portions; very reasonable prices; good sides. [$] *Average main: $12* ✉ *1236 S Federal Hwy., Intracoastal and Inland* ☎ *954/522–5046* 🌐 *tomjenkinsbbq.net* 🕘 *Closed Sun. and Mon.*

Hotels

Residence Inn Fort Lauderdale Intracoastal/Il Lugano

$ | HOTEL | This modern, clean hotel has studios and suites with fully equipped kitchens, private balconies with intracoastal views, plus amenities including a pool and fitness center. **Pros:** docking is available to guests; pet-friendly; bike rentals available. **Cons:** lacks character of other properties; business traveler vibes; not on the beach. [$] *Rooms from: $154* ✉ *3333 NE 32nd Ave, Intracoastal and Inland* ☎ *954/564–4400* 🌐 *www.marriott.com* 🛏 *105 rooms* 🍴 *Free Breakfast.*

☤ Nightlife

Bars and pubs along Fort Lauderdale's Intracoastal cater to the city's large, transient boating community along with its young professional population. Heading inland along Sunrise Boulevard, the bars around Galleria Mall target singles.

Blue Martini Fort Lauderdale

BARS/PUBS | A hot spot for the wild set, Blue Martini's menu is filled with tons of unconventional martini creations. The drinks are usually very good and the scene is fun for everyone, even those who aren't single and looking to mingle. ⊠ The Galleria at Fort Lauderdale, 2432 E Sunrise Blvd., Intracoastal and Inland ☎ 954/653–2583 ⊕ fortlauderdale.blue-martinilounge.com.

⬤ Shopping

The Galleria at Fort Lauderdale

SHOPPING CENTERS/MALLS | FAMILY | Fort Lauderdale's most sophisticated mall is just west of the Intracoastal Waterway. The split-level emporium comprises Neiman Marcus, Apple, H&M, Macy's, and dozens of specialty shops. You can chow down at The Capital Grille, Truluck's, P.F. Chang's China Bistro, or Seasons 52—or sip cocktails at Blue Martini. The mall itself is open Monday through Saturday 10–9, Sunday noon–6. The stand-alone restaurants and bars are open later. ⊠ 2414 E Sunrise Blvd., Intracoastal and Inland ☎ 954/564–1015 ⊕ www.galleria-mall-fl.com.

Wilton Manors and Oakland Park

North of Fort Lauderdale, Wilton Manors is the hub of gay life in the greater Fort Lauderdale area and has several popular restaurants and bars. Oakland Park, immediately to the north, also has several restaurants that are worth a visit.

☤ Restaurants

★ Eduardo de San Angel

$$$ | MEXICAN | Authentic chiles, spices, and herbs enhance classic seafood, meat, and poultry dishes at this inviting Mexican enclave known for its hospitality. The beloved restaurant has packed the house (which feels like a hacienda) for over 20 years, a testament to its excellent cuisine. **Known for:** upscale Mexican cuisine; exceptional service; cilantro soup. $ Average main: $30 ⊠ 2822 E Commercial Blvd., Oakland Park ☎ 954/772–4731 ⊕ eduardodesanangel. com ⊘ Closed Sun.

Lips

$$$ | AMERICAN | The '90s are still alive and well at Lips. The hit restaurant and drag-show bar is a hot spot for groups celebrating birthdays, bachelorette parties, and other milestones requiring glitz and glamour. **Known for:** drag performances while you dine; Sunday brunch; raucous celebrations. $ Average main: $23 ⊠ 1421 E Oakland Park Blvd., Oakland Park ☎ 954/567–0987 ⊕ www. fladragshow.com ⊘ Closed Mon.

Mai-Kai Restaurant and Polynesian Show

$$$$ | SOUTH PACIFIC | FAMILY | Touristy to some yet downright divine to others, Mai-Kai merges the South Pacific with South Florida. This torch-lit landmark is undeniably gimmicky, but it's the only place in town to drink tiki cocktails while watching Polynesian dances and fire shows. **Known for:** Peking duck; good wine list; long waits—reservations are essential. $ Average main: $39 ⊠ 3599 N Federal Hwy., Oakland Park ☎ 954/563–3272 ⊕ www.maikai.com ⊘ Closed Mon.

Stork's Café and Bakery

$ | CAFÉ | Stork's Café stands out as a friendly coffeehouse and café for gourmet sandwiches and salads. In addition to brewing eight types of coffee, Stork's has excellent baked goods that range from croissants, tortes, cakes, and pies to "monster cookies," including gingersnap and snickerdoodle. **Known for:** great coffee; baked goods; extensive sandwich menu. $ *Average main: $14* ✉ *2505 NE 15th Ave., Wilton Manors* ☎ *954/567–3220* ⊕ *storksbakery.com.*

Nightlife

The hub of Fort Lauderdale's gay nightlife is in Wilton Manors. Wilton Drive, aka "The Drive," has numerous bars, clubs, and lounges that cater to the LGBTQ community.

Georgie's Alibi Monkey Bar

BARS/PUBS | An anchor for the Wilton Manors gay community fills to capacity for cheap Long Island Iced Teas and stands out as a kind of gay "Cheers"—a chill neighborhood drinking hole with darts, pool, and friendly people. ✉ *2266 Wilton Dr., Wilton Manors* ☎ *954/565–2526.*

Rosie's Bar and Grill

BARS/PUBS | Rosie's is very lively, pumping out pop tunes and award-winning burgers. It's the go-to gay-friendly place for affordable drinks and great times. Sunday brunch, with its cast of alternating DJs, is wildly popular. ✉ *2449 Wilton Dr., Wilton Manors* ☎ *954/563–0123* ⊕ *www.rosiesbng.com.*

Shopping

Living Green Fresh Market

SPECIALTY STORES | **FAMILY** | Living Green Fresh Market is a fabulous alternative to overpriced behemoths for the health-conscious in Oakland Park. This green shop and café is bursting with colorful, local, fresh produce, wild-caught fish, prepared foods, and other goods. The quality is top-notch yet the prices are affordable. You can grab breakfast or lunch and cross things off your grocery list, while knowing that each item has a ton of integrity. Plus there's fair-trade coffee. ✉ *1305 E Commercial Blvd., Oakland Park* ☎ *954/771–9770* ⊕ *https://livinggreenfreshmarket.com.*

Western Suburbs and Beyond

West of Fort Lauderdale is an ever-evolving suburbia, where most of Broward's gated communities, golf courses, shopping outlets, casinos, and chain restaurants exist. As you reach the county's western side, the terrain takes on more characteristics of the Everglades, and you can see alligators sunning on canal banks with other exotic reptiles and birds.

Sights

Ah-Tah-Thi-Ki Museum

GARDEN | **FAMILY** | Beyond the western suburbs of Broward County and a couple of miles from Billie Swamp Safari is Ah-Tah-Thi-Ki Museum, which means "a place to learn, a place to remember" in the Seminole language. This Smithsonian Institution Affiliate documents the living history and culture of the Seminole Tribe of Florida through artifacts, exhibits, and experiential learning. There's a mile-long boardwalk above the swamplands (wheelchair-accessible) that leads you through the Big Cypress Seminole Indian Reservation. At the midpoint of the boardwalk, you can take a break at the re-created ceremonial grounds. ✉ *30290 Josie Billie Hwy., Clewiston* ☎ *877/902–1113* ⊕ *www.ahtahthiki.com* 🎫 *$10* ⊘ *Closed holidays.*

Billie Swamp Safari

GARDEN | **FAMILY** | Four different ecosystems in the "River of Grass" are preserved by the Seminole Tribe of Florida, and Billie Swamp Safari's daily tours can introduce you to the elusive wildlife that resides in each area—by airboat or swamp buggy. Sightings of deer, turtles, raccoons, wild hogs, hawks, eagles, and alligators are likely but certainly not guaranteed. Animal exhibits, a petting zoo, and snake/critter shows provide a solid contingency plan. For the rugged adventurer, overnight camping in a native-style chickee hut (thatched-roof dwelling) is available. If a sleepover is too much, Twilight Expeditions offers a campfire with storytelling followed by a nighttime tour. Head to the Swamp Water Café to try Native American dishes like Indian fry bread with honey, Indian tacos, and bison burgers. Check the website for showtimes and tour schedules. ✉ *30000 Gator Tail Trail, Clewiston* ☎ *863/983–6101* ⊕ *www.billieswamp.com* ✉ *Swamp Safari Day Package $50; Twilight Swamp Expedition $43* ⊗ *Closed Christmas Day.*

★ Butterfly World

GARDEN | FAMILY | More than 80 native and international butterfly species live inside the first butterfly house in the U.S. and the largest in the world. The 3-acre site inside Coconut Creek's Tradewinds Park has aviaries, observation decks, waterfalls, ponds, and tunnels. There are lots of birds, too: kids love the lorikeet aviary, where birds alight on every limb. ✉ *Butterfly World, 3600 W Sample Rd., Coconut Creek* ☎ *954/977–4400* ⊕ *www. butterflyworld.com* ✉ *$29.95* ⊗ *Closed holidays* ⌕ *A Tradewinds Park gate fee of $1.50 per person is in effect on weekends and holidays.*

Everglades Holiday Park

MARINA | FAMILY | Many episodes of Animal Planet's *Gator Boys* are filmed here, making this wetland "park" an extremely popular tourist attraction. Take an hour-long airboat tour, snap a selfie with a python, and catch alligators wrestling in the pit. ⚠ **The airboats tend to be supersized, and the overall experience can feel commercialized.** ✉ *21940 Griffin Rd.* ☎ *954/434–8111* ⊕ *www.evergladesh-olidaypark.com* ✉ *$33.39 for 60-minute airboat ride (includes group photo).*

Flamingo Gardens

GARDEN | FAMILY | Wander through the aviary, arboretum, wildlife sanctuary,

and Everglades museum inside the historic Wray Home at Davie's Flamingo Gardens. A half-hour guided tram ride winds through tropical fruit groves and wetlands, where the largest collection of Florida native wildlife lives (flamingos, alligators, bobcats, otters, panthers, and more). ✉ *Flamingo Gardens, 3750 S Flamingo Rd., Davie* ☎ *954/473–2955* ⊕ *www.flamingogardens.org* ✉ *$19.95.*

Sawgrass Recreation Park

NATURE PRESERVE | FAMILY | Catch a good glimpse of plants and wildlife—from ospreys and alligators to turtles, snakes, and fish—on a 30-minute airboat ride through the Everglades. The fee covers admission to all nature exhibits as well as a visit to a model Seminole village. ■ TIP→ **Nature truly comes alive at night. Sawgrass Recreation Park offers longer nighttime airboat rides on Wednesday and Saturday at 8 pm, reservatons required.** ✉ *1006 U.S. 27, Weston* ☎ *888/424–7262, 954/389–0202* ⊕ *www.evergladestours. com* ✉ *$22.95; Gator Night tours $40.*

🍴 Restaurants

★ Anthony's Coal Fired Pizza

$$ | PIZZA | FAMILY | Before this legendary South Florida pizzeria spread to more than 50 outposts across eight states, Anthony's original coal-fired oven was heating up Broward County in a big way. Its Miramar location packs the house with a simple menu of pizza made with fresh ingredients in an 800°F oven, chicken wings, and salads. **Known for:** approachable menu with pizza and Italian favorites; casual, fun atmosphere; coal-fired oven. ⓢ *Average main: $17* ✉ *3111 SW 160th Ave., Hollywood* ☎ *954/392– 3811* ⊕ *acfp.com/location/miramar.*

★ Village Tavern

$$ | CONTEMPORARY | FAMILY | Village Tavern is truly a neighborhood hub for those who love good food, good wine and cocktails, and great company. The bar scene is always fun, especially on Wine

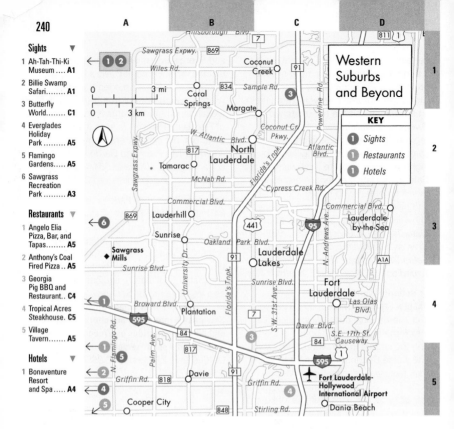

Sights ▼

1 Ah-Tah-Thi-Ki Museum **A1**
2 Billie Swamp Safari........ **A1**
3 Butterfly World........ **C1**
4 Everglades Holiday Park **A5**
5 Flamingo Gardens..... **A5**
6 Sawgrass Recreation Park **A3**

Restaurants ▼

1 Angelo Elia Pizza, Bar, and Tapas........ **A5**
2 Anthony's Coal Fired Pizza .. **A5**
3 Georgia Pig BBQ and Restaurant.. **C4**
4 Tropical Acres Steakhouse. **C5**
5 Village Tavern....... **A5**

Hotels ▼

1 Bonaventure Resort and Spa **A4**

Wednesdays when all the wines (even the premium labels) are $5 per glass. **Known for:** fresh ingredients; busy bar scene; outdoor dining. $ *Average main: $19 ⊠ Shops at Pembroke Gardens, 14555 SW 2nd St.* ☎ *954/874–1001* ⊕ *www.villagetavern.com/locations/ pembroke-pines-fl.*

Angelo Elia Pizza, Bar and Tapas

$$ | PIZZA | FAMILY | This casual Weston outpost is one of chef Angelo Elia's popular Tuscan-inspired restaurants in Broward County. Affordable small plates, salads, ceviches, and pizzas are neighborhood favorites. **Known for:** moderate prices; family-friendly atmosphere; housemade gelato. $ *Average main: $20 ⊠ Country Isles Shopping Center, 1370 Weston Rd., Weston* ☎ *954/306–0037* ⊕ *www. angeloeliapizza.com.*

Georgia Pig BBQ and Restaurant

$ | BARBECUE | FAMILY | When heading out to the area's western reaches, this postage-stamp-sized outpost can add down-home zing to your day—if you can find it, that is. Breakfast, which includes sausage gravy and biscuits, is served 7–11 am, but the big attraction is barbecue beef, pork, or chicken, on platters or in sandwiches for lunch and dinner. **Known for:** North Georgia–style barbecue sauce; chopped pork sandwiches; open-pit cooking. $ *Average main: $12 ⊠ 1285 S State Rd. 7 ⊹ U.S. 441, just south of Davie Blvd.* ☎ *954/587–4420* ▭ *No credit cards* ☉ *Closed Sun.* ⌖ *Credit cards are not accepted.*

Tropical Acres Steakhouse

$$$ | STEAKHOUSE | FAMILY | This old-school, family-owned steak house hasn't changed much since it opened

in 1949. Sizzling steaks are served from a fiery grill, and there are dozens of other entrées to choose from, such as Maine lobster, frogs' legs, rack of lamb, and boneless New York strip. **Known for:** nostalgia galore; family-friendly dining; popular happy hour. $ *Average main: $24* ⊠ *2500 Griffin Rd.* ☎ *954/989–2500* ⊕ *www.tropicalacres.com* ☉ *Closed Sun. in July–Nov. No lunch.*

🛏 Hotels

Bonaventure Resort and Spa

$ | RESORT | FAMILY | This suburban enclave targets conventions and business travelers as well as international vacationers who value golf, the Everglades, and shopping over beach proximity. **Pros:** lush landscaping; pampering spa; located near Sawgrass Mills, the outlet shopping mall. **Cons:** dated decor; 30-minute drive from airport; rental car necessary. $ *Rooms from: $120* ⊠ *250 Racquet Club Rd., Weston* ☎ *954/228–9030* ⊕ *https://www. bonaventureresortandspa.com* ⚓ *The semi-private Bonaventure Country Club is an 18-hole course designed by Joe Lee.* ⇆ *501 rooms* ⏐ *No meals.*

🍸 Nightlife

Florida's cowboy country, Davie, offers country-western fun out in the 'burbs. In addition, South Florida's Native American tribes have long offered gambling on Indian Territory near Broward's western suburbs. These casinos offer Vegas-style slot machines and even blackjack. Hollywood's Seminole Hard Rock Hotel & Casino offers the most elegant of Broward's casino experiences. *See Nightlife in Hollywood.*

Round Up Nightclub and Restaurant

MUSIC CLUBS | Round Up is South Florida's hot country-music and nightclub venue in the heart of Broward's horse country. In addition to line dancing, the venue offers great libations, dance lessons, large-screen TVs, and theme nights coinciding

with drink specials (Whiskey Wednesday, Beer Pong Thursday, Friday Ladies Night, and the like). Open Wedesday through Sunday from 6 pm to 4 am; closed Monday and Tuesday. ■ TIP→ **Happy hour is a good bet, from 6 to 9.** ⊠ *9020 W State Rd. 84, Davie* ☎ *954/423–1990* ⊕ *www. roundupnightclub.com.*

🛍 Shopping

★ **Sawgrass Mills**

OUTLET/DISCOUNT STORES | FAMILY | This alligator-shaped megamall draws millions of shoppers a year to its collection of over 350 outlet stores. Sawgrass Mills also has more than 70 luxury brand outlets, including Burberry, Diane von Furstenberg, GUCCI, Jimmy Choo, Prada, Salvatore Ferragamo Company Store, Tory Burch, and Versace at The Colonnade Outlets at Sawgrass Mills. According to the mall, it's the second-largest attraction in Florida—second only to Walt Disney World. Although this may sound like an an exaggeration, prepare for insane crowds. ⊠ *12801 W Sunrise Blvd., Sunrise* ☎ *954/846-2350* ⊕ *https://www. simon.com/mall/sawgrass-mills.*

🏃 Activities

BIKING

Among the most popular routes are Route A1A and Bayview Drive, especially in early morning before traffic builds, and a seven-mile bike path that parallels State Road 84 and New River and leads to Markham Park, which has mountain-bike trails. ■ TIP→ **Alligator alert: Do not dangle your legs from seawalls.**

AvMed Rides powered by Broward BCycle

BICYCLING | FAMILY | The big-city trend of bike sharing is alive and well in Broward County. With over 20 station locations in six cities, from as far south as Hallandale to as far north as Pompano Beach, bikes can be rented for as little as 30 minutes or as long as a week, and can be picked up and dropped off at any and all stations in Broward County. Most stations are found downtown and along the beach. This is an excellent green and health-conscious way to explore Fort Lauderdale. Download the BCycle app for up-to-date station availability. Please note that helmets are not provided at the kiosks. ⊕ broward.bcycle.com.

BIRD-WATCHING

Evergreen Cemetery

BIRD WATCHING | FAMILY | North of Fort Lauderdale's 17th Street Causeway sits an unexpected haven for bird-watchers. It's the city's oldest cemetery (established 1910), and the shade from its gumbo-limbo and strangler figs doubles as a place of repose for Bahama mockingbirds and other species flying through Broward. Warblers are big here, and there are occasional sightings of red-eyed vireos, northern water thrushes, and scarlet tanagers across 11 acres on Cliff Lake. ⊠ 1300 SE 10th Ave., Intracoastal and Inland ☎ 954/745–2140 ⊕ www.fortlauderdale.gov/departments/parks-recreation/cemeteries.

FISHING

Bahia Mar Yachting Center

BOATING | FAMILY | If you're interested in a saltwater charter, check out the offerings on the A Dock at the marina of the Bahia Mar Fort Lauderdale. Sportfishing and drift fishing bookings can be arranged. Snorkeling and diving outfitter Sea Experience also leaves from here, as does the famous Jungle Queen steamboat. In addition, the Water Taxi makes regular stops here. ⊠ 801 Seabreeze Blvd., Beachfront ☎ 954/627–6309 ⊕ bahiamaryachtingcenter.com.

RODEOS

Davie Pro Rodeo

RODEO | FAMILY | South Florida has a surprisingly established cowboy scene, concentrated in the western suburb of Davie. And for decades, the Bergeron Rodeo Grounds (also known as the Davie Pro Rodeo Arena) has hosted the area's riders and ropers. Throughout the year, the rodeo hosts national tours and festivals as well as the annual Southeastern Circuit Finals. Check the website for the exact dates of special events. ⊠ Bergeron Rodeo Grounds, 4271 Davie Rd., Davie ☎ 954/680–8005 ⊕ davieprorodeo.com.

SCUBA DIVING AND SNORKELING

Lauderdale Diver

SCUBA DIVING | FAMILY | This dive center facilitates daily trips on a bevy of hardcore dive boats up and down Broward's shoreline (they don't have their own boats, but they work with a handful of preferred outfitters). A variety of snorkeling, reef-diving, and wreck-diving trips are offered as well as scuba-diving lessons. ⊠ 1334 SE 17th St., Intracoastal and Inland ☎ 954/467–2822 ⊕ lauderdalediver.com.

★ Sea Experience

SCUBA DIVING | FAMILY | The Sea Experience I leaves daily at 10:15 am and 2:15 pm for glass-bottom-boat-and-snorkeling combination trips through offshore reefs. Beginner and advanced scuba-diving experiences are available as well. ⊠ Bahia Mar Fort Lauderdale Beach–A DoubleTree by Hilton Hotel, 801 Seabreeze Blvd., Beachfront ☎ 954/770–3483 ⊕ www.seaxp.com.

TENNIS

Jimmy Evert Tennis Center

LOCAL SPORTS | FAMILY | This grande dame of Fort Lauderdale's public tennis facilities is where legendary champ Chris Evert learned her two-handed backhand under the watchful eye of her now-retired father, Jimmy, the center's tennis pro for 37 years. There are 18 lighted clay courts and three hard courts. ⊠ Holiday Park, 701 NE 12th Ave., Intracoastal and Inland ☎ 954/828–5378 ⊕ www.fortlauderdale.gov/departments/parks-recreation/tennis-centers/jimmy-evert-tennis-center ⊠ $18 per day for non-residents.

Lauderdale-by-the-Sea

Lauderdale-by-the-Sea is 5 miles north of Fort Lauderdale.

Just north of Fort Lauderdale proper, the low-rise family resort town of Lauderdale-by-the-Sea boasts shoreline access that's rapidly disappearing in neighboring beach towns. The closest and most convenient of the A1A cities to Fort Lauderdale proper embraces its quaint personality by welcoming guests to a different world, drawing a mix of Europeans and cost-conscious families who are looking for fewer frills and longer stays.

GETTING HERE AND AROUND

Lauderdale-by-the-Sea is just north of Fort Lauderdale. From Interstate 95, exit at Commercial Boulevard and head east past the Intracoastal Waterway. From U.S. 1 (Federal Highway), go east at Commercial Boulevard. If driving north on State Road A1A, simply continue north from Fort Lauderdale Beach.

ESSENTIALS

VISITOR INFORMATION Lauderdale-by-the-Sea Chamber of Commerce. ✉ *4201 N Ocean Dr., Lauderdale-by-the-Sea* ☎ *954/776–1000* 🌐 *www.lbts.com.*

Beaches

★ Lauderdale-by-the-Sea Beach

BEACH—SIGHT | FAMILY | Preferred by divers and snorkelers, this laid-back beach is a gateway to magnificent coral reefs. When you're not underwater, look up and you'll likely see a pelican flying by. It's a super-relaxing retreat from the buzz of Fort Lauderdale's busier beaches. That said, the southern part of the beach is crowded near the restaurants at the intersection of A1A and Commercial Boulevard. The no-frills hotels and small inns for families and vacationers visiting for a longer stay are typically filled with Europeans. Look for metered parking around Commercial Boulevard and A1A. **Amenities:** food and drink; lifeguards; parking (fee). **Best for:** family outings; snorkeling; swimming. ✉ *Commercial Blvd. at State Rd. A1A, Lauderdale-by-the-Sea.*

Restaurants

Aruba Beach Café

$$$ | CARIBBEAN | FAMILY | This casual beachfront eatery is arguably Lauderdale-by-the-Sea's most famous restaurant. Aruba Beach serves Caribbean-American cuisine with standouts like conch chowder and conch fritters. **Known for:** Bimini bread with Aruba glaze; nightly live music; Sunday breakfast buffet. [$] *Average main: $22* ✉ *One Commercial Blvd., Lauderdale-by-the-Sea* ☎ *954/776–0001* 🌐 *www.arubabeachcafe.com.*

★ LaSpada's Original Hoagies

$ | AMERICAN | FAMILY | The crew at this seaside hole-in-the-wall puts on quite a show while assembling their sandwiches—locals rave that this indie chain has the best around. Fill up on the foot-long Monster (ham, turkey, roast beef, and cheese), Mama (turkey and Genoa salami), or hot meatballs marinara. **Known for:** the Monster, a foot-long sandwich with ham, turkey, roast beef, cheese; fresh bread; freshly sliced meats. [$] *Average main: $12* ✉ *233 Commercial Blvd., Lauderdale-by-the-Sea* ☎ *954/776–7893* 🌐 *www.laspadashoagies.com* ☞ *There are four additional locations in Broward County.*

Hotels

★ Blue Seas Courtyard

$ | B&B/INN | FAMILY | Husband-and-wife team Cristie and Marc Furth have run this whimsical Mexican-themed motel in Lauderdale-by-the-Sea since 1971. **Pros:** south-of-the-border vibe; friendly owners; across the street from the beach. **Cons:** no ocean views; old bathtubs in some rooms; small setting. [$] *Rooms*

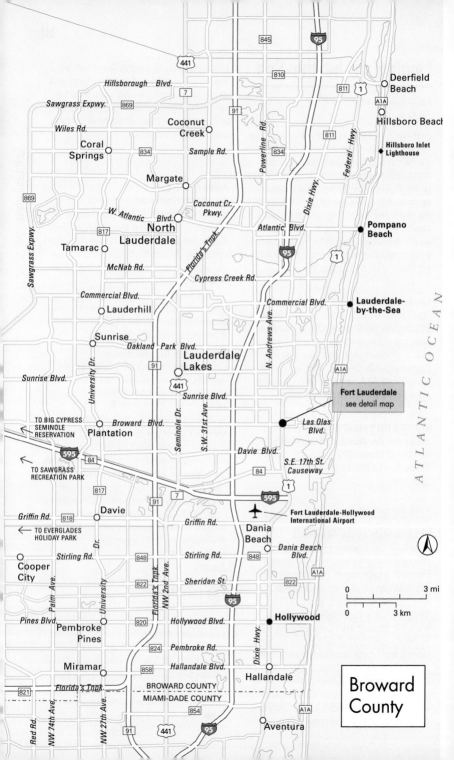

from: $178 ✉ 4525 El Mar Dr., Lauderdale-by-the-Sea ☎ 954/772–3336 🌐 www.blueseascourtyard.com 🛏 12 rooms 🍴 Breakfast.

High Noon Beach Resort
$ | **B&B/INN** | **FAMILY** | This highly-rated family-run hotel sits on 300 feet of beachy paradise with plenty of cozy spots, two heated pools, and an atmosphere that keeps visitors coming back for more. **Pros:** directly on the beach; free Wi-Fi; great staff. **Cons:** 45-day notice of cancellation; no maid service on Sunday; no guarantee for room type. [$] *Rooms from: $190 ✉ 4424 El Mar Dr., Lauderdale-by-the-Sea ☎ 954/776–1121 🌐 www.highnoonresort.com 🛏 41 rooms 🍴 Breakfast.*

Sea Lord Hotel and Suites
$ | **B&B/INN** | **FAMILY** | This gem is one of the nicest in Lauderdale-by-the-Sea. Many of the rooms have great ocean views, balconies, and full kitchens. **Pros:** gorgeous beach location; great staff; rooms with balconies and full kitchens. **Cons:** limited parking; aging decor; no fitness center. [$] *Rooms from: $190 ✉ 4140 El Mar Dr., Lauderdale-by-the-Sea ☎ 954/776–1505, 800/344–4451 🌐 sealordhotel.com 🛏 47 rooms 🍴 Breakfast.*

Activities

Anglins Fishing Pier
FISHING | **FAMILY** | A longtime favorite for 24-hour fishing, it's a spot where you may catch snapper, snook, cobia, blue runner, and pompano. It's also the longest pier in South Florida. The on-site bait-and-tackle shop can advise newbies to advanced anglers. ✉ *Two Commercial Blvd., Lauderdale-by-the-Sea ☎ 954/924–3613 🌐 www.boatlessfishing.com/anglins.htm.*

Pompano Beach

Pompano Beach is 3 miles north of Lauderdale-by-the-Sea.

The high-rise scene resumes as soon as Route A1A enters this town directly north of Lauderdale-by-the-Sea. Sportfishing is big in Pompano Beach, as its name implies, but there's more to beachside attractions than the popular Fisherman's Wharf. Behind a low coral-rock wall, Alsdorf Park (also called the 14th Street boat ramp) extends north and south of the wharf along the road and beach.

GETTING HERE AND AROUND

From Interstate 95, Pompano Beach exits include Sample Road, Copans Road, and Atlantic Boulevard.

Sights

There aren't many "sights" to see in Pompano Beach, but to the north, Route A1A traverses the so-called Hillsboro Mile (actually more than 2 miles), a millionaire's row featuring some of Broward's most beautiful and expensive homes. The road runs along a narrow strip of land between the Intracoastal Waterway and the Atlantic Ocean, with bougainvillea and oleander edging the way and yachts docked along the banks. Traffic often moves at a snail's pace, especially in winter, as vacationers (and sometimes even envious locals) gawk at the beauty.

Hillsboro Inlet Lighthouse
LIGHTHOUSE | **FAMILY** | About 2 miles north of Pompano Beach, you'll find a beautiful view across Hillsboro Inlet to a lighthouse, which is often called the brightest lighthouse in the Southeast and used by mariners as a landmark for decades. When at sea you can see its light from almost halfway to the Bahamas. Although the octagonal-pyramid, iron-skeletal tower lighthouse is on private property (inaccessible to the public),

it's well worth a peek, even from afar. The Hillsboro Lighthouse Preservation Society offers tours about eight times a year (sometimes on holiday weekends), and these include a boat ride to and from the lighthouse. Visit the society's website for the current schedule and tips on viewing vantage points. Tours cost around $35 per person. ✉ *2801, 907 Hillsboro Mile, Hillsboro Beach* ☎ *954/942–2102* 🌐 *www.hillsborolighthouse.org.*

🍴 Restaurants

Cap's Place Island Restaurant
$$$ | **SEAFOOD** | **FAMILY** | On an island that was once a bootlegger's haunt, this ramshackle seafood spot reached by launch has served the famous as well as the infamous, including the likes of Winston Churchill, FDR, JFK, and Al Capone. Cap was Captain Theodore Knight, born in 1871, who, with partner-in-crime Al Hasis, floated a derelict barge to the area in the '20s. [$] *Average main: $26* ✉ *Cap's Dock/Cap's Place, 2765 NE 28th Ct.* ☎ *954/941–0418* 🌐 *www.capsplace.com* 🕒 *Closed Mon. No lunch.*

🛏 Hotels

Cottages by the Ocean
$$ | **RENTAL** | **FAMILY** | For families favoring home-style comforts over resort-style bling, Cottages by the Ocean is one of five beach-area properties run by Beach Vacation Rentals. **Pros:** shops within walking distance; no resort fees (though there are cleaning fees); complimentary Wi-Fi. **Cons:** not directly on beach; no pool; slightly dated decor. [$] *Rooms from: $214* ✉ *3309 SE Third St.* ☎ *954/283–1111* 🌐 *4rentbythebeach.com/properties/cottages-by-the-ocean* 🛏 *6 rooms* 🍽 *No meals.*

🏃 Activities

SS Copenhagen Shipwreck
SCUBA DIVING | The wreck of the SS *Copenhagen* lies in 15- to 30-foot depths just outside the second reef on the Pompano Ledge, 3.6 miles south of Hillsboro Inlet. The 325-foot-long steamer's final voyage, from Philadelphia to Havana, began May 20, 1900, ending six days later when the captain—attempting to avoid gulf currents—crashed into a reef. In 2000, the missing bow section was identified a half mile to the south. The wreck, a haven for colorful fish and corals and a magnet for skin and scuba divers, became Florida's fifth Underwater Archaeological Preserve in 1994 and was listed on the National Register of Historic Places in 2001. Outfitters offer regular trips to the wreck site officially known as the SS Copenhagen State Underwater Archaeological Preserve. ✉ *Pompano Beach* 🌐 *museumsinthesea.com/copenhagen/index.htm.*

Hollywood

Hollywood has had several face-lifts to shed its old-school image, but there's still something delightfully retro about the city. New shops, restaurants, and art galleries open at a persistent clip, and the city has continually spiffed up its boardwalk—a wide pedestrian walkway along the beach—where local joggers are as commonplace as sun-seeking snowbirds from the North.

GETTING HERE AND AROUND

From Interstate 95, exit east on Sheridan Street or Hollywood Boulevard for Hollywood, or Hallandale Beach Boulevard for either Hollywood or Hallandale.

ESSENTIALS

VISITOR INFORMATION Hollywood Community Redevelopment Agency. ✉ *1948 Harrison St.* ☎ *954/924–2980* 🌐 *www.hollywoodcra.org.*

◉ Sights

★ Art and Culture Center/Hollywood

ARTS VENUE | FAMILY | The Art and Culture Center, which is southeast of Young Circle, has a great reputation for presenting übercool contemporary art exhibitions and providing the community with educational programming for adults and children. Check online for the latest exhibition schedule. ⊠ *1650 Harrison St.* ☎ *954/921–3274* ⊕ *www.artandculture-center.org* ⊟ *$7.*

ArtsPark at Young Circle

LOCAL INTEREST | FAMILY | In the center of downtown Hollywood, this 10-acre urban park has promenades and green spaces, public art, a huge playground for kids, a state-of-the-art amphitheater, and spaces for educational workshops like weekly glassblowing and jewelry making. There are food trucks and movie nights as well. ⊠ *1 N Young Cir.* ☎ *954/921–3500* ⊕ *www.hollywoodfl. org/65/ArtsPark-at-Young-Circle.*

Design Center of the Americas (*DCOTA*)

LOCAL INTEREST | Though access is typically reserved strictly to those in the design biz, the Design Center of the Americas still permits visitors to browse the myriad showrooms, which parade the latest and greatest in home furnishings and interior design. Note, however, that this is purely for inspiration, as direct consumer sales are not permitted. ⊠ *1855 Griffin Rd., Dania Beach* ☎ *954/920–7997* ⊕ *www. dcota.com* ⊗ *Closed weekends and major holidays.*

West Lake Park and Anne Kolb Nature Center

COLLEGE | FAMILY | Grab a canoe or kayak, or take a 40-minute guided boat tour at this lakeside park on the Intracoastal Waterway. At 1,500 acres, it's one of Florida's largest urban nature facilities. Extensive boardwalks traverse mangrove wetlands that shelter endangered and threatened species. A 65-foot observation tower showcases the entire park.

At the **Anne Kolb Nature Center,** there's a 3,500-gallon aquarium. The center's exhibit hall also has interactive displays explaining the park's delicate ecosystem. ⊠ *751 Sheridan St.* ☎ *954/357–5163* ⊕ *www.broward.org/Parks/West-LakePark/Pages/AnneKolbNatureCenter. aspx* ⊟ *Park: weekdays free, weekends and holidays $1.50.*

◓ Beaches

★ Dr. Von D. Mizell-Eula Johnson State Park

BEACH—SIGHT | FAMILY | Formerly known as John U. Lloyd Beach State Park, this 310-acre park was renamed Dr. Von D. Mizell–Eula Johnson State Park in honor of the duo who led efforts to change the "colored beach" into a state park in 1973, creating appropriate access for all residents. Native sea grapes, gumbo-limbo trees, and other native plants offer shade. Nature trails and a marina are large draws; canoeing on Whiskey Creek is also popular. The beaches are excellent, but beware of mosquitoes in summer **Amenities:** ample trails; parking (fee); toilets. **Best for:** solitude; sunrise; water sports. ⊠ *6503 N Ocean Dr., Dania Beach* ☎ *954/923–2833* ⊕ *www.floridastateparks.org/parks-and-trails/dr-von-d-mizell-eula-johnson-state-park* ⊟ *$6 per vehicle; $4 for lone driver.*

★ Hollywood Beach and Broadwalk

BEACH—SIGHT | FAMILY | The name might be Hollywood, but there's nothing hip or chic about **Hollywood North Beach Park,** which sits at the north end of Hollywood before the 2½-mile pedestrian Broadwalk begins. And this is a good thing. It's an easygoing place to enjoy the sun, sand, and sea. The year-round **Dog Beach of Hollywood,** between Pershing and Custer streets, allows canine companions to join the fun a few days a week. Walk along the **Broadwalk** for a throwback to the 1950s, with mom-and-pop stores and ice-cream parlors, where elderly couples go for long strolls and families

Did You Know?

You can ride the waves on the FlowRider attraction at the Margaritaville Resort, a popular tourist destination in Broward County.

build sand castles. The popular stretch has spiffy features like a pristine pedestrian walkway, a concrete bike path, a crushed-shell jogging path, an 18-inch decorative wall separating the Broadwalk from the sand, and places to shower off after a dip. Expect to hear French spoken throughout Hollywood since its beaches are a getaway for Québécois. **Amenities:** food and drink; lifeguards; parking (fee); showers; toilets. **Best for:** sunrise; swimming; walking. ✉ *101 S Broadwalk* 🌐 *www.hollywoodfl.org/1049/Hollywood-Beach* 🎫 *Parking in public lots: $3/hour weekdays and $4/hour weekends.*

🍴 Restaurants

★ Jaxson's Ice Cream Parlor and Restaurant

$$ | **AMERICAN** | **FAMILY** | This midcentury landmark whips up malts, shakes, and jumbo sundaes from ice cream that is made on-site daily. Owner Monroe Udell's trademarked Kitchen Sink—a small sink full of ice cream, topped by sparklers—is a real hoot for parties. **Known for:** license-plate decor; homemade ice cream; salads and sandwiches. [$] *Average main: $15* ✉ *128 S Federal Hwy., Dania Beach* ☎ *954/923–4445* 🌐 *www.jaxsonsicecream.com.*

The LeTub Saloon

$$ | **AMERICAN** | Despite molasses-slow service and an abundance of insects at sundown, this eatery is beloved by locals, and management seemed genuinely appalled when hordes of trend-seeking city slickers started jamming bar stools and tables after *GQ* and Oprah declared its thick, juicy Angus burgers the best around. Once a Sunoco gas station, this quirky waterside saloon has an enduring affection for claw-foot bathtubs; lunch will run you around $16 (burger $12; small fries $3.50). **Known for:** late-night service; vintage setting; great burgers and Key lime pie. [$] *Average main: $16* ✉ *1100 N Ocean Dr.* ☎ *954/921–9425* 🌐 *www.theletub.com.*

★ Monkitail

$$$$ | **JAPANESE** | Philadelphia-based chef and restaurateur Michael Schulson brings contemporary Japanese cuisine to the Diplomat Beach Resort's collection of popular restaurants. At Monkitail, superb ingredients and extremely fresh fish are complemented by the chef's precise techniques. **Known for:** superpremium ingredients; fantastic cocktails; traditional Japanese dishes. [$] *Average main: $45* ✉ *The Diplomat Beach Resort Hollywood, Curio Collection by Hilton, 3555 S Ocean Dr.* ☎ *954/602–8755* 🌐 *www.monkitail.com* 🕒 *Closed Mon.–Tues.*

Taverna Opa

$$$ | **GREEK** | **FAMILY** | It's a Greek throwdown every night at this Hollywood institution. Expect a lively night of great eats (including authentic hot and cold meze, wood-fire-grilled meats and seafood), table-top dancing, and awkward moments (especially when suburban parents with two left feet decide to get in on the act), and lots of wine to make it all okay. **Known for:** near Water Taxi stop; celebratory atmosphere; menu of Greek favorites. [$] *Average main: $29* ✉ *410 N Ocean Dr.* ☎ *954/929–4010* 🌐 *www.tavernaopa.com/locations/hollywood-fl.*

🛏 Hotels

★ The Diplomat Beach Resort

$$$ | **RESORT** | **FAMILY** | This colossal 39-story, contemporary, multitower resort property sits on a 50,000-square foot swath of Hollywood Beach's ocean and has a stunning new identity thanks to a $100 million renovation. **Pros:** coastal chic vibe; excellent dining; incredible ocean views. **Cons:** large complex; numerous conventioneers; expensive rates. [$] *Rooms from: $400* ✉ *3555 S Ocean Dr.* ☎ *954/602–6000* 🌐 *www.diplomatresort.com* 🛏 *1,000 rooms* 🍽 *No meals.*

★ Margaritaville Beach Resort

$$$ | **RESORT** | **FAMILY** | The funky boardwalk of Hollywood Beach has a tropical

destination inspired by Jimmy Buffett's lifelong search for paradise. **Pros:** oceanfront location; fun water activities; daily live entertainment. **Cons:** the surrounding area isn't very upscale; touristy vibe; must be a Jimmy Buffett fan. [$] *Rooms from: $370* ✉ *1111 N Ocean Dr.* ☎ *954/874-4444* 🌐 *www.margaritaville-hollywoodbeachresort.com* 🛏 *349 rooms* 🍴 *No meals.*

Seminole Hard Rock Hotel & Casino
$$$ | **HOTEL** | On the industrial flatlands of western Hollywood, the Seminole Hard Rock Hotel & Casino is a magnet for folks looking for Las Vegas–style entertainment (i.e., casinos that never close, clubbing, and hedonism). **Pros:** limitless entertainment; solid bars and restaurants; 24/7 gaming action. **Cons:** in an unsavory neighborhood; construction is under way on new hotel tower; rental car necessary. [$] *Rooms from: $379* ✉ *One Seminole Way* ☎ *866/502-7529* 🌐 *www.seminolehardrockhollywood.com* 🛏 *500 rooms* 🍴 *No meals.*

Nightlife

★ **Seminole Hard Rock Hotel & Casino**
CAFES—NIGHTLIFE | Seminole Hard Rock Hotel & Casino is a Vegas-inspired gaming and entertainment complex in a fairly forlorn area of Hollywood. Once inside the Hard Rock fortress, you'll feel the excitement immediately. In addition to the AAA Four Diamond hotel, there's a monster casino, a 5,500-seat performance venue (Hard Rock Event Center), plus dozens of restaurants, bars, and nightclubs. **TIP→ The Seminole Hard Rock Hotel & Casino is not to be confused with its neighbor, the Seminole Classic Casino.** ✉ *One Seminole Way* ☎ *866/502-7529* 🌐 *www.seminole-hardrockhollywood.com.*

Shopping

★ **Shops at Pembroke Gardens**
SHOPPING CENTERS/MALLS | **FAMILY** | The Shops at Pembroke Gardens is an outdoor oasis for consumers looking for a variety of shops, restaurants, salons, and spas. From shops like Ann Taylor and Sephora to local dining options like RA Sushi and Village Tavern, it's a popular hangout among locals and tourists. The wide range of retail options keeps this relatively upscale stretch accessible to shoppers on a budget. A small-scale farmers' market sets up in the center promenade on Sundays. ✉ *527 SW 145th Ter., Pembroke Pines* ☎ *954/450-1580* 🌐 *www.pembrokegardens.com.*

Chapter 7

PALM BEACH AND
THE TREASURE COAST

Updated by
Sara Liss

 Sights
★★★★☆

 Restaurants
★★★★☆

 Hotels
★★★★★

 Shopping
★★★★☆

 Nightlife
★★☆☆☆

WELCOME TO PALM BEACH AND THE TREASURE COAST

TOP REASONS TO GO

★ **Exquisite resorts:** Two grandes dames, The Breakers and the Boca Raton Resort & Club, perpetually draw the rich, the famous, and anyone else who can afford the luxury. The Eau Palm Beach and Four Seasons sparkle with service fit for royalty.

★ **Beautiful beaches:** From Jupiter, where dogs run free, to Stuart's tubular waves, to the broad stretches of sand in Delray Beach and Boca Raton, swimmers, surfers, sunbathers—and sea turtles looking for a place to hatch their eggs—all find happiness.

★ **Top-notch golf:** The Champion Course and re-envisioned Fazio Course at PGA National Resort & Spa are world renowned; pros sharpen up at PGA Village.

★ **Horse around:** Wellington, with its popular polo season, is often called the winter equestrian capital of the world.

★ **Excellent fishing:** The Atlantic Ocean, teeming with kingfish, sailfish, and wahoo, is a treasure chest for anglers.

1 Palm Beach. Tony beach town with luxury resorts and shopping.

2 West Palm Beach. No beach, but a great arts scene.

3 Lake Worth. Stop for its charming, artsy center.

4 Lantana. Its famous Key Lime House overlooks the water.

5 Boynton Beach. A family favorite with access to coral reefs.

6 Delray Beach. Its lively downtown is blocks from the ocean.

7 Boca Raton. Modern shopping mixes with historic buildings.

8 Palm Beach Gardens. Golf lovers flock to the PGA National Resort & Spa.

9 Singer Island. Easy access to snorkeling at Peanut Island.

10 Juno Beach. Famous for its sea turtles.

11 Jupiter and Vicinity. Calm respite with rugged coastline.

12 Stuart and Jensen Beach. Charming historic district and undeveloped beach.

13 Fort Pierce and Port St. Lucie. Ample fishing and surfing.

14 Vero Beach. Cosmopolitan yet understated.

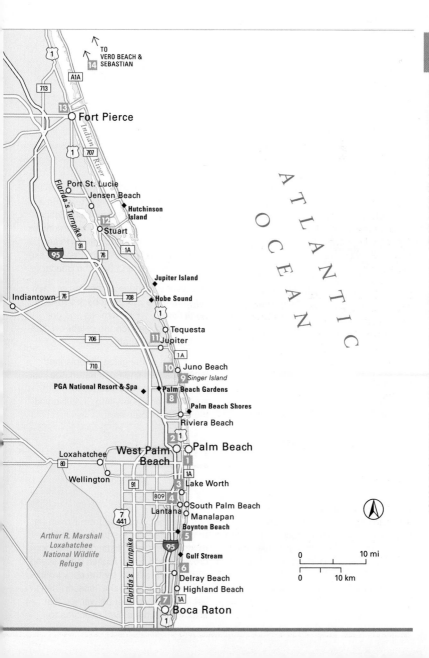

A golden stretch of the Atlantic shore, the Palm Beach area resists categorization, and for good reason: the territory stretching south to Boca Raton, appropriately coined the Gold Coast, defines old-world glamour and new-age sophistication.

To the north you'll uncover the comparatively undeveloped Treasure Coast—liberally sprinkled with seaside gems and wide-open spaces along the road awaiting your discovery.

Altogether, there's a delightful disparity between Palm Beach, pulsing with old-money wealth, and under-the-radar Hutchinson Island. Seductive as the gorgeous beaches, eclectic dining, and leisurely pursuits can be, you should also take advantage of flourishing commitments to historic preservation and the arts, as town after town yields intriguing museums, galleries, theaters, and gardens.

Palm Beach, proud of its status as America's first luxe resort destination and still glimmering with its trademark Mediterranean-revival mansions, manicured hedges, and highbrow shops, can rule supreme as the focal point for your sojourn any time of year. From there, head off in one of two directions: south toward Delray Beach and Boca Raton along an especially scenic estate-dotted route known as A1A, or back north to the beautiful barrier islands of the Treasure Coast. For rustic inland activities such as bass fishing and biking atop the dike around Lake Okeechobee, head west.

MAJOR REGIONS

About 70 miles north of Miami, off I-95, lies **Palm Beach**, which is actually on a barrier island. The greater Palm Beach area encompasses several communities on the mainland and to the north and south, including West Palm Beach, Lake Worth, Lantana, and Boynton Beach.

Just over the bridge at the Port of Palm Beach are the more laid-back towns of **North County**, which families and golf pros, not to mention the celebs on Jupiter Island, call home.

In contrast to the glitzy, überplanned Palm Beaches and Boca Raton, the more bucolic **Treasure Coast** stretches from south Martin County into St. Lucie and Indian River counties.

Planning

When to Go

The weather is optimal from November through May, but the trade-off is that roads, hotels, and restaurants are more crowded and prices higher. If the scene is what you're after, try the early weeks of December when the "season" isn't yet in full swing. But be warned that after Easter, the crowd relocates to the Hamptons, and Palm Beach feels like another universe. For some that's a blessing—and a great time to take advantage of lower summer lodging rates and dining deals—but you'll need to bring your tolerance for heat, humidity, and afternoon downpours.

Getting Here and Around

AIR TRAVEL

Palm Beach International Airport is in West Palm, but it's possible (and sometimes cheaper) to fly to Fort Lauderdale, Miami, or Orlando. Do rent a car if you plan on exploring. Scenic Route A1A, also called Ocean Boulevard or Ocean Drive, depending on where you are, ventures out onto the barrier islands. Interstate 95 runs parallel to U.S. 1, a main north–south thoroughfare in the region (also known as Federal Highway), but a few miles inland.

AIRPORT Palm Beach International Airport (*PBI*). ✉ *1000 Turnage Blvd., West Palm Beach* ✛ *From I–95, use the airport flyover exit; from Florida's Tpke., use the Southern Blvd. exit and drive east to the airport exit* ☎ *561/471–7420* ⊕ *www.pbia. org.*

AIRPORT TRANSFERS SuperShuttle. ☎ *800/258–3826* ⊕ *www.supershuttle. com.*

BUS TRAVEL

The county's bus service, Palm Tran, runs two routes (Nos. 44 and 40) that offer daily service connecting the airport, the Tri-Rail stop near it, and locations in central West Palm Beach. A network of 34 routes joins towns all across the area; it's $5 for a day pass. The free Downtown Trolley connects the West Palm Beach Amtrak station and the Tri-Rail stop in West Palm on its Green Line. Its Yellow Line makes continuous loops down Clematis Street, the city's main stretch of restaurants and watering holes interspersed with stores, and through

CityPlace, a shopping-dining-theater district, and to the Kravis Center. Hop on and off at any of the stops. The trolley's Yellow Line runs Sunday to Wednesday 11–9 and Thursday to Saturday 11–11. The trolley's Green Line, which stretches farther east, west, and south, and connects to Tri-Rail and Amtrak, runs weekdays 7–7, Saturday 9–7, and Sunday 11–7. A Blue Line, operating year-round, runs from downtown West Palm Beach to Northwood Village and the Palm Beach Outlets mall. Times are Thursday–Saturday, 11–10.

CONTACTS Downtown Trolley. ☎ *561/833–8873* ⊕ *www.downtownwpb. com/trolley/.* **Palm Tran.** ☎ *561/841–4287* ⊕ *www.pbcgov.com/palmtran.*

TAXI TRAVEL

Several taxi companies serve the area, including the Southeastern Florida Transportation Group. Also available are limousine services to Palm Beach or out of county. The ride-sharing services Uber (⊕ *www.uber.com*) and Lyft (⊕ *www.lyft. com*) are accessible as apps from your phone.

CONTACTS AmeriCab. ☎ *561/337–7777* ⊕ *www.americabtaxi.com* **Limos of Palm Beach.** ☎ *561/459–7128* ⊕ *www. limosofpb.com* **Palm Beach Yellow Cab.** ☎ *561/721–2222* ⊕ *www.palmbeachyellowcab.com* **Southeastern Florida Transportation Group.** ☎ *561/777–7777* ⊕ *www. yellowcabflorida.com.*

TRAIN TRAVEL

Amtrak stops daily in West Palm Beach. The station is at the same location as the Tri-Rail stop, so the same free shuttle, the Downtown Trolley, is available (via the trolley's Green Line).

Tri-Rail Commuter Service is a rail system with 18 stops altogether between West Palm Beach and Miami; tickets can be purchased at each stop, and a one-way trip from the first to the last point is $6.90 weekdays, $5 weekends. Three stations—West Palm Beach, Lake Worth, and Boca—have free shuttles to their downtowns, and taxis are on call at others.

A new high-speed train line, Virgin Trains USA (formerly called Brightline) began running in summer 2018. It connects downtown Miami to Fort Lauderdale and West Palm Beach in 30 and 60 minutes respectively.

CONTACTS Amtrak. ☎ *800/872–7245* ⊕ *www.amtrak.com.* **Virgin Trains USA** (*Formerly Brightline*). ⊕ *www.virgin.com.* **Tri-Rail.** ☎ *800/874–7245* ⊕ *www.tri-rail. com.*

Hotels

Palm Beach has a number of smaller hotels in addition to the famous Breakers. Lower-priced hotels and bed-and-breakfasts can be found in West Palm Beach, Palm Beach Gardens, and Lake Worth. Heading south, the ocean-side town of Manalapan has the Eau Palm Beach Resort & Spa. The Seagate Hotel & Spa sparkles in Delray Beach, and the posh Boca Beach Club lines the superlative swath of shoreline in Boca Raton. In the opposite direction there's the PGA National Resort & Spa, and on the opposite side of town on the ocean is the Marriott on Singer Island, a well-kept secret for spacious, sleek suites. Even farther north, Vero Beach has a collection of luxury boutique hotels, as well as more modest options along the Treasure Coast. To the west, towns close to Lake Okeechobee offer country-inn accommodations geared to bass-fishing pros.

Restaurants

Numerous elegant establishments offer upscale American, Continental, and international cuisine, but the area also is chock-full of casual waterfront spots serving affordable burgers and fresh seafood feasts. Snapper and grouper are especially popular here, along with the ubiquitous shrimp. Happy hours and early-bird menus, Florida hallmarks, typically entice the budget-minded with several dinner entrées at reduced prices offered during certain hours, usually before 5 or 6.

Hotel and restaurant reviews have been shortened. For full information, visit Fodors.com.

What It Costs			
$	**$$**	**$$$**	**$$$$**
RESTAURANTS			
under $15	$15–$20	$21–$30	over $30
HOTELS			
under $200	$200–$300	$301–$400	over $400

VISITOR INFORMATION
CONTACTS Discover the Palm Beaches. ✉ *1555 Palm Beach Lakes Blvd., Suite 800, West Palm Beach* ☎ *800/554–7256* ⊕ *www.thepalmbeaches.com.*

Palm Beach

70 miles north of Miami, off I–95.

Long reigning as the place where the crème de la crème go to shake off winter's chill, Palm Beach continues to be a seasonal hotbed of platinum-grade consumption. It's been the winter address for heirs of the iconic Rockefeller, Vanderbilt, Colgate, Post, Kellogg, and Kennedy families. Strict laws govern everything from building to landscaping, and not so much as a pool awning gets added without a town council nod. Only three bridges allow entry, and huge tour buses are a no-no.

All this fabled atmosphere started with Henry Morrison Flagler, Florida's premier developer, and cofounder, along with John D. Rockefeller, of Standard Oil.

Draped in European elegance, The Breakers in Palm Beach sits on 140 acres along the oceanfront.

No sooner did Flagler bring the railroad to Florida in the 1890s than he erected the famed Royal Poinciana and Breakers hotels. Rail access sent real-estate prices soaring, and ever since, princely sums have been forked over for personal stationery engraved with 33480, the zip code of Palm Beach (which didn't actually get its status as an independent municipality until 1911). Setting the tone in this town of unparalleled Florida opulence is the ornate architectural work of Addison Mizner, who began designing homes and public buildings here in the 1920s and whose Moorish-Gothic Mediterranean-revival style has influenced virtually all landmarks.

GETTING HERE AND AROUND

Palm Beach is 70 miles north of Miami (a 90-minute trip with traffic). To access Palm Beach off Interstate 95, exit east at Southern Boulevard, Belvedere Road, or Okeechobee Boulevard. To drive from Palm Beach to Lake Worth, Lantana, Manalapan, and Boynton Beach, head south on Ocean Boulevard/Route A1A;

Lake Worth is roughly 6 miles south, and Boynton is another 6. Similarly, to reach them from West Palm Beach, take U.S. 1 or Interstate 95. To travel between Palm Beach and Singer Island, you must cross over to West Palm before returning to the beach. Once there, go north on U.S. 1 and then cut over on Blue Heron Boulevard/Route 708. If coming straight from the airport or somewhere farther west, take Interstate 95 up to the same exit and proceed east. The main drag in Palm Beach Gardens is PGA Boulevard/Route 786, which is 4 miles north on U.S. 1 and Interstate 95; A1A merges with it as it exits the top part of Singer Island. Continue on A1A to reach Juno Beach and Jupiter.

Sights

Most streets around major attractions and commercial zones have free parking as well as metered spaces. If you can stake out a place between a Rolls-Royce and a Bentley, do so, but beware of the "Parking by Permit Only" signs, as a $50 ticket might take the shine off your spot. Better yet, if you plan to spend an entire afternoon strolling Worth Avenue, park in the Apollo lot behind Tiffany's midway off Worth on Hibiscus; some stores will validate your parking ticket.

Bethesda-by-the-Sea

HISTORIC SITE | This Gothic-style Episcopal church had a claim to fame upon its creation in 1926: it was built by the first Protestant congregation in southeast Florida. Church lecture tours, covering Bethesda's history, architecture, and more, are offered at 12:15 on the second and fourth Sunday each month from September to mid-May (excluding December) and at 11:15 on the fourth Sunday each month from end of May to August. Also notable are the annual Boar's Head and Yule Log festivals in January. Adjacent is the formal, ornamental Cluett Memorial Garden. ⊠ *141 S. County Rd.* ☎ *561/655–4554* ⊕ *www.bbts.org* ⊠ *Free.*

★ The Breakers

HISTORIC SITE | Built by Henry Flagler in 1896 and rebuilt by his descendants after a 1925 fire, this magnificent Italian Renaissance–style resort helped launch Florida tourism with its Gilded Age opulence, attracting influential wealthy Northerners to the state. The hotel, still owned by Flagler's heirs, is a must-see even if you aren't staying here. Walk through the 200-foot-long lobby, which has soaring arched ceilings painted by 72 Italian artisans and hung with crystal chandeliers. Meet for a drink and a round of eclectic small plates at the HMF, one of the most beautiful bars in the state. ■TIP→ **Book a pampering spa treatment or dine at the popular oceanfront Seafood Bar that was renovated in 2016. The $30 parking fee is waived if you spend at least $30 anywhere in the hotel (just have your ticket validated).** ⊠ *1 S. County Rd.* ☎ *561/655–6611* ⊕ *www.thebreakers.com.*

El Solano

HOUSE | No Palm Beach mansion better represents the town's luminous legacy than the Spanish-style home built by Addison Mizner as his own residence in 1925. Mizner later sold El Solano to Harold Vanderbilt, and the property was long a favorite among socialites for parties and photo shoots. Vanderbilt held many a gala fund-raiser here. Beatle John Lennon and his wife, Yoko Ono, bought it less than a year before Lennon's death. It's still privately owned and not open to the public, but it's well worth a drive-by on any self-guided Palm Beach mansion tour. ⊠ *720 S. Ocean Blvd.*

★ Henry Morrison Flagler Museum

HOUSE | The worldly sophistication of Florida's Gilded Age lives on at Whitehall, the plush 55-room "marble palace" Henry Flagler commissioned in 1901 for his third wife, Mary Lily Kenan. Architects John Carrère and Thomas Hastings were instructed to create the finest home imaginable—and they outdid themselves. Whitehall rivals the grandeur of European palaces and has an entrance hall with a baroque ceiling similar to Louis XIV's Versailles. Here you'll see original furnishings; a hidden staircase Flagler used to sneak from his bedroom to the billiards room; an art collection; a 1,200-pipe organ; and Florida East Coast Railway exhibits, along with Flagler's personal railcar, No. 91, showcased in an 8,000-square-foot beaux arts–style pavilion behind the mansion. Docent-led tours and audio tours are included with admission. The museum's Café des Beaux-Arts, open from Thanksgiving through mid-April, offers a Gilded Age–style early afternoon tea for $40 (11:30 am–2:30 pm); the price includes museum admission. ⊠ *1 Whitehall Way* ☎ *561/655–2833* ⊕ *www.flaglermuseum. us* ⊠ *$18.*

Mar-a-Lago

HISTORIC SITE | Breakfast-food heiress Marjorie Merriweather Post commissioned a Hollywood set designer to create Ocean Boulevard's famed Mar-a-Lago, a 114-room, 110,000-square-foot

Mediterranean-revival palace. Its 75-foot Italianate tower is visible from many areas of Palm Beach and from across the Intracoastal Waterway in West Palm Beach. Its notable owner, President Donald Trump, has turned it into a private membership club and has realized Marjorie Post's dream of turning the estate into a presidential retreat. Tourists have to enjoy the view from the car window or bicycle seat, but even the gates are impressive. ⊠ *1100 S. Ocean Blvd.* ☎ *561/832–2600* ⊕ *www.maralagoclub. com.*

Society of the Four Arts

ARTS VENUE | **FAMILY** | Despite widespread misconceptions of its members-only exclusivity, this privately endowed institution—founded in 1936 to encourage appreciation of art, music, drama, and literature—is funded for public enjoyment. The Esther B. O'Keeffe gallery building artfully melds an exhibition hall that houses traveling exhibits with a 700-seat theater. A library designed by prominent Mizner-peer Maurice Fatio, a children's library, a botanical garden, and the Philip Hulitar Sculpture Garden round out the facilities and are open daily. A complete schedule of programming is available on the society's website. ⊠ *2 Four Arts Plaza* ☎ *561/655–7227* ⊕ *www.fourarts.org* ⊠ *$5 gallery; special program costs vary.*

★ Worth Avenue

HISTORIC SITE | Called the Avenue by Palm Beachers, this half-mile-long street is synonymous with exclusive shopping. Nostalgia lovers recall an era when faces or names served as charge cards, purchases were delivered home before customers returned from lunch, and bills were sent directly to private accountants. Times have changed, but a stroll amid the Spanish-accented buildings, many designed by Addison Mizner, offers a tantalizing taste of the island's ongoing commitment to elegant consumerism. Explore the labyrinth of nine pedestrian "vias" off each side that wind

past boutiques, tiny plazas, bubbling fountains, and bougainvillea-festooned balconies; this is where the smaller, unique shops are. The Worth Avenue Association holds historic walking tours on Wednesdays at 11 am during "the season" (December through April). The $10 fee benefits local nonprofit organizations. ⊠ *Worth Ave.* ✛ *Between Cocoanut Row and S. Ocean Blvd.* ☎ *561/659–6909* ⊕ *www.worth-avenue.com.*

Beaches

Phipps Ocean Park

BEACH—SIGHT | About 2 miles south of "Billionaire's Row" on Ocean Boulevard sits this public ocean-side park, with two metered parking lots separated by a fire station. There are four entry points to the beach, but the north side is better for beachgoers. At the southern entrance, there is a six-court tennis facility. The beach is narrow and has natural rock formations dotting the shoreline, making it ideal for snorkelers. There are picnic tables and grills on-site, as well as the Little Red Schoolhouse, an 1886 landmark that hosts educational workshops for local kids. If a long walk floats your boat, venture north to see the mega-mansions, but don't go too far inland, because private property starts at the high-tide line. Parking is metered, and time limits strictly enforced. There's a two-hour time limit for free parking—but read the meter carefully: it's valid only during certain hours at some spots. **Amenities:** lifeguards; parking (no fee); showers; toilets. **Best for:** solitude; walking. ⊠ *2201 S. Ocean Blvd.* ☎ *561/227-6450 Ext. 8, 561/227–6450 tennis reservations* ⊕ *wpbparks.com/beaches/ phipps-ocean-park-and-beach* ⊠ *Free.*

Town of Palm Beach Municipal Beach

BEACH—SIGHT | You know you're here if you see Palm Beach's younger generation frolicking on the sands and locals setting up chairs as the sun reflects off their gleaming white veneers. The

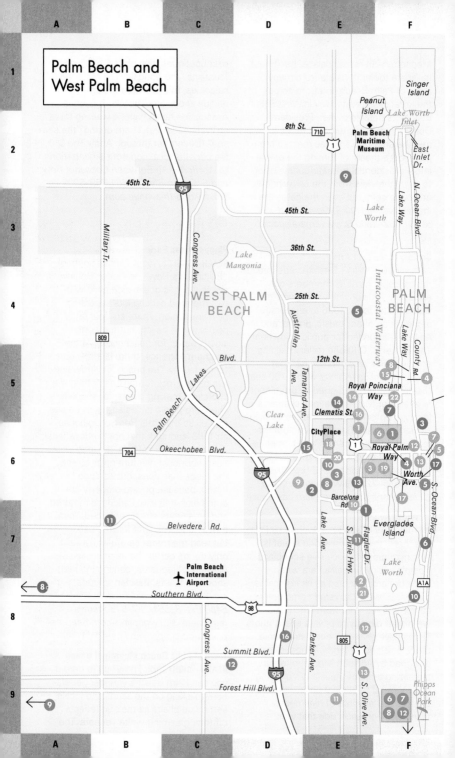

0 _____ 1 mile

0 _____ 1 km

A T L A N T I C   O C E A N

Sights ▼

1 Ann Norton Sculpture
Gardens.................. **E7**

2 Armory Art Center....... **E6**

3 Bethesda-by-the-Sea ... **F6**

4 The Breakers............. **F5**

5 Currie Park **E4**

6 El Solano................. **F7**

7 Henry Morrison Flagler
Museum **F5**

8 Lion Country Safari **A8**

9 Manatee Lagoon **E2**

10 Mar-a-Lago............... **F8**

11 Mounts
Botanical Garden....... **B7**

12 National Croquet
Center.................... **C9**

13 Norton Museum
of Art **E6**

14 Richard and Pat Johnson
Palm Beach County
History Museum **E5**

15 Society of the
Four Arts **D6**

16 South Florida
Science Center
and Aquarium.......... **D8**

17 Worth Avenue........... **F6**

Restaurants ▼

1 Avocado Grill............. **E6**

2 Belle and Maxwell's..... **E8**

3 Bice Ristorante **F6**

4 Bistro Chez
Jean-Pierre.............. **F5**

5 bûccan................... **F6**

6 Café Boulud **F6**

7 Café L'Europe............ **F6**

8 Echo...................... **F5**

9 Grandview
Public Market........... **D6**

10 Grato **E6**

11 Havana................... **E9**

12 Howley's **E8**

13 Marcello's La Sirena **E9**

14 Mediterranean
Market & Deli **E5**

15 PB Catch................. **F5**

16 Pistache French Bistro.. **E5**

17 Pizza Al Fresco........... **F6**

18 The Regional Kitchen &
Public House **E6**

19 Renato's.................. **F6**

20 RH Rooftop
Restaurant............... **E6**

21 Rhythm Cafe............. **E8**

22 Sant Ambroeus **F5**

Hotels ▼

1 The Brazilian
Court Hotel **F6**

2 The Breakers
Palm Beach **F5**

3 Casa Grandview West
Palm Beach **E6**

4 The Chesterfield
Palm Beach **F6**

5 The Colony............... **F6**

6 Eau Palm Beach **F9**

7 Four Seasons Resort
Palm Beach **F9**

8 Grandview Gardens
Bed & Breakfast......... **E6**

9 Hampton Inn & Suites
Wellington............... **A9**

10 Hilton West
Palm Beach **E6**

11 Hotel Biba **E7**

12 The Tideline
Resort & Spa............ **F9**

KEY

1 Sights

1 Restaurants

1 Hotels

The Mansions of Palm Beach

Whether you aspire to be a former president (Kennedy), a current one (Trump), or a rock legend (John Lennon, Rod Stewart, Jimmy Buffett—all onetime or current Palm Beach residents)—no trip to the island is complete without gawking at the megamansions lining its perfectly manicured streets.

No one is more associated with how the island took shape than Addison Mizner, architect extraordinaire and society darling of the 1920s. But what people may not know is that a "fab four" was really the force behind the residential streets as they appear today: Mizner, of course, plus Maurice Fatio, Marion Sims Wyeth, and John Volk.

The four architects dabbled in different genres, some more so than others, but the unmissable style is Mediterranean revival, a Palm Beach hallmark mix of stucco walls, Spanish red-tile roofs, Italianate towers, Moorish-Gothic carvings, and the uniquely Floridian use of coquina, a grayish porous limestone made of coral rock with fossil-like imprints of shells. As for Mizner himself, he had quite the repertoire of signature elements, including using differently sized and shaped windows on one facade, blue tile work inside and out, and tiered roof lines (instead of one straight-sloping panel across, having several sections overlap like scales on a fish).

The majority of preserved estates are clustered in three sections: along Worth Avenue; the few blocks of South County Road after crossing Worth and the streets shooting off it; and the 5-mile stretch of South Ocean Boulevard from Barton Avenue to near Phipps Ocean Park, where the condos begin cropping up.

If 10 miles of riding on a bike while cars zip around you isn't intimidating, the two-wheeled trip may be the best way to fully take in the beauty of the mansions and surrounding scenery. Many hotels have bicycles for guest use. Another option is the dependable Palm Beach Bicycle Trail Shop (☎ 561/659–4583 ⊕ *www.palmbeach-bicycle.com*). Otherwise, driving is a good alternative. Just be mindful that Ocean Boulevard is a one-lane road and the only route on the island to cities like Lake Worth and Manalapan, so you can't go too slowly, especially at peak travel times.

If gossip is more your speed, in-the-know concierges rely on Leslie Diver's Island Living Tours (☎ 561/868–7944 ⊕ *www.islandlivingpb.com*); she's one of the town's leading experts on architecture *and* dish, both past and present.

Top 10 Self-Guided Stops: (1) Casa de Leoni (✉ *450 Worth Ave.*, Addison Mizner); (2) Villa des Cygnes (✉ *456 Worth Ave.*, Addison Mizner and Marion Sims Wyeth); (3) Horgacito (✉ *17 Golfview Road*, Marion Sims Wyeth); (4) (✉ *220 and 252 El Bravo Way*, John Volk); (5) (✉ *126 South Ocean Boulevard*, Marion Sims Wyeth); (6) El Solano (✉ *720 S. Ocean Blvd.*, Addison Mizner); (7) Casa Nana (✉ *780 S. Ocean Blvd.*, Addison Mizner); (8) ✉ *920 and 930 South Ocean Boulevard*, Maurice Fatio); (9) Mar-a-Lago (✉ *1100 S. Ocean Blvd.*, Joseph Urban); (10) Il Palmetto (✉ *1500 S. Ocean Blvd.*, Maurice Fatio).

—Dorothea Hunter Sönne

Worth Avenue clock tower is within sight, but the gateways to the sand are actually on Chilean Avenue, Brazilian Avenue, and Gulfstream Road. It's definitely the most central and longest lifeguarded strip open to everyone and a popular choice for hotel guests from the Colony, Chesterfield, and Brazilian Court. Lifeguards are present from Brazilian Avenue down to Chilean Avenue. It's also BYOC (bring your own chair). You'll find no water-sports or food vendors here; however, casual eateries are a quick walk away. Metered spots line A1A. **Amenities:** lifeguards; showers. **Best for:** sunset; swimming. ✉ *S. Ocean Blvd.* ✣ *From Brazilian Ave. to Gulfstream Rd.* ☎ *561/838–5483 beach patrol* 🌐 *www.thepalmbeaches.com/central-region/town-palm-beach-municipal-beach.*

🍴 Restaurants

★ Sant Ambroeus

$$$ | ITALIAN | An outpost of the famed New York Italian spot, this chic café churns out crispy pizzas, delicate pasta dishes, and to-swoon-for desserts with polished service. The vibe is '60s era glam meets dreamy Milanese café, making it a hit with both socialites and shoppers who stop in for an espresso break in between jaunts to the boutiques at Royal Poinciana Plaza. **Known for:** heavenly cacio e pepe; opulent decor; gelato. [$] *Average main: $24* ✉ *340 Royal Poinciana Way* ☎ *561/285-7990* 🌐 *www.santambroeus.com/restaurant-sant-ambroeus-palm-beach.*

Bice Ristorante

$$$$ | ITALIAN | The bougainvillea-laden trellises set the scene at the main entrance on Peruvian Way, off posh Worth Avenue. Even though it's a chain, this is a favorite of Palm Beach society, and both the restaurant and the bar become packed and noisy during high season. **Known for:** seafood risotto; home-made pizzaccia bread with basil, chives, and oregano; outdoor dining where you can watch the scene on Worth Avenue. [$] *Average main: $35* ✉ *313½ Worth Ave.* ✣ *Entrance is on Peruvian Ave.* ☎ *561/835–1600* 🌐 *www.palmbeach.bicegroup.com.*

Bistro Chez Jean-Pierre

$$$$ | FRENCH | With walls adorned by avant-garde contemporary art, this family-run bistro is where the Palm Beach old guard likes to let down its hair, all the while partaking of sumptuous northern French cuisine along with an impressive wine selection. Forget calorie or cholesterol concerns, and indulge in scrambled eggs with caviar or house-made foie gras, or the best-selling Dover sole. **Known for:** Dover sole; foie gras prepared in-house; dessert soufflés. [$] *Average main: $39* ✉ *132 N. County Rd.* ☎ *561/833–1171* 🌐 *www.chezjean-pierre.com* ⏲ *Closed on Mon. from May–Nov. Closed Sun. No lunch.*

★ bûccan

$$$$ | ECLECTIC | An antidote to the sometimes stuffy and "jackets-encouraged" atmosphere of most restaurants on the island, chef-owner Clay Conley's ode to ecelectic American cuisine neatly straddles the line between fine dining and exciting gastropub. The restaurant attracts both old money and the younger set, with a buzzing bar-and-lounge scene and an open kitchen showcasing the culinary acrobatics on display. **Known for:** small sharing plates; hamachi tiradito; short rib empanadas. [$] *Average main: $32* ✉ *350 S. County Rd.* ☎ *561/833–3450* 🌐 *www.buccanpalmbeach.com* ⏲ *No lunch.*

★ Café Boulud

$$$$ | FRENCH | Palm Beach socialites just can't get enough of this prized restaurant by celebrated chef Daniel Boulud. This posh, French-American venue in the Brazilian Court hotel is casual yet elegant with a large and inviting bar that hosts a daily happy hour and a plush dining room that features a seashell-clad ceiling. **Known for:** house-cured charcuterie;

Dover sole; an extensive wine list. [$] *Average main: $38* ✉ *The Brazilian Court Hotel & Beach Club, 301 Australian Ave.* ☎ *561/655–6060* 🌐 *www.cafeboulud.com.*

Café L'Europe

$$$$ | INTERNATIONAL | Since 1980, the favorite spot of society's movers and shakers—and a few celebs—has remained a regular stop on foodie itineraries. Service and consistency are big reasons for its longevity. **Known for:** veal chops; romantic setting; champagne-and-caviar bar with extensive selections. [$] *Average main: $47* ✉ *331 S. County Rd.* ☎ *561/655–4020* 🌐 *www.cafeleurope.com* 🕒 *Closed Mon.*

Echo

$$$ | ASIAN | Palm Beach's window on Asia has a sleek sushi bar and floor-to-ceiling glass doors separating the interior from the popular terrace dining area. Chinese, Japanese, Thai, and Vietnamese selections are neatly categorized: Wind (small plates starting your journey), Water (seafood mains), Fire (open-flame wok creations), Earth (meat dishes), and Flavor (desserts, sweets). **Known for:** sushi and specialty rolls; fresh seafood; cocktails in the Dragonfly Lounge. [$] *Average main: $30* ✉ *230-A Sunrise Ave.* ☎ *561/802–4222* 🌐 *www.thebreakers.com/dining/echo* 🕒 *No lunch.*

PB Catch

$$$$ | SEAFOOD | As the name implies, it's all about fins and shells here, including the live ones that entertain diners in their tanks in the modern dining room. The menu includes a raw bar with a good selection of raw (or grilled) oysters, clams, and the chef's "seacuterie" platter, a build-your-own sampler of such choices as salmon pastrami, citrus-cured fluke, cured sea bass, or octopus torchon. **Known for:** in-house cured fish; shellfish tower from the raw bar; craft cocktails. [$] *Average main: $35* ✉ *251 Sunrise Blvd.* ☎ *561/655–5558* 🌐 *www.pbcatch.com.*

Pizza Al Fresco

$$ | PIZZA | The hidden-garden setting is the secret to the success of this European-style pizzeria, where you can dine under a canopy of century-old banyans in an intimate courtyard. Specialties are 12-inch hand-tossed brick-oven pizzas with such interesting toppings as prosciutto, arugula, and caviar. **Known for:** caviar-and-smoked-salmon pizza; fresh salads; garden setting. [$] *Average main: $19* ✉ *14 Via Mizner, at Worth Ave.* ✥ *Tucked in a courtyard off Worth Ave.* ☎ *561/832–0032* 🌐 *www.pizzaalfresco.com.*

Renato's

$$$$ | ITALIAN | Here, at one of the most romantic restaurants in Palm Beach, guests can dine Italiano. Sit in the beautiful courtyard, with stars above and twinkling lights on the bougainvillea, or in the intimate, low-lighted dining room flickering with candles and enhanced with fresh flowers and quiet classical music. **Known for:** fresh pasta dishes; homemade soups; romantic setting. [$] *Average main: $37* ✉ *87 Via Mizner* ☎ *561/655–9752* 🌐 *www.renatospalmbeach.com* 🕒 *No lunch Sun.*

Hotels

★ The Brazilian Court Hotel

$$$$ | HOTEL | This posh boutique hotel, stomping ground of Florida's well-heeled, is full of historic touches and creature comforts—from its yellow facade with dramatic white-draped entry to modern draws like the renowned spa and Daniel Boulud restaurant. **Pros:** stylish and hip local crowd; charming courtyard; free beach shuttle. **Cons:** small fitness center; nondescript pool; 10-minute ride to ocean and suggested 24-hour advance reservation for shuttle. [$] *Rooms from: $609* ✉ *301 Australian Ave.* ☎ *561/655–7740* 🌐 *www.thebraziliancourt.com* 🛏 *80 rooms* 🍴 *No meals.*

★ The Breakers Palm Beach

$$$$ | RESORT | FAMILY | More than an opulent hotel, The Breakers is a legendary 140-acre self-contained jewel of a resort built in a Mediterranean style and loaded with amenities, from a 20,000-square-foot luxury spa and grandiose beach club with four pools and a half-mile private beach to 10 tennis courts, croquet courts, and two 18-hole golf courses. **Pros:** impeccable attention to detail; beautiful room views; extensive activities for families. **Cons:** big price tag; short drive to reach off-property attractions. $ *Rooms from: $699* ⊠ *1 S. County Rd.* ☎ *561/655–6611, 888/273–2537* ⊕ *www.thebreakers.com* ⇘ *538 rooms* ○ *No meals.*

The Chesterfield Palm Beach

$$$$ | HOTEL | A distinctly upper-crust northern European feel pervades the peach stucco walls and elegant rooms here; the hotel sits just north of the western end of Worth Avenue, and high tea, a cigar parlor, and daily turndown service recall a bygone, more refined era. **Pros:** gracious, attentive staff; Leopard Lounge entertainment; free valet parking. **Cons:** long walk to beach; only one elevator; to some, can come off as a bit stuffy. $ *Rooms from: $495* ⊠ *363 Cocoanut Row* ☎ *561/659–5800, 800/243–7871* ⊕ *www.chesterfieldpb.com* ⇘ *52 rooms* ○ *No meals.*

The Colony

$$$$ | HOTEL | This exuberant and undeniably charming hotel underwent a five-year, $18 million top-to-bottom renovation in 2015 that gave the British-colonial-style a much-needed face-lift. **Pros:** unbeatable location; gorgeous decor; pillow-top mattresses. **Cons:** lobby is small; elevators are tight. $ *Rooms from: $600* ⊠ *155 Hammon Ave.* ☎ *561/655–5430, 800/521–5525* ⊕ *www.thecolonypalmbeach.com* ⇘ *90 rooms* ○ *No meals.*

★ Eau Palm Beach

$$$$ | RESORT | FAMILY | In the coastal town of Manalapan (just south of Palm Beach), this sublime, glamorous destination resort (formerly the Ritz-Carlton) showcases a newer, younger face of luxury, including a 3,000-square-foot oceanfront terrace, two sleek pools, a huge fitness center, and a deluxe spa. **Pros:** magnificent aesthetic details throughout; indulgent pampering services; excellent on-site dining; kids love the cool cyberlounge just for them. **Cons:** golf course is off property; 15-minute drive to Palm Beach. $ *Rooms from: $560* ⊠ *100 S. Ocean Blvd., Manalapan* ☎ *561/533–6000, 800/241–3333* ⊕ *www.eaupalmbeach.com* ⇘ *309 rooms* ○ *No meals.*

★ Four Seasons Resort Palm Beach

$$$$ | RESORT | FAMILY | Couples and families seeking relaxed seaside elegance in a luxe yet understated setting will love this manicured 6-acre oceanfront escape at the south end of Palm Beach, with serene, bright, airy rooms in a cream-colored palette and spacious marble-lined baths. **Pros:** Cabana Terrace Rooms have direct access to pool deck; all rooms have balconies; Michelin-starred chef heads Florie's restaurant; outstanding complimentary kids' program. **Cons:** 10-minute drive to downtown Palm Beach (but can walk to Lake Worth); pricey. $ *Rooms from: $739* ⊠ *2800 S. Ocean Blvd.* ☎ *561/582–2800, 800/432–2335* ⊕ *www.fourseasons.com/palmbeach* ⇘ *210 rooms* ○ *No meals.*

The Tideline Resort & Spa

$$$ | RESORT | This Zenlike boutique hotel has a loyal following of young, hip travelers, who appreciate the updated rooms and the full-service spa. **Pros:** most rooms have beautiful views of the private beach; ultracontemporary vibe; luxury setting. **Cons:** a hike from shopping and nightlife; the infinity pool is across the driveway. $ *Rooms from: $340* ⊠ *2842 S. Ocean Blvd.* ☎ *561/540–6440, 888/344–4321* ⊕ *www.tidelineresort.com* ⇘ *134 rooms* ○ *No meals.*

ⓨ Nightlife

Palm Beach is teeming with restaurants that turn into late-night hot spots, plus hotel lobby bars perfect for tête-à-têtes.

★ bûccan

BARS/PUBS | At this hip Hamptons-esque scene, society darlings crowd the lounge, throwing back killer cocktails like the French Pearl (gin, Pernod, lemon juice, mint) and Buccan T (vodka, black tea, cranberry, citrus, basil, and agave nectar). ⊠ 350 S. County Rd. ☎ 561/833–3450 ⊕ www.buccanpalmbeach.com.

Café Boulud

BARS/PUBS | A sleek, redesigned dining room bar with bar bites from a special menu plus an extended happy hour draws locals and visitors alike. ■TIP➔ Dress to impress. ⊠ 301 Australian Ave. ☎ 561/655–6060 ⊕ www.cafeboulud.com/palmbeach.

Cucina Palm Beach

BARS/PUBS | Though this spot is popular for lunch and dinner, it's even more popular later in the night. The younger, trendier set comes late to party, mingle, and dance into the wee hours. ⊠ 257 Royal Poinciana Way ☎ 561/655–0770 ⊕ www.cucinapalmbeach.com.

The Leopard Lounge

PIANO BARS/LOUNGES | In the Chesterfield hotel, this enclave feels like an exclusive club. The trademark ceiling and spotted floors of the renovated lounge are a nod to this hotel's historic roots, but the rest of the decor is new-age Palm Beach glam. Though it starts each evening as a restaurant, as the night progresses the Leopard is transformed into an old-fashioned club with live music for Palm Beach's old guard. The bartenders know how to pour a cocktail here. ⊠ The Chesterfield Palm Beach, 363 Cocoanut Row ☎ 561/659–5800 ⊕ www.chesterfieldpb.com.

🛍 Shopping

As is the case throughout South Florida, many of the smaller boutiques in Palm Beach close in the summer, and most stores are closed on Sunday. Consignment stores in Palm Beach are definitely worth a look; you'll often find high-end designer clothing in impeccable condition.

Betteridge Jewelers

JEWELRY/ACCESSORIES | Jewelry is very important in Palm Beach, and for more than 119 years the diverse selection here has included investment pieces. Window-shopping is allowed. ⊠ 236 Worth Ave. ☎ 561/655–5850 ⊕ www.betteridge.com.

The Church Mouse

OUTLET/DISCOUNT STORES | Many high-end resale boutique owners grab their merchandise at this thrift store run by the Episcopal Church of Bethesda-by-the-Sea, in business since 1970. The mouse accepts cheese from October to June, Monday–Saturday, 10–4. The store's end-of-season sale draws crowds that line the block. You can feel good about your purchases here: proceeds go to regional nonprofits. ⊠ 378 S. County Rd. ☎ 561/659–2154 ⊕ www.bbts.org/about-us/church-mouse/ ⊘ closed Sun.

★ Worth Avenue

SHOPPING NEIGHBORHOODS | One of the world's premier showcases for high-quality shopping runs half a mile from east to west across Palm Beach, from the beach to Lake Worth. The street has more than 200 shops (more than 40 of them sell jewelry), and many upscale chain stores (Gucci, Hermès, Saks Fifth Avenue, Neiman Marcus, Louis Vuitton, Chanel, Cartier, Tiffany & Co., and Tourneau) are represented—their merchandise appealing to the discerning tastes of the Palm Beach clientele. Don't miss walking around the vias, little courtyards lined with smaller boutiques; historic tours are available each month during "the season" from the Worth Avenue Association. ■ TIP➔ **For those looking to go a little lighter on the pocketbook, just north of Worth Avenue, the six blocks of South County Road have interesting and somewhat less expensive stores.** ⊠ *Worth Ave.* ✛ *Between Cocoanut Row and S. Ocean Blvd.* ⊕ *www.worth-avenue.com.*

🏃 Activities

Palm Beach Island has two good golf courses—The Breakers and the Palm Beach Par 3 Golf Course, but only the latter is open to the public. Not to worry, there are more on the mainland, as well as myriad other outdoor sports opportunities, including a new spring-training baseball stadium where two teams will play.

The Breakers Golf Courses

GOLF | The Breakers' historic par-70 Ocean Course, the oldest 18 holes in all of Florida, as well as its contemporary Breakers Rees Jones Course, are open exclusively to members and hotel guests. The Ocean Course, redesigned to bring back its "vintage" feel, is located on-site, on the grounds of the sprawling Breakers Palm Beach. The resort's sister course, designed by Rees Jones, is 10 miles west in West Palm Beach and replaces the former Breakers West course. A $210 greens fee for each includes range balls, cart, and bag storage; the John Webster Golf Academy at The Breakers offers private and group lessons. Discounts are given at the Ocean Course for afternoon starts, and for adults accompanied by kids, who play for free. ⊠ *The Breakers Palm Beach, 1 S. County Rd.* ☎ *561/655–6611* ⊕ *www.thebreakers.com/golf* 🏌 *$210 for 18 holes, cart included* 🏌 *Ocean Course: 18 holes, 6177 yards, par 72; Breakers Rees Jones Course: 18 holes, 7100 yards, par 72.*

Island Living Tours

Book a private mansion-viewing excursion around Palm Beach, and hear the storied past of the island's upper crust. Owner Leslie Diver also hosts an Antique Row Tour and a Worth Avenue Shopping Tour. Vehicle tours are 90 minutes for the Best of Palm Beach and 2½ hours for a more extensive architecture and history tour. Costs are from $60 to $150 per person, depending on the vehicle used. Leslie also runs 90-minute bicycle tours through Palm Beach ($45, not including bike rental). One bicycle tour explores the Estate Section and historic Worth Avenue; another explores the island's lesser known North End. Call in advance for location and to reserve. ☎ *561/309–5790* ⊕ *www.islandlivingpb.com.*

Lake Trail

BICYCLING | FAMILY | This palm-fringed trail, about 4 miles long, skirts the backyards of mansions and the edge of Lake Worth. The start ("south trail" section) is just up from Royal Palm Way behind the Society of the Four Arts; follow the signs and you can't miss it. As you head north, the trail gets a little choppy around the Flagler Museum, so most people just enter where the "north trail" section begins at the very west end of Sunset Avenue. The path stops just short of the tip of the island, but people follow the quiet residential streets until they hit North Ocean Boulevard and the dock there with lovely views of Peanut Island and Singer Island, and then follow North Ocean Boulevard the 4 miles back for a change of scenery. ⊠ *Parallel to Lake Way* ✛ *Behind Society of the Four Arts.*

★ Palm Beach Bicycle Trail Shop

BICYCLING | Open daily year-round, the shop rents bikes by the hour or day, and it's about a block from the north Lake Trail entrance. The shop has maps to help you navigate your way around the island, or you can download the main map from the shop's website. They are experts on the nearby, palm-fringed, 4-mile Lake Trail. ⊠ *50 Cocoanut Row, Suite 117* ☎ *561/659–4583* ⊕ *www.palmbeachbicycle.com.*

★ **Palm Beach Par 3 Golf Course**

GOLF | This course has been named the best par-3 golf course in the United States by *Golf Digest* magazine. The 18-hole course—originally designed by Dick Wilson and Joe Lee in 1961—was redesigned in 2009 by Hall of Famer Raymond Floyd. The par-3 course includes six holes directly on the Atlantic Ocean, with some holes over 200 yards. The grounds are exquisitely landscaped, as one would expect in Palm Beach. A lavish clubhouse houses Al Fresco, an Italian restaurant. A cart is an extra $15, but walking is encouraged. Summer rates are greatly discounted. ⊠ *2345 S. Ocean Blvd.* ☎ *561/547–0598* ⊕ *www. golfontheocean.com* ⊠ *$50 for 18 holes* ⅄ *18 holes, 2458 yards, par 58.*

West Palm Beach

Long considered Palm Beach's less privileged stepsister, West Palm Beach has come into its own. Its $30 million Centennial Square waterfront complex at the eastern end of Clematis Street, with piers, a pavilion, and an amphitheater, has transformed West Palm into an attractive, easy-to-walk downtown area—not to mention there's the Downtown Trolley that connects the shopping-and-entertainment mecca CityPlace with restaurant-and-lounge-lined Clematis Street. The Palm Beach Outlet Mall gives options to those looking for tony bargains. West Palm is especially well regarded for its arts scene, with unique museums and performance venues; a number of public art projects have appeared around the city.

The city's outskirts, vast flat stretches with strip malls and car dealerships, may not inspire but are worth driving through to reach attractions scattered around the southern and western reaches. Several sites are especially rewarding for children and other animal and nature lovers.

 Sights

Ann Norton Sculpture Gardens

GARDEN | This landmarked complex is a testament to the creative genius of the late American sculptor Ann Weaver Norton (1905–82), who was the second wife of Norton Museum founder, industrialist Ralph H. Norton. A set of art galleries in the studio and main house where she lived is surrounded by 2 acres of gardens with 300 species of rare palm trees, eight brick megaliths, a monumental figure in Norwegian granite, and plantings designed to attract native birds. ⊠ *253 Barcelona Rd., West Palm Beach* ☎ *561/832–5328* ⊕ *www.ansg.org* ⊠ *$10* ⊘ *Closed Mon.–Tues.*

Armory Art Center

COLLEGE | Built by the Works Progress Administration (WPA) in 1939, this art deco facility is now a nonprofit art school hosting rotating exhibitions and art classes throughout the year. The Armory Art Center became an institution for art instruction when the Norton Museum Gallery and School of Art dropped the latter part of its name in 1986 and discontinued art-instruction classes. ⊠ *1700 Parker Ave., West Palm Beach* ☎ *561/832–1776* ⊕ *www.armoryart.org* ⊠ *Free.*

Currie Park

NATIONAL/STATE PARK | FAMILY | Frequent weekend festivals, including an annual celebration of seafood, take place at this scenic city park next to the Intracoastal Waterway. Sit on one of the piers and watch the yachts and fishing boats pass by. Put on your jogging shoes—the park is at the north end of a 6.3-mile waterfront biking-jogging-skating path. Tennis courts, a boat ramp, and a playground are here, along with the Maritime Museum. DivaDuck tours launch from this park. ⊠ *N. Flagler Dr. at 23rd St., West Palm Beach* ☎ *561/804–4900* ⊕ *wpbparks. com/west-palm-beach-parks/currie-park.*

The Armory Art Center in West Palm Beach helps students of all ages create works of art in various mediums.

Lion Country Safari

AMUSEMENT PARK/WATER PARK | FAMILY | Drive your own vehicle along 4 miles of paved roads through a cageless zoo with free-roaming animals (chances are you'll have an ostrich nudging at your window) and then let loose in a 55-acre fun-land with bird feedings, games, and rides. A CD included with admission narrates the winding trek past white rhinos, zebras, and ostriches grouped into exhibits like Gir Forest that's modeled after a sanctuary in India and has native twisted-horned blackbuck antelope and water buffalo. (For obvious reasons, lions are fenced off, and no convertibles or pets are allowed.) Aside from dozens more up-close critter encounters after debarking, including a petting zoo, kids can go paddleboating, do a round of mini-golf, climb aboard carnival rides, or have a splash in a 4,000-square-foot aquatic playground (some extra fees apply). ⊠ *2003 Lion Country Safari Rd., at Southern Blvd. W, West Palm Beach* ☎ *561/793–1084* ⊕ *www.lioncountrysafari.com* ☜ *$35, $8 parking.*

★ Manatee Lagoon

LOCAL INTEREST | FAMILY | Once a casual spot next to the local electric plant's discharge waters, this center celebrating the manatee—South Florida's popular winter visitors—opened in 2016 at a spot where the peaceful creatures naturally congregate. The airy, two-story facility is surrounded by wraparound decks to accommodate sea-cow spotters from fall to spring. Educational, interactive displays tell the story of this once-endangered species. A long deck along the seawall leads to picnic pavilions from where you can watch the action at nearby Peanut Island and the Port of Palm Beach. Free admission makes it group-friendly; a live "manatee cam" shows manatee counts before you go. The center offers weekend art classes for children but requires advance registration; check their calendar for details. ⊠ *6000 N. Flagler Dr., West Palm Beach* ✛ *Entrance is on Flagler Dr., via 58th St. east of U.S. 1 and south of the Port of Palm Beach flyover* ☎ *561/626–2833*

⊕ www.visitmanateelagoon.com ✉ Free
⊘ Closed Mon.

Mounts Botanical Garden

GARDEN | The oldest public green space
in the county is, unbelievably, across the
road from the West Palm Beach airport;
but the planes are the last thing you
notice while walking around and relaxing
amid the nearly 14 acres of exotic trees,
rain-forest flora, and butterfly and water
gardens. The gift shop contains a selection of rare gardening books on tropical
climes. Frequent plant sales are held
here, and numerous plant societies with
international ties hold meetings open
to the public in the auditorium. Experts
in tropical edible and ornamental plants
are on staff. ✉ 531 N. Military Trail, West
Palm Beach ☎ 561/233–1757 ⊕ www.
mounts.org ✉ $5 (suggested donation).

National Croquet Center

SPORTS VENUE | The world's largest cro-
quet complex, the 10-acre center is also
the headquarters for the U.S. Croquet
Association. Vast expanses of orderly
lawns are the stage for fierce compe-
titions. There's also a clubhouse with a
pro shop and the Croquet Grille, with
verandas for dining and viewing (armchair
enthusiasts can enjoy the games for no
charge). You don't have to be a member
to try your hand out on the lawns, and
on Saturday morning at 10 am, there's a
free group lesson with an introduction to
the game, and open play; call in advance
to reserve a spot. ✉ 700 Florida Mango
Rd., at Summit Blvd., West Palm Beach
☎ 561/478–2300 ⊕ www.croquetnation-
al.com ✉ Center free; full day of croquet
$30.

★ Norton Museum of Art

MUSEUM | Fresh off an expansion, the
museum (constructed in 1941 by steel
magnate Ralph H. Norton and his wife,
Elizabeth) has grown to become one of
the most impressive in South Florida
with an extensive collection of 19th- and
20th-century American and European
paintings—including works by Picasso,
Monet, Matisse, Pollock, Cassatt, and
O'Keeffe—plus Chinese art, earlier European art, and photography. To accommodate a growing collection, the museum
is undergoing an extensive expansion
to include 12,000 additional square feet
of gallery space in a new west wing,
event spaces, and a great hall. A garden
will also be incorporated into the space.
■TIP→ **The popular Art After Dark, Thursday from 5 to 9 pm, is a gathering spot for
art lovers, with wine and music in the galleries.** ✉ 1451 S. Olive Ave., West Palm
Beach ☎ 561/832–5196 ⊕ www.norton.
org ✉ Free ⊘ Closed Mon.

Richard and Pat Johnson Palm Beach Coun-
ty History Museum

MUSEUM | A beautifully restored 1916
courthouse in downtown opened its
doors in 2008 as the permanent home
of the Historical Society of Palm Beach
County's collection of artifacts and
records dating back before the town's
start—a highlight is furniture and decorative objects from Mizner Industries (a
real treat since many of his mansions are
not open to the public). ✉ 300 N. Dixie
Hwy., West Palm Beach ☎ 561/832–4164
⊕ www.historicalsocietypbc.org ✉ Free
⊘ Closed Sun.

South Florida Science Center and Aquarium

MUSEUM | FAMILY | Both fresh- and
saltwater aquariums greet the curious at this interactive, family-friendly
science museum. Permanent exhibits
of Moon and Mars rocks and meteor-
ites, a giant sphere with global anima-
tion projection for Earth sciences, and
Everglades conservation exhibit teach
while entertaining. A planetarium with
daily themed shows and a conservation
9-hole mini-golf course designed by Gary
Fazio and Jim Niklaus are popular with
all ages and carry separate admission
charges. ✉ 4801 Dreher Trail N, West
Palm Beach ☎ 561/832–1988 ⊕ www.
sfsciencecenter.org ✉ $16.95; planetari-
um $5; mini-golf $7.

🍴 Restaurants

Avocado Grill
$$ | **ECLECTIC** | In downtown West Palm Beach's waterfront district, this hot spot is an alternative to the bar food, tacos, and burgers more common in the area. "Green" cuisine—seasonal salads, vegetarian dishes, and sustainably produced meats and seafood—is making waves at the avocado-themed restaurant. **Known for:** everything avocado, including wonderful guacamole; mushroom fricassee with cheddar grits; mixed seafood ceviche. [$] *Average main: $19* ✉ *125 Datura St., West Palm Beach* ☎ *561/623–0822* 🌐 *www.avocadogrillwpb.com.*

Belle and Maxwell's
$$ | **AMERICAN** | Palm Beach ladies who lunch leave the island for an afternoon at Belle and Maxwell's, while young professionals loosen up after work at the wine bar, part of the bistro's expanded dining area. Tucked along Antique Row, it looks like a storybook tea party at lunch, with eclectic furnishings and decor, and charming garden. **Known for:** classic chicken marsala; extensive list of lunch salads; homemade desserts. [$] *Average main: $18* ✉ *3700 S. Dixie Hwy., West Palm Beach* ☎ *561/832–4449* 🌐 *www.belleandmaxwells.com* ⏲ *Closed Sun. No dinner Mon.*

Grandview Public Market
$ | **ECLECTIC** | **FAMILY** | This laid-back food hall and community-centric market complete with colorful murals has been a crowd pleaser since it opened in the summer of 2017. There's plenty to taste, with 12 vendors selling everything from tacos to fried chicken to rolled ice cream. **Known for:** coffee; live music; tacos. [$] *Average main: $12* ✉ *1401 Clare Ave., West Palm Beach* ☎ *n/a* 🌐 *www.grandviewpublic.com.*

★ **Grato**
$$$ | **TUSCAN** | **FAMILY** | A sprawling cavern of wood-fired pizzas, pastas, and cocktails, this sibling to popular bûccan quickly became a hit when it opened on the mainland. Soaring ceilings, concrete floors, dark wood, and an open kitchen provide a buzzy backdrop to dishes of nicely charred pies (made with organic flour) and homemade pastas. **Known for:** wood-fired pizzas; fresh pastas; busy bar scene. [$] *Average main: $24* ✉ *1901 Dixie Hwy., West Palm Beach* ☎ *561/404–1334* 🌐 *www.gratowpb.com.*

Havana
$$ | **CUBAN** | **FAMILY** | Decorated with vintage travel posters of its namesake city, this two-level restaurant serves authentic Cuban specialties on the cheap, including great Cubano (pressed roast pork) sandwiches, arroz con pollo, and *ropa vieja.* The friendly place attracts a late-night crowd at its popular walk-up window. Get strong Cuban coffee (often awarded the best in Palm Beach County), sugary fried churros, and fruit juices in exotic flavors like mamey, mango, papaya, guava, and guanabana. **Known for:** late-night food service; Cuban sandwiches; picadillo Cubano. [$] *Average main: $15* ✉ *6801 S. Dixie Hwy., West Palm Beach* ☎ *561/547–9799* 🌐 *www.havanacubanfood.com.*

Howley's
$ | **AMERICAN** | Since 1950, this diner's eat-in counter and "cooked in sight, it must be right" motto have made it a congenial setting for meeting old friends and making new ones. Nowadays, Howley's prides itself on its kitsch factor and old-school eats like turkey potpie and a traditional Thanksgiving feast, as well as its retro-redux dishes like potato-and-brisket burrito. **Known for:** kitschy setting; retro diner specialties; late-night dining. [$] *Average main: $13* ✉ *4700 S. Dixie Hwy., West Palm Beach* ☎ *561/833–5691* 🌐 *www.sub-culture.org/howleys/.*

Marcello's La Sirena
$$$$ | **ITALIAN** | A longtime favorite of locals, this sophisticated Italian restaurant is in an unexpected, nondescript location on Dixie Highway away from

downtown and central hubs. But warm hospitality from a husband-and-wife team, along with smart service and delectable traditional dishes, await. **Known for:** fresh pasta dishes; award-winning wine list; great desserts. $ *Average main: $31* ⊠ *6316 S. Dixie Hwy., West Palm Beach* ☎ *561/585–3128* ⊕ *www.lasirenaonline.com* ◷ *Closed Sun.*

★ Mediterranean Market & Deli

$ | **MIDDLE EASTERN** | This hole-in-the-wall Middle Eastern bakery, deli, and market is packed at lunchtime with regulars who are on a first-name basis with the gang behind the counter. From the nondescript parking lot the place doesn't look like much, but inside, delicious hot and cold Mediterranean treats await the takeout crowd. **Known for:** lamb salad; gyros; freshly baked pita bread. $ *Average main: $10* ⊠ *327 5th St., West Palm Beach* ☎ *561/659–7322* ⊕ *www.mediterraneanmarketanddeli.com* ◷ *Closed Sun.*

Pistache French Bistro

$$$ | **FRENCH** | Although "the island" is no doubt a bastion of French cuisine, this cozy bistro across the bridge on the Clematis Street waterfront entices a lively crowd looking for an unpretentious good meal. The outdoor terrace can't be beat, and the fabulous modern French menu with twists such as roasted sliced duck with truffled polenta is a delight. **Known for:** fresh seafood; cheese and charcuterie; great desserts. $ *Average main: $27* ⊠ *101 N. Clematis St., West Palm Beach* ☎ *561/833–5090* ⊕ *www.pistachewpb.com.*

★ The Regional Kitchen & Public House

$$$ | **SOUTHERN** | *Top Chef* finalist and James Beard Award nominee Lindsay Autry debuted her own Southern-inspired American cuisine in CityPlace to the acclaim of local critics. The menu of updated comfort food includes fried green tomatoes, creamy tomato pie, pimento cheese done table-side, and shrimp and grits. **Known for:** reinvented Southern classics; table-side pimento cheese; weekend brunch. $ *Average main: $24* ⊠ *CityPlace, 651 Okeechobee Blvd., West Palm Beach* ⊕ *Directly across from the Convention Center* ☎ *561/557–6460* ⊕ *www.eatregional.com.*

★ RH Rooftop Restaurant

$$ | **AMERICAN** | **FAMILY** | Atop the glossy Restoration Hardware store adjacent to CityPlace is this regal, glass-enclosed atrium outfitted with white couches, crystal chandeliers, lush greenery, and a tinkling fountain. It's proven a hit with the old guard and the stroller-pushers alike; everyone basks in the sun-filled room and tucks into seasonal comfort food (prime rib french dip, truffled grilled cheese) and lingers on exceptionally comfortable couches. **Known for:** lobster roll; beautiful atrium; brunch. $ *Average main: $17* ⊠ *560 Okeechobee Blvd., West Palm Beach* ☎ *561/804–6826* ⊕ *www.restorationhardware.com/content/category.jsp?context=WestPalm.*

Rhythm Cafe

$$$ | **MODERN AMERICAN** | West Palm Beach's Rhythm Cafe is anything but Palm Beach formal (the decor includes a feathered pink flamingo perched on the terrazzo floor). Fun, funky, cheesy, campy, and cool all at once, the former 1950s-era drugstore-cum-restaurant on West Palm Beach's Antique Row features an ever-changing creative menu of homemade items with Italian, Greek, American, and Creole influences. **Known for:** "tapas-tizer" small plates; fresh fish; graham-cracker-crusted key lime chicken. $ *Average main: $24* ⊠ *3800 S. Dixie Hwy., West Palm Beach* ☎ *561/833–3406* ⊕ *www.rhythmcafe.com* ◷ *No lunch.*

🛏 Hotels

Casa Grandview West Palm Beach

$$ | **B&B/INN** | In West Palm's charming Grandview Heights historic district—and just minutes away from both downtown and the beach—this warm and personalized B&B offers a wonderful respite from

South Florida's big-hotel norm. **Pros:** daily dry cleaning of all linens; complimentary soft drinks, coffee, and snacks (and lots of them) in lobby; simple keyless entry (number code lock system). **Cons:** cottages and suites have seven-day minimum; free breakfast in B&B rooms only; art deco suites don't have air-conditioning. $ *Rooms from: $289* ⊠ *1410 Georgia Ave., West Palm Beach* ☎ *561/655–8932* ⊕ *www.casagrandview.com* ⤴ *17 rooms* ⦿ *Breakfast.*

Grandview Gardens Bed & Breakfast

$$ | **B&B/INN** | Defining the Florida B&B experience, this 1925 Mediterranean-revival home overlooks a serene courtyard pool and oozes loads of charm and personality, while the fabulous owners provide heavy doses of bespoke service. **Pros:** multilingual owners; outside private entrances to rooms; free bicycle use; innkeepers offer historic city tours. **Cons:** not close to the beach; in a residential area; rental car needed. $ *Rooms from: $225* ⊠ *1608 Lake Ave., West Palm Beach* ☎ *561/833–9023* ⊕ *www. grandview-gardens.com* ⤴ *5 rooms, 2 cottages* ⦿ *Breakfast.*

Hampton Inn & Suites Wellington

$$ | **HOTEL** | **FAMILY** | The only hotel near the polo fields in the equestrian mecca of Wellington—10 miles west of downtown Palm Beach—feels a bit like a tony clubhouse, with rich wood paneling, hunt prints, and elegant chandeliers; but inside the rooms are standard Hampton Inn fare. **Pros:** complimentary hot breakfast; free Wi-Fi; outdoor swimming pool; close to a large shopping center; near the county fairgrounds. **Cons:** no restaurant; Intracoastal Waterway is a 30-minute drive, and beach is farther. $ *Rooms from: $250* ⊠ *2155 Wellington Green Dr., West Palm Beach* ☎ *561/472–9696* ⊕ *hamptoninn3.hilton.com* ⤴ *122 rooms, 32 suites* ⦿ *Breakfast.*

Hilton West Palm Beach

$$ | **HOTEL** | **FAMILY** | In downtown, the contemporary business hotel situated next door to the county convention center has a pool with cabanas many resorts would envy. **Pros:** walking distance to convention center, CityPlace, Kravis Center; resort-style pool; amenities geared toward business travelers. **Cons:** long ride to the beach; noise from downtown construction and trains. $ *Rooms from: $279* ⊠ *600 Okeechobee Blvd., West Palm Beach* ✛ *Adjacent to the Palm Beach County Convention Center* ☎ *561/231– 6000* ⊕ *www3.hilton.com* ⤴ *400 rooms* ⦿ *No meals.*

Hotel Biba

$ | **HOTEL** | In the El Cid historic district, this 1940s-era motel has gotten a fun, stylish revamp from designer Barbara Hulanicki: each room has a vibrant mélange of colors, along with handcrafted mirrors, mosaic bathroom floors, and custom mahogany furnishings. **Pros:** cool, punchy design and luxe fixtures; popular wine bar; free continental breakfast with Cuban pastries. **Cons:** water pressure is weak; bathrooms are tiny; noisy when the bar is open late and trains run nearby; not all rooms have central air-conditioning. $ *Rooms from: $160* ⊠ *320 Belvedere Rd., West Palm Beach* ☎ *561/832–0094* ⊕ *www.hotelbiba.com* ⤴ *43 rooms* ⦿ *Breakfast.*

Nightlife

West Palm is known for its exuberant nightlife—Clematis Street and CityPlace are the prime party destinations. Downtown rocks every Thursday from 6 pm on with Clematis by Night (⊕ *www.wpb. org/clematis-by-night*), a celebration of music, dance, art, and food at Centennial Square.

Blue Martini

BARS/PUBS | The CityPlace outpost of this South Florida hot spot for thirty-, forty-, and fiftysomething adults gone wild has a menu filled with tons of innovative martini creations (42 to be exact), tasty tapas, and lots of cougars on the prowl, searching for a first, second, or even third husband. And the guys aren't complaining! The drinks are great and the scene is fun for everyone, even those who aren't single and looking to mingle. Expect DJs some nights, live music others. ✉ *City-Place, 550 S. Rosemary Ave., #244, West Palm Beach* ☎ *561/835–8601* ⊕ *www.bluemartinilounge.com.*

ER Bradley's Saloon

BARS/PUBS | People of all ages congregate to hang out and socialize at this kitschy open-air restaurant and bar to gaze at the Intracoastal Waterway; the mechanical bull is a hit on Saturdays. Live music's on tap five to seven nights a week. ✉ *104 Clematis St., West Palm Beach* ☎ *561/833–3520* ⊕ *www.erbradleys.com.*

★ Rocco's Tacos and Tequila Bar

BARS/PUBS | In the last few years, Rocco's has taken root in numerous South Florida downtowns and become synonymous with wild nights of chips 'n' guac, margaritas, and intoxicating fun. This is more of a scene than just a restaurant, and when Rocco's in the house and pouring shots, get ready to party hearty. With pitchers of margaritas continuously flowing, the middle-aged crowd is boisterous and fun, recounting (and reliving) the days of spring break debauchery from their pre-professional years. Get your party started here with more than 220 choices of tequila. There's another branch at 5250 Town Center Circle in Boca Raton; at 110 Atlantic Avenue in Delray Beach; and in Palm Beach Gardens in PGA Commons at 5090 PGA Boulevard. ✉ *224 Clematis St., West Palm Beach* ☎ *561/650–1001* ⊕ *www.roccostacos.com.*

🎭 Performing Arts

Palm Beach Dramaworks (*pbd*)

THEATER | Housed in an intimate venue with only 218 seats in downtown West Palm Beach, the modus operandi is "theater to think about," with plays by Pulitzer Prize winners on rotation. ✉ *201 Clematis St., West Palm Beach* ☎ *561/514–4042* ⊕ *www.palmbeachdramaworks.org.*

Palm Beach Opera

OPERA | Still going strong after nearly 60 years, three main-stage productions are offered during the season from January through April at the Kravis Center with English-language supertitles. There's an annual Children's Performance where all tickets are $5, plus a free outdoor concert at the Meyer Amphitheatre in downtown West Palm Beach. Tickets start at $25. ✉ *1800 S. Australian Ave., Suite 301, administrative office, West Palm Beach* ☎ *561/833–7888* ⊕ *www.pbopera.org.*

★ Raymond F. Kravis Center for the Performing Arts

ARTS CENTERS | This is the crown jewel amid a treasury of local arts attractions, and its marquee star is the 2,195-seat Dreyfoos Hall, a glass, copper, and marble showcase just steps from the restaurants and shops of CityPlace. The center also boasts the 289-seat Rinker Playhouse, 170-seat Persson Hall, and the Gosman Amphitheatre, which holds 1,400 total in seats and on the lawn. A packed year-round schedule features a blockbuster lineup of Broadway's biggest touring productions, concerts, dance, dramas, and musicals; the Miami City Ballet, Palm Beach Opera, and the Palm Beach Pops perform here. ✉ *701 Okeechobee Blvd., West Palm Beach* ☎ *561/832–7469* box office ⊕ *www.kravis.org.*

🛍 Shopping

★ Antique Row

SHOPPING NEIGHBORHOODS | West Palm's U.S. 1, "South Dixie Highway," is the destination for those who are interested in interesting home decor. From thrift shops to the most exclusive stores, it is all here within 40 stores—museum-quality furniture, lighting, art, junk, fabric, frames, tile, and rugs. So if you're looking for an art deco, French-provincial, or Mizner pièce de résistance, big or small, schedule a few hours for an Antique Row stroll. You'll find bargains during the off-season (May to November). Antique Row runs north–south from Belvedere Road to Forest Hill Boulevard, although most stores are bunched between Belvedere Road and Southern Boulevard. ⊠ *U.S. 1, between Belvedere Rd. and Forest Hill Blvd., West Palm Beach* ⊕ *www.westpalmbeachantiques.com.*

CityPlace

SHOPPING NEIGHBORHOODS | FAMILY | The 72-acre, four-block-by-four-block commercial and residential complex centered on Rosemary Avenue attracts people of all ages to restaurants like Italian-inspired Il Bellagio, bars like Blue Martini, a 20-screen AMC theater, the bowling alley and sports bar Revolutions, the Harriet Himmel Theater, and the Improv Comedy Club. In the courtyard, a 36,000-gallon water fountain and light show entertains, along with live bands on weekends. The dining, shopping, and entertainment are all family-friendly; at night, however, a lively crowd likes to hit the outdoor bars. Among CityPlace's stores are such popular national retailers as H&M, Tommy Bahama, and Restoration Hardware. Anushka Spa and Salon draws locals and visitors. ⊠ *700 S. Rosemary Ave., West Palm Beach* ☎ *561/366–1000* ⊕ *www. cityplace.com.*

Clematis Street

SHOPPING NEIGHBORHOODS | FAMILY | If lunching is just as important as window-shopping, the renewed downtown West Palm around Clematis Street that runs west to east from South Rosemary Avenue to Flagler Drive is the spot for you. Centennial Park by the waterfront has an attractive design—and fountains where kids can cool off—which adds to the pleasure of browsing and resting at one of the many outdoor cafés. Hip national retailers such as Design Within Reach mix with local boutiques like

third-generation Pioneer Linens, and both blend in with restaurants and bars. ⊠ *Clematis St., West Palm Beach* ✛ *Between S. Rosemary Ave. and Flagler Dr.* ⊕ *www.westpalmbeach.com/clematis.*

Palm Beach Outlets

OUTLET/DISCOUNT STORES | An outlet mall worthy of Palm Beach finally opened in 2014 in West Palm Beach. It features more than 130 retailers, with big names among the usual suspects. Off Fifth (Saks Fifth Avenue's store), Nordstrom Rack, White House | Black Market, Brooks Brothers, DKNY, and Calvin Klein are interspersed with stores selling shoes, discounted home decor, sports gear, kids' fashions, and more. The mall has several restaurants as well as coffee shops and a food court. And it continues to expand, so check the website for an updated list of shops. ■ TIP→ **The wine bar in Whole Foods Market is the "see and be seen" scene at this outdoor mall.** ⊠ *1751 Palm Beach Lakes Blvd., West Palm Beach* ☎ *561/515–4400* ⊕ *www. palmbeachoutlets.com.*

Activities

DivaDuck Amphibious Tours

BOAT TOURS | FAMILY | Running 75 minutes, these duck tours go in and out of the water on USCG-inspected amphibious vessels around West Palm Beach and Palm Beach. The tours depart two or three times most days for $29 per person (adults); there are discounts for seniors and kids. ⊠ *CityPlace, 600 S. Rosemary Ave., West Palm Beach* ✛ *Corner of Hibiscus St. and Rosemary Ave.* ☎ *877/844–4188* ⊕ *www.divaduck. com.*

Fitteam Ballpark of the Palm Beaches

BASEBALL/SOFTBALL | FAMILY | There's a lot to root for at the new-in-2017 state-of-the-art baseball stadium. It plays host to spring training for the Houston Astros and the Washington Nationals, along with farm team play and numerous tournaments in the summer on its many fields. Seating includes lawn, bleacher, field boxes, and suites, with full food service in the latter two. A full bar overlooks left field. With free (and plenty of) parking—as well as reasonably priced tickets—it's a value day out. Check the website to see the other teams coming to play in Florida's "Grapefruit League" against the home teams. The stadium complements Roger Dean Stadium in Jupiter, which hosts the spring games for the Miami Marlins and St. Louis Cardinals. Fields for lacrosse, football, and soccer are part of the massive complex and expected to draw those games; other community events are staged here. ⊠ *5444 Haverhill Rd., West Palm Beach* ✛ *Best exit off I-95 is 45th St.; off Florida's Tpke. is Okeechobee Blvd.* ☎ *561/500-4487* ⊕ *www.ballparkpalmbeaches.com* 🖻 *From $17.*

★ **International Polo Club Palm Beach**

POLO | Attend matches and rub elbows with celebrities who make the pilgrimage out to Palm Beach polo country (the western suburb of Wellington) during the January–April season. The competition is not just among polo players. High society dresses in their best polo couture week after week, each outfit more fabulous than the next; they tailgate out of their Bentleys and Rollses. An annual highlight at the polo club is the U.S. Open Polo Championship at the end of season.
■TIP➔ **One of the best ways to experience the polo scene is by enjoying a gourmet brunch on the veranda of the International Polo Club Pavilion; it'll cost you from $100 to $120 per person depending on the month, but it's well worth it.** ⊠ *3667 120th Ave. S, Palm Beach* ☎ *561/204-5687* ⊕ *www. internationalpoloclub.com.*

Lake Worth

For years, tourists looked here mainly for inexpensive lodging and easy access to Palm Beach, since a bridge leads from the mainland to a barrier island with Lake Worth's beach. Now Lake Worth has grown into an arts community, with several blocks of restaurants, nightclubs, shops, and galleries, making this a worthy destination on its own.

Sights

Museum of Polo and Hall of Fame

MUSEUM | The history of the sport of kings is displayed in a time line here, with other exhibits focusing on polo ponies, star players, trophies, and a look at how mallets are made. It provides a great introduction to the surprisingly exciting, hoof-pounding sport that is played live on Sundays from January to April in nearby Wellington. ⊠ *9011 Lake Worth Rd., Lake Worth* ☎ *561/969-3210* ⊕ *www.polomuseum.com* 🖻 *Free (donations accepted)* ⊘ *Closed Sun. Closed Sat. May–Dec.*

Beaches

Lake Worth Beach

BEACH—SIGHT | FAMILY | This public beach bustles with beachgoers of all ages thanks to the prolific family offerings. The waterfront retail promenade—the old-fashioned nongambling Lake Worth "casino"—has a Mulligan's Beach House Bar & Grill, a T-shirt store, a pizzeria, and a Kilwin's ice-cream shop. The beach also has a municipal Olympic-sized public swimming pool, a playground, a fishing pier—not to mention the pier's wildly popular daytime eatery, Benny's on the Beach (open for dinner weekends in season). Tideline Ocean Resort and Four Seasons guests are steps away from the action; Eau Palm Beach guests are a short bike ride away. **Amenities:** food and drink; lifeguards; parking (fee); showers; toilets; water sports. **Best for:** sunset; swimming. ⊠ *10 S. Ocean Blvd., at A1A and Lake Ave., Lake Worth* ⊕ *www.lakeworth.org* 🖻 *$1 to enter pier, $3 to enter and fish, $2 per hr for parking.*

The posh Palm Beach area has its share of luxury villas on the water; many are Mediterranean in style.

🍴 Restaurants

Benny's on the Beach

$ | **AMERICAN** | Perched on the Lake Worth Pier, Benny's has a walk-up bar, a take-out window, and a full-service beach-themed restaurant serving casual fare at bargain prices. "Beach Bread" is a take on a waffle sandwich; the fresh seafood is from Florida waters. **Known for:** Florida seafood; beach brunch; afternoon drinks. [$] *Average main: $12* ✉ *Lake Worth Beach, 10 S. Ocean Blvd., Lake Worth* ✣ *On Lake Worth Pier* ☎ *561/582–9001* 🌐 *www.bennysonthebeach.com.*

Paradiso

$$$$ | **ITALIAN** | Arguably downtown Lake Worth's fanciest restaurant, with sophisticated modern Northern Italian cuisine, this is a go-to place for a romantic evening. Waiters are on point and anticipate needs. **Known for:** whole branzino baked in a salt crust; extensive wine list; lighter lounge menu. [$] *Average main: $42* ✉ *625 Lucerne Ave., Lake Worth* ☎ *561/547–2500* 🌐 *www.paradisolakeworth.com.*

🛏 Hotels

Sabal Palm House

$ | **B&B/INN** | Built in 1936, this romantic, two-story B&B is a short walk from Lake Worth's downtown shops, eateries, and the Intracoastal Waterway, and each room is decorated with antiques and inspired by a different artist, including Renoir, Dalí, Norman Rockwell, and Chagall. **Pros:** on quiet street; hands-on owners; chairs and totes with towels provided for use at nearby beach. **Cons:** no pool; peak times require a two-night minimum stay; no parking lot. [$] *Rooms from: $159* ✉ *109 N. Golfview Rd., Lake Worth* ☎ *561/582–1090, 888/722–2572* 🌐 *www.sabalpalmhouse.com* 🔑 *5 rooms, 2 suites* 🍴 *Breakfast.*

Activities

Palm Beach National Golf and Country Club
GOLF | Despite the name, this classic 18-hole course resides in Lake Worth, not in Palm Beach. It is, however, in Palm Beach County and prides itself on being "the most fun and friendly golf course" in Palm Beach County. The championship layout was designed by Joe Lee in the 1970s and is famous for its 3rd and 18th holes. The 3rd: a par-3 island hole with a sand bunker. The 18th: a short par 4 of 358 yards sandwiched between a wildlife preserve and water. Due to the challenging nature of the course, it's more popular with seasoned golfers. The Steve Haggerty Golf Academy is also based here. Summer rates are significantly discounted. ✉ *7500 St. Andrews Rd., Lake Worth* ☎ *561/965–3381* 🌐 *www.palmbeachnational.com* 🎟 *$94 for 18 holes* ⛳ *18 holes, 6734 yards, par 72.*

Lantana

Lantana—just a bit farther south from Palm Beach than Lake Worth—has inexpensive lodging and a bridge connecting the town to its own beach on a barrier island. Tucked between Lantana and Boynton Beach is **Manalapan,** a tiny but posh residential community.

Beaches

Town of Lantana Public Beach
BEACH—SIGHT | Ideal for quiet ambles, this sandy stretch is also noteworthy for a casual restaurant, the no-frills breezy Dune Deck Café, which is perched above the waterline and offers great views for an oceanfront breakfast or lunch. The beach's huge parking lot is directly adjacent to the Eau Palm Beach (meters take credit cards), and diagonally across the street is a sizable strip mall with all sorts of conveniences, including boutiques and more eateries. Note: the beach is very narrow and large rocks loom in the water. Nevertheless, these are some of the clearest waters along the Florida coastline, and they make an idyllic background for long walks and great photos. **Amenities:** food and drink; lifeguards; parking (fee); showers; toilets. **Best for:** walking. ✉ *100 N. Ocean Blvd., Lantana* 🌐 *www.lantana.org* 🎟 *$1.50 per hr for parking.*

Restaurants

Old Key Lime House
$$ | **SEAFOOD** | **FAMILY** | An informal seafood spot—serving crab cakes, fish sandwiches, and fillets—and a favorite of locals and tourists, is perched on the Intracoastal Waterway with spectacular views. Observation decks with separate bars wrap around the back where boats can dock; indoors is more family-oriented. **Known for:** unpretentious, casual atmosphere; fried and grilled fish; great Key lime pie. [$] *Average main: $20* ✉ *300 E. Ocean Ave., Lantana* ☎ *561/582–1889* 🌐 *www.oldkeylimehouse.com.*

Jerk Oceano
$$ | **CONTEMPORARY** | Once a strictly pizza place—some say the best in the county—this tiny deck-fronted spot now serves eclectic American cuisine, with a once-a-week night of pizzas. Take cash and your patience along if you're going; everything is made to order, one order at a time. **Known for:** daily-changing menu; thin-crust made-to-order pizza; cash only. [$] *Average main: $16* ✉ *210 E. Ocean Ave., Lantana* ☎ *561/429–5550* 🌐 *www.pizzeriaoceano.com* 💳 *No credit cards* 🕓 *Closed Sun.*

Activities

Bar Jack Fishing
FISHING | Three deep-sea-fishing excursions aboard the *Lady K* deep-sea drift-fishing boat depart daily: 8–noon, 1–5, and 6:30–10:30. They don't take reservations; just show up 30 minutes before the boat is scheduled to leave.

The cost of the trip includes fishing license, bait, and tackle. ✉ *314 E. Ocean Ave., Lantana* ☎ *561/588–7612* 🌐 *www.barjackfishing.com* 🎟 *From $40.*

Boynton Beach

In 1884 when fewer than 50 settlers lived in the area, Nathan Boynton, a Civil War veteran from Michigan, paid $25 for 500 acres with a mile-long stretch of beachfront thrown in. How things have changed, with today's population at about 118,000 and property values still on an upswing. Far enough from Palm Beach to remain low-key, Boynton Beach has two parts, the mainland and the barrier island—the town of Ocean Ridge—connected by two bridges.

Sights

Arthur R. Marshall Loxahatchee National Wildlife Refuge

NATURE PRESERVE | **FAMILY** | The most robust part of the northern Everglades, this 221-square-mile refuge is one of two huge water-retention areas accounting for much of the "River of Grass" outside the national park near Miami. Start at the visitor center, which has fantastic interactive exhibits and videos like *Night Sounds of the Everglades* and an airboat simulator. From there, you can take a marsh trail to a 20-foot-high observation tower, or stroll a half-mile boardwalk lined with educational signage through a dense cypress swamp. There are also guided nature walks (including some specifically for bird-watching), and there's great bass fishing (bring your own poles and bait) and a 5½-mile canoe and kayak trail loop (both can be rented from a kiosk by the fishing pier). ✉ *10216 Lee Rd., Boynton Beach* ✣ *Off U.S. 441 between Rte. 804 and Rte. 806* ☎ *561/734-8303* 🌐 *www.fws.gov/refuge/arm_loxahatchee/* 🎟 *$5 per vehicle; $1 per pedestrian or bicyclist.*

Restaurants

Banana Boat

$$ | **AMERICAN** | A mainstay for local boaters who cruise up and down the Intracoastal Waterway, Banana Boat is easily recognizable by the lighthouse on its roof. On weekends casual crowds clad in tank tops, flip-flops, and bikinis dance to live island music while downing frozen drinks (try the Dirty Banana or Hurricane Wilma) and nibbling on bar foods like burgers and ribs. **Known for:** frozen bar drinks; burgers and other pub grub; brunch on Sunday. [$] *Average main: $18* ✉ *739 E. Ocean Ave., Boynton Beach* ☎ *561/732–9400* 🌐 *www.bananaboat-boynton.com.*

Delray Beach

15 miles south of West Palm Beach.

A onetime artists' retreat with a small settlement of Japanese farmers, Delray has grown into a sophisticated beach town. Delray's current popularity is caused in large part by the fact that it has the feel of an organic city rather than a planned development or subdivision—and it's completely walkable. Atlantic Avenue, which fell from a tony downtown to a dilapidated main drag, has been reinvented into a mile-plus-long stretch of palm-dotted sidewalks lined with stores, art galleries, and restaurants. Running east–west and ending at the beach, it's a happening place for a stroll, day or night. Another active pedestrian area, the Pineapple Grove Arts District, begins at Atlantic and stretches northward on Northeast 2nd Avenue about half a mile, and yet another active pedestrian way begins at the eastern edge of Atlantic Avenue and runs along the big, broad swimming beach that extends north to George Bush Boulevard and south to Casuarina Road.

GETTING HERE AND AROUND

To reach Delray Beach from Boynton Beach, drive 2 miles south on Interstate 95, U.S. 1, or Route A1A.

ESSENTIALS

VISITOR INFORMATION

Discover the Palm Beaches. ⊠ *1555 Palm Beach Lakes Blvd., Suite 800, West Palm Beach* ☎ *800/554–7256* ⊕ *www.thepalm-beaches.com.*

Sights

Colony Hotel

HOTEL—SIGHT | The chief landmark along Atlantic Avenue since 1926 is this sunny Mediterranean-revival-style building, which is a member of the National Trust's Historic Hotels of America. Walk through the lobby to the parking lot where original garages still stand—relics of the days when hotel guests would arrive via chauffeured cars and stay there the whole season. The bar is a locals' gathering spot. ⊠ *525 E. Atlantic Ave.* ☎ *561/276–4123* ⊕ *colonyflorida.com.*

Delray Beach Center for the Arts at Old School Square

ARTS VENUE | **FAMILY** | Instrumental in the revitalization of Delray Beach circa 1995, this cluster of galleries and event spaces was established in restored school buildings dating from 1913 and 1925. The **Cornell Museum of Art & American Culture** offers ever-changing exhibits on fine arts, crafts, and pop culture, plus a hands-on children's gallery. From November to April, the 323-seat **Crest Theatre** showcases national-touring Broadway musicals, cabaret concerts, dance performances, and lectures. ⊠ *51 N. Swinton Ave.* ☎ *561/243–7922* ⊕ *oldschoolsquare.org* ⊡ *$8 for museum* ⊙ *Closed Sun. and Mon.*

★ Morikami Museum and Japanese Gardens

GARDEN | **FAMILY** | The boonies west of Delray Beach seems an odd place to encounter one of the region's most important cultural centers, but this is exactly where you can find a 200-acre cultural and recreational facility heralding the Yamato Colony of Japanese farmers that settled here in the early 20th century. A permanent exhibit details their history, and all together the museum's collection has more than 7,000 artifacts and works of art on rotating display. Traditional tea ceremonies are conducted monthly from October to June, along with educational classes on topics like calligraphy and sushi making (these require advance registration and come with a fee). The six main gardens are inspired by famous historic periods in Japanese garden design and have South Florida accents (think tropical bonsai), and the on-site Cornell Café serves light Asian fare at affordable prices and was recognized by the Food Network as being one of the country's best museum eateries. ⊠ *4000 Morikami Park Rd.* ☎ *561/495–0233* ⊕ *www.morikami.org* ⊡ *$15* ⊙ *Closed Mon.*

Beaches

★ Delray Municipal Beach

BEACH—SIGHT | If you're looking for a place to see and be seen, head for this wide expanse of sand, the heart of which is where Atlantic Avenue meets A1A, close to restaurants, bars, and quick-serve eateries. Singles, families, and water-sports enthusiasts alike love it here. Lounge chairs and umbrellas can be rented every day, and lifeguards man stations half a mile out in each direction. The most popular section of beach is south of Atlantic Avenue on A1A, where the street parking is found. There are also two metered lots with restrooms across from A1A at Sandoway Park and Anchor Park (bring quarters if parking here). On the beach by Anchor Park, north of Casuarina Road, are six volleyball nets and a kiosk that offers Hobie Wave rentals, surfing lessons, and snorkeling excursions to the 1903 SS *Inchulva* shipwreck half a

Zen-like landscapes inspire relaxation at the Morikami Museum and Japanese Gardens in Delray Beach.

mile offshore. The beach itself is open 24 hours, if you're at a nearby hotel and fancy a moonlight stroll. **Amenities:** food and drink; lifeguards; parking (fee); showers; toilets; water sports. **Best for:** partiers; swimming; windsurfing. ✉ *Rte. A1A and E. Atlantic Ave.* 🌐 *www.mydelraybeach.com/departments/parks_and_recreation/delray_municipal_beach.php* 🎟 *$1.50 per 1 hr parking.*

🍴 Restaurants

Blue Anchor

$$ | BRITISH | Yes, this pub was actually shipped from England, where it had stood for 150 years in London's historic Chancery Lane. There it was a watering hole for famed Englishmen, including Winston Churchill; here you may hear stories of lingering ghosts told over some suds. **Known for:** fish-and-chips; beer selection; late-night food spot. [$] *Average main: $18* ✉ *804 E. Atlantic Ave.* ☎ *561/272–7272.*

★ **City Oyster & Sushi Bar**

$$$ | SEAFOOD | This trendy restaurant mingles the personalities and flavors of a New England oyster bar, a modern sushi eatery, an eclectic seafood grill, and an award-winning dessert bakery to create a can't-miss foodie haven in the heart of Delray's bustling Atlantic Avenue. Dishes like the oyster bisque, New Orleans–style shrimp and crab gumbo, tuna crudo, and lobster fried rice are simply sublime. **Known for:** large selection of oysters; excellent desserts; loud and busy, especially in high season. [$] *Average main: $26* ✉ *213 E. Atlantic Ave.* ☎ *561/272–0220* 🌐 *www.cityoysterdelray.com.*

★ **Max's Harvest**

$$$ | MODERN AMERICAN | A few blocks off Atlantic Avenue in the artsy Pineapple Grove neighborhood, a tree-shaded, fenced-in courtyard welcomes foodies eager to dig into its "farm-to-fork" offerings. The menu encourages people to experiment with "to share," "start small," and "think big" plates. **Known for:** menu aimed at sharing; cocktails made from artisanal spirits; Sunday brunch. [$] *Average main: $27* ✉ *169 N.E. 2nd Ave.* ☎ *561/381–9970* 🌐 *www.maxsharvest.com* 🕑 *No lunch Mon.–Sat.*

★ The Office

$$$ | AMERICAN | Scenesters line the massive indoor-outdoor bar from noon until the wee hours at this cooler-than-thou retro library restaurant, but it's worth your time to stop here for the best burger in town. There's a whole selection, but the Prime CEO steals the show: Maytag bleu cheese and Gruyère with tomato-onion confit, arugula, and bacon. **Known for:** upscale comfort food; weekend brunch; alcoholic shakes. [$] *Average main: $24* ✉ *201 E. Atlantic Ave.* ☎ *561/276–3600* 🌐 *www.theofficedelray.com.*

Hotels

Colony Hotel & Cabaña Club

$ | HOTEL | Not to be confused with the luxurious Colony in Palm Beach, this charming hotel in the heart of downtown Delray dates back to 1926; and although it's landlocked, it does have a cabana club 2 miles away for hotel guests only. **Pros:** pet-friendly; full breakfast buffet included with rooms; free use of cabanas, umbrellas, and hammocks. **Cons:** no pool at main hotel building; must walk to public beach for water-sports rentals. [$] *Rooms from: $195* ✉ *525 E. Atlantic Ave.* ☎ *561/276–4123, 800/552–2363* 🌐 *www.thecolonyhotel.com* 🛏 *70 rooms* 🍴 *Breakfast.*

Crane's Beach House Boutique Hotel & Luxury Villas

$$$ | HOTEL | A tropical oasis, this boutique hotel is a hidden jungle of lush exotic and tropical plants, only a block from the beach. **Pros:** private location within the city setting; short walk to the beach; free parking; property is smoke-free. **Cons:** pricey; no restaurants on-site; no fitness or spa facilities. [$] *Rooms from: $349* ✉ *82 Gleason St.* ☎ *866/372–7263, 561/278–1700* 🌐 *www.cranesbeachhouse.com* 🛏 *28 rooms, 4 villas* 🍴 *No meals.*

Delray Beach Marriott

$$$$ | HOTEL | FAMILY | By far the largest hotel in Delray Beach, the Marriott has two towers on a stellar plot of land at the east end of Atlantic Avenue—it's the only hotel that directly overlooks the water, yet it is still within walking distance of restaurants, shopping, and nightlife. **Pros:** fantastic ocean views; pampering spa; two pools. **Cons:** chain-hotel feel; charge for parking; must rent beach chairs. [$] *Rooms from: $499* ✉ *10 N. Ocean Blvd.* ☎ *561/274–3200* 🌐 *www.delraybeachmarriott.com* 🛏 *269 rooms* 🍴 *No meals.*

★ The Seagate Hotel & Spa

$$$$ | RESORT | FAMILY | Those who crave 21st-century luxury in its full glory (ultraswank tilework and fixtures, marble vanities, seamless shower doors) will love this LEED-certified hotel that offers a subtle Zen-coastal motif throughout. **Pros:** two swimming pools; fabulous beach club; exceptionally knowledgeable concierge team. **Cons:** main building not directly on beach; daily resort fee; separate charge for parking. [$] *Rooms from: $489* ✉ *1000 E. Atlantic Ave.* ☎ *561/665–4800, 877/577–3242* 🌐 *www.theseagatehotel.com* 🛏 *154 rooms* 🍴 *No meals.*

★ Sundy House

$$ | B&B/INN | Just about everything in this bungalow-style B&B is executed to perfection—especially its tropical, verdant grounds, which are actually a nonprofit botanical garden (something anyone can check out during free weekday tours) with a natural, freshwater swimming pool where your feet glide along limestone rocks and mingle with fish. **Pros:** charming eclectic decor; each room is unique; renowned restaurant with popular indoor-outdoor bar and free breakfast; in quiet area off Atlantic Avenue. **Cons:** need to walk through garden to reach rooms (i.e., no covered walkways); beach shuttle requires roughly half-hour advance notice; no private beach facilities. $ *Rooms from: $299* ⊠ *106 Swinton Ave.* ☎ *561/272–5678, 877/434–9601* ⊕ *www.sundyhouse.com* ⇆ *11 rooms* ⊚❙ *Breakfast.*

Nightlife

Boston's on the Beach
MUSIC CLUBS | You'll find beer flowing and the ocean breeze blowing at this beach bar and eatery, a local watering hole since 1983. The walls are laden with paraphernalia from the Boston Bruins, New England Patriots, and Boston Red Sox, including a shrine to Ted Williams. Boston's can get loud and rowdy (or lively, depending on your taste) later at night. Groove to reggae on Monday, live blues bands on Tuesday, and other live music from rock to country on Friday, Saturday, and Sunday. ⊠ *40 S. Ocean Blvd.* ☎ *561/278–3364* ⊕ *www.bostonsonthebeach.com.*

Dada
MUSIC CLUBS | Bands play in the living room of this historic house, though much of the action is outdoors on the lawn in fair weather, where huge trees and lanterns make it a fun stop for drinks or a group night out. It's a place where those who don't drink will also feel comfortable, however, and excellent gourmet nibbles are a huge bonus (a full dinner menu is available, too). A bohemian, younger crowd gathers later into the night. ⊠ *52 N. Swinton Ave.* ☎ *561/330–3232* ⊕ *www.sub-culture.org/dada.*

Jellies Bar at the Atlantic Grille
BARS/PUBS | Within the Seagate Hotel, the fun and fabulous bar at the Atlantic Grille is known locally as Jellies Bar. The over-thirty set consistently floats over to this stunning bar to shimmy to live music Tuesday to Saturday; the namesake jellyfish tank never fails to entertain as well. ⊠ *The Seagate Hotel & Spa, 1000 E. Atlantic Ave.* ☎ *561/665–4900* ⊕ *www.theatlanticgrille.com.*

Shopping

Atlantic Avenue and Pineapple Grove, both charming neighborhoods for shoppers, have maintained Delray Beach's small-town integrity. Atlantic Avenue is the main street, with art galleries, boutiques, restaurants, and bars lining it from just west of Swinton Avenue all the way east to the ocean. The now established Pineapple Grove Arts District is centered on the half-mile strip of Northeast 2nd Avenue that goes north from Atlantic; these areas are broadening as the downtown area expands south and east.

Furst
JEWELRY/ACCESSORIES | This studio-shop gives you the chance to watch designer Flavie Furst or her pupils at work—and then purchase their fine, handcrafted gold, gold-filled, and silver jewelry. The other half of this space is the Ronald Furst bespoke handbag store, selling unique bags, purses, and sacks. ⊠ *123 N.E. 2nd Ave.* ☎ *561/272–6422* ⊕ *www.flaviefurst.com.*

Snappy Turtle
CLOTHING | Jack Rogers sandals and Trina Turk dresses mingle with other fun resort fashions and beachy gifts for the home and family at this family-run store. ⊠ *1100 E. Atlantic Ave.* ☎ *888/762–7798* ⊕ *www.snappy-turtle.com.*

Activities

Delray Beach Tennis Center
TENNIS | Each year this complex hosts simultaneous professional tournaments where current stars like Ivo Karlovic and Marin Cilic along with legends like Andy Roddick, Ivan Lendl, and Michael Chang duke it out. Florida's own Chris Evert hosts the Pro-Celebrity Tennis Classic charity event here. The rest of the time, you can practice or learn on 14 clay courts and seven hard courts; private lessons and clinics are available, and it's

open from 7:30 am to 9 pm weekdays and until 6 pm weekends. Since most hotels in the area do not have courts, tennis players visiting Delray Beach often come here to play. ✉ *201 W. Atlantic Ave.* ☎ *561/243–7360* ⊕ *www.delraytennis. com.*

Richwagen's Bike & Sport

BICYCLING | Rent bikes by the hour, day, or week (they come with locks, baskets, and helmets); Richwagen's also has copies of city maps on hand. A seven-speed cruiser rents for $60 per week, or $30 a day. They also rent bike trailers, child seats, and electric carts. The shop is closed Sunday. ✉ *298 N.E. 6th Ave.* ☎ *561/276–4234* ⊕ *www.delraybeachbicycles.com.*

Boca Raton

6 miles south of Delray Beach.

Less than an hour south of Palm Beach and anchoring the county's south end, upscale Boca Raton has much in common with its fabled cousin. Both reflect the unmistakable architectural influence of Addison Mizner, their principal developer in the mid-1920s. The meaning of the name Boca Raton (pronounced boca rah- *tone*) often arouses curiosity, with many folks mistakenly assuming it means "rat's mouth." Historians say the probable origin is Boca Ratones, an ancient Spanish geographical term for an inlet filled with jagged rocks or coral. Miami's Biscayne Bay had such an inlet, and in 1823 a mapmaker copying Miami terrain confused the more northern inlet, thus mistakenly labeling this area Boca Ratones. No matter what, you'll know you've arrived in the heart of downtown when you spot the historic town hall's gold dome on the main street, Federal Highway. Much of the Boca landscape was heavily planned, and many of the bigger sights are clustered in the area around town hall and Lake Boca, a wide

stretch of the Intracoastal Waterway between Palmetto Park Road and Camino Real (two main east–west streets at the southern end of town).

GETTING HERE AND AROUND

To get to Boca Raton from Delray Beach, drive south 6 miles on Interstate 95, Federal Highway (U.S. 1), or Route A1A.

ESSENTIALS

VISITOR INFORMATION

Discover the Palm Beaches. ✉ *1555 Palm Beach Lakes Blvd., Suite 800, West Palm Beach* ☎ *800/554–7256* ⊕ *www.thepalmbeaches.com.*

Sights

Boca Raton Museum of Art

ARTS VENUE | **FAMILY** | Changing-exhibition galleries on the first floor showcase internationally known artists—both past and present—at this museum in a spectacular building that's part of the Mizner Park shopping center; the permanent collection upstairs includes works by Picasso, Degas, Matisse, Klee, Modigliani, and Warhol, as well as notable African and pre-Columbian art. Daily tours are included with admission. In addition to the treasure hunts and sketchbooks you can pick up from the front desk, there's a roster of special programs that cater to kids, including studio workshops and gallery walks. Another fun feature is the cell phone audio guide—certain pieces of art have a corresponding number you dial to hear a detailed narration. ✉ *501 Plaza Real, Mizner Park* ☎ *561/392–2500* ⊕ *www.bocamuseum.org* 💲 *$12* ⊘ *Closed Mon.*

Gumbo Limbo Nature Center

FISH HATCHERY | **FAMILY** | A big draw for kids, this stellar spot has four huge saltwater tanks brimming with sea life, from coral to stingrays to spiny lobsters, touch tanks, plus a sea turtle rehabilitation center. Nocturnal walks in spring and early summer, when staffers lead a quest to find nesting female turtles coming ashore to lay eggs, are popular; so are the hatching releases in August and September. (Call to purchase tickets in advance, as there are very limited spaces.) This is one of only a handful of centers that offer this. There is also a nature trail and butterfly garden, a ¼-mile boardwalk, and a 40-foot observation tower, where you're likely to see brown pelicans and osprey. ⊠ *1801 N. Ocean Blvd.* ☎ *561/544–8605* ⊕ *www. gumbolimbo.org* 🎟 *Free ($5 suggested donation); turtle walks $15.*

Old Floresta

HISTORIC SITE | This residential area was developed by Addison Mizner starting in 1925 and is beautifully landscaped with palms and cycads. Its houses are mainly Mediterranean in style, many with balconies supported by exposed wood columns. Explore by driving northward on Paloma Avenue (Northwest 8th Avenue) from Palmetto Park Road, then weave in and out of the side streets. ⊠ *Paloma Ave.* ✛ *North of W. Palmetto Park Rd.*

🌊 Beaches

Boca's three city beaches (South Beach, Red Reef Park, and Spanish River Park, south to north, respectively) are beautiful and hugely popular; but unless you're a resident or enter via bicycle, parking can be very expensive. Save your receipt if you care to go in and out, or park hop—most guards at the front gate will honor a same-day ticket from another location if you ask nicely. Another option is the county-run South Inlet Park that's walking distance from the Waterstone Resort (formerly the Boca Raton Bridge Hotel) at the southern end of Lake Boca; it has a metered lot for a fraction of the cost, but not quite the same charm as the others.

Red Reef Park

BEACH—SIGHT | FAMILY | The ocean with its namesake reef that you can wade up to is just one draw: a fishing zone on the Intracoastal Waterway across the street,

a 9-hole golf course next door, and the Gumbo Limbo Environmental Education Center at the northern end of the park can easily make a day at the beach into so much more. But if pure old-fashioned fun in the sun is your focus, there are tons of picnic tables and grills, and two separate playgrounds. Pack snorkels and explore the reef at high tide when fish are most abundant. Swimmers, be warned: once lifeguards leave at 5, anglers flock to the shores and stay well past dark. **Amenities:** lifeguards; parking (fee); showers; toilets. **Best for:** snorkeling; swimming; walking. ⊠ *1400 N. Rte. A1A* ☎ *561/393–7974, 561/393–7989 for beach conditions* ⊕ *www.mybocaparks. org/Red-Reef-Park* 🎟 *$16 parking (weekdays), $18 parking (weekends).*

South Beach Park

BEACH—SIGHT | Perched high up on a dune, a large open-air pavilion at the east end of Palmetto Park Road offers a panoramic view of what's in store below on the sand that stretches up the coast. Serious beachgoers need to pull into the main lot a quarter mile north on the east side of A1A, but if a short-but-sweet visit is what you're after, the 15 or so one-hour spots with meters in the circle driveway will do (and not cost you the normal $15 parking fee). During the day, pretty young things blanket the shore, and windsurfers practice tricks in the waves. Quiet quarters are farther north. **Amenities:** lifeguards; parking (fee); showers; toilets. **Best for:** sunset; swimming; walking; windsurfing. ⊠ *400 N. Rte A1A* ⊕ *www. myboca.us/Facilities/Facility/Details/ South-Beach-Park-56* 🎟 *$15 parking (weekdays), $17 parking (weekends).*

Spanish River Park

BEACH—SIGHT | At 76 acres and including extensive nature trails, this is by far one of the largest ocean parks in the southern half of Palm Beach County and a great pick for people who want more space and fewer crowds. Big groups, including family reunions, favor it because of the number of covered picnic areas for rent, but anyone can snag a free table (there are plenty) under the thick canopy of banyan trees. Even though the vast majority of the park is separated from the surf, you never actually have to cross A1A to reach the beach, because tunnels run under it at several locations. **Amenities:** lifeguards; parking (fee); showers; toilets. **Best for:** solitude; swimming; walking. ✉ *3001 N. Rte. A1A* ☎ *561/393–7815* 🌐 *www.myboca.us/Facilities/Facility/Details/Spanish-River-Park-55* 🎫 *$16 parking (weekdays), $18 parking (weekends).*

🍴 Restaurants

★ Casa D'Angelo Ristorante

$$$$ | **TUSCAN** | The lines are deservedly long at chef Angelo Elia's upscale Tuscan restaurant in Boca Raton. The outpost of his renowned Casa D'Angelo in Broward impresses with an outstanding selection of antipasti, carpaccios, pastas, and specialties from the wood-burning oven. **Known for:** wide range of antipasti; veal osso buco and scaloppine; extensive wine list. [$] *Average main: $38* ✉ *171 E. Palmetto Park Rd.* ☎ *561/996–1234* 🌐 *www.casa-d-angelo.com* 🕒 *No lunch.*

Farmer's Table

$$$ | **MODERN AMERICAN** | Taking up the local-food mantle, the menu here includes inventive dishes following the seasons using locally sourced meats, seafood, and vegetables. Whenever possible, the foods are organic or sustainable. **Known for:** Buddha bowl with stir-fried vegetables and udon; good wine, cocktails, and beer; some vegan options. [$] *Average main: $22* ✉ *Wyndham Boca Raton, 1901 N. Military Trail* ☎ *561/417–5836* 🌐 *www.farmerstableboca.com.*

Racks Downtown Eatery & Tavern

$$$ | **AMERICAN** | Whimsical indoor–outdoor decor and comfort food with a twist help define this popular eatery in tony Mizner Park. Instead of dinner rolls, pretzel bread and mustard get things started. **Known for:** menu made for sharing; raw bar; popular happy hour. [$] *Average main: $23* ✉ *402 Plaza Real, Mizner Park* ☎ *561/395–1662* 🌐 *www.racksboca.com.*

🛏 Hotels

★ Boca Beach Club

$$$$ | **RESORT** | **FAMILY** | Dotted with turquoise lounge chairs, ruffled umbrellas, and white-sand beaches, this contemporary resort, part of the Waldorf-Astoria collection, looks as if it were carefully replicated from a retro-chic postcard. **Pros:** great location on the beach; kids' activity center. **Cons:** pricey; shuttle ride away from the main building; resort fee. [$] *Rooms from: $542* ✉ *900 S. Ocean Blvd.* ☎ *888/564–1312* 🌐 *www.bocabeachclub.com* 🔑 *212 rooms* 🍽 *No meals.*

★ Boca Raton Resort & Club

$$$ | **RESORT** | **FAMILY** | Addison Mizner built this Mediterranean-style hotel in 1926, and additions over time have created a sprawling, sparkling resort, one of the most luxurious in all of South Florida and part of the Waldorf-Astoria collection. **Pros:** superexclusive—grounds are closed to the public; decor strikes the right balance between historic roots and modern comforts; plenty of activities. **Cons:** daily resort charge; conventions often crowd common areas. [$] *Rooms from: $309* ✉ *501 E. Camino Real* ☎ *561/447–3000, 888/543–1277* 🌐 *www.bocaresort.com* 🔑 *635 rooms* 🍽 *No meals.*

Waterstone Resort & Marina

$$ | **HOTEL** | The former Bridge Hotel was transformed into a sleek, modern resort with a $20 million restoration in 2014. **Pros:** short walk to beach; pet-friendly; waterfront views throughout. **Cons:** parking fee; no quiet common space; some rooms noisy from nearby bridge traffic. [$] *Rooms from: $289* ✉ *999 E. Camino Real* ☎ *561/368–9500* 🌐 *www.*

waterstoneboca.com 🛏 *139 rooms* 🍽 *No meals.*

Shopping

Mizner Park

SHOPPING CENTERS/MALLS | This distinctive 30-acre shopping center off Federal Highway, one block north of Palmetto Park Road, intersperses apartments and town houses among its gardenlike commercial areas. Some three dozen retailers—including Lord & Taylor, which moved in as the only national department store east of Interstate 95 in Boca—line the central axis. It's peppered with fountains and green space, restaurants, galleries, a jazz club, a movie theater, the Boca Raton Museum of Art, and an amphitheater that hosts major concerts as well as community events. ✉ *327 Plaza Real* 🕾 *561/362–0606* ⊕ *www. miznerpark.com.*

Royal Palm Place

SHOPPING CENTERS/MALLS | The retail enclave of Royal Palm is filled with independent boutiques selling fine jewelry and apparel. By day, stroll the walkable streets and have your pick of sidewalk cafés for a bite alongside Boca's ladies who lunch. Royal Palm Place assumes a different personality come nightfall, as its numerous restaurants and lounges attract throngs of patrons for great dining and fabulous libations. Parking here is free. ✉ *101 Plaza Real S* 🕾 *561/392–8920* ⊕ *www.royalpalmplace.com.*

Town Center at Boca Raton

SHOPPING CENTERS/MALLS | Over on the west side of the interstate in Boca, this indoor megamall has over 220 stores, with anchor stores including Saks and Neiman Marcus and just about every major high-end designer, including Kate Spade and Anne Fontaine. But not every shop here requires deep pockets. The Town Center at Boca Raton is also firmly rooted with a variety of more affordable national brands like Gap and

Banana Republic. ✉ *6000 Glades Rd.* 🕾 *561/368–6000* ⊕ *www.simon.com/ mall/town-center-at-boca-raton.*

Activities

Force-E

SCUBA DIVING | This company, in business since the late 1970s, rents, sells, and repairs scuba and snorkeling equipment—and organizes about 80 dive trips a week from the Palm Beach Inlet to Port Everglades in Broward County. The PADI–affiliated five-star center has instruction for all levels and offers private charters, too. They have two other outposts besides this Boca Raton location—one north in Riviera Beach and one south in Pompano Beach. ✉ *2621 N. Federal Hwy.* 🕾 *561/368–0555, 561/368–0555* ⊕ *www. force-e.com.*

Red Reef Park Executive Golf Course

GOLF | This executive golf course offers 9 holes with varying views of the Intracoastal and the Atlantic Ocean. The Joe Palloka and Charles Ankrom–designed course dates back to 1957. It was refreshed in 2001 through a multimillion-dollar renovation. The scenic holes are between 54 and 227 yards each—great for a quick round. Carts are available, but the short course begs to be walked. Park in the lot across the street from the main beach entrance, and put the greens fees receipt on the dash; that covers parking. ✉ *1221 N. Ocean Blvd.* 🕾 *561/391–5014* ⊕ *www.mybocaparks. org/Red-Reef-Executive-Golf-Course* 🏷 *$17 to walk; $27 to ride* 🏌 *9 holes, 1357 yards, par 32.*

Palm Beach Gardens

13½ miles north of West Palm Beach.

About 15 minutes northwest of Palm Beach is this relaxed, upscale residential community known for its high-profile golf complex, the **PGA National Resort & Spa.**

Although not on the beach, the town is less than a 15-minute drive from the ocean. Malls and dining are centered on the main street, PGA Boulevard, running east from the resort to U.S. 1.

🍴 Restaurants

Café Chardonnay

$$$$ | **AMERICAN** | A longtime local favorite, Café Chardonnay is charming, romantic, and has some of the most refined food in the suburban town of Palm Beach Gardens. Soft lighting, warm woods, white tablecloths, and cozy banquettes set the scene for a quiet lunch or romantic dinner. **Known for:** outstanding wine list; innovative specials; many locally sourced ingredients. [$] *Average main: $34* ✉ *The Gardens Square Shoppes, 4533 PGA Blvd., Palm Beach Gardens* ☎ *561/627–2662* 🌐 *www.cafechardonnay.com* 🕒 *No lunch weekends.*

★ **Coolinary Cafe**

$$$ | **AMERICAN** | It's tucked away in a strip mall and has only 50 seats inside (counting the bar) and a handful out on the sidewalk, but everything down to the condiments is made in-house here. Rabbit sausage and noodles or lamb meatball risotto are examples on the seasonal one-page menus the chef puts together daily. **Known for:** small, focused regular menu; fresh fish specials; long waits for dinner in season. [$] *Average main: $22* ✉ *Donald Ross Village Plaza, 4650 Donald Ross Rd., Suite 110, Palm Beach Gardens* ☎ *561/249–6760* 🌐 *www.coolinarycafe.com* 🕒 *Closed Sun.*

The Cooper

$$$ | **AMERICAN** | **FAMILY** | With a contemporary farm-to-table menu, and spacious dining rooms and bars, this spot in PGA Commons has plenty of local fans. Happy-hour crowds fill the patio bar-lounge area to sip the craft cocktails and nibble from a cheese or salumi board. **Known for:** wide-ranging American menu; extensive wine list; gluten-free options. [$] *Average main: $23* ✉ *PGA Commons, 4610 PGA Blvd., Palm Beach Gardens* ☎ *561/622–0032* 🌐 *www.thecooperrestaurant.com.*

Ironwood Steak & Seafood

$$$$ | **STEAKHOUSE** | Located in the PGA National Resort & Spa, this eatery draws guests, locals, and tourists alike eager for a taste of its fired-up Vulcan-cooked steaks (Vulcan to meat eaters is like Titleist to golfers—the best equipment around). Wagyu and Angus beef cuts are featured. **Known for:** wide range of steaks; raw bar; extensive wine list. [$] *Average main: $38* ✉ *PGA National Resort & Spa, 400 Ave. of the Champions, Palm Beach Gardens* ☎ *561/627–4852* 🌐 *www.pgaresort.com/restaurants/ironwood-grille.*

Spoto's Oyster Bar

$$$ | **SEAFOOD** | If you love oysters and other raw bar nibbles, head here, where black-and-white photographs of oyster fisherman adorn the walls. The polished tables give the eatery a clubby look. **Known for:** wide range of oysters and clams; fresh seafood; live music in the Blue Point Lounge. [$] *Average main: $26* ✉ *PGA Commons, 4560 PGA Blvd., Palm Beach Gardens* ☎ *561/776–9448* 🌐 *spotos.com.*

🛏 Hotels

Hilton Garden Inn Palm Beach Gardens

$$ | **HOTEL** | A hidden find in Palm Beach Gardens, this hotel sits on a small lake next to a residential area but near two shopping malls and close to PGA golf courses. **Pros:** 24-hour free business center; walk to two different malls with shops, restaurants, and movie theaters. **Cons:** outdoor self-parking; no bell service; pool closes at dusk; 15 minutes from the beach. [$] *Rooms from: $209* ✉ *3505 Kyoto Gardens Dr., Palm Beach Gardens* ☎ *561/694–5833, 561/694–5829* 🌐 *hiltongardeninn3.hilton.com* 🛏 *180 rooms* 🍴 *No meals.*

★ PGA National Resort & Spa

$$$ | RESORT | This golfer's paradise (five championship courses and the site of the yearly Honda Classic pro-tour tournament) is a sleek modern playground with a gorgeous zero-entry lagoon pool, seven different places to eat, and a full-service spa with unique mineral-salt therapy pools. **Pros:** dream golf facilities; affordable rates for top-notch amenities; close to shopping malls. **Cons:** no beach shuttle; difficult to get around if you don't have a car; long drive to Palm Beach proper. $ *Rooms from: $348 ⊠ 400 Ave. of the Champions, Palm Beach Gardens* ☎ *561/627–2000, 800/633–9150* ⊕ *www. pgaresort.com ⌨ 339 rooms* ⦿*❪ No meals.*

Shopping

Downtown at The Gardens

SHOPPING CENTERS/MALLS | FAMILY | This open-air pavilion down the street from The Gardens Mall has boutiques, chain stores, a grocery store, day spas, a 16-screen movie theater, and a lively restaurant and nighttime bar scene that includes the Dirty Martini and the Yard House, both of which stay open late. A carousel, children's barbershop, boutiques, and Cool Beans (an indoor playground), make this a family-friendly mall. ⊠ *11701 Lake Victoria Gardens Ave., Palm Beach Gardens* ☎ *561/340–1600* ⊕ *www.downtownatthegardens.com.*

★ The Gardens Mall

SHOPPING CENTERS/MALLS | FAMILY | One of the most refined big shopping malls in America, the 160-store Gardens Mall in northern Palm Beach County has stores like Chanel, Gucci, Louis Vuitton, and David Yurman, along with Saks Fifth Avenue and Nordstrom. There are also plenty of reasonably priced national retailers like H&M and Abercrombie & Fitch, Bloomingdale's, and Macy's. This beautiful mall has prolific seating pavilions, making it a great place to spend a humid summer afternoon. ⊠ *3101 PGA Blvd., Palm Beach Gardens* ☎ *561/775–7750* ⊕ *www. thegardensmall.com.*

 Activities

Spring-training fans travel to the area to see the Cardinals and Marlins tune up for their seasons at Roger Dean Stadium in Palm Beach Gardens, and to watch their AAA feeder teams in summer. Port St. Lucie and Vero Beach stadiums and more teams are only a short drive up Interstate 95.

★ PGA National Resort & Spa

GOLF | If you're the kind of traveler who takes along a set of clubs, you'll achieve nirvana on the greens of PGA National Resort & Spa. The five championship courses are open only to hotel guests and club members, which means you'll have to stay to play, but packages that include a room and a round of golf are reasonably priced. The Champion Course, redesigned by Jack Nicklaus and famous for its Bear Trap holes, is the site of the yearly Honda Classic pro tournament. The four other challenging courses are also legends in the golfing world: the Palmer, named for its architect, the legendary Arnold Palmer; the Fazio (formerly the Haig)) and the Squire, both from Tom and George Fazio; and the Karl Litten–designed Estates, the sole course not on the property (it is located 5 miles west of the PGA resort). Lessons are available at the David Leadbetter Golf Academy, and they also run a summertime kids' golf camp. ⊠ *PGA National Resort & Spa, 1000 Ave. of the Champions, Palm Beach Gardens* ☎ *561/627–1800* ⊕ *www.pgaresort.com/golf/pga-national-golf ⌨ $409 for 18 holes for Champion Course, Fazio Course, and Squire Course. $250 for 18 holes for Palmer Course and Estates Course. ⸓ Champion Course: 18 holes, 7048 yards, par 72. Palmer Course: 18 holes, 7079 yards, par 72. Fazio Course: 18 holes, 6806 yards, par 72. Squire Course: 18 holes, 6465 yards, par 72.*

Estates Course: 18 holes, 6694 yards, par 72.

Singer Island

6 miles north of West Palm Beach.

Across the inlet from the northern end of Palm Beach is Singer Island, which is actually a peninsula that's big enough to pass for a barrier island, rimmed with mom-and-pop motels and high-rises. Palm Beach Shores occupies its southern tip (where tiny Peanut Island is a stone's throw away); farther north are Riviera Beach and North Palm Beach, which also straddle the inlet and continue on the mainland.

Beaches

★ **John D. MacArthur Beach State Park**
BEACH—SIGHT | **FAMILY** | If getting far from rowdy crowds is your goal, this spot on the north end of Singer Island is a good choice. Encompassing 2 miles of beach and a lush subtropical coastal habitat, inside you'll find a great place for kayaking, snorkeling at natural reefs, bird-watching, fishing, and hiking. You might even get to see a few manatees. A 4,000-square-foot nature center has aquariums and displays on local flora and fauna, and there's a long roster of monthly activities, such as surfing clinics, art lessons, and live bluegrass music. Guided sea turtle walks are available at night in season, and daily nature walks depart at 10 am. Check the website for times and costs of activities. **Amenities:** parking (fee); showers; toilets; water sports. **Best for:** solitude; surfing; swimming; walking. ✉ *10900 Jack Nicklaus Dr., North Palm Beach* ☎ *561/624–6950* 🌐 *www.macarthurbeach.org* 🎟 *Parking $5, bicyclists and pedestrians $2.*

Peanut Island Park
BEACH—SIGHT | Partiers, families, and overnight campers all have a place to go on the 79 acres here. The island, in a wide section of the Intracoastal between Palm Beach Island and Singer Island with an open channel to the sea, is accessible only by private boat or water taxi, two of which set sail regularly from the Riviera Beach Municipal Marina (🌐 *peanutislandshuttleboat.com/*) and the Sailfish Marina (🌐 *www.sailfishmarina.com/water_taxi*). Fun-loving seafarers looking for an afternoon of Jimmy Buffett and picnics aboard pull up to the day docks or the huge sandbar on the north—float around in an inner tube, and it's spring break déjà vu. Walk along the 20-foot-wide paver-lined path encircling the island, and you'll hit a 170-foot fishing pier, a campground, the lifeguarded section to the south that is particularly popular with families because of its artificial reef. There are picnic tables and grills, but no concessions. A new ordinance means alcohol possession and consumption is restricted to permit areas. **Amenities:** lifeguards (summer only); showers; toilets. **Best for:** partiers; sunrise; swimming; walking. ✉ *6500 Peanut Island Rd., Riviera Beach* ☎ *561/845–4445* 🌐 *discover.pbcgov.org/parks/Locations/Peanut-Island.aspx* 🎟 *Beach free; water taxi $12; park stay $17.*

Hotels

Palm Beach Marriott Singer Island Beach Resort & Spa
$$$$ | **RESORT** | **FAMILY** | Families with a yen for the cosmopolitan but requiring the square footage and comforts of home revel in these one- and two-bedroom suites with spacious, marble-tiled, granite-topped kitchens. **Pros:** wide beach; genuinely warm service; plenty of kids' activities; sleek spa. **Cons:** no upscale dining nearby; unspectacular room views for an oceanside hotel. [$] *Rooms from: $509* ✉ *3800 N. Ocean Dr., Singer Island, Riviera Beach* ☎ *561/340–1700, 877/239–5610* 🌐 *www.marriott.com* 🛏 *202 suites* 🍴 *No meals.*

Sailfish Marina Resort

$ | HOTEL | A marina with deepwater slips—and prime location at the mouth to the Atlantic Ocean on the Intracoastal Waterway across from Peanut Island—lures boaters and anglers here to these rather basic rooms, studios, and efficiencies. **Pros:** inexpensive rates; great waterfront restaurant; has a water taxi; pretty grounds. **Cons:** no real lobby; not directly on beach; area attracts a party crowd and can be noisy; dated decor. [$] *Rooms from: $150* ✉ *98 Lake Dr., Palm Beach Shores* ☎ *561/844–1724* 🌐 *www.sailfishmarina.com* 🛏 *30 units* 🍴 *No meals.*

Activities

Sailfish Marina

FISHING | FAMILY | Book a full or half day of deep-sea fishing for up to six people with the seasoned captains and large fleet of 28- to 65-foot boats. A ship's store and restaurant are also on-site. ✉ *Sailfish Marina Resort, 98 Lake Dr., Palm Beach Shores* ☎ *561/844–1724* 🌐 *www.sailfishmarina.com.*

Juno Beach

12 miles north of West Palm Beach.

This small town east of Palm Beach Gardens has 2 miles of shoreline that becomes home to thousands of sea turtle hatchlings each year, making it one of the world's densest nesting sites. A 990-foot-long pier lures fishermen and beachgoers seeking a spectacular sunrise.

Sights

★ **Loggerhead Park Marine Life Center of Juno Beach**

NATURE PRESERVE | FAMILY | Located in a certified green building in Loggerhead Park—and established by Eleanor N. Fletcher, the "turtle lady of Juno Beach"—the center focuses on the conservation of sea turtles, using education, research, and rehabilitation. The education center houses displays of coastal natural history, detailing Florida's marine ecosystems and the life and plight of the various species of sea turtles found on Florida's shores. You can visit recovering turtles in their outdoor hospital tanks; volunteers are happy to tell you the turtles' heroic tales of survival. The center has regularly scheduled activities, such as Kid's Story Time and Junior Vet Lab, and most are free of charge. During peak nesting season, the center hosts night walks to experience turtle nesting in action. Given that the adjacent beach is part of the second-biggest nesting ground for loggerhead turtles in the world, your chances of seeing this natural phenomenon are pretty high (over 15,000 loggerheads nested here in 2017). ✉ *14200 U.S. 1* ☎ *561/627–8280* 🌐 *www.marinelife.org* 🎟 *Free.*

Beaches

Juno Beach Ocean Park

BEACH—SIGHT | FAMILY | An angler's dream, this beach has a 990-foot pier that's open daily, like the beach, from sunrise to sunset—but from November through February, pier gates open at 6 am and don't close until 10 pm on weeknights and midnight on weekends, making it an awesome place to catch a full sunrise and sunset (that is, if you don't mind paying the small admission fee). A concession stand on the pier sells fish food as well as such human favorites as burgers, sandwiches, and ice cream. Rods and tackle are rented here. Families adore this shoreline because of the amenities and vibrant atmosphere. There are plenty of kids building castles but also plenty of teens having socials and hanging out along the beach. Pets are not allowed here, but they are allowed on Jupiter Beach. **Amenities:** food and drink; lifeguards; parking (no fee); showers;

Away from developed shorelines, Jupiter's Blowing Rocks Preserve is rugged and otherworldly.

toilets. **Best for:** sunrise; sunset; swimming. ✉ *14775 U.S. 1* ☎ *561/799–0185 for pier* ⊕ *discover.pbcgov.org/parks/ Locations/Juno-Beach.aspx* ✉ *$4 to fish, $1 to enter pier; beach free.*

Jupiter and Vicinity

12 miles north of West Palm Beach.

Jupiter is one of the few towns in the region not fronted by an island but still quite close to the fantastic hotels, shopping, and dining of the Palm Beach area. The beaches here are on the mainland, and Route A1A runs for almost 4 miles along the beachfront dunes and beautiful homes.

Northeast across the Jupiter Inlet from Jupiter is the southern tip of Jupiter Island, which stretches about 15 miles to the St. Lucie Inlet. Here expansive and expensive estates often retreat from the road behind screens of vegetation, and the population dwindles the farther north you go. At the very north end, which

adjoins tiny Hobe Sound in Martin County on the mainland, sea turtles come to nest.

GETTING HERE AND AROUND
If you're coming from the airport in West Palm Beach, take Interstate 95 to Route 706. Otherwise, Federal Highway (U.S. 1) and Route A1A are usually more convenient.

CONTACTS Discover the Palm Beaches.
✉ *1555 Palm Beach Lakes Blvd., Suite 800, West Palm Beach* ☎ *800/554–7256* ⊕ *www.thepalmbeaches.com.*

Sights

★ **Blowing Rocks Preserve**
BEACH—SIGHT | FAMILY | Managed by the Nature Conservancy, this protected area on Jupiter Island is headlined by an almost otherworldly looking limestone shelf that fringes South Florida's most turquoise waters. Also protected within its 73 acres are plants native to beachfront dunes, coastal strand (the landward side of the dunes), mangrove

swamps, and tropical hardwood forests. There are two short walking trails on the Intracoastal side of the preserve, as well as an education center and a butterfly garden. The best time to come and see the "blowing rocks" is when a storm is brewing: if high tides and strong offshore winds coincide, the sea blows spectacularly through the holes in the eroded outcropping. During a calm summer day, you can swim in crystal clear waters on the mile-long beach and climb around the rock formations at low tide. Park in one of the two lots, because police ticket cars on the road. ⊠ 574 S. Beach Rd., CR 707, Hobe Sound ☎ 561/744–6668 ⊕ www.nature.org/blowingrocks ⊠ $2.

★ Hobe Sound Nature Center
NATURE PRESERVE | FAMILY | Though located in the Hobe Sound National Wildlife Refuge, this nature center is an independent organization. The exhibit hall houses live baby alligators, crocodiles, a scary-looking tarantula, and more—and is a child's delight. Just off the center's entrance is a mile-long nature trail loop that snakes through three different kinds of habitats: coastal hammock, estuary beach, and sand pine scrub, which is one of Florida's most unusual and endangered plant communities and what composes much of the refuge's nearly 250 acres.
■ TIP → Among the center's more popular events are the annual nighttime sea turtle walks, held between May and June; reservations are accepted as early as April 1. ⊠ 13640 S.E. U.S. 1, Hobe Sound ☎ 772/546–2067 ⊕ www.hobesoundnaturecenter.com ⊠ Free (donation requested) ⊗ Closed Sun.

★ Jonathan Dickinson State Park
NATIONAL/STATE PARK | FAMILY | This serene state park provides a glimpse of predevelopment "real" Florida. A beautiful showcase of Florida inland habitat, the park teems with gopher tortoises and manatees. From Hobe Mountain, an ancient dune topped with a tower, you are treated to a panoramic

view of this park's more than 11,000 acres of varied terrain and the Intracoastal Waterway. The Loxahatchee River, named a National Wild and Scenic River, cuts through the park, and is home to plenty of charismatic manatees in winter and alligators year-round. Two-hour boat tours of the river depart daily. Kayak rentals are available, as is horseback riding (it was reintroduced after a 30-year absence). Among the amenities are a dozen newly redone cabins for rent, tent sites, bicycle and hiking trails, two established campgrounds and some primitive campgrounds, and a snack bar. Palmettos on the Loxahatchee is a new food-and-beverage garden with wine, beer, and local foods featured. Don't skip the Elsa Kimbell Environmental Education and Research Center, which has interactive displays, exhibits, and a short film on the natural history of the area. The park is also a fantastic birding location, with about 150 species to spot. ⊠ 16450 S.E. U.S. 1, Hobe Sound ☎ 772/546–2771 ⊕ www.floridastateparks.org/jonathandickinson ⊠ Vehicles $6, bicyclists and pedestrians $2.

★ Jupiter Inlet Lighthouse & Museum
MUSEUM | FAMILY | Designed by Civil War hero Lieutenant George Gordon Meade, this working brick lighthouse has been under the Coast Guard's purview since 1860. Tours of the 108-foot-tall landmark are held approximately every half hour and are included with admission. (Children must be at least 4 feet tall to go to the top.) The museum tells about efforts to restore this graceful spire to the way it looked from 1860 to 1918; its galleries and outdoor structures, including a pioneer home, also showcase local history dating back 5,000 years. ⊠ Lighthouse Park, 500 Capt. Armour's Way, Jupiter ☎ 561/747–8380 ⊕ www.jupiterlighthouse.org ⊠ $12 ⊗ Closed Mon. May–Dec.

Beaches

Carlin Park

BEACH—SIGHT | About ½ mile south of the Jupiter Beach Resort and Indiantown Road, the quiet beach here is just one draw; otherwise, the manicured park, which straddles A1A, is chock-full of activities and amenities, and it has the most free parking of any beach park in the area. Several picnic pavilions, including a few beachside, two bocce ball courts, six lighted tennis courts, a baseball diamond, a wood-chip-lined running path, and an amphitheater that hosts free concerts and Shakespeare productions are just some of the highlights. Locals also swear by the Lazy Loggerhead Café that's right off the seaside parking lot for a great casual breakfast and lunch. **Amenities:** food and drink; lifeguards; parking (no fee); showers; toilets. **Best for:** swimming; walking. ✉ *400 S. Rte. A1A, Jupiter* 🌐 *discover.pbcgov.org/parks/Locations/Carlin.aspx.*

Hobe Sound National Wildlife Refuge

BEACH—SIGHT | Nature lovers seeking to get as far as possible from the madding crowds will feel at peace at this refuge managed by the U.S. Fish & Wildlife Service. It's a haven for people who want some quiet while they walk around and photograph the gorgeous coastal sand dunes, where turtles nest and shells often wash ashore. The beach has been severely eroded by high tides and strong winds (surprisingly, surfing is allowed and many do partake). You can't actually venture within most of the 735 protected acres, so if hiking piques your interest, head to the refuge's main entrance a few miles away on Hobe Sound (*13640 S.E. U.S. 1 in Hobe Sound*) for a mile-long trek close to the nature center, or to nearby Jonathan Dickinson State Park (*16450 S.E. U.S. 1 in Hobe Sound*). **Amenities:** parking (fee); toilets. **Best for:** solitude; surfing; walking. ✉ *198 N. Beach Rd., Jupiter Island* ✥ *At end of N. Beach Rd.* ☎ *772/546–6141* 🌐 *www.fws.gov/hobesound* 🎟 *$5.*

Jupiter Beach

BEACH—SIGHT | Famous throughout all of Florida for a unique pooch-loving stance, the town of Jupiter's beach welcomes Yorkies, Labs, pugs—you name it—along its 2½-mile oceanfront. Dogs can frolic unleashed (once they're on the beach) or join you for a dip. Free parking spots line A1A in front of the sandy stretch, and there are multiple access points and continuously refilled dog-bag boxes (29 to be exact). The dog beach starts on Marcinski Road (Beach Marker No. 25) and continues north until Beach Marker No. 59. Before going, read through the guidelines posted on the Friends of Jupiter Beach website; the biggest things to note are be sure to clean up after your dog and steer clear of lifeguarded areas to the north and south. **TIP→ Dogs fare best early morning and late afternoon, when the sand isn't too hot for their paws.** **Amenities:** showers; toilets. **Best for:** walking. ✉ *2188 Marcinski Rd., Jupiter* ✥ *Across the street from the parking lot* ☎ *561/748–8140* 🌐 *www.friendsofjupiterbeach.org.*

Restaurants

Guanabanas

$$ | **SEAFOOD** | Expect a wait for dinner, which is not necessarily a bad thing at this island paradise of a waterfront restaurant and bar. Take the wait time to explore the bridges and trails of the open-air tropical oasis, or grab a chair by the river to watch the sunset, listen to the live band, or nibble on some conch fritters at the large tiki bar until your table is ready. **Known for:** water views from the outdoor dining area; live music; weekend breakfast. [$] *Average main: $18* ✉ *960 N. Rte. A1A, Jupiter* ☎ *561/747–8878* 🌐 *www.guanabanas.com.*

Little Moir's Food Shack

$$ | SEAFOOD | This local favorite is not much to look at and a bit tricky to find, but well worth the search. The fried-food standards you might expect at such a casual, small place that uses plastic utensils are not found on the menu; instead there are fried tuna rolls with basil, and panko-crusted fried oysters with spicy fruit salad. **Known for:** fresh fish; good beer selection; long lines during the season. $ *Average main: $17* ⊠ *103 S. U.S. 1, Jupiter* ☎ *561/741–3626* ⊕ *www. littlemoirs.com/food-shack* ☾ *Closed Sun.*

Sinclair's Ocean Grill

$$$$ | SEAFOOD | This upscale restaurant at the Jupiter Beach Resort & Spa has a slick, contemporary look and is a favorite of locals in the know. The menu has a daily selection of fresh fish, such as Atlantic black grouper over lemon crab salad, sesame-seared tuna, and mahimahi with fruit salsa. **Known for:** fresh fish; weekend brunch; drinks in Sinclair's Lounge. $ *Average main: $31* ⊠ *Jupiter Beach Resort, 5 N. Rte. A1A, Jupiter* ☎ *561/746–2511* ⊕ *www.jupiterbeachresort.com.*

Taste Casual Dining

$$ | AMERICAN | Located in the center of historic Hobe Sound, this cozy dining spot with a pleasant, screened-in patio offers piano dinner music on Fridays. Locals like to hang out at the old, English-style wine bar; however, the food itself is the biggest draw here. **Known for:** fresh fish specials; slow-cooked prime rib; signature Gorgonzola salad. $ *Average main: $18* ⊠ *11750 S.E. Dixie Hwy., Hobe Sound* ☎ *772/546–1129* ⊕ *www. tasteaculinaryadventure.50megs.com* ☾ *May–Oct., closed Sun.*

 Hotels

★ Jupiter Beach Resort & Spa

$$$ | RESORT | FAMILY | Families love this nine-story hotel filled with rich Caribbean-style rooms containing mahogany sleigh beds and armoires; all rooms have balconies, and many have stunning views of the ocean and local landmarks like the Jupiter Lighthouse and Juno Pier. **Pros:** fantastic beachside pool area with hammocks and a fire pit; marble showers; great restaurant. **Cons:** $25 nightly resort fee; no covered parking; bathtubs in suites only. $ *Rooms from: $360* ⊠ *5 N. Rte. A1A, Jupiter* ☎ *561/746–2511, 800/228–8810* ⊕ *www.jupiterbeachresort.com* ⤳ *168 rooms* ⦿ *No meals.*

Wyndham Grand Jupiter at Harbourside Place

$$$ | HOTEL | This luxury waterfront hotel is in an upscale complex of business and retail development just minutes from the beach. **Pros:** convenient to plaza shops and restaurants; only minutes from the beach; boat docks and fitness center available. **Cons:** no covered walkway to restaurant; no green spaces; pricey. $ *Rooms from: $309* ⊠ *Harbourside Place, 122 Soundings Ave., Jupiter* ☎ *561/273–6600* ⊕ *www. wyndhamgrandjupiter.com* ⤳ *179 rooms* ⦿ *No meals.*

 Activities

Abacoa Golf Club

GOLF | Built in 1999, the tagline for this Joe Lee–designed 18-hole course in Jupiter is "public golf at its finest." Most of the courses in this golfing community are private, but the range at Abacoa is on par with them and membership (nor deep pockets) *isn't* required. Since 2013, $1 million has been spent to renovate the facilities throughout the course and clubhouse. One of the course's more interesting features includes the several elevation changes throughout, which is a rarity in flat Florida. The course caters to golfers at all skill levels. The greens fee ranges from $45 to $110 (including cart), depending on time of year, time of day, and weekday versus weekend. ⊠ *105 Barbados Dr., Jupiter* ☎ *561/622–0036* ⊕ *www.abacoagolfclub.com* ⛳ *$100 for 18 holes* ⛳ *18 holes, 7200 yards, par 72.*

Lake Okeechobee

Forty miles west of West Palm Beach, amid the farms and cattle pastures rimming the western edges of Palm Beach and Martin counties, is **Lake Okeechobee,** the second-largest freshwater lake completely within the United States. It's girdled by 120 miles of road yet remains shielded from sight for almost its entire circumference. (The best place to view it is in Port Mayaca on the north side—where you can get great sunset shots—and the Okeechobee docks on the northwest.) Lake Okeechobee—the Seminole's "Big Water" and the gateway of the great Everglades watershed—measures 730 square miles, at its longest roughly 33 miles north–south and 30 miles east–west, with an average natural depth of only 10 feet (flood control brings the figure up to 12 feet and deeper). Six major lock systems and 32 separate water-control structures manage the water and allow boaters to cross the state through its channels from the Atlantic Ocean to the Gulf of Mexico. Encircling the lake is a 34-foot-high grassy levee that locals call "the dike," and atop it, the Lake Okeechobee Scenic Trail, a segment of the Florida National Scenic Trail that's an easy, flat ride for bikers. Anglers have a field day here as well, with great bass and perch catches. ■ TIP→ There's no shade, so wear a hat, sunscreen, and bug repellent (a must). Be sure to bring lots of bottled water, too, because restaurants and stores are few and far between.

Golf Club of Jupiter

GOLF | Locally owned and operated since 1981, this Lamar Smith–designed golf club features a public, championship golf course—the "Jupiter" course—with 18 holes of varying difficulty. It has a course rating of 69.9 and a slope rating of 117 on Bermuda grass. There's a full-time golf pro on staff and an on-site bar and restaurant. ⊠ 1800 S. Central Blvd., Jupiter ☎ 561/747–6262 ⊕ www.golfclubofjupiter.com ⊠ $59 for 18 holes ⚒. 18 holes, 6275 yards, par 70.

★ Jonathan Dickinson State Park River Tours

TOUR—SPORTS | FAMILY | Boat tours of the Loxahatchee River and guided horseback rides, along with canoe, kayak, bicycle, and boat rentals, are offered daily. The popular Wilderness Guided Boat Tour leaves four times daily at 9 and 11 am and 1 and 3 pm (for best wildlife photos take the 11 or 1 tour). The pontoon cruises for 90 minutes up the Loxahatchee in search of manatees, herons, osprey, alligators, and more. The skipper details the region's natural and cultural history; and from Thursday to Monday the boat also stops at the Trapper Nelson Interpretive Site for a tour of the home of a local legend, the so-called Wildman of the Loxahatchee. ⊠ Jonathan Dickinson State Park, 16450 S.E. U.S. 1, Hobe Sound ☎ 561/746–1466 ⊕ www.jdstatepark.com/boat-tours ⊠ $6 park admission; boat tours $20.

Roger Dean Stadium

BASEBALL/SOFTBALL | It's a spring-training doubleheader: both the St. Louis Cardinals and the Miami Marlins call this 6,600-seat facility home base from February to April. The rest of the year two minor-league teams (Jupiter Hammerheads and Palm Beach Cardinals) share its turf. In the Abacoa area of Jupiter, the grounds are surrounded by a mix of restaurants and sports bars for pre- and postgame action. ⊠ 4751 Main St., Jupiter ☎ 561/775–1818 ⊕ www.rogerdeanstadium.com ⊠ From $12.

Stuart and Jensen Beach

10 miles north of Hobe Sound.

The compact town of Stuart lies on a peninsula that juts out into the St. Lucie River off the Indian River and has a remarkable amount of shoreline for its size. It scores huge points for its charming historic district and is the self-described "Sailfish Capital of the World." On the southern end, you'll find Port Salerno and its waterfront area, the Manatee Pocket, which are a skip away from the St. Lucie Inlet.

Immediately north of Stuart is down-to-earth Jensen Beach. Both Stuart and Jensen Beach straddle the Indian River and occupy Hutchinson Island, the barrier island that continues into the town of Fort Pierce. Between late April and August, hundreds, even thousands, of turtles come here to nest along the Atlantic beaches. Residents have taken pains to curb the runaway development that has created commercial crowding to the north and south, although some high-rises have popped up along the shore.

GETTING HERE AND AROUND

To get to Stuart and Jensen Beach from Jupiter and Hobe Sound, drive north on Federal Highway (U.S. 1). Route A1A crosses through downtown Stuart and is the sole main road throughout Hutchinson Island. Route 707 runs parallel on the mainland directly across the tidal lagoon.

◉ Sights

Strict architectural and zoning standards guide civic-renewal projects in the heart of Stuart. Antiques stores, restaurants, and more than 50 specialty shops are rooted within the two-block area of Flagler Avenue and Osceola Street north of where A1A cuts across the peninsula (visit ⊕ *www.stuartmainstreet. org* for more information). A self-guided walking-tour pamphlet is available at assorted locations to clue you in on this once-small fishing village's early days.

Elliott Museum

MUSEUM | FAMILY | Opened in March 2013, the museum's glittering, green-certified, 48,000-square-foot facility is double its previous size and houses a permanent collection along with traveling exhibits. The museum was founded in 1961 in honor of Sterling Elliott, an inventor of an early automated-addressing machine, the egg crate, and a four-wheel bicycle, and it celebrates history, art, and technology, much of it viewed through the lens of the automobile's effect on American society. There's an impressive array of antique cars, plus paintings, historic artifacts, and nostalgic goods like vintage baseball cards and toys. ⊠ *825 N.E. Ocean Blvd., Jensen Beach* ☎ *772/225–1961* ⊕ *elliott-museum.org* ⌲ *$14.*

Florida Oceanographic Coastal Center

NATURE PRESERVE | FAMILY | This hydro-land is the place to go for an interactive marine experience and live the center's mission "to inspire environmental stewardship of Florida's coastal ecosystems through education and research." Petting and feeding stingrays can be done at various times; in the morning, a sea turtle program introduces you to three full-time residents. Make sure to catch the "feeding frenzy" when keepers toss food into the 750,000-gallon lagoon tank and sharks, tarpon, and snook swarm the surface. Join a 1-mile guided walk through the coastal hardwood hammock and mangrove swamp habitats, or explore the trails on your own—you may see a dolphin or manatee swim by. ⊠ *890 N.E. Ocean Blvd., Stuart* ☎ *772/225–0505* ⊕ *www.floridaocean.org* ⌲ *$12.*

Gilbert's Bar House of Refuge Museum

MUSEUM | Built in 1875 on Hutchinson Island, this is the only remaining example of 10 such structures that were erected by the U.S. Life-Saving Service (a predecessor of the Coast Guard) to

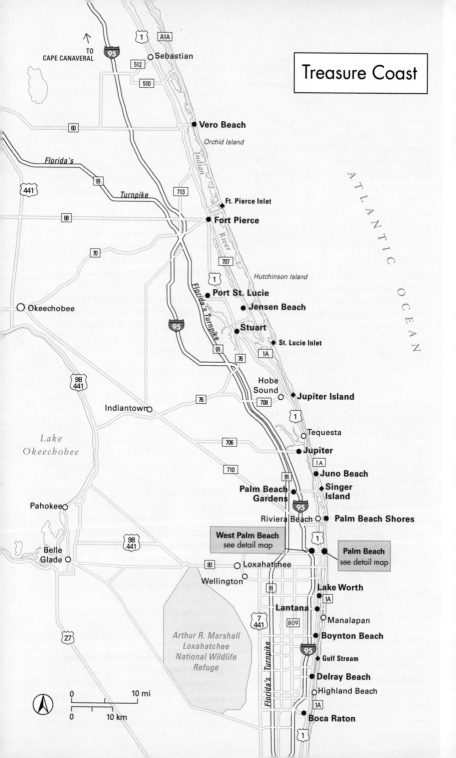

Florida's Sea Turtles: The Nesting Season

From May to October, turtles nest all along the Florida coast. Female loggerhead, Kemp's ridley, and other species living in the Atlantic Ocean or Gulf of Mexico swim as much as 2,000 miles to the Florida shore. By night they drag their 100- to 400-pound bodies onto the beach to the dune line. Then each digs a hole with her flippers, drops in 100 or so eggs, covers them up, and returns to sea.

The babies hatch about 60 days later. Once they burst out of the sand, the hatchlings must get to sea rapidly or risk becoming dehydrated from the sun or being caught by crabs, birds, or other predators.

Instinctively, baby turtles head toward bright light, probably because for millions of years starlight or moonlight reflected on the waves was the brightest light around, serving to guide hatchlings to water. Many coastal towns enforce light restrictions during nesting months. Florida homeowners are asked to dim their lights on behalf of baby sea turtles.

At night, volunteers walk the beaches, searching for signs of turtle nests. Upon finding telltale scratches in the sand, they cordon off the sites, so beachgoers will leave the spots undisturbed. (It is illegal to disturb turtle nests.) Volunteers also keep watch over nests when babies are about to hatch, and assist disoriented hatchlings.

Several local organizations offer nightly turtle walks during nesting season. Most are in June and July, starting around 8 pm and sometimes lasting until midnight. Expect a $10 to $15 fee. Call in advance to confirm times and to reserve a spot—places usually take reservations as early as April. If you're in southern Palm Beach County, contact Boca Raton's **Gumbo Limbo Nature Center** (☎ 561/338–1473 ⊕ www.gumbolimbo. org). The **John D. MacArthur Beach State Park** (☎ 561/624–6952 ⊕ www. macarthurbeach.org) is convenient for Palm Beach–area visitors at the northern end of Singer Island. **Hobe Sound Nature Center** (☎ 772/546–2067 ⊕ www.hobesoundnaturecenter.com) is farther up. Treasure Coasters in or near Vero Beach can go to **Sebastian Inlet State Park** (☎ 321/984–4852 ⊕ www.floridastateparks.org/ sebastianinlet).

aid stranded sailors. The displays here include antique lifesaving equipment, maps, artifacts from nearby wrecks, and boatbuilding tools. The museum is affiliated with the nearby Elliott Museum; package tickets are available. ⊠ 301 S.E. MacArthur Blvd., Jensen Beach ☎ 772/225–1875 ⊕ www.houseofrefuge-fl.org ☒ $8.

 Beaches

Bathtub Reef Beach

BEACH—SIGHT | FAMILY | Rough tides are often the norm in this stretch of the Atlantic Ocean, and frequently take away the beach, but a charming enclave at the southern end of Hutchinson Island—after the Marriott's beach and right by the Indian River Plantation luxury development—provides a perfect escape for families with young children and anyone who likes to snorkel. The waters are shallow and usually calm, and youngsters can walk up to the reef and see a dazzling assortment of fish. The parking lot is small, so get there early. Erosion is a problem, and sometimes lifeguards can't pull their hefty chairs out, leaving the beach unguarded (but it shouldn't deter you, because the sea isn't rough). **Amenities:** parking (no fee); lifeguards; toilets. **Best for:** snorkeling; swimming. ✉ *1585 S.E. MacArthur Blvd., Stuart* ☎ *772/320–3112* 🌐 *www.martin.fl.us/BathtubReefBeach.*

Stuart Beach

BEACH—SIGHT | **FAMILY** | When the waves robustly roll in, the surfers are rolling in, too. Beginning surfers are especially keen on Stuart Beach because of its ever-vigilant lifeguards, and pros to the sport like the challenges that the choppy waters here bring. But the beach is equally popular with surf fishers. Families enjoy the snack bar known for its chicken fingers, the basketball courts, the large canopy-covered playground, and the three walkways interspersed throughout the area for easy ocean access. **Amenities:** food and drink; lifeguards; parking (no fee); showers; toilets. **Best for:** surfing; swimming. ✉ *889 N.E. Ocean Blvd., Stuart* 🌐 *www.stuartfla.com/stuart/article/stuart-beach.*

🍴 Restaurants

11 Maple Street

$$$$ | **ECLECTIC** | This cozy spot is as good as it gets on the Treasure Coast. Soft music and a friendly staff set the mood in the antiques-filled dining room of this old house, which holds only 21 tables. **Known for:** nice selection of wines; good desserts; Old Florida setting in vintage house. [$] *Average main: $42* ✉ *3224 N.E. Maple Ave., Jensen Beach* ☎ *772/334–7714* 🌐 *www.elevenmaple.com* 🕓 *Closed Sun. and Mon. No lunch.*

Conchy Joe's

$$$ | **SEAFOOD** | Like a hermit crab sliding into a new shell, Conchy Joe's moved up from West Palm Beach in 1983 to its current home, a 1920s rustic stilt house on the Indian River. It's full of antique fish mounts, gator hides, and snakeskins, and is a popular tourist spot—but the waterfront location, very casual vibe, and delicious seafood lures locals, too. **Known for:** conch chowder; grouper marsala; live reggae Thursday–Sunday. [$] *Average main: $27* ✉ *3945 N.E. Indian River Dr., Jensen Beach* ☎ *772/334–1130* 🌐 *www.conchyjoes.com.*

District Table and Bar

$$$ | **SOUTHERN** | Farm-fresh foods with a Southern accent are served up at this chef-owned restaurant with a theater kitchen, where comfort foods are taken to new levels. (Slow Foods, a group that celebrates local foods and artisans, has given the restaurant a "Snail of Approval.") **Known for:** farm-to-table menu; lively bar scene; everything homemade, including condiments and jams. [$] *Average main: $23* ✉ *900 S.E. Indian St., Stuart* ☎ *772/324–8357* 🌐 *www.districttableandbar.com* 🕓 *Closed Mon.*

11 Maple Street

$$$$ | **ECLECTIC** | This cozy spot is as good as it gets on the Treasure Coast. Soft music and a friendly staff set the mood in the antiques-filled dining room of this old house, which holds only 21 tables. **Known for:** nice selection of wines; good desserts; Old Florida setting in vintage house. [$] *Average main: $42* ✉ *3224 N.E. Maple Ave., Jensen Beach* ☎ *772/334–7714* 🌐 *www.elevenmaple.com* 🕓 *Closed Sun. and Mon. No lunch.*

Ian's Tropical Grill

$$$ | **SEAFOOD** | Tucked inside a small plaza, the restaurant has a small, cozy dining room and covered alfresco patio. The menu changes often, depending on what's fresh in the markets and from local farms, which are named. **Known for:** fresh Florida seafood; primarily locally sourced ingredients; inventive cocktails. [$] *Average main: $25* ✉ *2875 S.E. Ocean*

Blvd., Stuart ☎ *772/334–4563* 🌐 *www.ianstropicalgrill.com* ⏰ *Closed Sun.*

Talk House

$$$ | FRENCH | Formerly known as Courtine's, Talk House changed hands in 2018 but kept much of the menu and staff. French and American influences are clear in the Swiss chef's dishes, from rack of lamb with Dijon mustard to grilled filet mignon stuffed with Roquefort and fresh spinach. **Known for:** refined Continental cuisine; elegant atmosphere; more casual bar menu. [$] *Average main: $25* ✉ *514 N. Dixie Hwy., Stuart* ☎ *772/692–3662* 🌐 *stuartstalkhouse.com* ⏰ *Closed Mon. No lunch.*

Hotels

Hutchinson Island Marriott Beach Resort & Marina

$$ | RESORT | FAMILY | With a 77-slip marina, a full water-sports program, a golf course, two pools, tons of tennis courts, and children's activities, this self-contained resort is excellent for families, most of whom prefer to stay in the tower directly on the ocean. **Pros:** attentive, warm staff; rooms are comfortable and casually chic; all rooms have balconies. **Cons:** only one sit-down indoor restaurant; common areas are a bit dated; no spa; daily resort fee. [$] *Rooms from: $230* ✉ *555 N.E. Ocean Blvd., Stuart* ☎ *772/225–3700, 800/775–5936* 🌐 *www.marriott.com/hotels/travel/pbiir-hutchinson-island-marriott-beach-resort-and-marina* 🛏 *274 rooms* 🍴 *No meals.*

Pirate's Cove Resort & Marina

$ | RESORT | This cozy enclave on the banks of the Manatee Pocket with ocean access at the southern end of Stuart is the perfect place to set forth on a day at sea or wind down after one—it's relaxing and casual, and has amenities like a swimming-pool courtyard, restaurant, and fitness center. **Pros:** spacious tropical-themed rooms; great for boaters, with a 50-slip, full-service, deepwater marina; each room has a balcony overlooking the water; free Wi-Fi and parking. **Cons:** lounge gets noisy at night; decor and furnishings are pretty but not luxurious; pool is on the small side. [$] *Rooms from: $150* ✉ *4307 S.E. Bayview St., Port Salerno* ☎ *772/287–2500* 🌐 *www.piratescoveresort.com* 🛏 *50 rooms* 🍴 *No meals.*

Shopping

More than 60 restaurants and shops with antiques, art, and fashion draw visitors downtown along Osceola Street.

B&A Flea Market

OUTDOOR/FLEA/GREEN MARKETS | A short drive from downtown and operating for more than two decades, the oldest and largest weekend-only flea market on the Treasure Coast has a street-bazaar feel, with shoppers happily scouting the 500 vendors for the practical and unusual. A produce market carries local tropical fruits and vegetables. If you have an open mind and love to shop garage sales, you'll do just fine here. ✉ *2885 S.E. U.S. 1, Stuart* ☎ *772/288–4915* 🌐 *www.bafleamarket.com* 🎟 *Free.*

Activities

***Island Princess* Cruises**

BOAT TOURS | Cruise the Indian River and St. Lucie River as well as Jupiter Sound aboard the *Island Princess,* an 82-footer that docks at the Sailfish Marina in Stuart. In season, there are nature cruises and cruises that go through the St. Lucie River locks. Have lunch during their Jupiter Island cruise, embarking Tuesday and weekends year-round. The schedule, which changes often, is posted on the company's website. All ages are welcome, and advance reservations are required. ✉ *Sailfish Marina, 3585 S.E. St. Lucie Blvd., Stuart* ☎ *772/225–2100* 🌐 *www.islandprincesscruises.com* 🎟 *Cruises from $28.*

Sailfish Marina of Stuart

FISHING | Nab a deep-sea charter here to land a sailfish, a popular sport fish that is prolific off the St. Lucie Inlet. This is the closest public marina to the St. Lucie Inlet. Recently expanded, it is home to *Island Princess* Cruises, which takes visitors to Vero Beach or Jupiter via the Intracoastal Waterway. ⊠ *3565 S.E. St. Lucie Blvd., Stuart* ☎ *772/283–1122* ⊕ *www.sailfishmarinastuart.com.*

Fort Pierce and Port St. Lucie

11 miles north of Jensen Beach.

About an hour north of Palm Beach, Fort Pierce has a distinctive rural feel—but it has a surprising number of worthwhile attractions for a town of its size, including those easily seen while following Route 707 on the mainland (A1A on Hutchinson Island). The downtown is expanding, and sports new theater revivals, restaurants, and shops. A big draw is an inlet that offers fabulous fishing and excellent surfing. Nearby Port St. Lucie is largely landlocked southwest of Fort Pierce and is almost equidistant from there and Jensen Beach. It's not a big tourist area except for two sports facilities near Interstate 95: the St. Lucie Mets' training grounds, Tradition Field, and the PGA Village. If you want a hotel directly on the sand or crave more than simple, motel-like accommodations, stay elsewhere and drive up for the day.

GETTING HERE AND AROUND

You can reach Fort Pierce from Jensen Beach by driving 11 miles north on Federal Highway (U.S. 1), Route 707, or Route A1A. To get to Port St. Lucie, continue north on U.S. 1 and take Prima Vista Boulevard west. From Fort Pierce, Route 709 goes diagonally southwest to Port St. Lucie, and Interstate 95 is another choice.

VISITOR INFORMATION St. Lucie County Tourist Development Council. ⊠ *2300 Virginia Ave., Fort Pierce* ☎ *800/344–8443* ⊕ *www.visitstluciefla.com.*

Sights

Heathcote Botanical Gardens

GARDEN | Stroll through this 3½-acre green space, which includes a palm walk, a Japanese garden, and a collection of 100 bonsai trees. There is also a gift shop with whimsical and botanical knickknacks. Guided tours are available by appointment for an extra fee. ⊠ *210 Savannah Rd., Fort Pierce* ☎ *772/464–0323* ⊕ *www.heathcotebotanicalgardens.org* ⊠ *$6* ⊙ *Closed Mon.*

National Navy UDT-SEAL Museum

MILITARY SITE | **FAMILY** | Commemorating the more than 3,000 troops who trained on these shores during World War II when this elite military unit got its start, there are weapons, vehicles, and equipment on view. Exhibits honor all frogmen and underwater demolition teams and depict their history. The museum houses the lifeboat from which SEALs saved the *Maersk Alabama* captain from Somali pirates in 2009. Kids get a thrill out of the helicopters and aircraft on the grounds. ⊠ *3300 N. Rte. A1A, Fort Pierce* ☎ *772/595–5845* ⊕ *www.navysealmuseum.com* ⊠ *$15* ⊙ *Closed Mon.*

Savannas Recreation Area

NATURE PRESERVE | **FAMILY** | Once a reservoir, the 550 acres have been returned to their natural wetlands state. Today the wilderness area has campgrounds, interpretive trails, and a boat ramp, and the recreation area is open year-round. Canoe and kayak rentals are available Thursday through Monday. A dog park (open daily) is also on-site. Amenities include showers, toilets, and free Wi-Fi for campers. ⊠ *1400 E. Midway Rd., Fort Pierce* ☎ *772/464–7855* ⊕ *www.stlucieco.gov/*

parks/savannas.htm 🎟 *Free; $25.25 for campers (full service).*

Beaches

Fort Pierce Inlet State Park

BEACH—SIGHT | Across the inlet at the northern side of Hutchinson Island, a fishing oasis lures beachgoers who can't wait to reel in snook, flounder, and bluefish, among others. The park is also known as a prime wave-riding locale, thanks to a reef that lies just outside the jetty. Summer is the busiest season by a long shot, but don't be fooled: it's a laid-back place to sun and surf. There are covered picnic tables but no concessions; however, from where anglers perch, a bunch of casual restaurants can be spotted on the other side of the inlet that are a quick drive away. Note that the area of Jack Island Preserve has been closed indefinitely. **Amenities:** lifeguards (summer only); parking (fee); showers; toilets. **Best for:** solitude; surfing; walking. ✉ *905 Shorewinds Dr., Fort Pierce* ☎ *772/468–3985* 🌐 *www.floridastateparks.org/parks-and-trails/fort-pierce-inlet-state-park* 🎟 *Vehicle $6, bicyclists and pedestrians $2.*

Hotels

Dockside Inn

$ | **HOTEL** | This hotel is the best of the lodgings lining the scenic Fort Pierce Inlet on Seaway Drive (and that's not saying much); it's a practical base for fishing enthusiasts with nice touches like two pools and a waterfront restaurant. **Pros:** good value; overnight boat docking available; reasonable rates at marina; parking included. **Cons:** basic decor; some steps to climb; grounds are nothing too fancy but have great views. [$] *Rooms from: $125* ✉ *1160 Seaway Dr., Fort Pierce* ☎ *772/468–3555, 800/286–1745* 🌐 *www.docksideinn.com* 🔑 *36 rooms* 🍴 *No meals.*

Activities

The region's premier dive site is actually on the National Register of Historic Places. The *Urca de Lima* was part of the storied treasure fleet bound for Spain that was destroyed by a hurricane in 1715. It's now part of an underwater archaeological preserve about 200 yards from shore, just north of the National Navy UDT-SEAL Museum and under 10 to 15 feet of water. The remains contain a flat-bottom, round-bellied ship and cannons that can be visited on an organized dive trip.

Dive Odyssea

SCUBA DIVING | This full-service dive shop offers kayak rentals, tank rentals, and scuba lessons. The shop can arrange a scuba charter in Jupiter or Palm Beach (two-tank dive trips typically start at $65), but Dive Odyssea no longer offers dive trips of its own. ✉ *Fort Pierce Inlet, 621 N. 2nd St., Fort Pierce* ☎ *772/460–1771* 🌐 *www.diveodyssea.com.*

First Data Field

BASEBALL/SOFTBALL | Out west by Interstate 95, this Port St. Lucie baseball stadium, formerly known as Tradition Field, is where the New York Mets train; it's also the home of the St. Lucie Mets minor-league team. ✉ *525 N.W. Peacock Blvd., Port St. Lucie* ☎ *772/871–2115* 🌐 *www.milb.com/st-lucie.*

PGA Village

GOLF | Owned and operated by the PGA of America, the national association of teaching pros, PGA Village is the winter home to many Northern instructors, along with permanent staff. The facility is a little off the beaten path and the clubhouse is basic, but serious golfers will appreciate the three championship courses by Pete Dye and Tom Fazio and the chance to sharpen their skills at the 35-acre PGA Center for Golf Learning and Performance, which has nine practice bunkers mimicking sands and slopes from around the globe. Between the Fazio-designed Wanamaker Course, the

Ryder Course, and the Dye-designed Dye Course, there are 54 holes of championship golf at PGA Village. Also affiliated is the nearby St. Lucie Trail Golf Club, another Fazio design. Beginners can start out on the lesser known (and easier) 6-hole PGA Short Course. Holes are 35 to 60 yards each, and course play is free. ⊠ *1916 Perfect Dr., Port St. Lucie* ☎ *772/467–1300, 800/800–4653* ⊕ *www.pgavillage.com* ✉ *Wanamaker Course $131; Ryder Course $131; Dye Course $131; St. Lucie Trail Golf Club $89* ⚑. *Wanamaker Course: 18 holes, 7123 yards, par 72; Ryder Course: 18 holes, 7037 yards, par 72; Dye Course: 18 holes, 7279 yards, par 72; St. Lucie Golf Club Trail Course: 18 holes, 6901 yards, par 72.*

Vero Beach

12 miles north of Fort Pierce.

Tranquil and picturesque, this upscale Indian River County town has a strong commitment to the environment and culture, and it's also home to eclectic galleries and trendy restaurants. Downtown Vero is centered on the historic district on 14th Avenue, but much of the fun takes place across the Indian River (aka the Intracoastal Waterway) around Orchid Island's beaches. It was once home to the Dodgers Spring Training base, and there's still a strong affinity for baseball here, and it's kid-friendly, with the former Dodgertown Stadium hosting Little League tournaments, and plenty of parks around. Its western edges still are home to cattlemen and citrus growers, so there is a juxtaposition of country and gentry.

GETTING HERE AND AROUND

To get here, you have two basic options: Route A1A along the coast (not to be confused with Ocean Drive, an offshoot on Orchid Island), or either U.S. 1 or Route 605 (also called Old Dixie Highway) on the mainland. As you approach

Vero on the latter, you pass through an ungussied-up landscape of small farms and residential areas. On the beach route, part of the drive bisects an unusually undeveloped section of the Florida coast. If flying in, consider Orlando International Airport, which is larger and a smidge closer than Palm Beach International Airport.

VISITOR INFORMATION

CONTACTS Indian River County Chamber of Commerce. ⊠ *1216 21st St.* ☎ *772/567–3491* ⊕ *www.indianriverchamber.com.*

Sights

Environmental Learning Center

NATURE PRESERVE | Off Wabasso Beach Road, the 64 acres here are almost completely surrounded by water. In addition to a 600-foot boardwalk through the mangrove shoreline and a 1-mile canoe trail, there are aquariums filled with Indian River creatures. Boat and kayak trips to see the historic Pelican Island rookery are on offer along with guided nature walks and touch-tank encounters. Call or check the center's website for times. ⊠ *255 Live Oak Dr.* ☎ *772/589–5050* ⊕ *www. discoverelc.org* ✉ *$5* ⊗ *Closed Mon.*

★ McKee Botanical Garden

GARDEN | On the National Register of Historic Places, the 18-acre plot is a tropical jungle garden—one of the most lush and serene around. This is *the* place to see spectacular water lilies, and the property's original 1932 Hall of Giants, a rustic wooden structure that has stained-glass and bronze bells, contains what is claimed to be the world's largest single-plank mahogany table at 35 feet long. There's a Seminole bamboo pavilion, a gift shop, and café (open for lunch Tuesday through Saturday, and Sunday in season), which serves especially tasty snacks and sandwiches. ⊠ *350 U.S. 1* ☎ *772/794–0601* ⊕ *www.mckeegarden. org* ✉ *$12* ⊗ *Closed Mon.*

Pelican Island National Wildlife Refuge

NATURE PRESERVE | Founded in 1903 by President Theodore Roosevelt as the country's first national wildlife refuge, the park encompasses the historic Pelican Island rookery itself—a small island in the Indian River lagoon and important nesting place for 16 species of birds such as endangered wood storks and, of course, brown pelicans—and the land surrounding it overlooking Sebastian. The rookery is a closed wilderness area, so there's no roaming alongside animal kingdom friends; however, there is an 18-foot observation tower across from it with direct views and more than 6 miles of nature trails in the refuge. Another way to explore is via guided kayak tours from the Florida Outdoor Center. Make sure to bring a camera—it's a photographer's dream. ☒ Rte. A1A ✢ 1 mile north of Treasure Shores Park. Take A1A and turn on Historic Jungle Trail ☎ 772/581–5557 ⊕ www.fws.gov/pelicanisland 🖼 Free.

Beaches

Most of the hotels in the Vero Beach area are clustered around South Beach Park or line Ocean Drive around Beachland Boulevard just north of Humiston Park. Humiston Park is smack-dab in the main commercial zone with restaurants galore, including the lauded Citrus Grillhouse at its southern tip.

Humiston Park

BEACH—SIGHT | Just south of the Driftwood Resort on Ocean Drive sits Humiston Park, one of the best beaches in town. Parking is free and plentiful, as there's a large lot on Easter Lily Lane and there are spots all over the surrounding business district. The shore is somewhat narrow and there isn't much shade, but the vibrant scene and other amenities make it a great choice for people who crave lots of activity. With lifeguards on call daily, there's a children's playground, plus a ton of hotels, restaurants, bars, and shops within walking distance.

Amenities: food and drink; lifeguards; showers; toilets. **Best for:** partiers; sunsets; swimming; walking. ☒ 3000 Ocean Dr., at Easter Lily La. ☎ 772/231–5790.

★ Sebastian Inlet State Park

BEACH—SIGHT | FAMILY | The 1,000-acre park, which runs from the tip of Orchid Island across the passage to the barrier island just north, is one of the Florida park system's biggest draws, especially because of the inlet's highly productive fishing waters. Views from either side of the tall bridge are spectacular, and a unique hallmark is that the gates never close—an amazing feature for die-hard anglers who know snook bite better at night. Two jetties are usually packed with fishers and spectators alike. The park has two entrances, the entrance in Vero Beach and the main entrance in Melbourne (9700 Rte. A1A). Within its grounds, you'll discover a wonderful two-story restaurant that overlooks the ocean, a fish and surfing shop (by the way, this place has some of the best waves in the state, but there are also calmer zones for relaxing swims), two museums, guided sea turtle walks in season, 51 campsites with water and electricity, and a marina with powerboat, kayak, and canoe rentals. **Amenities:** food and drink; parking (fee); showers; toilets; water sports. **Best for:** sunrise; sunset; surfing; walking. ☒ 14251 N. Rte. A1A ☎ 321/984–4852 ⊕ www.floridastateparks.org/parks-and-trails/sebastian-inlet-state-park 🖼 $8 vehicles with up to 8 people, $4 single drivers, $2 bicyclists and pedestrians.

Wabasso Beach Park

BEACH—SIGHT | FAMILY | A favorite for local surfboarding teens and the families at the nearby Disney's Vero Beach Resort, the park is nestled in a residential area at the end of Wabasso Road, about 8 miles up from the action on Ocean Drive and 8 miles below the Sebastian Inlet. Aside from regular amenities like picnic tables, restrooms, and a dedicated parking lot

(which really is the "park" here—there's not much green space—and it's quite small, so arrive early), the Disney crowd walks there for its lifeguards (the strip directly in front of the hotel is unguarded) and the local crowd appreciates its conveniences, like a pizzeria and a store that sells sundries, snacks, and beach supplies. **Amenities:** food and drink; lifeguards; parking (no fee); showers; toilets. **Best for:** surfing; swimming. ✉ *1820 Wabasso Rd.*

🍴 Restaurants

The Lemon Tree

$ | **DINER** | **FAMILY** | If Italy had old-school luncheonettes, this is what they'd look like: a storefront of yellow walls, dark-green booths, white linoleum tables, and cascading sconces of faux ivy leaves and hand-painted Tuscan serving pieces for artwork. It's self-described by the husband-and-wife owners (who are always at the front) as an "upscale diner," and locals swear by it for breakfast (served all day) and lunch. **Known for:** shrimp scampi; treats on the house; waits during the high season. [$] *Average main: $11* ✉ *3125 Ocean Dr.* ☎ *772/231-0858* 🌐 *www.lemontreevero.com* 🕓 *No lunch or dinner Sun. No dinner June–Sept.*

Ocean Grill

$$$ | **SEAFOOD** | Opened in 1941, this family-owned Old Florida–style restaurant combines its ocean view with Tiffany-style lamps, wrought-iron chandeliers, and paintings of pirates. Count on at least three kinds of seafood any day on the menu, along with steaks, pork chops, soups, and salads. **Known for:** just OK food; great drinks; the Pusser's Painkiller. [$] *Average main: $28* ✉ *1050 Beachland Blvd.* ☎ *772/231–5409* 🌐 *www.ocean-grill.com* 🕓 *Closed 2 wks around Labor Day. No lunch Sun.*

★ The Tides

$$$ | **ECLECTIC** | A charming cottage restaurant west of Ocean Drive prepares some of the best food around—not just in Vero Beach, but all of South Florida. The chefs, classically trained, give a nod to international fare with disparate dishes such as tuna tataki, Asian-inspired carpaccio with satay, penne *quattro formaggi,* and classic lobster bisque. **Known for:** fresh Florida fish; jumbo crab cakes with corn-and-pepper sauce; chef's table with wine pairings. [$] *Average main: $29* ✉ *3103 Cardinal Dr.* ☎ *772/234–3966* 🌐 *www.tidesofvero.com* 🕓 *No lunch.*

🛏 Hotels

★ Costa d'Este Beach Resort

$ | **RESORT** | This stylish, contemporary boutique hotel in the heart of Vero's bustling Ocean Drive area has a gorgeous infinity pool overlooking the ocean and a distinctly Miami Beach vibe—just like its famous owners, singer Gloria Estefan and producer Emilio Estefan, who bought the property in 2004. **Pros:** all rooms have balconies or secluded patios; huge Italian marble showers; complimentary signature mojitos on arrival. **Cons:** spa is on small side; rooms have only blackout shades; daily resort fee. [$] *Rooms from: $139* ✉ *3244 Ocean Dr.* ☎ *772/562–9919* 🌐 *www.costadeste.com* 🔑 *94 rooms* 🍽 *No meals.*

Disney's Vero Beach Resort

$$$ | **RESORT** | **FAMILY** | This oceanfront, family-oriented retreat tucked away in a residential stretch of Orchid Island has a retro Old Florida design and not too much Mickey Mouse, which is a welcome surprise for adults. **Pros:** a great pool with waterslide and kiddie splash pool; campfire circle; several dining options on property. **Cons:** far from shopping and dining options; minimal Disney-themed decor. [$] *Rooms from: $365* ✉ *9250 Island Grove Terr.* ☎ *772/234–2000, 407/939–7540* 🌐 *www.disneybeachresorts.com/vero-beach-resort/* 🔑 *181 rooms* 🍽 *No meals.*

The Driftwood Resort

$ | **RESORT** | **FAMILY** | On the National Register of Historic Places, the two original buildings of this 1935 inn were built entirely from ocean-washed timbers with no blueprints; over time more buildings were added, and all are now decorated with such artifacts as ship's bells, Spanish tiles, a cannon from a 16th-century Spanish galleon, and plenty of wrought iron, which create a quirky, utterly charming landscape. **Pros:** central location and right on the beach; free Wi-Fi; laundry facilities; weekly treasure hunt is a blast. **Cons:** older property; rooms can be musty; no-frills furnishings. $ *Rooms from: $150* ⊠ *3150 Ocean Dr.* ☎ *772/231–0550* ⊕ *www.verobeachdriftwood.com* ⚑ *100 rooms* ¶⊙¶ *No meals.*

★ Vero Beach Hotel & Spa

$$ | **RESORT** | **FAMILY** | With a sophisticated, relaxed British West Indies feel, this luxurious five-story beachfront hotel at the north end of Ocean Drive is an inviting getaway and, arguably, the best on the Treasure Coast. **Pros:** beautiful pool; complimentary daily wine hour with hors d'oeuvres. **Cons:** separate charge for valet parking; some rooms overlook parking lot. $ *Rooms from: $299* ⊠ *3500 Ocean Dr.* ☎ *772/231–5666* ⊕ *www. verobeachhotelandspa.com* ⚑ *102 rooms* ¶⊙¶ *No meals.*

Shopping

The place to go when in Vero Beach is **Ocean Drive.** Crossing over to Orchid Island from the mainland, the Merrill P. Barber Bridge turns into Beachland Boulevard; its intersection with Ocean Drive is the heart of a commercial zone with a lively mix of upscale clothing stores, specialty shops, restaurants, and art galleries.

Just under 3 miles north of that roughly eight-block stretch on A1A is a charming outdoor plaza, the **Village Shops.** It's a delight to stroll between the brightly painted cottages that have more unique, high-end offerings.

Back on the mainland, take 21st Street westward and you'll come across a small, modern shopping plaza with some independent shops and national chains. Keep going west on 21st Street, and then park around 14th Avenue to explore a collection of art galleries and eateries in the historic downtown.

Exclusively Coastal

CRAFTS | Stop here for lovely handcrafted goods inspired by the sea, many by local artisans. Choose from jewelry, candles, gifts for kids, home decor items, and artwork. ⊠ *3119 Ocean Dr.* ☎ *772/234–4790* ⊕ *exclusivelycoastal.com.*

Maison Beach

GIFTS/SOUVENIRS | Formerly called Christine, the owner changed the name of this cute shop and moved to Pelican Plaza. It still is *the* place to find gorgeous hostess and dining entertainment gifts like Mariposa napkin holders, Julia Knight bowls, and Michael Aram picture frames, along with trendy Mudpie household ware. ⊠ *Pelican Plaza, 4895 Hwy. A1A* ☎ *772/492–0383* ⊕ *maisonbeach.myshopify.com.*

Sassy Boutique

CLOTHING | One of the chicest spots in town sells bright, punchy, and pretty women's designer fashions such as Tory Burch, Kate Spade New York, Kenneth Jay Lane, Stacia, and Nanette Lepore. ⊠ *3375 Ocean Dr.* ☎ *772/234–3998* ⊕ *www.sassyboutique.com.*

Vero Beach Outlets

OUTLET/DISCOUNT STORES | Need some retail therapy? Just west of Interstate 95 off Route 60 is a discount shopping destination with 50 high-end brand-name stores, including Ann Taylor, Calvin Klein, Christopher & Banks, Dooney & Bourke, Polo Ralph Lauren, Restoration Hardware, and White House/Black Market. ⊠ *1824 94th Dr.* ✦ *On Rte. 60, west*

of I–95 at Exit 147 ☏ *772/770–6097*
⊕ *www.verobeachoutlets.com.*

 ## Activities

Sandridge Golf Club

GOLF | The Sandridge Golf Club features two public 18-hole courses designed by Ron Garl: the Dunes course, with 6 holes located on a sand ridge; and the Lakes course, named for—you guessed it—the ubiquitous lakes around the course. The Dunes course, opened in 1987, follows a history-steeped pathway once used during mining operations. The Lakes course, opened in 1992, is renowned for the very challenging, par-4 14th hole with an island green. There's a pro shop on-site offering lessons and clinics. Florida and Indian River County residents can get membership cards to book tee times eight days out—and get discounts for play. ⊠ *5300 73rd St.* ☏ *772/770–5000* ⊕ *www.sandridgegc.com* 🗟 *$50 for 18 holes with cart* 🏌 *Dunes course: 18 holes, 6817 yards, par 72; Lakes course: 18 holes, 6181 yards, par 72.*

Index

Photo Credits

Front Cover: Tono Balaguer / age fotostock [Description: Miami Beach Ocean Boulevard Art Deco District in Florida, USA.] Back cover, from left to right: Chuck Wagner/Shutterstock; Tap10/Shutterstock; ShaneKato/iStockphoto. Spine: Michael Phillips/iStockphoto. Interior, from left to right: James A. Harris/Shutterstock (1). Mia2you/Shutterstock (2-3). PBorowka/Shutterstock (5). **Chapter 1**: Experience South Florida: S.Borisov/Shutterstock (6-7). Sean Pavone/Shutterstock (8-9). Art Deco Tours (9). CK Ma/Shutterstock (9). William Rodrigues Dos Santos | Dreamstime.com (10). Pola Damonte/Shutterstock (10). Juneisy Q. Hawkins/Shutterstock (11). Romrodphoto/Shutterstock (12). Courtesy Miami Design District (12). Ball & Chain/Michael Strader Marko (12). Courtesy of Hemingway Home (12). Courtesy of Miami Dolphins (13). Sean Pavone/Shutterstock (13). comeirrez/Shutterstock (16). Olyina/Shutterstock (16). voloshin311/Shutterstock (16). Hunt Consulting/Shutterstock (16). bonchan/Shutterstock (17). norikko/Shutterstock (17). Andrew Meade (17). Neosiam | Dreamstime.com (17). Alexander Demyanenko/Shutterstock (18). Kamira/Shutterstock (18). Luke Popwell | Dreamstime.com (18). Simon Dannhauer/Shutterstock (19). Dmitry Vinogradov | Dreamstime.com (19). Courteesy of Art Basel `(20). Richard Goldberg/Shutterstock (20). Zachary Balber/Courtesy of The Bass, Miami Beach (20). Wangkun Jia/Shutterstock (20). Felix Mizioznikov | Dreamstime.com (21). Daniel Bock/Courtesy of Museum of Contemporary Art North Miami (MOCA) (21). Oriol Tarridas Photography (21). Comayagua99/Wikimedia.org (21). **Chapter 3**: Miami and Miami Beach: pisaphotography/Shutterstock (35). Roxana Gonzalez/Shutterstock (38). Alena Haurylik / Shutterstock (39). Jupiterimages/Brand X/Alamy (39). dk / Alamy (67). Nicholas Pitt / Alamy (67). Nicholas Pitt / Alamy (69). Ryan Forbes / Avablu (69). Nicholas Pitt / Alamy (69). Ryan Forbes / AVABLU (69). Tinamou | Dreamstime.com (69). Ian Patrick / Alamy (70). Interfoto Pressebildagentur / Alamy (70). culliganphoto / Alamy (70). Garth Aikens/Miami Beach Convention Center (71). Robert Harding Picture Library Ltd / Alamy (82). John Tunney | Dreamstime.com (92). photravel_ru/Shutterstock (104). **Chapter 4**: The Everglades: Brian Lasenby/Shutterstock (107). tbkmedia.de / Alamy (112-113). inga spence / Alamy (116). FloridaStock/Shutterstock (116). Andrewtappert (116). David R. Frazier Photolibrary, Inc. / Alamy (116). wikimedia.org (116). Larsek/Shutterstock (117). Caleb Foster/Shutterstock (117). mlorenz/Shutterstock (117). umar faruq/Shutterstock (117). Peter Arnold, Inc. / Alamy (117). John A. Anderson/Shutterstock (118). Norman Bateman/Shutterstock (118). FloridaStock/Shutterstock (118). FloridaStock/Shutterstock (118). David Drake & Deborah Jaffe (119). Krzysztof Slusarczyk/Shutterstock (119). Norman Bateman/Shutterstock (119). Jerry Zitterman/Shutterstock (119). Steven Widoff / Alamy (126). Marc Muench / Alamy (130). jimfeng (134). Visit Florida (139). **Chapter 5**: The Florida Keys: Romrodphoto/Shutterstock (143). Gregory Wrona / Alamy (146). Claudio Lovo/Shutterstock (147). Michael Ventura / Alamy (147). Stephen Frink/ Florida Keys News Bureau (155). flasporty/Flickr, [CC BY-ND 2.0] (162). Korzeniewski | Dreamstime.com (167). PBorowka/Shutterstock (169). Melissa Schalke/iStockphoto (171). Henryk Sadura / Alamy (178). CedarBendDrive/Flickr, [CC BY-ND 2.0] (189). Visit Florida (191). John P Franzis (193). Starwood Hotels & Resorts (205). Daniel Korzeniewski / Shutterstock (207). **Chapter 6**: Fort Lauderdale: Kamira/Shutterstock (215). Sean Pavone/Shutterstock (231). Pola Damonte/Shutterstock (234). Lago Mar Resort & Club (236). Fotoluminate LLC (248). **Chapter 7**: Palm Beach and the Treasure Coast: Pola Damonte/Shutterstock (251). Sargent Photography (257). mrk_photo/Flickr, [CC BY-ND 2.0]. (269). FloridaStock/Shutterstock (277). EdwinWilke/Shutterstock (281). FloridaStock/Shutterstock (292). Visit Florida (306). About Our Writers: All photos are courtesy of the writers except for the following: Galena Mosovich, Courtesy of ra-haus fotografie, LLC.

Every effort has been made to trace the copyright holders, and we apologize in advance for any accidental errors. We would be happy to apply the corrections in the following edition of this publication.

Notes

Notes

Fodor's SOUTH FLORIDA

Publisher: Stephen Horowitz, *General Manager*

Editorial: Douglas Stallings, *Editorial Director*; Margaret Kelly, Jacinta O'Halloran, Amanda Sadlowski, *Senior Editors*; Kayla Becker, Alexis Kelly, Teddy Minford, Rachael Roth, *Editors*

Design: Tina Malaney, *Design and Production Director*; Jessica Gonzalez, *Graphic Designer*; Mariana Tabares, *Design & Production Intern*

Production: Jennifer DePrima, *Editorial Production Manager*; Carrie Parker, *Senior Production Editor*; Elyse Rozelle, *Production Editor*; Jackson Pranica, *Editorial Production Assistant*

Maps: Rebecca Baer, *Senior Map Editor*; David Lindroth, Mark Stroud (Moon Street Cartography), *Cartographers*

Photography: Jill Krueger, *Director of Photo*; Namrata Aggarwal, Ashok Kumar, Carl Yu, *Photo Editors*; Rebecca Rimmer, *Photo Intern*

Business & Operations: Chuck Hoover, *Chief Marketing Officer*; Robert Ames, *Group General Manager*; Tara McCrillis, *Director of Publishing Operations*; Victor Bernal, *Business Analyst*

Public Relations and Marketing: Joe Ewaskiw, *Senior Director Communications & Public Relations*; Esther Su, *Senior Marketing Manager*; Ryan Garcia, Thomas Talarico, Miranda Villalobos, *Marketing Specialists*

Fodors.com Jeremy Tarr, *Editorial Director*; Rachael Levitt, *Managing Editor*

Technology: Jon Atkinson, *Director of Technology*; Rudresh Teotia, *Lead Developer*; Jacob Ashpis, *Content Operations Manager*

Writers: Sara Liss, Jill Martin, Galena Mosovich, Lane Nieset, Paul Rubio

Editor: Kayla Becker

Production Editor: Carrie Parker

15th Edition

ISBN 978-1-64097-142-4

ISSN 1526–2219

Library of Congress Control Number 2018914621

All details in this book are based on information supplied to us at press time. Always confirm information when it matters, especially if you're making a detour to visit a specific place. Fodor's expressly disclaims any liability, loss, or risk, personal or otherwise, that is incurred as a consequence of the use of any of the contents of this book.

SPECIAL SALES
This book is available at special discounts for bulk purchases for sales promotions or premiums. For more information, e-mail SpecialMarkets@fodors.com.

PRINTED IN THE UNITED STATES OF AMERICA

10 9 8 7 6 5 4 3 2 1

About Our Writers

Sara Liss has been a freelancer for lifestyle publications for more than 10 years. She served as founding editor of UrbanDaddy Miami is now the Senior Food Writer at Miami.com. Her main beat is food but she dabbles in travel and design writing and has started Saffron Supper Club, a roving Middle-Eastern culinary experience and Friday Beach, a neighborhood celebration that happens in her town of Surfside. Her current outlets include Modern Luxury publications, *Condé Nast Traveler*, the *Miami Herald* and *WHERE* magazine. She updated the Palm Beach and Treasure Coast chapter of this edition.

Updating the Florida Keys and much of the Lower Gulf Coast is Miami native, **Jill Martin**. As a freelance writer, she has blogged more than 1,000 articles for the state's tourism website, Visit Florida, and also writes for various travel sites and print magazines. She has appeared on numerous TV and radio shows as a Florida travel expert and is the creator of Sunshine Brain Games, a trivia card game all about Florida. She resides full time in the Redland and part time on Sanibel.

Galena Mosovich, who wrote parts of the Experience chapter and updated Fort Lauderdale and the Everglades, is known for covering cutting-edge developments and personalities in cocktail culture, gastronomy, travel, and visual art for top publications. Galena was raised in Coral Springs, in the northwest corner of Broward County, and she now lives in North Carolina with her two dogs and two birds.

Lane Nieset is a South Florida native who graduated from the University of Florida with degrees in French and Journalism. She spent three years as the Florida editor for *Recommend* magazine in Miami, where she also wrote a weekly dining column for Ocean Drive. She now splits her time between Miami and Paris working as a freelance writer covering a mix of travel, lifestyle, wine and food for publications such as *National Geographic Travel*, *Travel + Leisure*, *Vogue.com* and *Food & Wine*. She has appeared as a guest host in the Cannes episode of BBC Travel's *RSVP Abroad* series. Lane has eaten and sipped her way around more than 50 countries on all seven continents, trying everything from snowshoeing in Antarctica to glacier trekking in the French Alps. Lane wrote parts of the Experience chapter for this edition.

Award-winning travel writer **Paul Rubio** has penned stories on adventures and experiences in 130 countries (and counting). Paul is a Harvard graduate with a master's degree in public administration and a master's degree in economics. He also holds a bachelor's degree from Boston University with a double major in economics and environmental policy and a minor in conservation biology. Paul worked in the field of wildlife conservation before embracing his writing talents full-time in 2008. Since then, he has won more than two dozen national awards for his exemplary work in travel journalism. The prolific writer contributes to a number of top-tier international, national, and regional publications including *Condé Nast Traveler*, *Palm Beach Illustrated*, *Private Clubs* magazine, and *Robb Report*.